**Local
Government
Finance**

# Local Government Finance

Capital Facilities Planning and
Debt Administration

**Alan Walter Steiss**
*Virginia Polytechnic Institute and
State University*

**Lexington Books**
D.C. Heath and Company
Lexington, Massachusetts
Toronto       London

352.1
S823l

Library of Congress Cataloging in Publication Data

Steiss, Alan Walter.
    Local government finance.

    Includes index.
    1. Capital budget.  2. Municipal budget.  3. Municipal bonds.
I. Title.
HJ9111.S84                   352'.1                75-18344
ISBN 0-669-00126-0

Copyright © 1975 by D.C. Heath and Company

All rights reserved. No part of this publication may be reproduced or transmitted in any form or by any means, electronic or mechanical, including photocopy, recording, or any information storage or retrieval system, without permission in writing from the publisher.

Published simultaneously in Canada

Printed in the United States of America

International Standard Book Number: 0-669-00126-0

Library of Congress Catalog Card Number: 75-18344

# Contents

| | |
|---|---|
| **List of Figures** | ix |
| **List of Tables** | xi |

**Chapter 1**
**Capital Facilities Planning**

| | |
|---|---|
| Government Responsibility | 1 |
| The Role of Capital Facilities Planning | 6 |
| Definition of Terms | 8 |
| Allocation of Responsibilities | 13 |
| Summary and Conclusions | 16 |

**Chapter 2**
**Evaluation Criteria and Procedural Steps**

| | |
|---|---|
| Criteria for the Evaluation of Capital Budgets | 19 |
| Procedural Steps in Capital Facilities Planning | 28 |
| Priority Classification Systems | 35 |
| Program Formulation—Summary of Procedural Steps | 41 |

**Chapter 3**
**The Role of Economic Analysis**

| | |
|---|---|
| Origins of Economic Analysis | 45 |
| Theoretical Constructs of Urban Economics | 47 |
| Regional Techniques | 50 |
| Economic Base Studies | 63 |
| Summary | 71 |

**Chapter 4**
**Formulation of A Debt Policy**

| | |
|---|---|
| Constitutional and Statutory Limits on Borrowing | 73 |
| Purposes of Government Borrowing | 76 |

Measuring the Capacity to Pay ........................................... 79
The "Supply Side" of the Urban Economy ................................ 82

**Chapter 5**
**Forecasting Local Expenditures and Financial Resources**

Expenditure Forecasts ................................................... 85
Estimates of Financial Resources ........................................ 94

**Chapter 6**
**Methods of Financing Capital Facilities and Choice of Debt Form**

Methods of Financing ................................................... 103
Choice of Debt Form ................................................... 111
Summary ............................................................... 125

**Chapter 7**
**Marketing Municipal Bonds**

Issuance of Municipal Bonds ............................................ 127
Underwriting Municipal Bonds .......................................... 141
Summary ............................................................... 151
Appendix 7A: Financial Information Required in Municipal Bond Prospectus for General Obligation and Special Tax Bonds ............................................................ 153

**Chapter 8**
**Revenue Bonds**

Security of Revenue Bonds .............................................. 155
Historical Background .................................................. 155
Appropriate Uses of Revenue Bonds ..................................... 157
Revenue Bond Laws .................................................... 158
Sources of Revenue ..................................................... 159
Planning the Sale of Revenue Bonds ..................................... 161
Maturity Provisions ..................................................... 163
Covenants on Revenue Bonds ........................................... 164
Distribution of Revenues ................................................ 166
Issuance of Additional Bonds ............................................ 167
Summary ............................................................... 168

## Chapter 9
## Debt Administration

| | |
|---|---|
| Debt Records and Reporting | 169 |
| Short-term Borrowing | 179 |
| Debt Service and Retirement | 185 |
| Refunding, Conversion, and Defaults | 191 |
| Summary | 197 |

## Chapter 10
## Cost-Benefit and Cost-Effectiveness Analysis

| | |
|---|---|
| Cost-Benefit Analysis | 199 |
| Cost-Effectiveness Analysis | 230 |

## Chapter 11
## The Role of Program Budgeting

| | |
|---|---|
| Major Components of Program Budgeting | 261 |
| Limitations to Implementation | 265 |
| Formulation of a Capital Facilities/Program Budget | 266 |
| Summary and Conclusions | 274 |

| | |
|---|---|
| **Notes** | 277 |
| **Glossary** | 287 |
| **Author Index** | 295 |
| **Subject Index** | 297 |
| **About the Author** | 301 |

## List of Figures

| | | |
|---|---|---|
| 3-1 | The Supply Side of an Urban Economy | 53 |
| 3-2 | The Demand Side of an Urban Economy | 54 |
| 3-3 | The Kennedy Basic-Nonbasic Wash Bucket Principle | 55 |
| 3-4 | Urban Economic Structure: Classification by Market Location and Consumer Commodity | 65 |
| 3-5 | Macro-Micro Synthesis of Dominant Industry Groups | 70 |
| 3-6 | Dominant Industry-Economic Indicator Relation (Micro Level) | 71 |
| 10-1 | Life Cycle Costs Plotted Against Time | 211 |
| 10-2 | Solving for $r$: Benefits in Excess of Costs | 219 |
| 10-3 | Radner's Graph of Optimal Scales | 228 |
| 10-4 | Sector Division of Each Cell in the Matrix | 235 |
| 10-5 | Cost-Goal Analysis in Graphic Form | 237 |
| 10-6 | Cost-Effectiveness Analysis in Graphic Form | 239 |
| 10-7 | Cost-Constraint Analysis in Graphic Form | 240 |
| 10-8 | Trainee Capacity and Systems Costs Versus Number of Training Centers for Alternative Systems A and B | 251 |
| 10-9 | Trainee Capacity Versus System Costs for Alternative Systems A and B | 252 |
| 10-10 | Systems Costs Versus Number of Centers for Alternative Systems A, B, and C | 254 |
| 10-11 | Trainee Capacity Versus System Costs for Alternative Systems A, B, and C | 255 |

## List of Tables

| | | |
|---|---|---|
| 2-1 | Estimates for Six-year Capital Improvements Program (Form A) | 32 |
| 2-2 | Individual Project Estimate for Six-year Capital Improvements Program (Form B) | 33 |
| 2-3 | General Criteria for Capital Improvements Priority System | 38 |
| 3-1 | Basic Format for Input-Output Analysis | 57 |
| 5-1 | General Expenditures of Local Governments | 86 |
| 5-2 | Level of Indebtedness of Homeville 1965-79 | 93 |
| 5-3 | Local Government Revenues | 95 |
| 6-1 | Debt Service Charges on $1 Million for Ten Years Under Straight Serial and Annuity Serial Bonding | 115 |
| 6-2 | $70 Million San Francisco Bay Area Rapid Transit District General Obligation Bonds, Series G, Issued June 1967, Due Serially June 15, 1972 to 1999, Inclusive | 119 |
| 7-1 | Cost per $1,000 for Marketing Municipal Bonds | 135 |
| 7-2 | Percentage Distribution of Total Costs for Marketing Municipal Bonds | 135 |
| 7-3 | Costs per $1,000 for Marketing Municipal Bonds: Specific Cost Categories | 136 |
| 7-4 | Comparison of Municipal Bond Rating Systems | 137 |
| 7-5 | Underwriters' Calculation of "Production" for $70 Million BART Bond Issue | 145 |
| 9-1 | Bond and Interest Register | 171 |
| 9-2 | Bonded Debt Ledger | 172 |
| 9-3 | Interest Payable Ledger | 173 |
| 9-4 | Debt Statement | 176 |
| 9-5 | Financial Statement for Revenue Bonds | 180 |
| 9-6 | Number of Recorded Defaults on Municipal Bonds, Selected Dates, 1933-38 | 194 |
| 10-1 | Discounting $1,000 Over Ten Years | 213 |
| 10-2 | Internal Rate of Return Calculations on Five-year Project | 217 |
| 10-3 | Benefit Investment Analysis as Illustrated by Six Investment Alternatives | 220 |
| 10-4 | Calculations of Net Benefits Using Two Different Discount Rates | 224 |
| 10-5 | Benefit-Cost Calculations for Two Alternatives | 227 |
| 10-6 | Cost-Effectiveness Analysis: Fixed Budget | 242 |

| | | |
|---|---|---|
| 10-7 | Cost-Effectiveness Analysis: Indivisible Projects | 243 |
| 10-8 | Cost-Effectiveness Analysis: Project Complementarities | 244 |
| 10-9 | Cost-Effectiveness for Aggregate and Disaggregate Data | 247 |
| 10-10 | Cost-Effectiveness Analysis with Incidence Considered | 249 |
| 10-11 | Alternative Program Costs | 250 |
| 10-12 | Total Costs Over Ten Years | 250 |
| 10-13 | Alternative Program Costs | 254 |
| 10-14 | Cost-Effectiveness with Externalities | 257 |
| 10-15 | Calculation of Weighted Cost-Effectiveness Ratios | 257 |

**Local
Government
Finance**

# 1 Capital Facilities Planning

**Government Responsibility**

It has been said that the primary purpose of government is to provide on a collective basis that which cannot be achieved through individual action. Two fundamental activities of government lay at the foundation of this statement: (1) the regulation of individual actions to ensure that they will not be detrimental to the general public; and (2) the provision of public facilities and services for the mutual benefit of all citizens. Both of these fundamental activities stem from the broad objectives of government to "promote the general health, safety, morals, and public welfare."

The beginnings of laws governing and controlling the actions of individuals are lost in antiquity. Although the imposition of new regulations often has met with public objections, it is generally taken for granted, even under the laissez-faire philosophy of "government governs best when it governs least," that laws developed in the public interest are vital to ensuring orderly conduct in our society.

While the imposition of regulations and controls in the public interest is as old as history itself, the provision of public facilities and services is a relatively new activity of government. Public education has been universally accepted in this country for little more than 100 years. The provision of many health facilities still remains a joint undertaking of the public and private spheres. Less than 100 years ago, fire protection in many built-up areas of the country was provided on an individual contract basis.

Although of much more recent origins, the provision of public facilities and services is widely accepted as a basic responsibility of government in contemporary society. While segments of the public may complain bitterly when taxes are increased to provide new school facilities or to expand public health and welfare programs, it is generally acknowledged that significant economies can be achieved by such governmental activities—economies that could not be derived if each citizen had to provide for these facilities and services on an individual basis.

*Emergence of Public Budgeting*

With the expanding complexities of our society, the general public has come to look with increasing frequency to government for the provision of public services and facilities of a suitable type, size, and quality, when and where they are needed. As government began to assume greater responsibilities in these areas, however, only the most evident needs were addressed, and these were dealt with in a somewhat haphazard fashion. If any financial resources remained after these initial obligations were met, other programs might be initiated. As recently as 1910 state and local governments made no provision for the overall supervision and regulation of public expenditures through a comprehensive budgetary process.

As public service programs increased in size and complexity, demanding increased public revenue and, more importantly, evincing the need for more effective allocation of these limited fiscal resources, it became evident that a more systematic approach was necessary to avoid the hit-and-miss results that characterized many early efforts. Consequently, public budgeting procedures have evolved gradually over the past 65 years. It is possible to identify three successive stages in the development of modern procedures for public budgeting.[1] In the first stage, dating roughly from 1920 to 1935, the dominant emphasis was on the development of adequate mechanisms for the control of expenditures. The second stage, which began with the New Deal of the Roosevelt administration and reached its peak in the early fifties with the introduction of performance budgeting, provided a focus on management considerations. The third stage can be traced to current efforts to link the processes of strategic planning and budgeting in a multipurpose budget system.

*Assumptions Underlying the Planning-Budgeting Relationship*

The first assumption regarding the need for more systematic planning and budgeting of public facilities and services is not so much of an assumption as it is a fact—substantial changes in current rates of governmental spending have resulted from corresponding changes in the level and/or kinds of services and facilities provided. If governments are to provide suitable responses to these public needs, of appropriate quality, when and where they are required, greater attention must be given to the long-range planning and budgeting of such expenditures as are necessary within limited available fiscal resources.

From this the second basic assumption can be drawn, namely, that the responsibility for establishing public policy, and in particular, policy relating to the standards of public service, rests with the elected representatives of the general public. This assumption lies at the foundation of our democratic system of government. It is essential, therefore, that a systematic and comprehensive appraisal of goals and objectives be undertaken as a foundation for the establishment of public policy. Such an investigation serves as the core of the strategic planning process. A strategic plan is the product of considerable effort on the part of various agencies working in concert with appropriate private groups and organizations to outline prospects for future growth and change, to explore alternative courses of action to guide this growth and development toward desirable goals and objectives, and to recommend to decision makers ways in which the positive aspects of change can be maximized and the negative by-products minimized. This information is vital if elected officials are to make meaningful and effective policy decisions with regards to public action.

A third basic assumption is that policy statements must be capable of being translated into standards of service. Within the scope established by the overall policies of government with regards to the provision of public facilities and services, it is incumbent on each government to determine what standards or levels of service are desirable for its programs and what these mean in terms of its capital plant. These standards very often can be expressed in measurable, quantitative terms. For example, standards for open space and recreational facilities can be expressed in terms of acres per given unit of population or in terms of the optimum time or distance required for residents to travel to enjoy a given type of recreational experience. Standards for hospitals can often be expressed in terms of beds per thousand population; educational facilities in terms of classroom-pupil and faculty-student ratios; library facilities in terms of capacity and time-distant factors; and so forth. While many standards are more intangible and difficult to quantify, those that are measurable provide an important means of assessing existing facilities and programs in light of desirable objectives.

To translate standards of service into future capital needs, it is necessary to have a well-founded estimate of future population and its geographic distribution in fairly detailed breakdowns. Such estimates permit each agency, working in conjunction with the planning agency, to measure these fixed standards against its potential "clientele." Therefore, detail projections of population are an important contribution arising from the formulation of the strategic plan. Applying these projections, it is possible to determine the extent of new or additional facilities needed in the capital program and the sequence or timing required to ensure that these facilities are available when the need arises.

A fourth assumption relating to the planning of public services and facilities is that standards of service must have a degree of built-in flexibility. To be meaningful, standards must be representative of actual performance or benefits. Therefore, as new operational techniques are introduced or as new demands arise, it is important that such standards be flexible enough to permit adjustment to meet these changing conditions. This is not to suggest that such standards should be varied from year to year; if they were, their value would be greatly diminished. Standards of service must be established as agreed upon and justifiable guidelines that have validity over time. However, in our dynamic society public needs are continually changing, and, therefore, standards for public services must be designed to accommodate and reflect these changes without destroying their long-term validity.

As an example of the impact of technology or innovation on such standards of service, the development of more intensive treatment procedures and the use of outpatient techniques has shortened the length of time necessary for patients to stay in mental hospitals. This, in turn, has partially relieved the pressing need for facilities and has necessitated an adjustment in standards. Similarly, innovations in methods for dealing with certain types of criminals have led to significant changes in the penal system and in the facilities required.

A fifth assumption is that government must have long-term plans for its operating budget as well as for its capital budget and that these two elements of the budgetary process must be placed in proper relationship, one to another. Too often a capital budget is developed with insufficient attention to the effects it will have on the operating budget. Thus, a major construction program may be authorized that, rather than having the anticipated impact on the government's fiscal capacity, has a much more significant impact because inadequate consideration was given to the operating costs this new facility would generate. Therefore, it is important that long-range capital facilities plans, formulated in conjunction with appropriate line agencies as a part of the strategic plan, include estimates of operating costs, at least for the initial period following the completion of the project.

The final assumption serves as a collorary to the previous one; that is, many expenditure items that are relatively fixed in the short run become highly variable when analyzed from a long-range viewpoint. Here again the need is manifest for the long-range viewpoint in the planning of such expenditures that can be provided through a strategic planning process.

### Government's Capacity to Borrow

The power to borrow is one of the most important assets of government. Few governments have the capability to finance vital public facilities strictly on a "pay-as-you-go" basis through annual tax yields. From the outset of this discussion it should be made clear that there are a number of important advantages to financing capital expenditures out of current revenues or on a pay-as-you-go basis. Such an approach encourages government to "live within its income"; it minimizes the premature commitment of funds that should be reserved for operating expenditures; and it conserves the credit of government for times of emergency when ample credit may be vital. Since the pay-as-you-go approach avoids the added costs of interest payments, it is less costly than borrowing.

The pay-as-you-go approach, on the other hand, may result in an undue burden being placed on the present taxpayer to finance some future need from which he may not fully benefit. Thus, it may be argued that public projects providing services over many years should be paid for by people according to their use or benefit—should be financed on a pay-as-you-use basis. In order to secure user-benefit equity, a public facility should be financed so that the burden does not fall to one generation of users but is spread over the life of the facility, that is, equity requires that benefits received and payments made should coincide.[a] By borrowing, the government relieves taxpayers of part of their immediate tax burden and shifts this burden to future taxpayers. In so doing, of course, tax liabilities are increased due to the interest charges, the hope being that the population (taxpayers) will increase sufficiently at some future point to offset the increased liability.

Like all government powers, however, the capacity to borrow must be used with critical regard for its justifiable purposes and with a clear understanding of its safe and reasonable limits. A sound borrowing policy is one that seeks to conserve rather than exhaust credit. The ability to borrow when necessary on the most favorable terms afforded by the market is an objective that applies to governments just as it does in the private sector. In general, government should borrow sparingly and repay as rapidly as possible.

A government's credit standing, servicing expenses, the cost of new borrowing, and its very ability to borrow to meet normal or crisis needs—all depend in large part upon how well it handles its outstanding debt. The consequences of governmental debt management, however, go far beyond costs of borrowing. Government debt management now affects the entire economic system of the community, its degree of prosperity, and the relative welfare of its citizens.

Since the Civil War total debt outstanding against the credit of state and local governments has risen in every decade. The rate of increase was slowed during World War I and was virtually eliminated during the thirties. As bonds were retired during World War II and little new construction was financed, the total amount of debt outstanding dropped to a pre-Depression level. The postwar construction boom in local public facilities, however, quickly used up the surpluses accumulated during wartime and generated unprecedented new borrowing to finance public projects, many of which were undreamed of in earlier periods.

In 1966 the Joint Economic Committee concluded that long-term borrowing had financed about half of the $220 billion in capital outlays by state and

---

[a]According to Musgrave this principle is particularly important in municipal finance "where the composition of the resident group is subject to more or less frequent change." (Richard A. Musgrave, *The Theory of Public Finance* (New York: McGraw-Hill, 1959), p. 563) An elderly person who becomes a resident in a locality that, soon thereafter, makes large expenditures for durable items, financed on a pay-as-you-go basis, would be treated inequitably.

local governments in the postwar period from 1946 to 1966. The committee projected that, between 1965 and 1975, the dollar amount of tax-exempt bonds outstanding would increase from $94 to $199 billion.[2] Current estimates of the municipal bond market would suggest that this projection of a doubling of municipal debt in ten years was rather conservative.

The long-range planning of capital projects and the administration of municipal debt have become major responsibilities of local governmental officials. It is surprising, therefore, that with few exceptions the subjects of capital facilities planning and public debt management have been relegated to a relatively few pages in a concluding chapter of most standard works on public finance. While libraries are replete with books on capital budgeting in the private sector, only the more astute student of local government can find the limited monographs on the subject as it relates to the responsibilities of government.

### The Role of Capital Facilities Planning

Few areas of importance to local government administration are changing more rapidly than the field of budgeting. While the modern concepts of program budgeting are making gradual inroads into the more traditional techniques for managing local finances, long-range capital improvements planning has lagged significantly behind other developments in the field of local financial administration. As the Advisory Commission on Intergovernmental Relations reported in 1965:

> The usefulness, indeed the necessity, of long-term capital planning cannot be over-emphasized. While most States have statutory requirements as to annual budgeting by local governments and some require the filing of local operating budgets with State agencies, the need for a capital budget is only beginning to be recognized. The states should foster the development of local capital budgets and, in conjunction with their programs of technical assistance to local debt management, should require that such budgets be filed with the State agency administering such assistance.[3]

Thus, the commission's report concluded that no aspect of budgeting is of more importance than the planning of long-term capital expenditures. "Indispensable as are data of the past and current condition of local governments, debts are paid in the future; and a knowledge of future financing, even on an estimated basis, is a tool of the first importance in both the local and State evaluation of proposed bond issues."[4]

There is a growing recognition that it is impossible to achieve the maximum returns from public investments if they are made on a year-to-year basis. To ensure the proper balance of revenues and expenditures, it is necessary to develop a sound long-range capital facilities plan. Such a plan must include estimates of government expenditures both for the operation and maintenance of public services and for capital improvements, together with estimates of revenues from taxes, borrowing, and other sources necessary to finance these expenditures. To be effective a capital facilities plan must be developed for a relatively long period, must allow flexibility for adjustment as new conditions arise, and must be based upon an overall strategic plan that includes a long-range program for the provision of public services.

In developing a capital facilities plan, it is necessary to give separate consideration to operating and maintenance expenditures, on the one hand, and expenditures for capital improvements on the other. Operating programs can be changed fairly rapidly to meet changing conditions, but a major facility that is misplaced or misdesigned constitutes a continual drain on governmental resources.

### *Components of Capital Facilities Planning*

While going under a variety of names, such as public works planning, long-range capital improvements programming, capital outlay planning, public investment planning, and capital budgeting, the principles of capital facilities planning are the same—to guide the provision of major public facilities having a relatively long life within the limits of available public resources. Thus, effective capital facilities planning must involve planning, staging, and financing.

The *planning* phase begins with the formulation of policies (goals and objectives) as to the desired levels of public service. These goals and objectives must be related to population and economic trends and projections to ascertain future demands for public services and facilities. By comparing needs with the capacity of existing facilities, it is possible to determine the magnitude of the additional supply necessary to meet the anticipated demand.

The need for the *staging* of capital improvements arises from the limited tax resources available to any level of government. Staging should be based on a system of priorities tied to the goals and objectives set forth in the planning phase and a system for the continuous evaluation of public services and facilities.

The *financing* phase relates to an analysis of how payments are to be made and the source of funds to be drawn upon. As discussed later, there are a number of ways in which capital facilities can be financed—on a pay-as-you-go basis, from reserve funds, through long- or short-term borrowing, and so on. These methods must be evaluated in terms of the overall fiscal capacity and in light of the particular capital improvement needs.

*Advantages of Capital Facilities Planning*

A long-range capital facilities plan has many obvious advantages. It provides a means of assuring that projects will be carried out in accordance with a well thought-out and defendable system of priorities reflecting both public needs and government's ability to pay. It promotes coordination among the various departments and agencies of government and thereby circumvents overlapping or conflicting programs. It protects against the undue influences of pressure groups representing special interests that, from time to time, may attempt to force their pet projects through at the expense of more urgent or more meritorious improvements.

Through capital facilities planning required bond issues or the need for other revenue producing measures can be foreseen and action taken before the need becomes so critical as to require emergency financing measures. Advance programming lengthens the period available for the proper technical design of projects and facilities. It also permits a continual, systemic appraisal of personnel and equipment needs that can result in a number of economies. And, finally, the planning of capital facilities may provide justification for the advance acquisition of properties needed for improvements, thereby taking advantage of a lower market value.

The shortage of existing revenues compared with the demands for new and improved programs makes it imperative that expenditures be planned on a systematic basis. Failure to plan for capital investments can result in violent fluctuations of capital expenditures from year to year and an increased tendency to borrow, thus increasing overall financing costs and resulting in a number of diseconomies in the allocation of personnel and equipment.

A capital facilities plan will not solve all of the financial problems of government. It may or may not result in a reduction of taxes or public debt. However, it should result in a more expeditious and wise expenditure of public funds, whereby each dollar spent yields a more effective return in terms of the desired improvements.

## Definition of Terms

To gain a clearer understanding of the workings of a capital facilities plan, it is first necessary to define a number of terms associated with this aspect of public budgeting procedures. Several of these terms have application in other phases of governmental operations but assume particular meaning in relation to the planning of capital expenditures.

*Relationship Between Planning
and Programming*

To begin with, a fundamental distinction should be made between capital facilities planning and capital improvements programming. *Capital facilities planning* is concerned with those areas of the overall public planning process that relate to the determination of needs for new and improved public facilities. Such planning involves consideration of the many factors that may influence the growth and development of a community, the formulation of desirable goals and objectives that can be translated into policy decisions, and the analysis and recommendation of alternative courses of action to achieve these goals and objectives. Thus, the central concern of capital facilities planning focuses upon a determination of long-range needs related to particular categories of public facilities and tied to future points in time or levels of population to be served.

*Capital improvements programming* involves the arrangement of proposed capital facilities projects in a sequential order, extending over a relatively long period and based on a schedule of priorities, and involves the assignment of a "price tag" to their development over a more immediate time period. Planning points up needs; programming provides a basis for ordering the sequence in which these needs can be met most effectively.

A further distinction must also be made between program planning and programming. At first glance these activities may seem to be one in the same. However, *program planning* involves the formulation and carrying out of programs designed to implement the objectives and responsibilities delegated to line agencies in an effort to achieve agreed-upon governmental policies. As such, program planning may include elements of programming to the extent that the responsibilities of any particular line agency may involve the development and maintenance of capital facilities.

From the foregoing definitions it may be seen that planning and programming are closely interrelated and complementary activities; both are essential to the efficient operations of modern government. While short-range program decisions may be made in the absence of planning because needs are so evident, the long-range implications of capital expenditures cannot be anticipated without the firm foundation of a comprehensive plan. The planning process provides a basis for determining the likely magnitude and distribution of population, the location of industry and other economic activities, the relationship between development and resources, both human and natural, and offers important inputs concerning the evaluation, analysis, and establishment of project priorities. Until such a planning process is established as a regular function of government, any estimates of a jurisdiction's long-range needs and responsibilities for capital facilities are likely to be in the realm of guesswork. While planning may be carried out without programming and the programming of proposed public improvements may be undertaken in the absence of adequate planning, in either case the results are likely to be an ineffective and wasteful use of governmental resources. To achieve the best results, programs are required to effectuate plans, and plans are needed to ensure that the full value of programming is realized. Therefore, the capital improvements program should not only be *based* on a comprehensive plan, it should be an *integral part* of such a plan.

*What is a Capital Facility or Capital Improvement?*

Generally speaking, the terms *capital facility* or *capital improvement* refer to projects of large size, fixed nature, and/or long life (usually a minimum of 15 to 20 years), involving expenditures of a nonrecurring nature, designed to provide new or additional governmental facilities for public service. Thus, funds allocated for the design and construction of a new health clinic would be considered as a capital expenditure, whereas monies appropriated to sustain the operations of such a facility, in terms of salaries, supplies, equipment replacement (except as such replacement might constitute a significant outlay of funds), would be more properly considered as an operational expenditure to be included as an annual budget request.

One test of a true capital outlay is whether it adds substantially to the value of the fixed assets of government. Equipment required at the time of acquisition or construction of a facility is often included as part of the capital improvement program. However, expenditures for minor equipment acquisitions and most repair work should not be included as part of the capital expenditures.

*What is a Capital Budget?*

The term capital budget, as it has been used by various writers, has given rise to considerable confusion. At times the term is reserved for the allocation of funds for the ensuing fiscal year under the total capital facilities plan to parallel the concept of an annual budget. Others have used the term to refer to the total capital improvements program. However, since the phrase capital budget is frequently treated as a specific authorization by the legislative body against which annual appropriations are made, the shorter term definition is used in this discussion. The total program for capital construction is referred to as the capital improvements program.

*Programming Period*

Capital improvements programs are developed for a specific time period, usually six years. While the overall capital facilities plan should extend over a much longer period, it is obvious that such a plan is subject to many uncertainties. It is neither possible nor necessary to be as specific and exacting in planning over this longer period as it is in determining the schedule for capital expenditure for the more immediate future. Therefore, within the broader framework of the long-range facilities plan, the more immediate portions are generally developed in greater detail and are incorporated into a six-year capital improvements program. There is no magic to the number "six," but governments have generally found that this is a convenient period for detail programming of capital expenditures, permitting sufficient lead time for the design and other preliminary work required by such projects.

Initially in capital improvements programming procedures, the practice was to divide the longer time period into a number of distinct program periods and to develop a capital program for each of these periods. Conceptually, following the completion of the first six-year program, a second was embarked upon, and when that had been turned into bricks, mortar, and asphalt, the third six-year program was initiated.[5] In practice, however, it was found that, as soon as the first year of the first program was nearly completed, it was necessary to reevaluate all future programs in light of changing needs and to modify, refine, and adjust these programs. Thus, the program for the six-year period from 1973 to 1978 evolves into a program for 1974 to 1979, which in turn becomes the program for 1975 to 1980, and so forth. As a result, each successive capital budget becomes the first of a six-year program. If undertaken within the framework of the long-range capital facilities plan and parallel program plans, this procedure provides several advantages. It affords an opportunity for greater flexibility and feedback and promotes continuity in the programming process. It permits the gradual refinement and detailing of projects. And, in general, such an approach is more adoptable to projects of varying durations.

*Other General Terms*

Several additional terms that will be used in subsequent discussion require definition. A complete glossary of terms used in the planning of capital facilities is included at the end of this book.

**Financing Methods.** As indicated in the introduction, there are several methods of financing capital expenditures. Generally these methods are used in various combinations depending upon the nature of the individual project, the availability of revenue sources, and the stability of funds. The pay-as-you-go method, for example, is particularly adaptable to programs that can be developed on an incremental basis and/or those for which funds are relatively stable and not subject to periodical fluctuations. As an example, the construction of highway facilities, financed by motor fuel taxes, or the acquisition and development of public hunting and fishing grounds, financed by revenues derived from license fees, are projects at the state level for which the pay-as-you-go method of financing might be applicable.

A second method of financing involves long- or short-term borrowing[b] and/or the issuance of revenue bonds. This method is generally appropriate in cases where the initial outlay of funds for a particular project or series of projects would create a substantial drain on the financial resources of government. Therefore, it is necessary to spread these costs over a much longer period. A substantial number of capital improvements are financed in this manner.

A third approach appropriate to the orderly process of capital improvements programming is financing from reserve or "sinking" funds. This method is perhaps the most economical and reliable and is made possible in connection with long-range capital facilities planning and capital improvements programming procedures. It involves the setting aside from general annual revenues a given sum in advance of the projected needs in order to have sufficient capital on hand to initiate the project when the need arises. This method has the advantage of avoiding the interest charges incurred with the issuance of bonds (and, in fact, if these reserve funds are invested, they can produce additional revenues) and is not as subject to fluctuations as in the case of the pay-as-you-go approach. The problem is to provide sufficient safeguards to ensure that these funds are adequate to meet the demands and that they are not "tapped" for some other project or operating expense as they are being built up.

As has been suggested, these financing methods are generally used in varying combinations. Thus, a major toll road may be constructed with funds derived from a bond issue. The annual revenues from this facility may be sufficient not only to meet the annual interest and principal charges necessary to retire the bonds, but also to build up a reserve for future major improvements or additions to the facility. Eventually, it may be possible to finance other projects from the revenues that this facility produces either on a pay-as-you-go basis or through the establishment of a sinking fund.

**Annual Costs, Tax Burden, and Debt Burden.** The annual costs of any improvement program are determined by the planning, staging, and methods of financing together with the projected operating costs. To be most effective the programming of capital improvements should undertake to level off annual costs and to avoid erratic fluctuations. Annual costs, when measured against tax resources and available subsidies, determine the tax burden generated by the capital program. Total capital costs, together with the staging and financing methods, determine the overall debt burden. Where the tax or debt burden becomes too great for public resources, it may be necessary to reduce the improvements scheduled within the capital program until their costs fit to these resources.

---

[b]Grant-in-aid programs and other similar financing devices fall under this general category.

**Standards of Service.** An essential element in the capital facilities plan relates to the establishment of goals and objectives for public service programs and the determination of a desirable standard or level of service for carrying out these programs. While the formation of goals and standards is practiced by most departments in day-to-day operations, it is all too easy to lose sight of these goals and to continue to work on a historical basis only. It is even more easy to lose sight of overall public goals in deciding on goals of any particular agency.

**Priorities.** The heart of a good capital improvements program, the development and application of a sound system of priorities, provides the method by which each project is measured against the total capital expenditure needs of government and through which a schedule is developed. While a priority system should have some degree of flexibility, it must be stable enough to offer substantive justification for the scheduling of projects and the allocation of funds within the capital improvements program. Since a considerable number of elements contribute to the establishment of a priority system, these are discussed at length in a later section.

### Allocation of Responsibilities

As with any planning activity in a democratic society, the responsibilities for capital facilities planning are shared by a number of groups and individuals within government. The chief executive, the legislative body, the various operating departments, the finance agency, and the planning agency each play an important role in the decision-making process. As Robert E. Coughlin has observed: "Each group attempts to look at the program as a whole and make decisions about its parts. But, because of its particular function and position, each group sees the problems with a slightly different emphasis." [6]

*Staff Functions: The Finance and Planning Agencies*

Operating departments, primarily concerned with their own efficiency, are likely to view the entire capital improvements program in terms of its impact on their own project requests. As a consequence, they tend to overemphasize the importance of their own project requests in the assignment of priorities. As the watchdog of expenditures, the position of the finance agency is somewhat counter to that of the operating departments in that it must be primarily concerned with maximizing the returns from individual projects while achieving economies in the total program. The finance agency must view each proposal critically to evaluate the potential "needs" that it is designed to serve. Very often this results in a heavy emphasis being placed by the finance agency on the short-run implications of the capital facilities plan.

The planning agency, in turn, must have a greater concern for the long-range implications and the functional relationship among projects as they fit together to further the objectives of the capital facilities plan. Frequently this requires that the planning agency project beyond the immediate needs embodied in the "justifications" submitted by the operating departments to explore some of the more subtle ramifications of individual project requests.

*Chief Executive and Legislative Body*

Ultimately, the decisions regarding capital expenditures must rest with the chief executive and the legislative body. As the elected representatives of the people, these officials must share a primary concern for the broader interests and the welfare of their constituents. However, their particular function and position dictates that they emphasize different aspects of the capital facilities plan. The chief executive must assume a position that places primary emphasis upon middle-range objectives, falling somewhere on the continuum between the short-range emphasis of the finance agency and the longer-range viewpoint of the planning agency. He must also pay particular attention to the political consequences of the decisions that are made concerning capital expenditures. The legislative body must also take cognizance of the political implications of their decisions, but generally tend to gravitate toward the more immediate objectives of the program, placing particular emphasis on the cost factors involved.

*Framework for Capital Expenditure Decisions*

This pluralistic approach, with its system of checks and balances characteristic of a democratic form of government, obviates the overly authoritarian approach to governmental expenditures and thus protects the interest of the general public. "The program is submitted to each of these groups in turn and, in theory, the successive application of these slightly different points of view result in a program that is 'balanced' for the common good of the community."[7]

Of course, the drawbacks to this approach are obvious, in terms of the time required to carry out this process and in terms of the compromises that often are necessary. As one student of government has put it: "Rome wasn't built in a day—but it would have taken a heck of a lot longer if the construction proposals had to go through our modern form of democratic government." To circumvent the delays that arise from this pluralistic approach, the capital improvements program must be developed with a spirit of close coordination and cooperation among the various groups involved. Unfortunately, all too often these groups view each other as adversaries rather than as allies serving complimentary functions.

It should be evident from the foregoing discussion that the decision-making process relating to capital expenditures does not merely involve one simple decision or even a series of related decisions at one clearly defined level. Further, any decision that is made has significant ramifications beyond the more obvious one that a project is or is not to be built. For example, the decision to delay the extension of certain highway facilities may have a substantial impact on the economy of an area or may mean that the full potential of some other public facility or improvement may fail to be realized because of the lack of access. A more subtle ramification might arise from a decision to postpone the construction and/or expansion of higher educational facilities, which may force qualified students to seek a college education out-of-state, thereby eventually depriving the state's industries of the minds and talents of many of these young individuals. This, in turn, could have a significant impact on the economy of the state.

Thus, capital facilities planning "calls for a set of consistent decisions at several levels, ranging from the high level at which, for example, choice is made between investment in direct social welfare facilities as opposed to investment in economic base facilities, to the low level at which, for example, choice is made of one among a number of desirable industrial redevelopment projects or one of a number of desirable playground improvements."[8]

While the various levels of decision may correspond to the various levels of responsibility within the administrative structure of government, there is not a direct one-to-one relationship. The decision-making process can be either "accumulative" or "dispersive," and in practice it is generally a mixture of both. Thus, a major top-level decision may be the end product of a number of lower level decisions (accumulative) and the motivation for such a decision may have been initiated at a much lower level, or the process may begin with the top-level decision that sets the general parameters for successively more specific decisions throughout the administrative structure (dispersive).

The following example illustrates the distinction between these two approaches. Studies initiated by the planning agency as a part of a comprehensive planning program point to the need for more open space and recreational facilities. In conjunction with the operating department responsible for the acquisition and maintenance of recreation facilities, the planning agency, after thoroughly studying the problem, recommends an annual acquisition program to span a ten-year period. After various alternatives are explored, the decision is made by the chief executive to undertake a more intensive acquisition program over a shorter period and to float a bond issue to finance this program. Council agrees to adopt the program, conditioning their approval with the stipulation that a given percentage of the funds appropriated be earmarked for facilities in the inner city. Thus, the line agencies, in carrying out the program, must work within the board framework in selecting sites for acquisition.

This very simplified example illustrates both approaches to the decision-making process. The decision of the chief executive to undertake an open space acquisition program was based on a series of decisions initiated at lower levels with the administrative structure. As these decisions filtered up to the top, various alternative courses of action were undoubtedly considered and rejected or modified by decisions made elsewhere in the system. Once the decision was made by the chief executive and approved by the legislative body, the process was reversed. The policy framework within which operational decisions were to be made was established at the top of the structure and then was disseminated downward to the line agencies responsible for carrying out the program.

Quite obviously, at any point in the process both approaches may be in evidence. The decision to initiate the comprehensive planning program that led to the documentation of open space deficits may have come from the top. Similarly, the motivation for the legislatures decision to emphasize the urban needs may have been initiated at some lower point in the structure. Thus, in actual practice, the process of developing a capital program often begins at the more specific levels, where the need for a particular set of improvements is first established. Then specific needs are translated into program requirements on the operational level and once these programs are filtered up to the top and the whole picture is seen, policy decisions are made to serve as guides for subsequent operational decisions.

### Summary and Conclusions

The literature of public finance and administration contains many studies dealing with the history and theory of public budgeting. While the early literature reflected a concern for honest administration of governmental resources, more recent studies have emphasized the services provided through the allocation of limited public resources, that is, the performance effectiveness of governmental programs. This shift in the literature is reflective of a shift in public budgeting procedures, from a concern for input and process to one of output and effectiveness.[c] Performance budgeting, introduced in the forties, directed attention to the measurement of cost and accomplishment of detailed activities. Program budgeting, gaining acceptance in the sixties, focuses to top level review and decision-making and stresses comprehensive planning and programming as integral phases in the budgetary process. Although given only passing attention in most contemporary public finance texts, this new emphasis on comprehensiveness has particular significance for the activities of capital facilities planning and public debt administration.

Capital facilities planning involves a unified series of steps to carry out the policy aims of government. The end product of these activities—a capital

---

[c]In the broader context of public management, this shift is also reflected in the new emphasis on public policy analysis and evaluation.

budget—sets forth in financial terms critical policy decisions concerning the distribution of available resources among the activities for which a jurisdiction has responsibility. Capital facilities planning must recognize the interrelated character of all expenditures, whether for new or existing program or capital outlays, and must provide for their joint evaluation in arriving at expenditure decisions. As a management tool, capital facilities planning provides a coordinative mechanism for all phases of capital construction—estimation, submission, approval, execution, and post audit.

It should be borne in mind that the executive branch of government has two categories of responsible officials. First, the services of government are performed by various operating departments (often referred to as line agencies). Second, the executive officials and staff agencies must coordinate and reconcile the activities of the operating departments with the resources at government's command. In spite of this necessary distinction, orderly capital facilities planning requires a considerable degree of collaboration between these two categories of public actors. The staff agencies must seek the inputs of the operating departments in the initiation of the capital facilities planning process. The operating departments must decide initially the order of priorities for accomplishing the service goals that are their responsibility. Departmental decisions, however, cannot be final, since further decisions must be made in order to coordinate all programs. Many factors may affect the final decision, including the availability of resource, the political environment, changes in federal and state programs, and expanded borrowing authority for capital outlays.

Budgeting, and in particular, capital budgeting, is a political process. With reference to community decision making, Roscoe C. Martin and others hypothesize that the capital budget is likely to be the single focus of political conflict if it finds a single focus.[9] While any budget contains some "automatic" decisions, the important fact is that most decisions relating to capital investment are policy decisions. Economic and other criteria are employed in the capital facilities planning process, but they are defined within and conditioned by the broader political context. Moreover, the efficiency and effectiveness of the capital facilities plan is measured by the results of executive and legislative action.

This book is concerned primarily with capital facilities planning as a management tool, concentrating on the procedural steps in the formulation of a capital facilities plan and capital improvements program, the issuance of municipal bonds, and the administration of the resulting long-term debt. However, since questions relating to the formulation of a debt policy are central to these management issues, the politics of capital facilities planning, as reflected in the administrative and institutional framework of capital outlay decisions, is also discussed.

# 2 Evaluation Criteria and Procedural Steps

**Criteria for the Evaluation of Capital Budgets**

A theory of capital facilities planning does not exist within the governmental sphere comparable to that developed for the evaluation of business investment decisions. Consequently, no abstract body of principles is available to judge the adequacy of capital budgeting systems in the public sector. In part, this absence of theory arises from an inability to improve upon the imprecise measures (i.e., social benefits and social costs) with which government must deal in making investment decisions in contrast with comparably more precise measures in the private sector (e.g., profits, net cash proceeds, pay-back periods, "book values" on investments, etc.). Thus, while governments for some time have recognized the value of budgeting for operating expenses, only recently has the budgeting of capital expenditures been accorded this same status. Early writers made considerable effort to establish a conceptual framework for the public budgetary process.[a] These early formulations, however, made no explicit reference to the capital budget. Consequently, with minor exceptions, the *theory* of capital budgeting has not been set forth; rather the emphasis in subsequent years has been on devising and improving the *techniques* of capital budgeting.[b]

In spite of the imprecise measures for capital expenditure decisions in government, criteria must be devised if the budgetary process is to be used as a management tool in making investment decisions. These criteria must be based on a realization that social benefits and costs often are "guesstimated" on both economic and political bases, and as a consequence, unwise expenditure decisions frequently result.

In the absence of a body of abstract principles by which to judge current capital budgeting efforts in the public sector, it is necessary to resort to more conventional factors, including: (a) budgetary comprehensiveness and unity; (b) integration of planning processes—strategic, capital facilities, program, and

---

[a]The early works of A.E. Buck, for example, performed this task. The efforts of the New York Bureau of Municipal Research, during the twenties, conceptually made budgeting an integral part of the "economy and efficiency" movement in government.

[b]The economic theory of capital budgeting has been explored somewhat more extensively. However, among economists, far more attention has been directed to the use of the capital budget as an economic stabilizer for national governments.

financial; (c) elements of organization; (d) priority classifications; and (e) budget execution.[1] Since these factors are integral to the overall procedures of capital budgeting, they can be considered as "criteria" for purposes of evaluation.

*Budget Comprehensiveness and Unity*

Fundamentally, the principle of *comprehensiveness* means that all governmental expenditures and revenues should enter into basic budgetary procedures and be subjected to standard budgetary mechanism of evaluation. In short, this principle holds that no programs should be exempt from the central budgetary process regardless of their source of funding or unique characteristics. The principle of *unity* reinforces this concept by asserting that all budget requests should be judged according to the same criteria. Budgetary unity must extend to all phases of the process, that is, preparation, submission, approval, execution, and auditing.

Since capital outlays and operating expenditures, in the view of many public officials, represent two distinct aspects of the budget process, in practice they have been accorded almost completely separate treatment without any regular effort to link these processes together. In some municipalities, capital outlays are considered only incidentally if a surplus has developed in the preceding fiscal period. Thus, the approach followed in many communities of separate treatment of capital and operating budgets represents an initial violation of the basic principles of budget comprehensiveness and unity.

The most widely held argument favoring the separate treatment of the capital and operating budget is that capital expenditures are nonrecurrent. The nonrecurrent criterion is also the basic justification for financing capital expenditures through borrowing. On somewhat different grounds, borrowing for capital facilities may be justified in order to ensure equity to each generation of taxpayers in paying for capital outlays.[2]

Additional arguments advanced in favor of the separate treatment of capital outlays include: (1) Capital expenditures represent additional investment in the basic facilities owned by the community; (2) capital outlays are conceived and appropriations made on a project rather than a program basis; (3) capital budgeting requires the generation of different types of information; and (4) capital outlays are future oriented, important to the economic and social well-being of the community.[3] These same arguments have led some authors to conclude that, while the operating budget properly falls within the realm of responsibility of fiscal watchdog agencies (e.g., the budget office, office of the comptroller, etc.), the planning of capital improvements should be the responsibility of the comprehensive planning agency. Coleman Woodbury has suggested, in fact, that a "new" definition of comprehensive planning should be that of "capital facilities planning," for it is in this realm that the policies and projections embodied in a comprehensive plan are converted into reality. Unfortunately, the organizational separation of budget development responsibilities may further erode the principles of comprehensiveness and unity.

The argument of nonrecurrency, while applicable to some small communities, is no longer valid in the case of larger municipalities or state governments, where capital expenditures are as recurrent on an annual or biennial basis as are operating expenditures, that is to say, it is reasonable to expect that such governments will spend funds during each fiscal period for some types of physical facilities. This concept of functional recurrency has budgetary significance, in that it places capital and operating expenditures in the same broad category, competing for the same scarce resources. In economic terms the last dollar spent for capital outlays should provide an amount of satisfaction (benefit) equal to similar expenditures for operating purposes. Therefore, both capital outlays and operating expenditures should be dealt with in the same broad conceptual framework of budget comprehensiveness and unity.

Violations of the principles of comprehensiveness and unity are not limited to the distinction made between the operating and capital budgets, however. In theory, a capital budget should include all public expenditures, in excess of some established minimum, designed to provide new or additional governmental facilities. In practice, however, various programs have been partially or totally exempted from consideration as part of the capital budget. The main justification for exempting certain activities stems from the fact that these programs are financed by dedicated funds specifically earmarked for land acquisition and/or capital construction in these areas and, therefore, cannot be "manipulated" through general capital budgeting procedures. However, this and other such "justifications," for the most part, are little more than rationalizations. As Hillhouse and Howard have observed: "The arguments about constitutional and statutory provisions, earmarked revenues, and control by independent authorities do not have much merit. Each of these situations is the result of a deliberate and reversible decision." [4]

Necessarily, capital and operating outlays must be confronted jointly at some point in (or preferably throughout) the budgetary process. Thus, budgetary comprehensiveness and budgetary unity are applicable criteria for judging capital budgeting activities in the public sector, because they provide the most thorough basis for jointly evaluating capital outlays and operating expenditures. Attention must be focused on the inclusiveness of the budget document (i.e., whether the budget is conceived and administered as a single mechanism or as separate mechanisms devised for consideration of various aspects of the budget), on the criteria applied in the evaluation of budget requests, and on the degree to which these criteria are uniformly applied in all phases of the budget process.

*Integration of the Planning Process*

By definition, the capital budget is the end product of four interrelated planning activities. The performance of these planning functions, in large measure, will determine the success of capital budgeting within any jurisdiction. Therefore, the degree to which program planning, capital facilities planning, and financial planning are integrated—as essential ingredients of long-range strategic planning—provides a further criterion for the evaluation of the capital budget.

Strategic planning provides the basis for the other phases of the capital budgeting process. Its initiation is dependent on two key elements: (a) a statement of broad objectives of government over a relatively long period of years, and (b) the provision of quantitative data, such as population projections and economic trends, upon which specific program projections can be based. This information is used by operating (line) agencies to define program goals and to estimate the costs of reaching these goals. The core of program planning, therefore, involves: (a) refinement of existing programs in light of emerging trends, (b) continuing review and revision of immediate and perhaps long-range goals in light of these trends, and (c) redirection of existing programs toward the accomplishment of long-range objectives.[5]

Program planning generates the information necessary to formulate decisions in capital facilities planning, through which trends and program goals are translated into requirements for physical facilities and overall coordination is provided by the establishment of a priority listing of projects. Central staff review of these projects produces cost estimates and a determination of feasibility in light of anticipated revenues. If acceptable, projects must be integrated into a complete program plan for the whole of government operations, that is, the strategic plan.

Occurring simultaneously with or perhaps preceding these basic planning activities, financial planning has two principal aspects. First, long-term fiscal policies must be devised, involving consideration of present and alternative revenue sources, cost and levels of service to be provided, levels of capital expenditures, and sources of funds.[6] The second aspect of financial planning is tied directly to the program and capital facilities plans and focuses on the determination of costs and revenues available for financing the more immediate capital improvements program. By indicating the impact of proposed capital outlays on revenues, operating costs, and debt service, this phase of financial planning provides decision makers with the information necessary to make responsible commitments.

These planning activities are the heart of capital budgeting. Program planning and capital facilities planning require the coordinated effort of line and central staff agencies, with principal emphasis on the decision-making functions of program agencies. The latter activity—financial planning—generates the types of information, relating to such questions as the available revenues, added borrowing capacity, or increased intergovernmental support, that the chief executive and legislative body need to make decisions necessary to ensure a coordinated program of public services and facilities.[7]

In examining any capital budgeting operation, therefore, several questions can be posed. Have long-range public service goals been established for the community and are they integrated into a comprehensive plan? Have general fiscal policies been developed with sufficient forethought to be applicable over an extended time period and, at the same time, with sufficient flexibility to adapt to changing conditions? To what extent are operating (line) agencies performing long-range program planning with central staff assistance? Have capital facility needs been clearly identified in light of program plans? Is the central staff in a position to advise decision makers on a budget to satisfy the established long-term public service delivery goals of the community? Are there adequate channels for communication among the representative agencies? Answers to these and similar questions will provide important insights into the overall integration of planning responsibilities supportive of the capital budget.

*Organization for Capital Budgeting*

Several organizational arrangements are possible for the development of a capital budget.[c] The *department approach* places the planning and budgeting functions in a single department, usually within one or more divisions of an administrative staff agency responsible to the chief executive. From this position, coordination is achieved by these staff functions "speaking with one voice." A second approach assigns planning, budget preparation, and budget execution responsibilities to separate departments. Coordination may be achieved through interagency task forces, by procedural means such as sequential responsibilities, or by central direction from the office of the chief executive. A third approach places capital budgeting in the hands of a *board or commission* responsible for submitting recommendations to the chief executive or the legislative body or perhaps both. Such a commission may receive staff support from one or more of the agencies involved in the planning and budgeting of capital projects.

None of these organizational schemes, however, is an absolute ideal for the achievement of effective of capital budgeting; any one of them may be the best choice within a given institutional setting. The administrative structure applicable to the achievement of any given purpose must reflect the overall political and social context within which it operates. There is no one ideal system, and consequently, none of these approaches, in and of themselves, can be used to evaluate the effectiveness of the organizational system adopted by a particular jurisdiction in its approach to capital budgeting.

---

[c]These distinctions are drawn from Jackson McClain's study, *Capital Budgeting in Selected States,* pp. 15–17. A.M. Hillhouse and S. Kenneth Howard (*State Capital Budgeting,* pp. 9–18) describe organization according to the agency exercising principal responsibility for capital budget preparation, for example, planning agency, construction agency, operating budget agency, or legislative and executive commission or board. McClain asserts that a distinction should be made between the legislative and executive commission, since in the former the controls of the chief executive are usually quite limited.

It is possible, however, to analyze organizations from other than a structural point of view. The purposes for which an organization exists, that is, communication, coordination, and decision making, offer other important organizational criteria for evaluation. Thus, Chester I. Barnard has defined a formal organization as "a system of consciously coordinated activities or forces of two or more persons," emphasizing the communication and coordination functions of organizations.[8] Alex Bavelas and Dermot Barrett suggest that an organization is a mechanism for processing information. "The goals an organization selects, the methods it applies, the effectivness with which it improves its own procedures—all of these hinge upon the quality and availability of the information in the system."[9] The importance of communication to the overall operation of an organization and, in particular, to the decision-making process, has been discussed in some detail by Herbert A. Simon.[10] An organization can be conceptualized as a configuration of communication patterns that connect individuals and collectivities of varying sizes, shapes, and degrees of stability and cohesiveness and thereby establishes patterns of contact among individuals and groups.[11]

Public budgeting is integrally involved with the decision-making process—the budget is a vehicle for policy formulation and the process is one of the more important mechanisms in government through which required program and financial information is brought together to arrive at policy decisions.[12] This conceptualization recognizes that almost every public decision has budgetary implications, because it involves the allocation of scarce public resources.[13] Thus, within any administrative organization there is a hierarchy of decision centers. Each successively lower center implements the goals established by the center immediately above, and each successively higher level coordinates the activities undertaken to implement these goals by centers at the next lower level.[14] Within this hierarchy, a communication network transmits decisions from the top downward and information from the bottom upward. As McClain has observed:

> The organization for capital budgeting illustrates the three functions of communication, coordination, and decision making. The process is based upon decisions as (a) to long-range service goals and (b) to the development of a long-term fiscal policy. A hierarchy of decision-centers exists with the governor or a policy-making body at the apex and the program activity at the base with the program, department, and budget agency in the intermediate steps. A communication network is available initially to transmit the long-range service goals downward and later to transmit forms and instructions for program and capital improvement planning downward and program and capital improvement plans upward.[15]

As Victor A. Thompson, Jerald Hage, and others have observed, the increased complexity of the problems confronting modern organizations—and public agencies in urban government—has resulted in a high degree of role specialization and task fragmentation in order to achieve more workable solutions.[16] In the public sector, the information required for any particular decision is dispersed among numerous individuals and groups in diverse positions. Generally, no one person has sufficient information to make a decision without first engaging in an extensive communication process. The necessary information is generated at many different points within government, with much of the information relevant to a decision originating at operating levels. Thus, while goals relating to the delivery of public services are generally acknowledged to be policies of the highest order and, therefore, assumed to be established at the top of the communication network by those officials elected or appointed to make policy, many of these policies have their origins at lower levels in the hierarchy and are transmitted formally or informally up the communication system.

The effectiveness of an organizational structure for capital budgeting, therefore, can be analyzed in terms of the degree to which it facilitates the flow of communications in support of the decision-making processes. Coordination at each successive level in the organizational hierarchy is also vital to the success of such activities.

*Priority Classification*

Priority classification is one of the most difficult aspects of capital facilities planning. Priority classification is an attempt to order the range of projects generated by various agencies in an objective fashion; however, the methodology has been insufficiently developed to permit a very high degree of objectivity.[17] Herein lies the difficulty. While it may be possible in some capital projects to quantify economic benefits and costs with a relative degree of sophistication, with one or two possible exceptions, social benefits and costs have yet to reach this level of quantification. Thus, methodological inadequacies result in the listing of projects according to some subjective scale of value preferences. Even if it were possible to develop more sophisticated techniques for measuring both social and economic benefits and costs, however, the value preference aspect of priority classification is not likely to be eliminated.

Two basic decisions must be made relevant to each project under consideration: (1) its *importance* relative to all other projects; and (2) its desirable *sequence* relative to other projects. Initially, all proposed improvements should be evaluated to determine if they are in conformance with the general goals and objectives of the community. Each project should be reviewed in terms of its location, size, services provided, relationship to its service area, impact on surrounding land use, effect on transportation facilities, likely ramifications in terms of population distribution and density patterns, and conformity to overall policies. In short, each project should be "tested" against standards contained in a long-range strategic plan for the development of the community. Since capital facilities planning is explicitly concerned with the timing of projects, a parallel evaluation of the sequence in which these projects are to be undertaken must accompany the identification of their relative importance. Thus, in terms of the overall goals and objectives of a government's development and service policies, two or more projects may have the same relative importance. However, in terms of their sequence, it may be necessary to initiate project A well in advance of projects B or C in order to derive the maximum benefits from all three capital expenditures. Therefore, considerations of importance and sequence together provide a fundamental basis for the determination of priority.

There are two basic approaches to the assignment of priorities. Some authorities on capital facilities planning have suggested that it is first necessary to make decisions concerning the priority of projects within a specific function. Thus, in submitting its list of proposed projects, each department may be required to include a priority list based upon their own departmental program planning objectives. In establishing the initial order or sequence, each department is expected to indicate which of their various project proposals should come first and why. This approach involves the combining of many small plans to create one large plan with the central staff, working closely with the individual departments, serving as the overall "coordinator."[18]

A second approach begins with a broad determination of the relative proportion of the total capital improvements allocation to be earmarked in each functional category. Individual projects are then apportioned within each functional group.[19] This second approach emphasizes the broad goals of capital facilities planning but provides for a minimum of direct comparison between individual departmental project requests.

In actual practice the establishment of priorities must involve a synthesis of these two basic approaches. Thus, each department must set priorities within its own area of interest and expertise; at the same time an overall financial framework must be devised along functional lines. Maintaining continual liaison with the individual departments, the central staff agency must then examine and evaluate the departmental priority lists, making recommendations that will provide both internal and total program consistency within the established financial framework.

Further issues regarding the methodology used for establishing a priority system are discussed in a subsequent section. Suffice it to say in the context of the overall evaluation of capital budgeting procedures that the extent to which a defendable priority system is developed and consistently applied will bear heavily on the success of a jurisdiction's capital facilities planning efforts.

*Budget Execution*

Relatively little has been written about the budget execution phase of capital budgeting. It is critical, however, that methods for monitoring the progress of construction be developed so as to provide management personnel with effective tools for the day-to-day administration of the capital facilities plan.

In budget execution both program and budget administrators may be confronted with a large number of projects at different stages of completion. Control problems may arise, such as construction schedules that are not met or project designs that exceed budgetary allocations, unless management can formulate procedures to provide continuous financial and technical information to relate current status with program plans for each project. A project record must be developed to facilitate both the execution of the capital budget and the accumulation of data to aid future programming. Data relating to the adequacy of cost estimates, problems associated with various types of construction, the frequency and character of change orders, and so forth must be reappraised as a regular part of budget execution procedures in order to improve future capital facilities planning decisions.

Thus, the final criteria of evaluation for capital budgeting efforts focuses on the degree to which a jurisdiction has developed and utilizes on-line project data. This evaluation should be based on the answers to such questions as: Are data available to indicate the current status of each project? To what extent have the techniques of operations planning (e.g., PERT and CPM) been applied in the scheduling and control of projects? Does the flow of information permit the application of the principle of "management by exception"? Does management have the necessary information to make operational decisions on each project? In current year execution, has the capital budget been closely coordinated with the operating budget? To what degree are the available data used in the programming of future construction projects?

*Summary*

The purpose of this presentation has been to outline some basic criteria to be applied in the evaluation of any capital budgeting effort. These criteria include: comprehensiveness and unity, planning integration and effectiveness, organizational aspects in terms of communication, coordination, and decision making, priority classification systems, and budget execution. These basic criteria can be applied in the evaluation of established procedures for capital facilities planning and capital budgeting, or as guidelines to assist in the formulation of such procedures.

Although operating and capital expenditures may be analyzed separately, conceptually budgeting must encompass both fiscal dimensions of governmental responsibilities. Thus, in the planning, preparation, and execution of the capital budget, techniques for coordination with operating expenditure decisions and the relationship of staff and line agencies participating in the budgetary process must be of prime importance.

## Procedural Steps in Capital Facilities Planning

While the procedures for developing a capital facilities plan may vary in response to legislative directives and according to the size of the jurisdiction, a number of basic steps should be followed in the formulation of an effective capital budget. Among these procedural steps are: (1) an inventory of existing public facilities, (2) the cataloging of proposed projects, (3) the establishment of a priority classification system, (4) the estimation of resources and obligations, and (5) the determination of fiscal policies. The last two steps are the subject of subsequent chapters. Attention is directed in the remainder of this chapter to the first three procedural items that serve as a preface to the necessary decisions concerning capital expenditure commitments by local governments.

### *Inventory of Existing Facilities*

The development of a capital facilities plan must begin with a complete and accurate inventory of all existing public facilities under the jurisdiction's responsibility. Only after this information is compiled and analyzed is it possible to determine the extent to which public service standards can be met by matching existing capital equipment against future needs.

Few jursidictions have an adequate record of their existing capital facilities and generally what records are available are scattered among many agencies and maintained in a variety of forms with little thought to compatibility or cross referencing of data. In the early seventies, with the increased use of electronic data processing equipment in government, it is now possible to maintain an accurate inventory of capital facilities with relatively little difficulty. However, most jurisdictions are faced with the substantial task of updating and making uniform their current records and files on existing capital facilities.

What sort of information should be included in such an inventory? First, accurate maps should be developed and maintained of all public-owned lands, including a description of the purposes for which these lands are used, extent of improvements on these properties (roads, water, utilities, etc.), acquisition price and current value, and general short- and long-range proposals for use and development. Second, precise floor and area plans for all public buildings, structure and utilities, accompanied by information on the date and type of construction, present condition, and remaining useful life period must be prepared and continually updated. Facilities that are used on a long- or short-term basis should be recorded with some estimates of the capital expenditure for comparable facilities.[d] If the municipality contains several public agencies independent or quasi-independent in fiscal matters, they may be included, provided their programs are set up as separate parts of the total inventory. Whenever possible, overlapping local governmental units, such as school district, county, or metropolitan sewerage district, should be prevailed upon to collaborate in a joint inventory of facilities under some cooperative procedures.

These data should be cross-indexed and tabulated according to location, function, capacity, and other relevant factors, While primary records may be kept by agencies directly responsible for the capital facilities, duplicate sets of records should be maintained in a central system and should be readily available to staff agencies responsible for coordinating capital improvements programming activities.

As noted previously, difficulties often arise in capital facilities planning from a failure to give adequate attention to the relationships between the capital and operating budgets. Therefore, for each entry in the existing facilities inventory, parallel information should be maintained as to personnel and administrative costs, equipment and supplies (capital and noncapital), and the annual cost of maintenance and upkeep.

The inventory phase of capital facilities planning, while initially involving considerable time, money, and manpower, should nevertheless result in substantial saving by eliminating and preventing overlap and duplication. As an example, assume that a major department, such as the board of health, has outgrown its present quarters. The question is raised, should the existing facility (which still has a considerable life period left) be enlarged or should new facilities be acquired or constructed or leased. This decision should not be made by giving consideration to the needs of the health department alone. Assume for purposes of discussion that there are several other governmental activities housed in various types of leased and owned buildings that are also in need of improvement and/or expansion. By examining the broader needs of a number of agencies, it may be possible to determine that considerable economies could be achieved by consolidating these offices and activities into a single facility. At the same time, another agency may be found that would be accommodated in the space vacated by the board of health. It is equally important that decisions of this sort be made not only in terms of short-run considerations but with an eye to the long-range implications of such shifts and adjustments.

A second example of economies that could arise from a detailed inventory

---

[d]These data serve to assess the advisibility of leasing facilities as measured against the construction or improvement of existing facilities to house various activities of government.

of existing capital facilities relates to secondary uses that may be made of multipurpose facilities. In an eastern state an extensive search was conducted in an effort to find an adequate site for a new state mental hospital. The line agency working in conjunction with the state's planning staff determined the potential service area for the new facility and then narrowed their search to this district. At the same time as this study was being conducted, a detailed inventory of the total capital facilities was in progress. By matching up the site requirements of this new hospital with the inventory of existing state-owned lands within its service area, a suitable location with a number of site improvements was found within a large state forest. After further study and discussion among various staff and line agencies it was determined that this new facility would be compatible with the primary function of the state forest and, in fact, would contribute to carrying out this primary mission by providing additional access points, thus opening new areas to hunting, fishing, and other recreational activities.

*Cataloging of Proposed Projects*

Since a primary purpose of capital facilities planning is to establish a logical sequence for the construction of major projects, involving the expenditure of considerable public funds, the listing of various projects or improvements required (or desired) together with pertinent explanatory data for each project serves as the second important step in the capital facilities planning process. The capital budget is thus formed from a catalog of projects that are, at least, compatible with the capital facilities plan and, at best, called for explicitly by the plan.

Procedures for developing this catalog are relatively straightforward. The chief administrator or coordinating staff agency sends out forms and instructions annually, soliciting project requests from each department or agency to guide in the preparation of the capital improvements program at least a year prior to the beginning of the fiscal year for which the capital budget is being formulated. The letter of instructions should indicate briefly the purpose and use to which the requested information will be put, the date on which the information should be completed, and to whom it should be submitted. It should also indicate the procedures to be followed in providing information relative to plans and estimates for projects. It may be pointed out, for example, that the long-range capital facilities plan, previously adopted, contains numerous recommendations for physical improvements, and that in addition to these improvements, there may be many others required to keep pace with the needs of the community or to replace worn out or obsolete equipment.

General procedures require that two or three brief forms be completed by each agency in compiling its project list. These forms should be returned promptly to the designated coordinating agency or commission in accordance with the overall budget timetable. If the requested improvements are not included in the comprehensive plan (or capital facilities plan), the agency's project listing should be accompanied by a recommendation that the plan be modified or enlarged to include such indicated improvements. (Capital expenditures covering equipment frequently are not part of a comprehensive plan but may be included in a capital facilities plan.) To the extent possible, all projects should be indicated on a map(s) of the jurisdiction, color-coded according to the proposed year of construction. In filling out these forms, the agencies should be cognizant that the desired cost and priority estimates include all construction projects for public improvements that have a relatively long life expectancy (ordinary repairs and maintenance should not be recorded as a capital project).

Form A (see Table 2-1) provides an overall summary of the anticipated projects to be undertaken within the program responsibilities of a given department or agency. This form is used to record all construction projects and their equipment, including purchase of land, major alterations and repairs of existing buildings, or grading and development of land, and should indicate the distribution of financing over the programming period (five to six years), the recommended method of financing, and additional operating expenditures arising from the improvement. Each project should be given a priority assignment, listing the major criteria considered for each project in order of relative importance. Only such projects as are, in the opinion of the agency, required during the next six years should be entered on Form A with the anticipated expenditure shown in the year in which it should be made. The column "prior" should show the sums of money, if any, that have been made available previously for projects for which additional funds are requested. The column "later" should show the amount needed for project completion after the current six-year programming period, as appropriate.

It is particulary important to fill in the column showing "additional operating costs" whenever a project involves such items. These costs constitute a continuing annual expense that may result in a serious fiscal burden for the jurisdiction and, therefore, must be considered carefully. Any anticipated operating income should also be entered for similar consideration. If a new project will involve a savings in operating and maintenance expenses, this should be so indicated under "remarks."

Form B (see Table 2-2) is for recording the more detailed information as to costs and the supporting justification for each project entered on Form A, including the purpose of the project, its location and physical description, estimated total cost (encompassing such items as land, right-of-ways, preliminary plans and designs, building and structural costs, equipment and installations, architectural and/or engineering fees, utilities, landscaping, etc.), expenditures requested during programming period, effects on operating budget, additional capital expenditures needed to make the project fully usable, suggested

## Table 2-1
## Estimates for Six-year Capital Improvements Program (Form A)

*Recommended Financing*

| | | | |
|---|---|---|---|
| GR | General revenues | FA | Federal aid |
| SC | Service charges | SA | State aid |
| UT | Utility revenue | SR | Specific reserves |
| GOB | General obligation bonds | WC | Working capital |

City of _____

Summary sheet of _____

Date submitted _____

*Status of Plans*

| | | | | |
|---|---|---|---|---|
| 0 | No plans needed | | 5 | Sketch plans in preparation |
| 1 | First request | | 6 | Sketch plans completed |
| 2 | Preliminary estimate received | | 7 | Detailed plans in preparation |
| 3 | Surveys completed | | 8 | Detailed plans & specifications |
| 4 | Work on plans scheduled | | | |

| Prop. Prior. | Proj. No. | Name & Location of Project | Finance Method | Total Estimated Cost | Year in Which Expenditure is Needed ||||||| Additional Operating Costs | Status of Plans | Remarks (Benefits) and References to Overall Capital Facilities Plan |
|---|---|---|---|---|---|---|---|---|---|---|---|---|---|
| | | | | | 1975–1976 | 1976–1977 | 1977–1978 | 1978–1979 | 1979–1980 | 1980–1981 | Prior | Later | | | |
| | | | | | | | | | | | | | | | |
| | | | | | | | | | | | | | | | |
| | | | | | | | | | | | | | | | |
| | | | | | | | | | | | | | | | |
| | | | | | | | | | | | | | | | |

### Table 2-2
### Individual Project Estimate for Six-year Capital Improvement Program (Form B)

Program Period _____

City of _____     Project number _____

                                                                  Date _____ 19 _____

1. Department _____
2. Division of _____

3. Description of project
   (a) Name, physical description, location

   (b) Purpose

   (c) Shown on map attached
       ( ) yes     ( ) no

4. Need for project (use separate sheet if necessary)

5. In capital facilities or comprehensive plan?
   Reference _____

6. Estimated cost
   A. Planning (totals a, b, c) _____
      (a) Architect fees _____
      (b) Engineering _____
      (c) Inspection _____
   B. Land _____
   C. Construction _____
      (a) Labor _____
      (b) Nonlabor _____

   D. Misc. equipment _____
   E. Furnishings _____
   F. Other _____
   Total estimated cost _____
   Prior funding _____

7. Relation to other projects, where applicable

8. Future burden _____
   (a) Annual cost _____
   (b) New staff _____
   (c) Future expenditure for equipment _____

9. Income from project (estimated annual, direct and indirect)

10. Construction period

11. Status of plans and specifications

12. Proposed method of construction (contract or day labor)

13. Project expenditures by years
    1975–76 _____
    1976–77 _____
    1977–78 _____
    1978–79 _____
    1979–80 _____
    1980–81 _____

*Endorsement* (to be completed by department head)

14. Priority rating
15. Year recommended for construction
16. Method of financing

method of financing, and so forth. Particular attention should be directed to the sections pertaining to purpose and need for the proposed project. These data constitute the justifications for the project and should include such reasons or benefits as the particular service to be rendered, the character of the area to be served, number of people, and value of property served. This second form may be accompanied by any pictures, drawings, plans, or other supporting documentation concerning the project request. In addition to stating the relationship to any other specific project within the same department or a project by another department, Form B should describe specific needed facilities or utilities (i.e., sewage, water, power, roads, sidewalks, etc.) that have to be coordinated with the project. Also, other agencies, groups, or organizations (federal, state, or local) that are concerned or associated with the project should be identified.

The third form, which is sometimes combined with the first, is concerned with a review and updating of previously requested projects. For projects that are currently in the program, this third form serves as a "progress report." For projects that have been deferred from early programs, this form serves notice of their deferred status and provides an opportunity for reevaluation of such project needs.

As one capital budgeting officer put it, the listing of an agency's projects according to their own estimates of priority and need are likely to range from "a poor man's shopping list" to a "letter to Santa Claus" in the initial years of a full-fledged capital facilities planning process. After a relatively short period, however, experience has shown that these individual agency priority estimates become more realistic and provide a most useful device to assist the planners and programmers in the compilation of overall priority schedules.

The agency in charge of preparing the capital budget should provide guidance to department heads in preparing their estimates. Operating departments personnel may not have given much consideration to the long-term needs of the jurisdiction. The staff agency can also help interpret the instructions and aid in filling out the forms. Such assistance will save considerable time later on and will help assure uniformity of procedures. In some cities operating departments will need the advice of not only the city planner and budget agency, but also of the finance director, city engineer, and city attorney.

Perhaps the greatest assistance that the planning and budget agency staff can render is in connection with determining priorities, means of financing, and justifications. For example, the staff can help departments consider such questions as:

1. What is the relationship of the proposed project to the overall development of the city?
2. How many citizens will be helped by the project and how many citizens will be harmed or inconvenienced if the project is not constructed?

3. Will the proposed project replace a present outworn service or structure or is it an additional responsibility of government?
4. Will the project add to the value of the area and thereby increase the valuation of city property?
5. Will the construction of the improvement add to the city's operation and maintenance budget?
6. Will the project increase the efficiency of performance or reduce the cost of performance for a particular service?
7. Will the project provide a service required for economic growth and development of the municipality?
8. Is the estimated cost of the improvement within the city's ability to pay?

The principal function of these forms is to provide a uniform and standardized method of indicating the *justification* for projects to be included in the capital improvements program. The justification should not only include a statement concerning the importance of the individual project requests but also an indication of how the project relates to overall goals and objectives, as well as the more specific service program of the agency and the interrelation among the various projects. While more elaborate procedures and forms have been developed,[e] these three basic items serve as a foundation for the compilation and coordination activities of the planning and programming staffs.

## Priority Classification Systems

After the lists of departmental project needs have been compiled, an initial review will frequently indicate certain proposals that are impractical or impossible to undertake in the current program period. These projects should be

---

[e] In New York State, for example, a nine-part format recently was initiated. In addition to the basic information concerning capital facility requirements, the New York procedures include a statement by each agency concerning: (1) present or future forces and factors influencing program substance and activity; (2) the total need and demand for any given type of service or facility regardless of what level of government may be responsible to meet these needs; (3) the role of private enterprise, the federal and local levels of government, etc., in providing these programs; (4) a breakdown of the program activities within state government; (5) an identification of specific program goals, plans, and objectives; (6) personnel requirements and justifications; (7) data on the "dollar support" required to implement the program plans; (8) areas requiring further research. It should be noted that these requirements go well beyond the basic information directly necessary to formulate a capital improvements program, and in fact, overlaps into the basic areas of responsibility included in the planning process. However, these materials are not sufficient to take the place of a thorough ongoing and comprehensive planning program and, in fact, there is some question as to the propriety in splitting these responsibilities along such lines. The additional information required, while important to the overall deliberations, tends to obscure the proper balance that must be reached between the programming and planning functions of government.

eliminated from further consideration. The remaining proposed projects must then be arranged in order of priority based upon certain criteria of need and of ability to finance.

Regardless of the approach used, decisions with regards to the relative importance of projects should be based upon some systematic method of evaluation that should include some defendable and measurable criteria for establishing priorities for capital improvements. Various sets of general criteria have been proposed by agencies and authorities having experience in establishing capital improvement priorities. In general, these attempts at developing a systematic approach to assigning priorities can be divided into two classes: (1) those that stress the intangible values, and (2) those that undertake to quantify the various criteria and to develop a scoring system. Each of these approaches has its merits and its shortcomings, and to the extent possible, elements from each should be incorporated into a sound system of priorities evaluation.

**The Intangible Approach.** Priorities systems developed under this approach begin by giving preference to projects vital for "the protection of life, health, and public safety." A second important consideration under this approach gives priority to projects designed to meet current deficiencies in existing facilities based on some standard of service. While these deficiency criteria often are expressed in rather general terms, it may be possible to establish some quantifiable measures or "weights" that can be applied to determine the essential level of service and the harm arising from a deficiency of service. The problem here is that it often is difficult to develop measures or indices that are comparable across functional lines.

A third area of consideration gives preference to those projects designed to conserve or maintain existing properties, resources or investment, or that demonstrate some substantial economic or social benefit. Projects on which existing facilities may be dependent in order to realize their full potential also would be given a high priority, as would projects that are self-liquidating or that generate increased governmental revenues or resources. Special consideration may also be given to projects for which substantial federal or state subsidies are available for only a limited period. Finally, under this "intangible" approach, special consideration may be given to emergency situations.

It should be evident that, although this approach tends to emphasize intangible values, several of these items can be "quantified."

> Everything else being equal, within any single functional field, the segment of need showing the greatest deviation from the established standard should receive the first priority. Among functional fields, that field which is farthest behind in meeting its standards—everything else being equal again—has the highest relative urgency.[20]

However, in addition to the problem of making comparisons between different

# EVALUATION CRITERIA AND PROCEDURAL STEPS

areas of service (e.g., parks versus institutions), many of these standards are based partially on serious studies and partially on folk wisdom. Using standards that are based more on intuition than on careful analyses of needs may make this particular method appear far more "scientific" than it really is.

The concept of "essentiality of service" has been introduced to overcome partially the problem of comparability of standards of service. However, here again,

> The weights attached to gauge relative essentiality among services are not often capable of exact measurement—at least not in the way in which functional standards are determined. Some services are obviously pre-requisites if the community is to survive. Others help in supporting essential service but are not in themselves critical. Still others provide the amenities of life, and while desirable, they are not essential.[21]

The factor of time or sequence rounds out this approach to priority determination.

> To equalize deviations over the entire period, all services should be brought along at about the same rate. Generally speaking, backlogs and current needs will still be given precedence in developing a list of relative urgencies. Exceptions become necessary, however, when the time factor is considered and the function facing the greatest demand in the immediate future may take precedence over that with the largest actual deviation.[22]

Based on the foregoing discussion it seems appropriate to suggest a tentative priority system reflecting the intangible approach. Such a system must be flexible and can serve as a working hypothesis until a more perfect system is developed. A six-way breakdown of priorities is suggested: (1) urgent (highest priority); (2) essential; (3) necessary; (4) desirable; (5) acceptable; and (6) deferable (lowest priority). The last of these categories—deferable—is largely reserved for the adjustment of priorities following the initial review by the programmers and the planners. The various suggested criteria for assigning project proposals to these six categories are shown in Table 2-3. While these six priority categories are based largely on the "intangibles" approach, examination of the various suggested criteria will reveal several areas in which more measurable indices could be developed.

**Point System Priorities.** In an effort to establish a more "scientific" basis for evaluating project proposals and for determining capital improvements priorities, some attention has been given to the development and application of mathematical formulas. To date, however, these attempts have largely been limited to measuring the relative importance of individual projects within

Table 2-3
General Criteria for Capital Improvements Priority System

| Category | General Criteria |
| --- | --- |
| 1. Urgent | Projects that cannot reasonably be postponed; projects that would remedy a condition dangerous to public health, welfare, or safety; projects required to maintain a critically needed departmental program; projects needed to meet an emergency situation. |
| 2. Essential | Projects required to complete or make fully usable a major public improvement; projects required to maintain a minimum standard as part of a continuing departmental program; desirable projects that are self-liquidating; projects for which outside funds for over 65 percent of the costs are available for only a limited period. |
| 3. Necessary | Projects that should be carried out within a few years to meet clearly demonstrated anticipated needs; projects designated for replacement of unsatisfactory or obsolete facilities; projects designated for remodeling for continued use. |
| 4. Desirable | Adequately planned projects needed for the expansion of current departmental programs; projects designed to initiate new programs that are considered proper for a progressive community in competition with other communities; projects for the conversion of existing facilities to other uses. |
| 5. Acceptable | Adequately planned projects that could be used for ideal operations, but that can be postponed without detriment to present operations if budget reductions are necessary. |
| 6. Deferable | Projects that are definitely recommended for postponement or elimination from immediate consideration in the current capital program since they are questionable in terms of overall needs, adequate planning, or proper timing. |

the same functional group. The objective of this approach is to provide a means of standardizing recommendations by which all projects submitted to the programming agency by the individual departments are subjected to a uniform procedure in their processing.

The purpose of these more mathematically oriented priority systems is to develop a series of weighted scores that reflect the relative relationship among the various "intangibles" set forth in the previous discussion. That criterion which is judged to be most important or most significant as a determining factor in establishing capital improvements priorities is given the highest score (frequently based on units of ten or some multiple ot ten) and all other factors are then ranked in relation to this score. Thus, "protection of life and maintenance of public health" may be ranked as the most important criteria and given a score of 100. "Conservation of resources" may be judged to be nearly as important, and therefore, given a score of 90. On the other hand, "aesthetic and cultural values" may be ranked relatively low, scoring only 20 points. These categories are often further subdivided into a number of subcategories and scores accumulated for any given project. It should be evident that any effort to develop such an "objective" approach must be based, to a large degree, on subjective judgments.

Perhaps the most advanced *point system* approach was established some years ago in the state of Rhode Island. The Rhode Island point system has seven general categories of priority considerations: (1) circumstances influencing preference; (2) general purposes; (3) specific needs in terms of functions served; (4) availability of outside funds; (5) priority requested by sponsoring agency; (6) time of desired undertaking; and (7) impact on operating costs. It may be observed that these categories closely parallel the various considerations cited under the "intangibles" approach.

However, the Rhode Island system took this approach one step further by applying "ratings" to the various projects according to subdivisions in each of these categories. For example, "general purposes" (item #2) are rated as follows:

| | |
|---|---|
| Social service | 200 points |
| Education | 190 points |
| Public service (parks, highways, airports, etc.) | 180 points |
| Special services (police, institutions, National Guard) | 170 points |
| Conservation | 160 points |

Within each functional group a score is derived for each project by accumulating the points assigned in each of these seven categories. Some effort is then made to cross-reference these scores among the various functional groups to develop an overall priority list.

Quite obviously, such a point system cannot be applied rigidly, but rather must be used as a guide for decisions on capital improvements priorities. The priority system, whether it be developed on a more subjective, "intangibles" basis or on a point system, must be tailored to the particular goals and objectives of the individual jurisdiction. One locality may be interested primarily in furthering industrial growth and development; another may have as its main objective the development of tourism and the recreation industry; a third may place primary emphasis on the preservation of a well-maintained residential atmosphere. It should be evident that within any state these objectives may differ from area to area.

Finally, it must be emphasized that no written or mathematical formula can be substituted for human judgment. In the final analysis the planner must exercise his best professional judgment in working with the various operating agencies in assigning priorities, while at the same time recognizing that in government "... the actual choice and establishment of final priorities are still accompanied by the political process of compromise, a give-and-take between all groups concerned." [23]

*Staff Responsibilities in Determining Priorities*

As noted throughout the foregoing discussion, the establishment of priorities must involve the direct participation of the programmer, the planner, and representatives of the various departments and agencies initiating project requests. Since at present a reliable scientific approach to the weighing and comparing of the various "intangibles" has not yet been developed, it becomes the primary responsibility of the planning agency to point out the implications of alternative projects to the executive and legislative bodies. In the final analyses it is the responsibility of these decision makers to select among these alternatives and in so doing, a further "intangible" must be considered, that is, "will the proposed improvements be acceptable to the voters?"

As noted previously, the public services program and the capital facilities plan, as part of the overall strategic planning process, should serve as the principal basis for determining general priorities. These plans embody the overall goals and objectives of government and the parallel policies necessary to achieve these goals and objectives. It is against these policy statements that the planning agency must test the various capital improvements project requests. For example, assuming that one of the primary objectives of government is to strengthen the overall economic base of the community by attracting new industry and protecting existing economic activities, the planners should undertake studies and provide recommendations as to which improvements would be of the most value to industry. Thus, on the one hand, various transportation improvements may be required to meet the needs of certain types of industries, whereas improved water supply and power facilities may serve to attract others. Still other types of economic activities may seek locations near institutions of higher education to benefit from the research facilities that such institutions can provide. It becomes the planner's task to recommend a program that will achieve the delicate balance among these and other parallel objectives. In short, each project has its obvious and more subtle ramifications. The more obvious ramifications arise out of the primary need that motivates the sponsoring agency to submit the initial proposal. The more subtle ones, however, often require a comprehensive examination and interrelation of a variety of objectives. It is to this task that the planner must direct his attention.

## Program Formulation—Summary of Procedural Steps

As suggested earlier, the initiation of comprehensive capital improvements programming procedures must begin with an examination of the existing legislative authorization to determine if it has sufficient scope to achieve the overall programming objectives. If necessary, legislative measures should be introduced to define clearly the objectives of and responsibilities for the capital improvements program.

Once the proper legislative authorization has been established, the next step is for the chief executive to call for the submission of all capital improvements projects proposed by the various operating departments. In announcing the initiation of a capital improvements program, the chief executive also may wish to make any fiscal or general policy statements that may be appropriate. The timetable under which these projects will be considered should also be specified in the chief executive's announcement.

The planning agency must then take the initiative in establishing liaison with the various operating departments. Working with these departments and the financial planners, the planning agency should establish a set of standard procedures by which proposals for capital improvements are set forth, including the necessary forms on which the proposals should be reported and the written set of instructions to be followed in completing these forms. Generally, with the initiation of a new capital improvements program, it will be necessary to review these forms after the initial requests are submitted and perhaps make revisions and adjustments to "iron out any bugs" in the procedures.

At the same time as procedures are being developed for the submission of project proposals, the finance office should undertake an analysis of the financial status and the existing and potential fiscal resources. Working with the planning agency, the finance agency should then assess the amount of funds that will be available to finance the total operation of government and prepare recommendations as to what portion of these funds should be earmarked for capital improvements.

As a part of its liaison with the various operating departments, the planning agency should assist the operating departments in the compilation of their project listings, in establishing priorities within functional groups, as well as advising on the desirability of projects before they are formally submitted. After the various departments have submitted their proposals, the planning agency must review all of the catalogued projects and the supporting data in light of the goals and objectives set forth in the comprehensive development plan, the policies that have been formulated to implement this plan, and the financial analysis that has been developed in conjunction with the financial planners. In undertaking this analysis, to the extent that the information is available, consideration should be given to the possible impact of the improvements that are scheduled by other levels of government and by the private sector.

In order to provide clarification and/or redefinition of proposals (where necessary) the planning agency and the programmers should maintain a continual dialogue with the operating departments. One vehicle for this liaison that has achieved some success when applied elsewhere is the creation of an "interagency committee." Such a committee also provides a forum for discussion concerning the interrelationships that might exist among the various project proposals.

When all departmental project proposals have been examined and discussed, a composite capital improvements program should be prepared for presentation to the chief executive. If any projects are recommended for omission or postponement, reasons for these recommendations should be clearly stated. This program is then reviewed and adopted, with appropriate modifications, by the chief executive and the legislative body.

When the capital program is adopted it should be made available in report form to all civic groups and interested citizens in addition to being distributed to members of the legislative body and the operating departments. The capital program report should cover three main topics:

1. Explanation of the various considerations and policies that were brought to bear on the development of priorities, that is, legal requirements, magnitude or projected capital needs, the jurisdictions fiscal resources, etc.
2. A listing of major capital projects now under construction or for which funds have been appropriated
3. A detailed edscription of the capital improvements program and budget for (a) the next fiscal year; and (b) for the following five years with a listing of projects by agency and by priority

The detailed description of each project should include a brief statement as to its general purpose and the reason for its inclusion in the program. Capital costs, operating costs, the sources of funds, and the method of financing and the financing schedule for each project should be set forth in the report.

The report should be as brief and as graphic as is reasonably possible. For purposes of explanation and clarification, it should include charts, graphs, tables, and maps wherever appropriate, indicating the projected clientele of each project and the physical layout of each project, as well as charts showing estimated revenues, operating expenses, and debt service costs. Finally, the report should include a brief description of the development plan, including relevant departmental programs, policies, and standards of service.

To reiterate a point made earlier, even after legislative action has been taken in adopting or rejecting proposals for capital improvements, funds must still be made available. Therefore, although a capital budget may be adopted, there is still another opportunity for review at the time that appropriations are made, or in the case of bond issues, at the time of referendum is placed before the voters. Of course, even after appropriations are made, changes and adjustments are still possible prior to construction. However, if the original project requests are based upon a sound planning foundation, the need for such changes should be minimal.

# 3 The Role of Economic Analysis

Underlining any analysis of long-term expenditures and revenues of local governments must be a general concern with the aggregate local public economy—with "the problems of the cities." As the Council of Economic Advisors has observed, "too many cities realize the worst of all possible worlds, with strained budgets, inadequate expenditures for public services ranging from education to law enforcement, burdensome property taxes which spur the exodus of wealthier taxpayers and discourage job-creating business, and partial, excessively costly solution to problems that extend far beyond the city's jurisdiction and control."[1] While economists and political scientists must seek generalized solutions to these mounting problems, local officials must be much more concerned with quantitative and qualitative measurements of their own local governments operations, and with their consequent interaction. In short, sound capital facilities planning must be based on a firm understanding of the structure and interactive processes of the local economy.

## Origins of Economic Analysis

In the early twenties, as the neophyte planning profession turned its attention from the "City Beautiful" to the "City Practical," there emerged a general recognition of the need for a more comprehensive approach insofar as physical planning was concerned.

> Cities awakened to the fact that it is not reasonable to have one group of men plan the highways of the city, another the park system, another areas to be set aside for industry, business, and residence, and still another the sewage and water supply system. They began to realize that such procedures are fatal unless arrangements are made for these men to work closely together following an agreed-upon general plan, so each may know what the other is doing.[2]

Thus, there emerged the first truly American contribution of the planner's kit bag—the Master Plan—an overall scheme for the development of the physical plant of the city.

The widespread acceptance of the concept of the Master Plan led to another important "discovery"—that the planning of the physical plant of a city was closely tied to its ability and willingness to pay for public facilities and services. Thus, capital expenditure budgets were initiated by many local governments to provide a more orderly program of public investment. It was soon recognized, however, by more progressive city planning officials that the ability of local government to pay for these necessary facilities and services was conditioned, in large measure, by the community's revenue base. In an effort to gain a better understanding of the community's resource base and to devise means of strengthening it, many local governments in the thirties initiated so-called "economic base studies." Thus, another important technique was added to the public planner's repertoire. These studies, in many instance, led to an active "courting" of new industry by local government in the forties and fifties.

Although capital budgeting at the local level had its origins, in most instances, in the offices of the planning agency or at the initiation of local planning officials, as the field of public administration began to exercise greater influence in the affairs of local government during the thirties, the function of budgeting became a central tool of policy administration, and with it, responsibilities for capital improvements programming shifted from the planner to the office of the comptroller or the department of finance. Planners did little to resist this shift of activities; in most cases, they were too busy with their other new-found toys (tools). It is significant that the 1948 edition of the International City Managers' Association (ICMA) publication, *Local Planning Administration,* cited above has a very brief chapter near the end of the book on procedures for capital facilities planning.

The financial plight of state and local governments was given relatively little attention in the years immediately following World War II, as economists, political scientists, and public administrators devoted their energies to pressing problems of national growth, business cycles, economically depressed regions, and national goals. During the war years concern had been expressed regarding the potential role of local governmental expenditures in counteracting a postwar depression anticipated by many economists. Thus, the Council of State Governments urged state and local jurisdictions to restrict operations, pay off debts, and prepare for large expenditures after the war. Other economists were troubled by the then-current trend of locating new economic activities in more rural areas beyond the reach of the taxing authority of urban communities, a trend they foresaw as creating "extremely embarrassing" fiscal situations for local governments, as indeed has been the case.[3] The accumulated distortions in local governmental affairs following nearly 15 years of depression and war, the impact of inflation on local expenditures, and the underlying deficiencies and maladjustments in the fiscal, economic, and governmental structures of states and localities also received some attention.[4] Expressions of these concerns, however, were relatively disconnected from the principal focus of economists and political scientists of this period, and the resulting prescriptions reflected the limited "state of the art" in understanding the complexities of the urban economy.

## Theoretical Constructs of Urban Economics

The urban economy must be regarded as a complex system of production, distribution, and consumption that embraces the sum total of economic productive activities within an urban center and that portion of its hinterland dependent upon the facilities and services available within the city. Productive activities refer not only to manufacturing, agriculture, and extractive industries in which products are processed and/or marketed, but also to trade, finance, transportation and communications, government, and other services using the urban center as a base of operations.

*Regional Approaches*

Economists are rather late-comers to the study of the city. Until recently, regional and urban economics were viewed (and continued to be viewed by some theorists) as a single field. In a 1963 survey, for example, John R. Meyer included metropolitan studies within the purview of regional economics, although he acknowledged that urban problems were beginning to play an increasingly important role in regional analysis.[5] This lack of separate identity has inhibited the full development of urban economics as a field of study. Courses in urban economics have only recently been added to standard university curricula, even in the more progressive schools of economics.

The field of regional economics itself experienced an identity crisis in its emergence as a discipline. Various definitions of the field still exist. Some writers emphasize the interdisciplinary links of regional economics, suggesting that a unified "regional science" exists in which economics, geography, sociology, and demography form an indivisible whole for purposes of regional analysis.[6] A second approach to defining regional economics is based on the notion that a specific group of problems forming the subject matter of regional economics can be distinguished and, as such, serves as a definition of the field—the precise opposite of the first approach.[7] A third approach regards regional economics as the economics of spatial separation—the problems of social economic adjustments in a spatially differentiated world.[8] Still another definition conceives regional economics as the economics of resource immobility, that is, the consequence of an uneven distribution of resources.[9] In an effort to resolve these differing points of view, Vinod Dubey suggests the following definition:

> Regional economics is . . . the study, from the viewpoint of economics, of the differentiation and interrelationships of areas in a universe of unevenly distributed and imperfectly mobile resources, with particular emphasis in application on the planning of the social overhead capital investments to mitigate the social problems created by these circumstances.[10]

A more succinct definition is offered by Dubey when he observes: "Regional economics is not the study of the economic problems of regions. . . . Rather, it is the study of all the problems of regions from the economic viewpoint."[11]

A basic premise of the regional approach to the study of economics is that economic activities in any urban center are affected by other centers of activity in its immediate region and are ultimately linked to the national economy as a whole. Thus, this approach holds that the *present* economic position of an urban center must be analyzed in relation to other urban areas and is dependent upon its share of the regional and national total of goods and services produced. Its *future* position, in turn, is dependent on its capacity to develop new productive resources and to expand existing ones in competition with other urban centers. Using such methods as descriptive analysis, location theory, economic impact studies, input-output analysis, and income and product accounts, regional economists are concerned with why some urban areas are richer, more egalitarian, or more economically stable than others, why there are differential growth rates in income and production, and whether there are economies or diseconomies of city size.

While regional economics can provide important insights into the impact of national economic forces and trends and their influences in larger regions and subregions, to derive a fully rounded understanding of the urban economy, it is also necessary to examine local productive activities and resources, distributive resources, and capital resources for financing new or expanding existing activities, that is, the supply side of the local economy. Only in this way is it possible to determine the capacity of the local economy to sustain its present position and to expand its productive activities within a broader regional context.

### *Partial Theories of the Economic City*

Economists see the urban structure in two lights. First, they pursue a descriptive approach that views the city as a matrix of locations for firms—a necessary translation of a national economy into spatial terms. Second, and somewhat more pertinent to the present discussion, urban economists see the city itself as an economic unit—as a kind of super firm, based upon relations between buyers and sellers, contractors, and subcontractors (with the household as the smallest firm), all involved in a giant export-import business. The city is a center of production, trade, and distribution, the basic units of which are economic organizations. Even local government, in this view, can be equated to a firm. The economic city rests upon a division of labor among firms. This division of labor involves competition and cooperation within the framework of the marketplace, with certain advantages and disadvantages accruing; these, in turn, can be analyzed in terms of location theory, multiplier effects, economies of scale, and marginal economies of operation. The city as a whole is "in business," and its economic position may be estimated in terms of a balance of trade.

The city is a system that, among other things, provides contact and interaction for the production and consumption of goods. Buyers and sellers meet at all levels; goods are assembled and distributed; labor and materials are brought together for manufacture. Power is produced and supplied; communication and transportation channels are developed and utilized. Financial mechanisms are concentrated in the city to assemble and allocate, through monetary processes, the capital goods used in production; these mechanisms also supply the medium of exchange. Space for economic functions is sorted out to the various users—itself a productive activity. Government services are also a major factor of production, since they supply critical human wants—security, control, and regulation. Thus, it must be recognized that the economic system is composed of a number of subsystems, each of which must be identified and studied in order to understand more fully the total economic system and its interaction with other dimensions of the urban environment.

Several core areas of study may be identified within the field of urban economics, including studies of:

1. *Structure and growth of the urban economy.* The city is viewed in its role as a component of the national economy—an element in a national system of cities. Problems of city growth and decline may be included under this heading.
2. *Intrametropolitan organization and change.* This subfield focuses on the spatial dimensions of the urban economy, in terms of organization of economic activities within the metropolis and the relation of the city form and the allocation of economic resources. Land use, urban housing, and urban transportation are specific topics of interest.
3. *Urban public services and welfare.* This area is concerned with the urban public economy, addressing problems associated with efficient allocation of public resources and the interaction of the public and private sectors. Topics covered include federal, state, and local finance in an urban context and the demand for and supply of urban public services.
4. *Economics and urban human resources.* Focal topics of this area are households as suppliers of labor services in the urban market and the urban population as a consumer of final products of the economy. Migrations, poverty, and investments in human capital (including education) are examined in an urban context.
5. *Regional accounts.* The systematic organization of information flows needed for economic analysis is the primary focus of this core area. The urban region is the relevant unit for the application of urban economic analysis.

These subfields have grown at different rates and some are still relatively underdeveloped (the economics of urban poverty and discrimination, for example). In particular, the area of human resource economics has lagged behind when compared to the growth in other subfields, reflecting in part the lack of group cohesion among researchers concerned with specific topics under this heading. Labor economists, consumption economists, human ecologists, and fledgling human resource economists have rather diverse points of view, so that communication among potential contributors to this area of concern often has been difficult.

## Regional Techniques[a]

A central consideration in regionally oriented approaches to the study of the urban economy is the concept of linkages or regional interdependencies. Differential distribution of natural resources and variations in the degree of labor specialization, economic organization, and technological development have contributed to an increased interdependence among economic regions in the United States. Thus, these regional techniques build upon the theory that local productive activities are significantly influenced by a complex interplay of forces at the regional and national levels.

### *Descriptive Approaches*

Among the oldest conceptual frameworks for studying regional economies are the descriptive approaches that emphasize the structure of the economy rather than processes or functions. The region has been used independently as a unit of study and analysis by a number of disciplines. As might be expected when a concept is used in a wide variety of contexts, it has acquired a number of meanings.

There are two basic approaches to the definition of economic regions. The *nodal approach,* stemming for the most part from studies of demographers, sociologists, and geographers, seeks ways of describing metropolitan spheres of influence and linkages among cities in a region according to their dependence on a single dominant center or node. Such regions tend to be heterogenous, emphasizing economic linkages between the center and its hinterland.

The nodal region may be associated with internal unity. Unity of organization can encompass a great diversity of elements that are bound

---

[a]As a consequence of their limited application to the analysis of specific local economies, these regional techniques are discussed in a somewhat superficial fashion.

together in a systematic way by interconnections, interactions, or flows.[12]

In contrast, the focus on *economic homogeneity* gives more direct recognition to the spatial distribution of productive activities, reflecting the influence of resources and raw materials on the location of such activities, and taking into account the specialized nature of areas in selected economic pursuits. Such an approach builds on the notion that an industrialized nation can be subdivided into geographic areas of specialization that reflect contemporary trends in the territorial division of labor, distributions of resources, and the flows of commodities (goods, services, and capital) among regions. Thus, economic regions have been designated by several criteria: (a) economic factors (an industry complex and its labor and/or materials supply area), (b) physical factors (e.g., commodity regions, natural resource regions, river basins, etc.), (c) human resource factors (e.g., availability of organizational or intellectual resources, capital for investment, etc.), and (d) political boundaries (a city, county, state, or nation).

Economic regions can be rural or urban. Most economic theories are easiest applied and most valid in a nonurban context. The assumption is frequently made, however, that once the structure and process of these theories are understood, they can be expanded in application to urban regions. Unfortunately, this expansion never took place in a number of cases.

*Location Theory*

In an economy governed by market forces, the locational decision of a given enterprise is (or rationally should be) based on the selection of that site evidencing the lowest sum of all costs incurred in servicing the market or markets in which its products are sold. Thus, as developed by regional economists, location theory is largely an extension of economic price theory—the study of allocation of scarce resources among competing ends is extended to the allocation in space.[13] Location theory deals with what kinds of economic structure is where and why this structure began and how it has survived. As such, it can be regarded as normative locational economics—what *ought* to be where, if only private goods are considered, or as positive locational economics—what is where, if social costs and/or benefits do exist and do not escape the profit calculus of the private entrepreneur.

Location theory focuses on the following problem areas:

1. *Locations of an economic activity*—involving locational choice, plant location, localized inputs, and location within transportation networks
2. *Location of an industry*—including the classification of market and supply

areas, alternative allocation of sales, price policy, general principles or relocation, free entry, and optimal distribution of plants

3. *Allocation of land*—including consideration of von Thunen's theory and patterns of demand
4. *Study of central places*—including the hierarchy model, flow model, and transportation networks
5. *Consideration of equilibrium*—including pricing in spatially separated markets (homogeneous or heterogeneous goods), equilibrium in a continuously extended spatial market, and the study of long-run equilibrium
6. *Location effects of economic growth*—including spatial price equilibrium, the growth of firms, industrial dynamics, the dynamics of central places, economic growth in a one-product economy, and localized resources.

Location theory can be applied on both a macroeconomic and microeconomic scale. Figures 3-1 and 3-2 illustrate the complex economic factors involved in the location of an economic activity. In dealing in a causative manner with major shifts in the structure of the economy, a location theorist may consider: (1) a shift in demand away from products with relatively high materials cost toward highly finished and complex products with minor materials cost (supply factor); (2) shifts in the transportation structure (in terms of rates) against the cost of materials and finished goods (supply factor); (3) introduction of labor-saving technologies in stages of processing (supply factor); (4) shifts in the price structure for raw materials, finished goods, or labor (demand factor); (5) increased competition and substitution of products by consumers (demand factor); and/or (6) increased affluence and a rising demand for more differentiation in products that are manufactured most effectively in close proximity to the mass market (demand factor). These and other similar considerations contribute significantly to where a particular economic activity will locate and survive.

*Economic Impact Studies*

Economic impact studies examine the phenomena of: (a) dollar *inputs* entering a regional economic structure; (b) the *process* of dollars circulating throughout the system; and (c) the process of dollars leaving the system as *regional output* and the total wealth generated and its distribution (see Figure 3-3). Economic inputs create: (a) economic impacts (employment, taxes, etc.), (b) political impacts (public revenues, service demands, etc.), and (c) physical impacts (spatial expansion-contraction, social diseconomies, pollution, etc.). The function of economic impact depends on whom one asks. Idealistically, its function should be socioeconomic welfare. If the process of substantial economic impact does not attain the function of economic welfare, it is some-

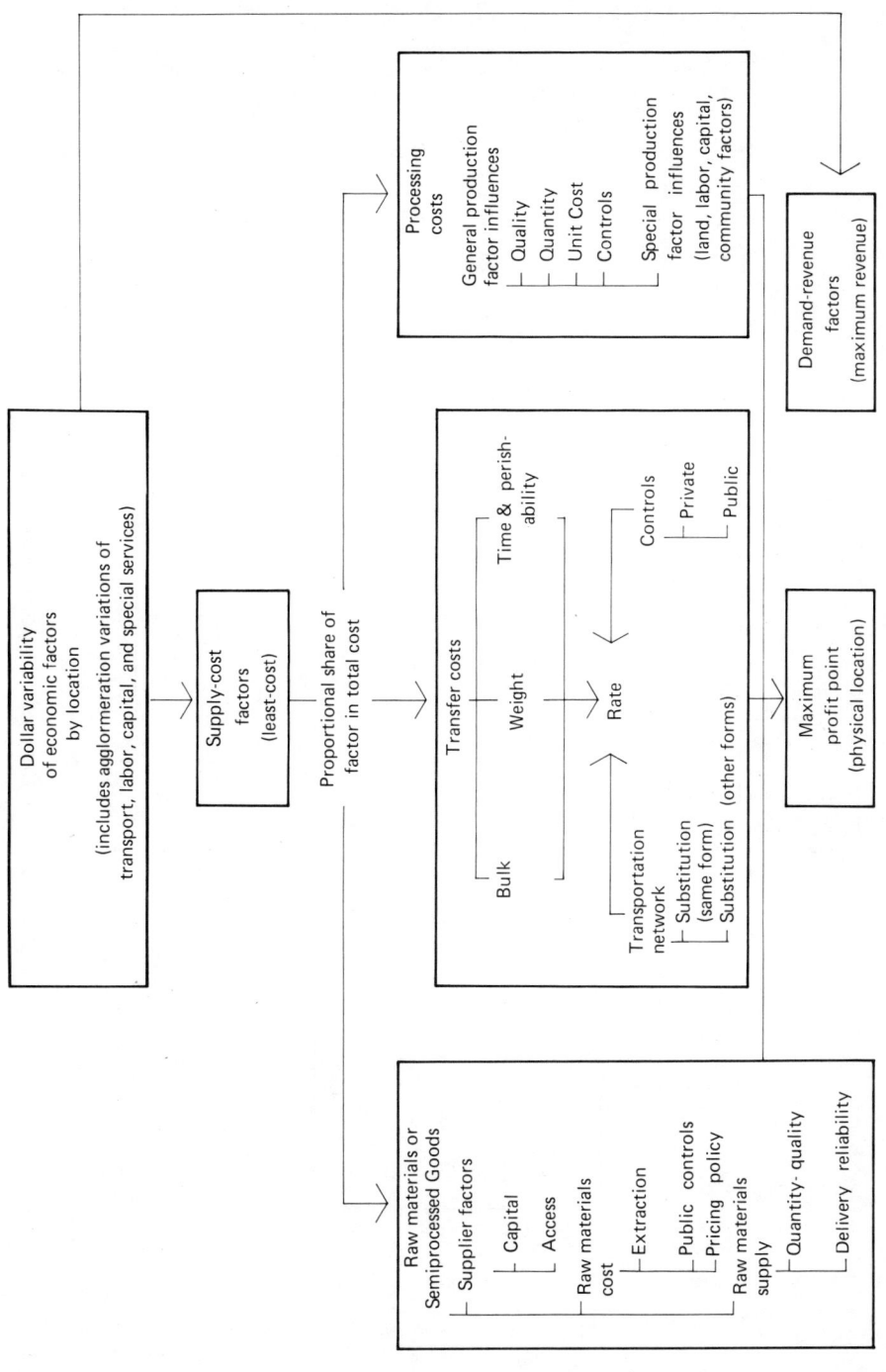

**Figure 3-1.** The Supply Side of an Urban Economy

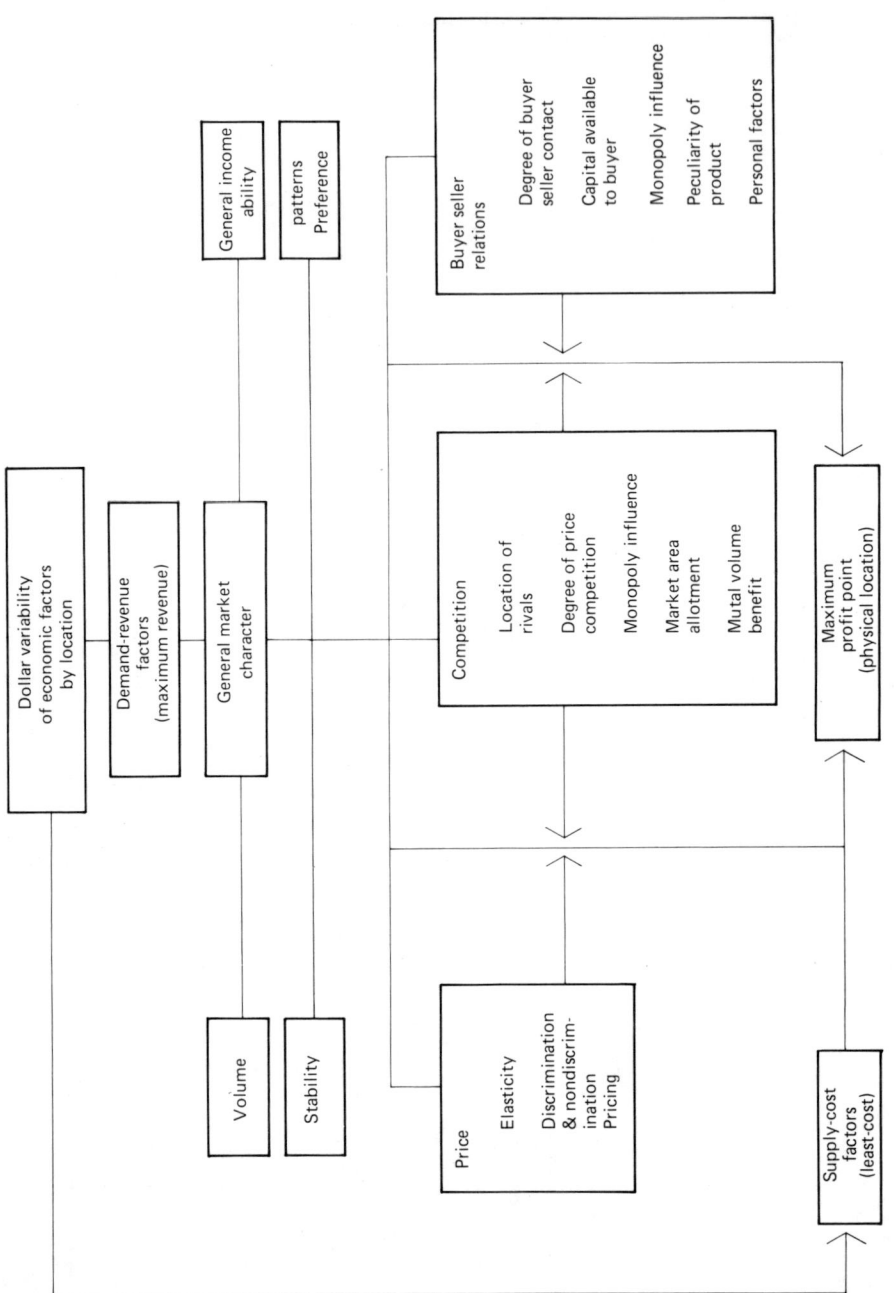

**Figure 3-2.** The Demand Side of an Urban Economy

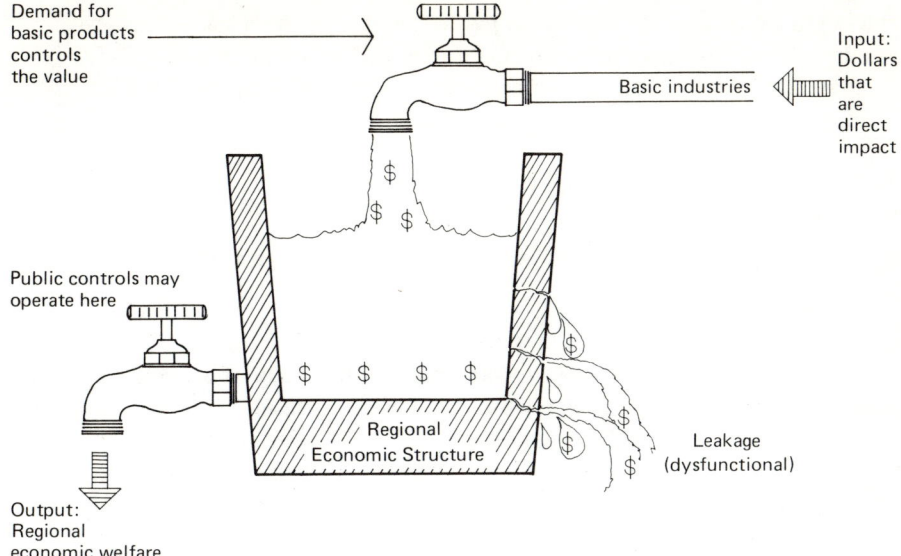

(Adapted from: James Kennedy, "Urban Conceptual Subsystems," January 1971.)

**Figure 3-3.** The Kennedy Basic-Nonbasic Wash Bucket Principle

times called exploitation. Traditionally, economic impact has always been associated with the functional concept of *progress.* [14]

Wilbur Thompson discusses economic impact in terms of stages of urban growth.[15] In the first stage—the stage of export specialization—the local economy is dominated by a single industry, that is, one firm or several firms from the same industrial category. Secondary economic activities are highly dependent upon the economic well-being of the principal industry. As the economic system is broadened and new industries, customers, and/or local suppliers are added, the region moves to the stage of export complex. Critical linkages exist between basic industries and their suppliers and customers. The third stage, that of economic maturity, is reached when imports are replaced by new "own use" or "home grown" productive activities; in this stage the service sector has reached puberty. In the fourth stage the localized economy has become a node—a regional metropolis—connecting and controlling neighboring cities in its hinterland. In this stage the export of services becomes a major economic function. Thompson defines a fifth stage beyond the regional metropolis that he labels the stage of technical-professional virtuosity. In this stage the economic system has achieved national eminence in some specialized economic function. Thompson notes that economic growth may hesitate and stagnate between any of these stages if the momentum at the end of a phase is not strong enough to carry the economy to the point at which the next stage is achieved. He also introduces the concept of the "urban ratchet"—when the economy reaches a size in which certain functions are "locked-in" (due to capital investment, markets, etc.), it will not slip backward. While it is not possible to accept any of these classifications as the *complete* answer to the impact of economic growth, they serve as a necessary first step in gaining a fuller understanding of these phenomena.

*Input-Output Analysis*

A somewhat more sophisticated approach to the study of economic impact is found in input-output analysis, which defines and measures the economic structure of a community or region in terms of an interindustry system or matrix. Input-output theory has existed since 1877, when Leon Walras first conceived the basic model in the context of general equilibrium theory. The model was further developed by Françoise Quesmoy in *Tableau Economique*. It was not until 1931, however, that the method had its first practical application in the work of Wassily W. Leontief. Unlike other forms of complex urban systems analysis, the theoretical framework for input-output analysis existed long before computer technology made practical the extensive inversions of mathematical matrices. Its widespread application to an analysis of the urban economy has been hampered, however, by the lack of adequate models and data deficiencies.

Input-output analysis seeks to model the technological interrelationships of production and distribution in the economy through a system of simultaneous equations that can be solved for the total input and output requirements of any particular set of economic activities. As applied to a regional economy, it provides a complete structural description of the transactions taking place and links each intermediate flow among sectors of the regional economy to exogenous demand, that is, demand arising from outside of the region. Thus, input-output theory postulates that any given line of economic activity bears a measurable relationship to every other industry in the economy, and that these relationships can be set forth in a series of equations (readily solved by computers). Once the regional economy is subdivided into appropriate sectors of individual industries (for example, food processing, shoe manufacturing, banking, and so forth), or groups of similar industries (for example, agriculture, finance, retail trade, and so on), interindustry relationships can be expressed in terms of what Leontief has called a huge revenue expenditure accounting system or transaction table.[16]

Consider the economic system to be made up of $n$ sectors. These sectors may be arrayed in a double-entry table (Table 3-1), with each sector appearing on the column side as a purchaser of goods and services from other sectors and

## Table 3-1
### Basic Format for Input-Output Analysis

|  |  | Purchasing Sectors of Economy | | | | | | Final Demand Sectors $Y_i$ | Total Output |
|---|---|---|---|---|---|---|---|---|---|
|  |  | 1 | 2 | 3 | 4 | 5 ... | n | ($i$ = 1, 2, 3 ... n) |  |
|  | 1 | $x_{11}$ | $x_{12}$ | $x_{13}$ | $x_{14}$ | $x_{15}$ | $x_{1n}$ | $Y_1$ | $X_1$ |
|  | 2 | $x_{21}$ | $x_{22}$ | $x_{23}$ | $x_{24}$ | $x_{25}$ | $x_{2n}$ | $Y_2$ | $X_2$ |
|  | 3 | $x_{31}$ | $x_{32}$ | $x_{33}$ | $x_{34}$ | $x_{35}$ | $x_{3n}$ | $Y_3$ | $X_3$ |
|  | 4 | $x_{41}$ | $x_{42}$ | $x_{43}$ | $x_{44}$ | $x_{45}$ | $x_{4n}$ | $Y_4$ | $X_4$ |
|  | 5 | $x_{51}$ | $x_{52}$ | $x_{53}$ | $x_{54}$ | $x_{55}$ | $x_{5n}$ | $Y_5$ | $X_5$ |
|  | . | . | . | . | . | . | . | . | . |
|  | n | $x_{n1}$ | $x_{n2}$ | $x_{n3}$ | $x_{n4}$ | $x_{n5}$ | $x_{nn}$ | $Y_n$ | $X_n$ |
| Charges against final demand |  | $V_1$ | $V_2$ | $V_3$ | $V_4$ | $V_5$ | $V_n$ |  |  |
|  |  | (Payments for labor, taxes, imports, etc.) | | | | | |  |  |
| Total |  | $X_1$ | $X_2$ | $X_3$ | $X_4$ | $X_5$ | $X_n$ |  |  |

Outputs (Receipts or Sales) →

on the row side as a supplier of products to other sectors. Thus, the revenue side of the ledger sheet shows how the output of every industry is distributed to other industries (sectors) in the economy, while the expenditure side records for each industry the distribution of inputs per unit of output from all other industries (generally expressed as coefficients,[b] derived by dividing each input in a given column by the total of all inputs in that column, that is, $V_j$).[c] The economic sectors shown in the transaction table may be classified as internal (within the regional economy) or external (outside the regional economy); obviously, the greatest detailed sectorial breakdown is with those internal to the region. While some models disaggregate external sectors in some detail, often only one "rest of the world" (ROW) sector accounts for all external sectors; in Table 3-1 the so-called "final demand sector" includes external sectors as

---

[b] Two types of coefficients are applied. The *constant production coefficient* is used in noninterregional models (those dealing with a closed economy), while the *constant interareal input coefficient* (involving constant supply channels) is applied in the interregional models where inputs come from many areas and outputs (products) leave the region. Various writers have suggested that these coefficients are the key weakness in input-output analysis. Changes in price and volume of sales, shifts in technology, product substitution, etc. all result in a need to change the coefficients.

[c] In the matrix, $x_{ij}$ is the sales of sector $i$ to sector $j$; $V_i$ is charges against the final demand; and $X_i$ is the total sales of sector $i$. $V_i$ can also be interpreted as the value added by sector $i$.

well as household expenditures, government purchases, and investments through private capital formation.

The accounting system derived from an input-output table displays consistency because the following balance conditions prevail:

1. *Row balances.* Total output ($X_i p_i$, where $p_i$ is the price per unit) equals the sum of all transactions between sectors $i$ and $j$ ($x_{ij} p_i$) plus the final demand sector ($Y_i p_i$).
2. *Column balances.* Total inputs ($X_j p_j$) equals the sum of all transactions between sectors $i$ and $j$ ($x_{ij} p_i$) plus the charges against final demand ($V_j p_j$).
3. *Overall balance.* Therefore, by definition $X_i = X_j$.

It is assumed that the amount of goods and services delivered by any sector $i$ to the other sectors is a linear and homogeneous function of the output levels of the purchasing sectors $j$.

In its basic form input-output theory focuses on an interindustry analysis within a given region. Walter Isard has developed a space-economy analysis by expanding this approach through a series of iterations that establish relationships in the flow of commodities between regions that arise in fulfilling the input-output requirements in the interindustry analysis.[17] Early formulations of this model, however, involved a questionable assumption: Inputs for a given sector in one region require fixed portions of output from other sectors in other regions. Thus, changes in the shape of the space economy and changes in regional flows might constrain the use of the model to relatively short-run applications. Isard has attempted to solve this problem through a three step process, involving: (1) the solution of a national input-output table for all sectors exogenous to the regions into which the nation is to be divided; (2) allocation of national output among regions; and (3) given estimates of final regional demand, the solution of an input-output table for each region to obtain total regional production, including residentiary output.[18] Isard proposed the use of gravity models to allocate output among regions.

Input-output analysis is well suited to comparative studies, statistical analyses, and dynamic problem solving. It can provide a precise "snapshot" of the intricacies of a regional economy. Such an approach illustrates the specific indirect impacts of economic activities, so that dollars can be traced throughout the system. By holding the structure of the economy constant, it can be used to test the effects of changes in income flow (inputs).

Input-output analysis has certain disadvantages, however. It is relatively expensive and difficult to do. As a consequence it often is accepted as a precise and flawless tool (which it is not). Since it is complex, impressive, and has intellectual status, analysts may couch their biased arguments in esoteric terms to accomplish predetermined goals. There are potential errors in the collection of data, and improper sector groupings can mask many important economic welfare consideration. Input-output analysis is a relatively static approach; it assumes that the economic structure (supply channels and production costs) remains constant over extended time periods. Without frequent (and costly) revisions, it rapidly becomes dated in a changing economy. Finally, input-output models accentuate the economic base dependence of the entire economy; as Thompson has emphasized, economic base theory loses its relevance as economies become large and complex.[19]

*Industrial Complex Analysis*

Regional scientists are particularly sensitive to the inability of interregional input-output analysis to handle adequately economies of scale, localization economies, urbanization economies, and regional price variations resulting in or associated with the use of different proportions of the factors of production. Therefore, the techniques of industrial complex analysis have been devised to compensate for some of the deficiencies in the coefficients applied in input-output approach, to improve upon the earlier industry-by-industry method of analysis by synthesizing industries into groups, and to provide a bridge to comparative cost and locational analyses. An *industrial complex* may be defined as a set of activities occurring at a given location and belonging to a group (or subsystem) of activities that are subject to import, production, marketing, or other interrelations.[20] The selection of specific industrial complexes to be analyzed is relative to the purpose of the study, availability of data, research resources at hand, and the inclinations of the researchers.

Industrial complex analysis begins in a rather traditional fashion with a reconnaisance of resources in order to identify desirable industrial linkages. The entire economy of the region must be examined in order to isolate the several important considerations that might govern the appropriate type of industrial complex. The commodity balance of trade is examined, as are basic considerations influencing economic development, for example, economies of scale. From engineering sources information may be accumulated on minimum feasible plant sizes for different intermediate and end products. As with comparative cost studies of a single economic activity, detailed knowledge is required as to the precise weights and quantities of raw materials and intermediates, of power, labor, and capital inputs, and of the several outputs of the industrial complex. Internal interrelations, that is, interactivity linkages, must be expressed explicitly in quantitative terms. It is at this point that the interindustry matrix of input-output analysis comes into play.

A table is constructed showing the amount of various inputs and outputs associated with operating each individual or combined productive process (activity) associated with a specific industrial complex at a "unit" level.[d] Unlike

---

[d]The determination of the unit level for any activity is arbitrary and is defined merely to facilitate computation and understanding.

input-output tables, which typically are built in dollar terms based on census data, the industrial complex table is based on physical data obtained from engineering studies. The columns represent activities, while the rows represent commodities. When a commodity is used in a process as an input, it is indicated by a minus sign; when it is produced as an output, it is indicated by a plus sign. Only those inputs and outputs whose amounts vary in direct proportion with the scale of productive activity are listed. Labor and capital services are excluded (but are considered at a later stage), since generally they vary in nonlinear fashion with scale of operation. Once the table is constructed the analysis proceeds to a detailed examination of the structure of each of a number of industrial complexes (step 2). The total inputs and outputs associated with each of the selected production complexes are computed (step 3), and the total labor and capital requirements of the selected complexes are estimated (step 4). The investigator next determines the structure of specific complexes, each detailed in terms of precise weights and quantities of raw materials and intermediate inputs, of labor, power, and capital inputs, and of the several outputs (step 5). Having employed an interactivity matrix (i.e., an extended interindustry matrix encompassing data on both relevant factors for nonlinear inputs as well as their unit requirements), the investigator is in a position to proceed with a comparative cost framework (step 6).

The six-step procedure of industrial complex analysis outlined above provides a highly useful analytical tool in terms of the interaction of related elements of regional economy. Industrial complex analyses are particularly useful in industrial development planning. It is, of course, a relatively complicated and difficult technique to administer, requiring extensive understanding of input-output analysis as well as comparative cost analysis. The weaknesses of this approach center on its limited treatment of the service sector and its inherent inapplicability to industries with low levels of integration.

*Income and Product Accounts*

As its name implies, the income and product accounts approach to regional economic analysis involves a system of double-entry bookkeeping (similar to that used in input-output analysis). Unlike input-output analysis, however, these accounts are established on the basis of asset changes without tracing interchanges in physical inventories. Therefore, a more inclusive view of all forms of income producing activities can be obtained under this approach.

Until recently income and product accounts have been viewed primarily as tools for the study of the national economy. Over the past 30 years, Gross National Product and other income statistics have become familiar indicators on national economic well-being, on the basis of which annual analyses of economic growth and economic projections have been developed. The application of these concepts at the regional level, however, poses some very different problems. In national accounts, closure in the economic system can be achieved by introduction of a "rest-of-the-world" account. At the regional scale this approach has several pitfalls because boundaries must be established arbitrarily and may cut across important ties with other regions. As Werner Hochwald has observed, on the regional level:

> ... strategic production decisions are made in response to expected "foreign" market demand rather than local expenditures Regional accounts therefore are "open" to trace the impact of external forces on local production flows; their design depends on the choice of exogenous and endogenous sectors used to trace relations between the region and the "Rest of the World."[21]

Other criticisms of income and product accounts focus on the problem of obtaining reliable data on a regularly reported basis and the consequent cost of establishing and maintaining an adequate and complete set of accounts for regions. An increasing number of economists, however, see the data problem as a temporary one, and therefore, look with favor on the use of a properly designed system of regional accounts for selected kinds of economic analysis. They suggest that local surveys, including sampling studies, can be undertaken to supply the requisite data, and with careful interpretations of interregional economic relations, income and product accounts can be used in the study of local economic development and urban growth. When "across-the-boards" analyses are eventually introduced as a comparative base, regional studies can be provided with the necessary breadth of perspective to facilitate the interpretation of a local systems of accounts.

In a system of income and product accounts, the economy is seen as a mechanism for the production of goods and services for final disposition as: (a) export sales, (b) private investment in industry and business, (c) governmental purchases, and (d) household consumption. The first three areas of final demand may be viewed as exogenous elements, independent of total income, while the fourth element (household consumption) is endogenous and is dependent on total income. If total income is the sum of exogenously and endogenously determined income, then a basic relationship can be established between current and future levels of consumption. For example, if exogenous activity accounts for 60 percent of total income, a regional multiplier of 1.67 can be applied to determine the impact of shifts in either local economic activity or total income. Such a multiplier ($K$) can be derived from the following formula.[22]

$$K = \frac{1}{1 - Y/T}$$

where $Y$ is the value added in the local market (40 percent in the above example) and $T$ is total income (100 percent). In other words, assuming that the multiplier value remains constant, for every million dollars of additional value added for export, there will be approximately $670,000 of additional local economic activity. Or, if an increase of $100,000 is experienced in the local income level, eventually total income will increase by $167,000. While these figures are based on the assumption that the multiplier remains constant, this need not be the case. If new lines of activity are introduced into a region or other events lead to changes in its relative competitive advantages vis-à-vis other regions, the multiplier may be modified in making projections. The use of regional multipliers in economic forecasting requires the preparation of projections that, presumably, are in balance with anticipated economic growth in all regions in the nation.

*Ratio-Stepdown Methods of Analysis*

A somewhat less complex and less costly (albeit less meaningful) approach to regional economic analysis is found in the so-called ratio-stepdown or approximation methods. Under this approach comparative analyses are developed as to a region's share in national productive activity, using such standard measures as value added by manufacture, wholesale sales, retail sales, and receipts from services. Comparisons are drawn as to the relative position of the study area in each line of activity, expressed as a percentage of the larger economic region and/or nation. By making such comparisons over time, it is possible to determine if the position of the study area is improving, remaining constant, or deteriorating. Where projections are desired, this approach—as with the techniques of input-output and regional accounts—requires a "given" forecast of national (or regional) productive activity. Such forecasts, of course, must be available in terms of the standard measures being employed, that is, value added, wholesale and retail sales, and receipts from services. Past values for these relationships are arranged in a time series and extrapolated by fitting a mathematical curve to the data. The projected region-to-nation (or subregion-to-region) ratio is then applied to the "given" absolute figures of the nation to obtain values for the region. The apportionment technique, a variation on the ratio-stepdown approach, introduces an element of control by making parallel analyses of all subareas of the larger region and balancing the results with the total before proceedingsto the actual stepdown.

Ratio-stepdown methods reflect the combined effects of interindustry and interregional flows and indicate where gross changes are occurring over time. However, since they cannot trace flows between industries within and among regions, they do not provide a direct measure of linkage, but rather, only a crude cross-sectional view of gross effects of commodity flows as they influence total transactions.

*Econometric Models*

In the late sixties and early seventies, efforts were made on an experiemental basis to apply the techniques of econometrics to the analysis of regional and urban economic systems. Econometrics consists of the application of modern statistical techniques and procedures to theoretical models formulated in mathematical terms. The models in question, however, suffer from at least two serious limitations: (1) the inadequacy of mathematical models in general, and (2) the fact that statistical methods frequently are based on assumptions that do not hold strictly for the data under analysis.

Econometric models are derived from certain basic economic assumptions or axioms, for example, the "law of supply and demand" and the "theory of the market." Economists assume, for example, that the consumer maximizes his utility, while the prices of all commodities and services and his income are given independently of his actions. From this assumption certain properties can be derived with regard to individual demand functions for all commodities and services. Econometricians attempt to take these relationships and quantify and "formulafy" them into statistically testable models. To date, while these models seem to hold a great deal of potential, their application to urban economic systems has been relatively limited and the complexity of the formula involved has prevented wider testing.

## Economic Base Studies

As a consequence of the late adaption of regional approaches to urban economic studies, the complexities of their analytical procedures, and the data obstacles discussed previously, input-output analysis, regional accounts systems, and econometric models have been used infrequently in the study of the urban economy. In contrast, economic base studies, which employ less complicated analytical procedures and are designed to utilize regularly reported, standard data sources, have received rather widespread application. As noted at the outset of this discussion, the economic base study has been a standard technique of analysis for the planner for nearly 40 years.

*Export-Base Hypothesis*

The underlying foundation of economic base studies has been stated by Thompson as follows: Cities survive by selling products or services to the "outside world," thereby gaining the wherewithal with which to pay for indispensable imports, i.e., goods not produced in the local economy. By extension, cities rise and fall with the growth and decline of their export industries.[23]

Economic base studies thus begin by dividing the urban economy into two categories: (1) *basic (or export) industries,* that is, those industries producing goods and services (and capital) for distribution to markets outside a defined local economic area; and (2) *nonbasis or service industries,* the goods and services of which are consumed within the confines of the local economic area. Thus, in economic base studies the distinction is made between those economic activities that bring new money into the community (basic industries) and those that simply result in the recirculation of money (service industries), the assumption being that expansion in basic activities usually results in growth in service activities and thus growth in the total economy. Some economic base theorists draw parallels between this approach and international trade theory. Economic base studies focus attention on "export balances," which become a measure of the strength of the urban economy much in the same manner that export balances have an important influence on the position of the national economy. As with international trade theory, rising export balances have positive implications, while declining balances, if allowed to continue, have negative repercussions. In economic base theory fluctuation in the level of a community's exporting base is a prime cause of changes in urban economic activity. Consequently, forecasts of urban economic growth may be based on multipliers that relate residentiary (local) activities to exports.

*Classification of Activities*

Richard Andrews, who has made perhaps the most exhaustive analysis of the economic base concept,[24] has suggested that a "purely" basic or nonbasic industry is something of a rarity; for the most part, industries serve a mixture of export and local markets and may be more basic or more nonbasic but seldom exclusively so. Therefore, Andrews proposes several additional subcategories for each of these divisions, as follows:

I. Export (basic)
   A. Movement of commodity (goods, services, and/or capital) to consumers or purchasers
   B. Movement of consumers of purchasers to commodity
II. Local (nonbasic)
   1. Importation of commodities (goods, services, and/or capital) for local distribution or local fabrication and local distribution
   2. Local origination of commodity for fabrication and local distribution
   3. Either class 1 or 2 business that enter into sales arrangements with firms of either base or local market; no or few sales to final or household consumers

Andrews suggests a further division of these categories to distinguish between those firms in which 80 to 100 percent of their sales is either export-oriented or locally oriented (high export or high local) and those in which 50 to 80 percent of their sales has such identifiable orientations. He also subdivides class 3 firms (which he calls "subsidiaries") into 3A: base subsidiaries and 3B: local market subsidiaries. Examples of base subsidiaries would include advertising, mailing services, machine parts, package manufacturing, etc., while local market subsidiaries might be represented by accounting and legal services, delivery companies, industrial laundry services, "canteen" suppliers, and so forth. Andrews classification system is summarized in Figure 3-4.

*Delineation of the Base Area*

Where the boundaries of the base area are drawn can have a significant influence on the determination of what activities are basic and what activities are service or local-oriented. Using the political boundaries of a jurisdiction may result in too narrow a definition, thereby distorting the analysis; expanding the boundaries too far may result in an "encroachment" on the base area of other economic centers. Several criteria have been developed and some have been tested to determine the best technique for delineation. N.B.S. Gras advanced the following guidelines in 1922: (1) shifts in systems of transportation, (2) service areas of daily newspapers and other advertising media, (3) dependence of outlying financial institutions on

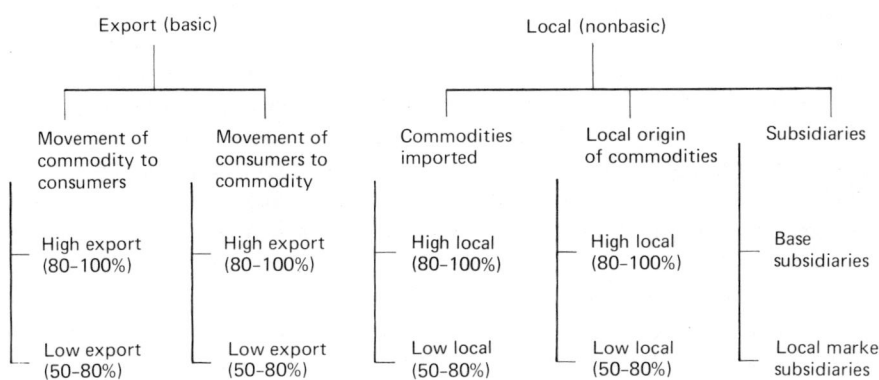

Figure 3-4. Urban Economic Structure: Classification by Market Location and Consumer Commodity

center for clearances and reserves, (4) provision of auxiliary services to hinterland firms, (5) extent to which local facilities are used for storage, shipping, and marketing by firms in the "hinterland," (6) "service area" for cultural facilities, institutions of learning, and recreational facilities. In the late twenties and early thirties, William J. Reilly developed an empirical approach to this problem through an examination of some 132 American urban areas. His Law of Retail Gravitation states that ". . . two cities attract retail trade from any intermediate city or town in the vicinity of the breaking point approximately in direct proportion to the populations of the two cities and in inverse proportion to the square of the distances from these two cities to the intermediate town,"[25] distance being measured along the most direct improved highway. More recently developed techniques for delineating the retail trade area include: (1) consumer surveys, using household interviews on a sampling basis, (2) sampling surveys of retail and service establishment to determine "customer draw," and (3) parking surveys, whereby automobile license plate numbers are recorded in the central business district or regional shopping centers and checked for home addresses against license registration books. Whatever approach or combination of approaches is used, the final results usually are translated into jursidictional boundaries so that standard sources of data can be utilized.

*Techniques of Measurement*

One of the most challenging problems in economic base analysis involves the selection of a unit or units of measurement by which to distinguish and quantify the basic and service components of the urban economy under study. Andrews has identified six units of measurement that are either in use or have been proposed for use: (1) employment, (2) payrolls, (3) value added, (4) value of production, (5) physical production, and (6) dollar income and expenditure accounts. Each of these measures has shortcomings, and, therefore, Andrews recommends that all feasible measuring techniques be used in any study. Using employment as the measure of economic activity encounters the problems of seasonal and part-time workers. In addition, output per worker (productivity) may increase without parallel increases in employment; rise in productivity may be associated with an increase in the rate and total wage assigned to the individual job. While payrolls provide a more significant indicator of economic activity and economic opportunity than the mere number of jobs, these data are open to highly significant price change adjustments. Payrolls may provide a clue to the standard of living to be expected in a community if these data can be obtained in terms of annual renumeration distributions. Physical production, value added, and value of production have advantages for analysis within particular sectors of the economy; however, these measures do not apply to some sectors and therefore have limited application. Further, value added and value of production may be clouded by complex price movements and encounter problems associated with intangible inputs and value products (i.e., educational institutions). While dollar income and expenditure accounts, in combination with employment data, would provide the most comprehensive measure of economic activity, the complexity and difficulty of tracing monetary transactions, coupled with data reporting problems, limit the application of these measures. As a consequence, the two primary measures of economic base studies have been employment and payroll data.

*Economic Base Multipliers and Location Quotients*

Homer Hoyt, whose experimental work in economic base analysis has provided the contemporary operational model, observed that when employment is used as a measure, a ratio occurs between basic and nonbasic activities. While Hoyt suggested that this ratio was about 1 to 1, empirical studies have shown that it varies over a relatively narrow range of from 1 to 0.5 to 1 to 2 (with the base activity component computed as the constant). Some writers have interpreted these ratios to mean that for every worker in the basic sector of the economy, a given number of jobs are "created" in the service sector. Therefore, if the basic to service ratio is 1 to 2, the basic to total employment ratio would be 1 to 3; if 50 percent of the total population is in the labor force, the basic to total population would be 1 to 6. These multipliers have been used in making population projections, as well as projections of employment and economic activities (assuming a constant or predictably changing ratio). Unfortunately, these values do not necessarily remain constant for long periods of time, that is, the ratio can exhibit significant shifts, depending upon changes in the economy of the urban area and national economic conditions.

Employment data are also used to calculate *location quotients,* sometimes, called coefficients of localization or specialization. If a given community is highly specialized relative to the nation (or region) in the production of a particular commodity, the product may be presumed to be an export item. Therefore, solving the following equation for $X$ determines the number of workers that would be employed in industry $i$ if the community produced just enough of that industry's product to supply its own needs.[26]

$$\frac{X}{\text{total local employment}} = \frac{\text{national employment in industry } i}{\text{total national employment}}$$

If actual employment is in excess of $X$, then industry may be assumed to be export oriented; if actual employment is below $X$, then products of this industry are assumed to be imported.

While the use of location quotients provides a relatively inexpensive way of measuring exports for a given community, the results obtained depend on the level of Standard Industrial Classifications (SIC) applied, that is, no variation may be noted until four digits or lower are used. Other criticisms of location quotients include the arguments that residents of one community may have significantly different tastes than those in other communities or the nation as a whole and the possibility that a community may be more productive then the national average in terms of output per employee (and therefore would have a lower employment ratio in a given industry).

### Criticisms of the Economic Base Approach

Much of the present-day appeal of economic base studies stems from their seemingly simplistic application. However, this simplicity can also lead to fallacious and contradictory results. As Ralph W. Pfouts points out, the panacea of base industries have led communities into an economic development policy not unlike the doctrine of mercantilism.[27] While studies have shown that an appreciable proportion of basic industry is necessary for urban growth and development, it does not follow that this alone is sufficient for growth and development. Pfouts' tests suggest that the service component may be more important as an indicator of growth potential than the basic component. Therefore, he proposes a community income analysis as a substitute approach for economic base studies.

Hans Blumenfeld has also identified what he considers to be a number of misconceptions and contradictions in the economic base concept.[28] He notes that the applicability of the economic base approach tends to decrease with increasing size of an urban center and tends to increase with increasing specialization and division of labor between centers. Therefore, large, highly diverse metropolitan centers survive and grow because highly developed and diverse business and consumer services enable such centers to attract new basis industries for those that may decline. Blumenfeld concludes that the nonbasic activities of such centers are the permanent and constant element—the truly "basic" sector of their economy. Blumenfeld proposes the substitution of studies that would consider the potential vulnerability of local economic activities to outside competition and the potential capacity of local economic activities to expand into outside markets, coupled with "balance of payment" studies that would consider all types of payments, giving equal weight to both imports and exports.

## Economic Dominants Analysis

One of the most conspicuous flaws in existing systems of urban economic analysis is that they are not dynamic or continuous. As a consequence of methodological limitations and cost factors, most of these approaches are applied on a one-time basis. More dynamic techniques, such as systems of accounts and industrial complex analysis, suffer from the data limitations discussed previously. Given these limitations, Andrews has proposed an approach that provides an in-depth analysis of selected industry groups rather than broad or universal enterprise coverage; this approach he calls *economic dominants analysis.* [29] Andrews notes that the appropriate objectives in the study of urban and other small region economies are: (a) the determination of optimum size and character of the economic system, and (b) the attainment of maximum operating efficiency of the dominant economic parts of the system as measured by means of carefully conceived goals. Dominants may be export or local in their market orientation and, as industry groups, claim an arbitrary minimum proportion of total area employment—three, four, or five percent depending on local economic structure (and cost constraints of conducting the study). Selective dynamic in-depth analysis is based on the hypothesis that the quantitative and qualitative character of the total urban or regional economy can be understood and roughly predicted by means of a continuing study of those industries or economic activity groups that dominate the area in terms of employment and other strategic factors. Empirically it was found that, on first application, employment dominance was an adequate guide to a more complete picture of economic dominance. Therefore, other determinants, such as payroll and productivity, were shifted to later stages where they were used as weighting factors in the determination of relative importance of dominants in the formulation of development policy.[30]

Under this approach selected economic dominants (industry groups) are subjected to a depth analysis that includes: (a) macroanalysis—a system involving national, regional, and state level analyses of dominant industry group economic trend characteristics; (b) microanalysis—a method of detailed economic examination of a sample of local firms within each dominant industry groups; and (c) integration of macro and micro findings to determine the nature and degree of deviation between local level firm performance, and trends of the same industry groups at national, regional, and state levels (see Figure 3-5). The principal objectives of the macroanalysis are: (1) to provide a more complete understanding of the nature and functioning of the broad industry group of which a local dominant export industry group is a small part; and (2) to establish a scale of performance and develop trend patterns at state, regional and national levels against which the performance characteristics and trends of a local dominant industry group can be measured. A basic assumption of the

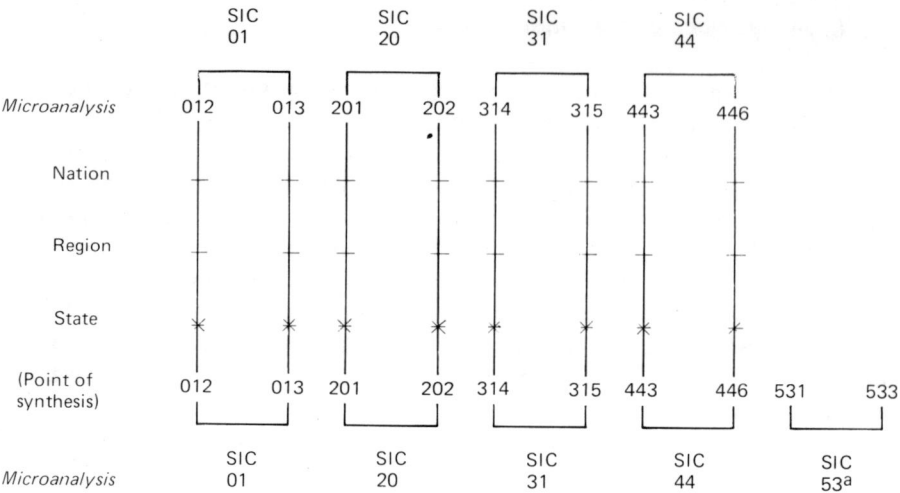

[a]Dominant industry groups oriented to local markets are not subject to macro-analysis but are included in the micro approach.

**Figure 3-5.** Macro-Micro Synthesis of Dominant Industry Groups

procedure is that the pattern of conformities and divergencies resulting from comparisons of macro with micro data will provide substantial clues to the prognosis of local area activity. The objectives of the microanalysis are: (1) establishment of a data and analysis bond between local industry groups and their broadscale counterparts identified under macroanalysis; (2) identification of single problem and problem patterns of dominant industry groups at the local level not revealed by the macroanalysis; and (3) extension of data coverage beyond the macroanalysis in order to objectify local problem situations more clearly and thereby provide the detail necessary for positive economic planning. The product of this analytical procedure is an understanding of the individual strengths, weaknesses, locational peculiarities, tendencies, and general growth potential of each of the dominant industry groups that make up the local economy.

Across-the-board integration of selected industry group data concludes the macro-micro synthesis and is accomplished by means of the following two steps: (1) formal analytical identification of primary linkage relationships among export and ancillary (local) dominant industry groups at the local level; and (2) summation of the individual dominants on an employment basis for the current (base) year. With the macro-micro synthesis complete, it is a relatively simple matter to show the significant relationships between the total employment of the dominants and each of several economic indicators for the current year (see Figure 3-6).

Subdominant industry groups also may be identified. These are industry

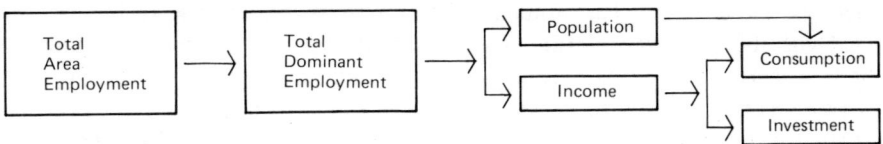

**Figure 3-6.** Dominant Industry-Economic Indicator Relation (Micro Level)

groups whose employment shares are just below the minimum level of dominance used in an area but still of significant size, that is, one to two percent. Subdominants are not subjected to first round macroanalysis and microanalysis. They are included in the system because they represent an underlying "seedbed" of established economic activity that is vital to ultimate selective development planning.

This approach, like the others discussed, is not without its shortcomings. Andrews has identified the following weaknesses in his approach: (1) the inference of the balance of the economy from trends evident in the dominants—problem of generalizing from a less than total universe; (2) statistically, the analysis does not deal with a random sample which is inherent in the concept of dominance; (e) inability to determine whether the share of total represented by dominant industry groups is adequate; and (4) application must be on a continuing basis to be effectively used.[31] Given these limitations, however, the economic dominants approach holds a good deal of promise. It is relatively simple to mount, and it lends itself to the more dynamic objectives of a continuous study. Furthermore, in-depth surveys of local industry groups can provide a good deal of spinoff information that cannot be obtained from abstract statistical analyses.

**Summary**

While the economist has been a latecomer into the field of urban analysis, he has a rich tradition of theory and a systematic ethic to build upon. In some respects urban economists are at a stage parallel to that of the field of economics as a whole when Marshall began his work in the late nineteenth century. Many current theories of urban economics still can be traced to the early doctrines of mercantilism and classicism. It will not take a century for the field to "catch-up," however. Significant strides are being made as more and more attention is devoted to the problems of the urban environment, their economic "roots," and the role of government in the total economic system.

To date the urban economy has been studied primarily in terms of three conceptual systems—input-output analysis, income and product accounts analysis, and economic base studies. Efforts to develop evaluative techniques to deal with the whole range of factors affecting the vitality of the economy may be viewed as subjective extensions of the economic base type of analysis. It should be apparent that there are a number of similarities in these three conceptual approaches. By shifting emphasis, changing units of measurement, or expanding or reducing the number of sectors included, on approach becomes more like one of the other two. As data sources become more extensive and more refined, and as the data handling capacity of high speed computers receives wider utilization, it is likely that the "rough edges" of these three models will be smoothed away so that they more nearly fit as a single system of analysis. When this is accomplished the integration of broader theoretical concerns of economics will be possible.

# 4 Formulation of a Debt Policy

Like the power to tax, the power to borrow is inherent in all sovereign governments. Consequently, state governments have full inherent power to borrow, subject only to such limitations as imposed in the federal Constitution and in their own state constitutions. Local governments, in turn, have such powers to incur debt as are delegated to them by state constitutions and statutes. Within these legal limits state and local administrative authorities have a wide range for the application of sound judgment or for the contrary. Many state laws fall far short of providing dependable standards for borrowing, and the best of them afford an inadequate substitute for the responsibility of public officials. Therefore, among other factors, a debt policy must be formulated in accordance with legal requirements, available financing methods, and the capacity to pay.

## Constitutional and Statutory Limits on Borrowing

In ratifying the federal Constitution the states sacrificed only one detail of their inherent borrowing powers—they prohibited themselves from issuing debt instruments in the form of "bills of credit" intended to circulate as money. Although wide latitude remained, the borrowing powers of state governments today are sharply restricted in many state constitutions.

Virtually all states have constitutional debt restrictions. In about half of the states bond issues over some specified limit can be authorized only by constitutional amendment, a most cumbersome process;[a] and in over one-third of the states, bond proposals must be submitted to the electorate by referendum.[b] Where legislative approval of debt issues is limited, the limitation is generally in the form of a fixed sum; a few states limit public debt to a percentage of the assessed valuation of property within their borders. State constitutions also cover various terms of state borrowing. In most cases the debt must be for a specific purpose; maximum maturities for state bonds are con-

---

[a]The limit within which the legislature may act upon its own initiative may reflect a low figure for general borrowing and a higher one for some special purposes.

[b]This requirement may apply to all proposals or only to issues that exceed some constitutionally established limit.

stitutionally established in many states; state constitutions commonly require the legislature to levy a special tax sufficient to cover debt service; and provisions forbidding legislatures to lend state credit to individuals or corporations have been written into most state constitutions.[c]

Constitutional limitations on state borrowing have often proved problematic and frequently have led to circumvention.[d] They are a rather crude and superficial method of controlling expenditures, representing the imposition of the judgment of one generation on another that inevitably is confronted with different conditions. Faced with the problems of constitutional revision in order to overcome these limitations, many states have resorted to the creation of other agencies—authorities, boards, commissions, and/or governmental corporations—whose debts the courts generally have held are not debts against the state (and therefore not subject to the same constitutional limitations). Interest rates on the bonds of these "substitute" agencies, however, generally are higher than on obligations secured by the full faith and credit of the state.

Constitutional restrictions continue to be defended in many quarters as a protection against the abuse of state credit. It is argued that the delay and publicity involved in securing authorization by special referendum or constitutional amendment provides a check against one session of the state legislature yielding to pressures that may bind taxpayers for a full generation. While the tendendy is for most "borrowing" amendments to be approved by state electorates, per capita state debts are lower in those states requiring such approvals than in states with essentially no limits on legislative borrowing; and presumably (although not necessarily), the level of public services in states with such restrictions is lower as well.

Local borrowing powers generally are regulated in greater detail than are those of state governments.[e] The purposes for which local governments may borrow, the methods of incurring debts, the amount of local debt, its interest rate, term, and provisions for retirement, and the form of local debt issues are all regulated, in one state or another, by constitutional or statutory provision. The most common limitation is on the amount of local borrowing, usually taking the form of a provision that the outstanding total indebtedness cannot exceed a specified proportion of the assessed value of property within the borrowing jurisdiction. Different assessment-ratio debt limits may be established for various classes of local governments, with the greatest restrictions placed on smaller communities and the highest ratios established for school districts.

---

[c]Prior to 1850 several states underwrote the bonds of railroad companies that subsequently failed, leaving the governments saddled with substantial debts. This provision was enacted to prevent any recurrence of such commitments.

[d]During the thirties a number of states found themselves temporarily unable to obtain federal relief funds because they could not borrow to match the federal grants.

[e]Counties, townships, towns, special districts, and incorporated municipalities under a specified population size are not permitted to incur any debt in some states.

This assessment-ratio limitation frequently excludes self-supporting debt (i.e., debt that is not backed by the full faith and credit of local government). A majority of states provide that all or certain of their local governments can issue bonds only after approval by local referenda. A number of states fix the maximum interest rate that municipal bond issues may carry and provide that local bonds must not be sold below par (i.e., at a discount that often is required by investors to increase their return on such long-term investments). Some states set maximum durations for local bond issues, such as the life of the improvement to be financed, or specific periods for various types of improvements. Finally, several states restrict the form of bond issue, thus limiting the alternatives available to municipalities in managing their debt.

There can be little question that some restriction on local borrowing power is desirable. The wisdom of many of the present constitutional and statutory limitations, however, is open to questions.

While it may seem logical, for example, to relate debt limits to assessed valuations, since assessments partly determine property tax levies and the property tax is the major source of local revenues to pay debt service charges, assessment ratios vary significantly among communities. Therefore, a uniform debt limit based on unequalized assessment operates with differing degrees of restriction among local units of government. Moreover, local governments have learned how to circumvent such limitations by raising the ratio of their property assessments while lowering the tax rate or millage, thus raising their debt limits.[f] Furthermore, since local governments increasingly are obtaining revenue from sources other than the property tax, local debt limits based only on assessments are economically obsolete.

The logic of debt limits being tied to assessed valuations has been further eroded by the actions of some state legislatures that have adopted provisions enabling localities to exceed constitutional debt limits through the creation of special government units to take over particular functions of the original debt-laden governments. Each new unit is given an additional debt-incurring capacity; the superimposition of such new districts in one state, for example, made possible in some cases a total debt over four times that established by constitutional limits based on assessed valuations.

The provision that the term of borrowing shall not exceed the life of the improvement initially was conceived as a safeguard against irresponsibility by

---

[f]Property taxes are determined by two variables: (1) the level of assessment or the ratio between assessed value and true value; and (2) the rate of taxation, usually expressed in terms of a given number of mills per unit of assessed value (or dollars per thousand dollars of assessed value). Therefore, a property in one community may be assessed at 40 percent of true value and carry a tax rate of $40 per thousand, whereas in another community, a similar property may be assessed at 80 percent of true value but carry a tax rate of only $20 per thousand; both properties would yield similar levels of revenue. Therefore, it may be readily seen how a community can change its debt limit by manipulating these two variables without producing any real increase in revenues.

public officials and the electorate in incurring debts of such durations that most of the burden would be shifted to future generations. However, these limitations on maturities have proved of limited value. Too often, local officials interpret the limitation as an authorization, taking as a standard the period intended to be a maximum.

The Advisory Commission on Intergovernmental Relations (ACIR) has concluded that present restrictions "... are in most states critically in need of intensive review and major change. Basic revision is widely needed; patching has been inadequate, and in some instances actually harmful." Thus the ACIR recommends greater freedom in local government borrowing practices, the removal of limitations tied to property taxation, greater weight given to interest cost, less dependence on local referenda, and more state technical assistance in debt administration.

### Purposes of Government Borrowing

Since borrowing merely postpones the payment of a public expenditure and in the meanwhile a continuing item of interest is added to the cost, a government must have special reasons to justify debt financing. Authorities on public finance are in rather general agreement as to proper purposes for muncipal borrowing; four such reasons are: (1) to finance large emergency or irregular expenditures, (2) to finance capital construction projects, (3) to harmonize divergent patterns of current expenditures and revenues, and (4) to refinance existing debt.[1] A fifth reason that has received much discussion—to stimulate the economy when business is sluggish—has little application to local government; its application to the state and federal level of government has also been a subject of considerable debate of late by both economists and politicians.

The devastation of a natural catastrophe—flood, fire, tornado, or earthquake—may give rise to immediate large financial needs for which the taxing power of local government is not sufficiently responsive. Such widespread disaster also tends to weaken temporarily the financial structure of the affected communities, and therefore, expediency may dictate a reduction of existing taxes rather than an increase to permit recovery. Even if special taxes are feasible and are quickly levied to provide needed funds, there is likely to be a considerable time lapse before the receipts are actually available. Therefore, emergency expenditures necessitated by such natural disasters are properly financed by borrowing.

A genuine emergency may arise with the advent of a serious business depression, and although local governments may be unable to "pump-prime" the economy directly, it may be desirable to provide some tax relief to the consequent unemployed. The utilization of borrowing to finance needed government services in the face of a decline in taxpaying capacity and the threat that higher taxes may further handicap recovery has special justification.

"Emergency" justification may be extended to certain other public borrowings where the expenditures required, although not strictly "emergency" in characters are large-scale and irregular. For example, cities quite properly finance heavy snow removals by special intermediate-term debt. A sudden, large influx of population may require that facilities ordinarily financed gradually out of current revenues on a "pay-as-you-go" basis be acquired all at once, leaving no practical alternative but to borrow. Such circumstances may arise as a consequence of new industrial development in the community or the expansion of the community through annexation of an area previously lacking in certain public services.[g]

An emergency borrowing program can be undertaken with impunity, however, only when the borrowing practices of the municipality have been sound. If a community's borrowing policy has been lacking in foresight, an emergency may find it without a market for its bonds. If, on the other hand, a credit reserve has been established in times of prosperity, a community can issue bonds for emergency purposes without dangerously mortgaging its future. This is a strong argument for a partial pay-as-you-go policy for the financing of capital improvements.

Certain types of capital construction expenditures may be financed safely and reasonably by long-term borrowing. The capital cost of such public enterprises as water and sewer systems may be met by borrowing, provided the amortization of the debt is sufficiently rapid to keep ahead of depreciation and obsolescence. A municipality that operates such an enterprise in a manner to cover both current and capital costs by the rates charged for services would be following standard business practices if it were to borrow to finance capital construction. It would be wasteful to forego construction or expansion rather than borrow, if the full costs of the borrowed funds were less than the full value of the additional services the community would obtain.[h] Debt incurred for such government enterprises, the charges of which cover interest and principal payments as well as operating costs, is commonly called "self-supporting debt." Unlike ordinary government debt, it represents no additional drain on tax receipts, and consequently, state constitutions and statutes recognize this distinction and exempt "self-supporting debt" from many of the limitations

---

[g] The annexation laws of most states require that a municipality provide the annexed area within a specified period the same level of public servcies as afforded the existing jurisdiction. Since annexation procedures may require several years for resolution of the issue, such municipalities may only be partially justified in using "emergency" borrowing, since there may be adequate time for proper planning of the expansion of facilities.

[h] In strict economic terms resources should be put into capital construction, or even into an intangible long-term investment such as education or health, up to the point where the present value of the services of additional investment (determined by discounting the value of future services at an appropriate rate of interest) will just equal the value of the current consumption sacrificed. (See: A.C. Harberger, "The Interest Rate in Rate in Cost-Benefit Analysis," *Federal Expenditure Policy for Economic Growth and Stability* (Washington, D.C.: Government Printing Office, 1958), pp. 239–41.) In practice, however, the *economic* principal of borrowing is largely inadequate as a guide for *political* action.

that apply to other municipal borrowing. Should a municipality elect to set service charges so low that the revenues received do not cover debt service commitments, or should improper management of such facilities reduce revenues below capital costs, then such an enterprise is not "self-supporting" since part of the cost of the debt must be met by funds from the municipality's general revenues.

Capital expenditures for other than "self-supporting" enterprises can be classified in two groups with reference to sound methods of financing: (1) projects that are large and costly in relation to a municipality's current fiscal resources, that have long utility, and are not of a frequently recurrent type; and (2) capital requirements that are almost as steadily recurrent as a municipality's operating expenses, such as various types of equipment and the routine extension and replacement of existing facilities. A prudent borrowing policy would exclude the second category of capital expenditures, since borrowing for such purposes tends to pyramid municipal debt. Annual recurring capital costs should be met directly from taxation, since their deferment through borrowing merely results in their duplication at a later date.[i]

With regards to the first category of capital expenditures, a capital facility is a good investment in economic terms if the full costs of borrowing are less than the expected benefits. In practice, however, the calculations necessary to arrive at such a decision are most complex. Even rough measurements of the full collective benefit of a public investment are extremely difficult, as are the measurements of cost or sacrifices that taxpayers are willing to make to service the debt. Consequently, public officials have had to resort to less precise concepts, such as "lasting benefit" and "nonrecurring costs," in lieu of more sophisticated economic measures applicable in the more controlled environment of the private sector.

Borrowing for such projects permits payment on the installment plan, during the useful life of the project, of an expense that would be prohibitive if imposed upon the community at any one time. Long-term programming of capital construction should enable municipal and state governments to preplan continuing capital expenditures in reasonably even annual installments, permitting the adoption of a pay-as-you-go program and the accumulation of capital reserves.[j] Borrowing can then be properly limited for emergencies, for occasional unavoidable "peaks" of capital outlay, and for special projects not

---

[i]A municipality should never resort to long-term borrowing to finance ordinary current expense. Borrowings are a supplement to taxation and not actual revenue, since they create an equivalent liability that must be met from future taxes.

[j]Two factors reduced the appeal of pay-as-you-go financing during the period from the end of World War II to the early sixties: (a) low interest rates on municipal bonds, and (b) rising costs of construction. Delays in construction during this period often proved more costly than borrowing. While construction costs continue to rise at a phenomenal rate, current federal fiscal and monetary policies have resulted in a significant increase in the rate of interest on municipal securities.

foreseen in the budgeted program. A "capital construction" tax levy or a stipulated "set-aside" from each annual budget for capital expenditures, as discussed previously, is the soundest basis for a municipality's borrowing policy.[k] By planning its normal capital expenditures at least five years ahead and incorporating each year's requirement in that year's budget, a municipality can reserve its capacity to borrow for those large projects that do not frequently recur. In this way it can retain a good credit rating that is favorable to the successful marketing of such bonds as are necessary.

Municipal governments, and occasionally state governments, have found it necessary to resort to short-term borrowing to adjust for irregularities in the patterns of expenditures and receipts during a fiscal year. Borrowing in anticipation of current taxes and other revenues has become a routine procedure in the majority of municipalities. This is a form of borrowing that could and should be rendered unnecessary through improved financial planning, thereby enabling many governments to reduce interest payments. If the first tax due date were made to coincide with the beginning of the fiscal year, and if a quarterly or semiannual installment method of tax payments were instituted, this type of borrowing could be reduced to a minimum.[l]

While the refinancing of existing debt through the adjustment of maturity dates to take advantages of lower interest rates is a very sound principle, relatively few state or local governments have been able to take advantage of this approach in recent years. Rising interest rates for both long-term and short-term money preclude the application of this concept in most cases; there is little prospect that interest rates will drop below the level at which most existing debt was incurred. Refunding maturing bonds by a new issue, on the other hand, often means that the government has failed to accumulate sufficient funds to retire the loan and is irresponsibly continuing the debt.

### Measuring the Capacity to Pay

The limits on government debt that may be safely incurred are as fully important as the purposes for which a municipality may justifiably borrow. In general, capacity of a community to incur debt must be gauged by the amount and quality of its resources and by its legal and practical ability to draw upon these resources. While there is no precise method for determining how much

---

[k]Contrary to widely recommended economic principles, capital outlays of large cities and states have tended to follow a cyclical pattern, which results in increased expenditures in periods of business optimism and significant contractions in expenditures in periods of depression. The adoption of a "capital construction" tax levy or stipulated "set-aside" for capital projects from the annual budget, based on the average level of capital expenditures over a five- to ten-year period, would tend to ameliorate the cyclical pattern.

[l]The concept of "cash basis operation" for local government is discussed more fully in a subsequent section.

debt a municipality can carry, there are several simple procedural guidelines that can be applied in the formulation of a sound borrowing policy.[m]

The first step in formulating the basis for such a policy is to determine the "burden" of government debt—the actual obligations facing the community. The concept of debt burden relates to the question of how much taxpayers must give up in monetary terms to finance debt service, that is, debt retirement and interest on outstanding debt. A complicating factor in this analysis is the overlapping system of local government that may result in various local governing units borrowing for the same community. While a city administration can only directly control its own debt, it must be cognizant of the overlapping debt of county government, school districts, public authorities, and other special purpose districts, all of which constitute commitments to the taxpayers of any community. In short the overall debt burden of a municipality must be computed on the basis of its direct debt plus the proportionate share of the debt of overlapping units that its citizens are called upon to support.

In the computation of overall municipal debt it is first necessary to determine the direct debt, from which can be deducted all debt from self-supporting projects in order to show the actual amount to be supported by tax levies. To this figure must then be added the proportionate share of overlapping debt, based on percentages of district and county tax levies paid by taxpayers within the municipality.

By themselves, taxes paid in support of debt services constitute *gross debt burden.* Two other measures of debt burden are equally important in the analysis of debt capacity: (1) *net debt burden,* that is, the balance of debt remaining after subtracting the "benefits" derived from the project or projects, and (2) *relative debt burden,* the comparison of gross debt to some measure of tax-raising capacity, such as population, property values, or personal income.

Analysis of net burden of the taxes that finance debt service is facilitated by separating the "debt burden" into two parts, one covering debt retirement and the other interest. It must be assumed that the spending of government that is financed by borrowing produces collective benefits equal to or greater than the cost of the project. If this is not the case, then any criticism of "burden" in excess of benefit should be directed to the spending, not to the resulting debt. In other words, it is the decision on the project that has created the imbalance in cost-benefit terms and not the schedule of debt retirement itself. Assuming that expenditures for capital projects have been wisely conceived, retirement of debt over a period of years creates a sequence of gross burdens whose total falls short of, or just equals, the benefits resulting from the expenditure financed by the borrowing. In short, the present worth of the project or projects, when the stream of costs and benefits are discounted to

---

[m]The legal borrowing limit established by most states is not a safe standard to follow; at best, it provides a maximum limit. Thus, the only sound policy is to determine a realistic limit that fits the community and falls well within the legal limits set by state legislation.

present values, is positive without reference to the net debt burden arising from interest costs.[n]

Interest payments represent the cost of "buying time." Time for debt repayment can be "bought" wisely or unwisely. If wisely bought there is a benefit to offset the subsequent burden of taxes to support interest payments. If time for debt repayment is unwisely bought the taxes required to support interest payments will impose a net burden, perhaps a significant one. Stripping this discussion of the economic jargon, the important point to bear in mind in analyzing net debt burden is that both the cost of the project (the principal), regardless of its method of financing, and the cost of interest must be considered separately. The justification of the project or projects in cost-benefit terms should not be clouded by decisions relating to the terms of borrowing.

The most commonly used methods of measuring relative debt burden are: (a) by population, expressed in per capita figures, and (b) by the valuation of taxable property, expressed as a ratio of assessed valuation adjusted to estimated full value. The validity of per capita debt burden data is subject to question since such data often fail to take into account any of the economic variables that affect the tax-raising capacity of a governmental area. Per capita figures can have a reasonable degree of utility for comparative purposes, however, if allowances are made for the variations in per capita resources (through the use of income data) from municipality to municipality. While property values also give a distorted measure of general economic capacity and are complicated by the difficulties in making an exact determination of full value, they can be applied in comparing debt burden among local units of government, or for one unit over a period of years, when the property tax is the sole or major revenue source for such units. It must be recognized, however, that in a period of inflation, if the debt of any government remains fixed, its relative burden will decrease over time as the measure for comparison expands. Even where a government's debt is increasing, the relative burden might decrease if the increase of the debt is less rapid than the increase of the measure.

Once measures of relative debt have been ascertained for a given community, it is important to compare these data with similar measures for other municipalities of generally similar size, type, and economic composition. This comparison permits a determination of where the debt load ranks. Although not a definitive measure, it does permit an appraisal of relative strengths and weaknesses in the management of debt obligations.

In appraising the direct debt of a municipality it often is assumed that the margin of safety rests in annual principal and interest requirements that do not rise above 25 percent of the budget. However, such a standard might encourage

---

[n] Even though overall benefits of a debt-financed outlay equals or exceeds overall burden (cost), there can be widely inequitable imbalance of individual net benefit and net burden. For example, a debt-retirement period that is substantially shorter than the benefit period places a burden balance on early members of the taxpaying group and gives a benefit balance to late members.

a false sense of security if applied to a municipality that has deferred the bulk of its debt service requirements far into the future. A more sound rule-of-thumb is that the funds require to retire five percent of the outstanding principal on all bonds plus cover the total annual interest requirements should not exceed 25 percent of a normal budget. Thus, if the annual interest charges for the general obligation bonds of a municipality were $180,000 on $3 million of unretired principal, the total municipal budget should be in excess of $1.32 million (25 percent of which would be $330,000, which equals the annual interest charges of $180,000 plus 5 percent of the outstanding debt or $150,000).

## The "Supply Side" of the Urban Economy

As noted previously, the more common methods of measuring relative debt burden, and, thereby, the capacity to pay for new borrowing, frequently fail to take into account the economic variables that affect the tax-raising capacity of a municipality. Therefore, a sound debt policy must also reflect a thorough analysis of the level and rate of growth of local economic activities.

Traditional methods for studying the urban economy have been criticized for an overemphasis on the role of demand in determining the economic well-being of localities. In a widely cited article Benjamin Chinitz has written that: ". . . . our efforts so far have been almost exclusively devoted to the demand dimensions of interdependence. The supply side has been virtually ignored." [2] This comment applies equally to the techniques of input-output analysis and the more sophisticated simulation methods as it does to the relatively simple basic-nonbasic and multiplier models. The fact that the input-output and simulation methods depict the flows of goods and services between the sectors of local industry in great detail does not obviate this shortcoming. Chinitz argues that an economic analysis should include not only the flows between local industries but also a thorough examination of the ways in which the structure of the local economy affects such factors as the price of supply, production costs, and entrepreneurial behavior within the local economy. He suggests, for example, that the supply of risk capital and the entrepreneurship required for launching new ventures may be significantly greater in a city where the industrial structure is largely competitive than in one dominated by a few very large firms. Thus, the organizational structure of local industry, in the long run, may affect the way the local economy responds to opportunities for growth and diversification.

Charles M. Tiebout has suggested that a study of the supply side ". . . deals with the nature of the local economy as an economic environment." [3] An examination of the supply side should attempt to uncover the strengths and weaknesses of the community as a place in which to conduct business and to live. Once these factors are known, local policy makers could set about to capitalize on its strengths and ameliorate its weaknesses in order to increase the area's productivity and attractiveness and help to ensure long-run growth of its output and living standards.

It is a limitation, if not a defect, of the methods of economic base analysis that they ascribe changes in the level of local activity entirely to changes in the level of an exogenously determined final demand, that is, the extent to which exports from the local economy can be increased. As John F. Kain has pointed out, this approach to the local economy inevitably focuses attention on matters over which local governments have little or no control—the exogenously determined components of demand—while distracting attention from the very thing localities can influence—the nature and attractiveness of the local economic environment.[4] In the short run local economic activity will fluctuate in large measure in response to shifts in outside demands; however, this well recognized factor of economic analysis is no reason to neglect the importance of internal supply factors in determining the course of events over the long run.

More precisely, location and feasibility studies should be made to discover what industries can best make use of the area's physical location and attributes and economic advantages. An examination should be made of the community's local supply of labor, land, capital, and entrepreneurship to see whether these factors can be marshalled more effectively for economic growth. Finally, a survey should be made of the community's entire "infrastructure"—housing, transportation facilities, schools, medical facilities, recreational areas, public service delivery systems, and so forth—to determine if they are ample, well-balanced, and life-enhancing, that is, contribute to the "good community life."

It should be evident that such an analysis of the "supply side" of a local economy is inextricably intertwined with a community's fiscal policies. Excessive debt will produce an undersirable economic environment in terms of rapidly rising tax rates, inequities of user-benefits, and an uncertain debt burden. The failure to meet capital expenditure responsibilities likewise will contribute to an unhealthy local economy. thus, a sound borrowing policy can play an important role in the economic well-being of any municipality.

# 5

## Forecasting Local Expenditures and Financial Resources

**Expenditure Forecasts**

While all municipalities prepare future budgets, at least for the year ahead, rarely can these be defined as true forecasts of anticipated revenues and expenditures. Agencies of local government typically are not required to submit long-term budget projections, and as a consequence, they often fail to examine adequately the impact of both existing and new programs on future expenditure patterns.[a] Changes in revenue flows or rapid shifts in expenditures for particular services can result in critical financial problems that might have been avoided if such forecasts had been made.

*Rapidly Rising Local Expenditures*

Since the end of World War II expenditures of local governments have been rising at a phenomenal rate. Between 1960 and 1971 the rates of growth of local expenditures for major public functions ranged from a high of 12.2 percent per year for public welfare to a low of 5.0 percent per year for streets and roads (see Table 5-1). These data have even greater impact when it is recognized that a 12.2 percent annual growth rate produces a 216 percent increase in costs over ten years. The combined total for all local public functions has grown regularly at a faster rate than the Gross National Product (GNP); between 1960 and 1971 local government expenditures financed from all sources increased at a compound rate of 9.7 percent per year, while during the same period, the GNP rose at an annual average rate of 6.9 percent.

The reasons for the growth in local expenditures are many and complex. For analytical purposes, however, public expenditures may be regarded as the product of two interactive factors: the number of units of service provided and the average cost of providing a single unit. Significant increases in both of these factors have contributed to the rapid growth of total local expenditures.

---

[a]The need for long-term budget projections has been more clearly established at the federal level, where agencies are now required to prepare and submit multiyear budget plans to the Office of Management and Budgeting as part of annual budgetary procedures.

## Table 5-1
### General Expenditures of Local Governments

| Expenditure Category | Compound Annual Rate of Growth | |
|---|---|---|
|  | 1950-60 | 1960-71 |
| Total Expenditures | 9.0% | 9.7% |
| Education | 9.9 | 10.0 |
| Public welfare | 4.5 | 12.2 |
| Health & hospitals | 9.0 | 10.7 |
| Streets & roads | 6.8 | 5.0 |
| Police | 8.8 | 9.6 |
| Fire protection | 7.9 | 7.9 |
| Sanitation & Sewerage | 7.0 | 8.2 |
| Parks & recreation | 9.9 | 8.6 |
| Housing & renewal | 6.5 | 10.4 |
| All other | 9.1 | 10.3 |

Sources: U.S. Bureau of the Census, *Census of Governments, 1962*, and *Governmental Finances in 1970-71*

### The "Elasticity" of Local Expenditures

A useful measure to examine the relationship between change in local government expenditures and changes in the Gross National Product has been suggested by James Heilbrun.[1] This measure, which Heilbrun calls the "elasticity of local spending," is defined by the following formula:

$$E_{LS} = \frac{\text{Percentage Change in Local Governmental Expenditures}}{\text{Percentage Change in GNP}}$$

When local government expenditures are increasing at a faster rate than the GNP, the value of $E_{LS}$ will be greater than one. From the data in Table 5-1, between 1960 and 1971, the $E_{LS}$ for all local governments had a value of 1.406 (i.e., 9.7% divided by 6.9%), whereas during the preceding decade, 1950-60, the value was 1.525 (9.0% divided by 5.9%).

Heilbrun also suggests that it is possible to define the elasticity of local revenue sources in a similar fashion, that is, by dividing the percentage change in local tax revenues by the percentage change in GNP. This measure, $E_{LT}$, can also be used to indicate the relationship between changes in the revenue derived from any particular tax and changes in the GNP, assuming that tax rates and the definition of the tax base are held constant. Since economic growth usually produces a growth in the base of a given community's revenue sources, revenue derived from a particular tax changes when GNP changes, even though tax rates and base definitions are held constant. Thus, $E_{LT}$ can be thought of as a measure of tax base elasticity as well as a measure of revenue elasticity with rates held constant.

If the value of the elasticity of local revenue sources for a given community was equal to the value of the elasticity of local spending, and if all expenditures were paid for out of local sources, then local government could finance the growth of expenditures year-by-year with no increase in tax rates, that is, the growth of the GNP would induce just enough expansion in the local tax base to provide the revenues needed to pay for growing expenditures. However, the fact that the value of $E_{LT}$ in the years since the end of World War II has been far below the value of $E_{LS}$ has contributed to the persistent financial pressure under which local governments have been forced to operate.[b]

While the elasticity of local government expenditures can be calculated directly from readily observable data on total expenditures and GNP, tax elasticity is more difficult to calcuate since the objective is to measure changes in the size of the tax base, with definitions and rates held constant, rather than changes in observable tax revenues. The property tax accounts for about 85 percent of local tax revenue; estimates of its elasticity for the United States as a whole vary from a low of 0.8 to a high of 1.3, with the majority of such estimates placing the value in the range between 0.8 and 1.0.[2] Sales and gross receipts taxes rank second in importance, producing eight percent of local revenue. On a national basis, the general sales tax collected by local governments is estimated to have an elasticity of between 1.0 and 1.27, with the majority of estimates falling at 1.0; in other words, the growth of revenues from the general sales taxes closely parallel the growth of the GNP. Other sources of general revenue (excluding intergovernmental aid), such as taxes on particular commodities and miscellaneous fees and charges, tend to have elasticities well below 1.0.[3] When these parts are added together, it appears that $E_{LT}$ for the aggregate of local taxes and charges, at best, is about 1.0 and perhaps somewhat lower.

With an expenditure elasticity of about 1.4 and a tax or revenue elasticity of 1.0 or less, it should be clear why local governments find themselves under constant pressure to raise tax rates or to adopt new taxes if they are to finance local growth in expenditures from local revenue sources. Fortunately, part of the gap between rapidly growing outlays and slowing rising tax bases has been partially offset by grants from the federal and state governments. Intergovernmental revenues have been one of the fastest growing categories of local support; by 1971 they supplied 37 percent of all local revenues.

Since the growth of intergovernmental grants has not closed the gap

---

[b]It should be pointed out that the elasticity of expenditures may depend, in part, on the elasticity of the tax base. When the latter is smaller than the former, it is likely that a restraining influence is exerted, that is, expenditures will increase less rapidly when such increases require a higher tax rate.

completely, however, tax rates at the local level have been increasing steadily. Thousands of overlapping local government jurisdictions collect many different taxes; it is impossible, therefore, to calculate a meaningful average rate of local taxation by which to measure this trend. Heilbrun has suggested an approximate trend calculated from indirect measurements, however.[4] Assuming that during the last two decades the elasticity of local revenue sources had a value of 1.0, if tax rates remained constant and no new taxes were added by local governments, then by definition the percentage change in tax revenue would have been equal to the percentage change in GNP. During this period the GNP increased by 268 percent; if local tax revenues had increased by the same percentage, they would have amounted to $29.4 billion in 1971. The fact is that they had risen to $43.3 billion in 1971, implying rate increases (plus new taxes adopted) of approximately 48 percent (i.e., $43.3 divided by $29.4 = 1.476).[c]

*Projections Versus Commitments*

In view of the rapidly expanding demands for increased local expenditures, it is difficult to understand why more thorough projections are not made in order to provide a better basis for financial planning. One of the most common arguments is that the publication of these expenditure projections would commit public officials to particular programs or courses of action that, in turn, would limit the flexibility of government. This view arises from a misconception as to what a forecast really is. Expenditure forecasts do not imply commitments but merely establish what expenditures are likely to be under a variety of conditions. By stressing the conditional aspects in public presentation, officials can avoid misunderstandings. Such forecasts, made under different assumptions, can underscore the variety of options open to a community.

Even when the goal of local government is to provide the same level of service over a period of years, disruptions in service delivery may result unless likely changes in demand for such services are anticipated with sufficient lead time to make necessary adjustments. Increases in population receiving a particular service may necessitate added personnel and often additional capital equipment and facilities. A school, for example, should not be constructed after the need exists; there is a five- to six-year lead time required to ensure the availability of such public facilities at the time the demand becomes critical. Therefore, forecasting is required simply to prevent current levels of service from rapidly becoming inadequate. Furthermore, the uncertainties surrounding federal revenue sharing programs and other forms of intergovernmental assis-

---

[c]Assuming that the elasticity of local revenues had a value of only 0.9 instead of 1.0, then the figures imply a tax rate increase of 60 percent instead of 48 percent.

tance give rise to the need for long-range forecasting, both to justify requests for such funds and to map out contingency plans if these funds are not forthcoming.

*Current Projection Practices*

During the years that public budget officials and planners have been making expenditure projections, their techniques, except for a relatively few, have remained virtually unchanged. Some simply make "best guesses" about future levels of expenditures. The common tendency is to allow the patterns of previous expenditures influence projections; next year's expenditures are determined by applying the observed percentage change in expenditures between this fiscal year and the last fiscal year. Alternatively, a trend line may be developed by fitting a series of historical data and then extrapolating this trend line to obtain the projections.

The current "state of the art" may be illustrated by a recent publication by the Management Information Serivce of the International City Management Association.[5] The projection process advocated consists of dividing revenue and expenditures into "readily definable major categories" and then projecting these categories for five to six years on the basis of past trends. Income and cost projections are compared to provide some notion of "future free fiscal capacity," that is, the uncommitted monies that can be used for capital expenditures, to establish capital reserves, or for debt service.

While this approach has the advantage of simplicity, it leaves many problems unsolved. Although the advocates of the approach stress the fact that such things as the tax base and tax rates may change and that local government officials should be consulted to determine the possibility of deviations from historical trends, allowance seldom is made for any such possibilities in the projections themselves. On the contrary, population is treated as if it will remain stable regardless of recent rates of growth, and the rate of salary increase of public employees is treated as if it will remain constant.

*A New Approach: The New Haven Expenditure Model*

A major departure from these traditional approaches has recently been proposed by Claudia DeVita Scott, a member of the staff of Planning Research Corporation, while working under contract with the City of New Haven. This revenue/expenditure model has been fully described in a recent publication of The Urban Institute, entitled *Forecasting Local Government Spending* (1972).

Projections arising from the model are based on three kinds of variables:

1. Population variables, including projections of the size, age, and racial composition of the population
2. Salary variables, that is, projections of the levels or rates of increase for public employees in various salary and wage classes
3. Service variables, that is, projections of the way in which the level of service or manner in which services are provided will change, given some assumed change in the demand for services by the population

Unlike other forecasting techniques, the New Haven model has a fairly flexible structure. Each particular class of expenditure can be projected according to various explicit assumptions regarding the supply and demand associated with a particular service. Each projection is associated with specific statements concerning the values of the major variables, supplied by those officials of the local government best qualified to predict as a consequence of their access to pertinent facts. Even where a high degree of confidence cannot be attached to a particular projection (due to uncertainty), the model permits the testing of different assumptions (through a sensitivity analysis approach). Explicit statements concerning service levels required by the model permit the testing of the impact of decisions to expand or contract particular services in some defined period. The model requires separate information inputs for each year over which the projections are made, and therefore, unlike extrapolation techniques, the model yields projections that are more independent (i.e., are not influenced by past trends.) The model can deal with a wide range of assumptions simultaneously—some services may be expanded, some contracted, others held at their present level. This capacity to test differing alternatives is not readily available in the more traditional techniques.

The model is designed to produce separate estimates of future expenditures (and future revenue needs) for nine major categories: (1) education, (2) library services, (3) police and public safety, (4) fire protection, (5) health, (6) welfare, (7) public works, (8) parks and recreation, and (9) administration and development. For complex categories subdivisions are made so that separate activities within departments can be examined in some detail. Additional categories, where appropriate, can be readily added; this is one of the advantages of the independent projection feature of the model. Since the model specifies separate equations for major activities, it is possible to depict interrelationships between activities within the same category and to examine the implications of various expenditure patterns arising from different program mixes.

*Basis for Projections*

The projections of expenditures are built on two basic sets of factors: (1) estimates of expenditures arising from personnel; and (2) estimates of nonpersonnel related expenditures. For each department (category), projections must be obtained regarding the total number of employees and their distribution among various skill and wage levels. With this as a base, both the number of workers in a particular wage or salary class and the average annual salary or wage for that class are projected and summed to produce total personnel expenditures. Personnel projections are related both to the demographic characteristics of the population (which are used to measure the demand for public services) and to policy decisions (or policy alternatives) as to the level and quality of services provided. The change in personnel is computed as a function of two other changes—the change in demand for the service and the change in the supply of the service. Policy variables are introduced as multiplicative factors—they permit assumptions to be made regarding the response in supply as a multiple or fraction of some historically observed relationship between the supply response to a change in demand.

Nonpersonnel items consist of materials and supplies, transportation, utilities, and contractual and debt service charges. These items are projected in two parts. One part excludes debt service and utilizes a linear regression equation that expresses a functional relationship between nonpersonnel expenditures and personnel expenditures (or, alternatively, total numbers of personnel). The second part involves the calculation of debt service through the use of an accounting model that employs information on the amount of debt outstanding, plans for new capital expenditures, and expectations regarding future interest rates (an exogenous factor) to derive forecasts of the principal and interest payments on the public debt. Policy variables are specified concerning the mix of financing techniques for long-term capital expenditures.

### Debt Service and Capital Improvements

While too involved to discuss in detail (it takes Ms. Scott 135 pages to set forth the complete model), it would seem appropriate to examine further the debt service and CIP phase of the model, since it has direct bearing on the present subject of capital expenditure forecasting. In so doing an attempt has been made to simplify the notations used by Ms. Scott which, at times, seems rather awkward.

In any year the dollar expenditure for debt service (i.e., principal and interest payments) is a function of: (a) the amount of debt outstanding, (b) the interest structure over all bonds, and (c) the term of the bonds, that is, their maturities. A bond issue distributes the burden of a community's capital expenditures over a number of years. Therefore, the value of the debt service is affected by the timing of a bond issue, the distribution of its value among bonds of different maturities, the rate of interest, and the timing of the principal and interest payments over the life of the issue. In a subsequent section an examination will be made of the different types of payment and interest schedules; suffice it to say at this point that principal and interest payments can occur in a variety of ways: for example, in equal installments like a home mortgage (where the portion of the debt service going to the principal increases as the portion going to meet interest charges decreases); on a declining balance basis (where each payment becomes slightly less since the interest charges apply only to the unpaid balance); on a deferred principal basis (where interest charges are a constant level for some period since the principal is not being paid down); and so forth. The total amount of principal and interest payment due in some future year (call it $k$) may be conceived as arising from debt incurred during or before the present year (call it $t$) and from debt incurred in years $t + 1, t + 2, \ldots, t + k$.

Assume the simplest (and most common) form of municipal bond issue, where a series of bonds are issued in year $t$, with an interest payment in year $t$ but no principal payment until year $t + 1$; principal is then paid in equal amounts over $m - 1$ years, where $m$ is the maturity (or life span) of the bond issue. An interest rate of $r$ percent is paid on the outstanding principal. Therefore, the debt service in the first year of the issue ($t$) is equal to the rate of interest times the total outstanding debt, whereas in each succeeding ($t + 1, \ldots t + k, \ldots, t + (m - 1)$), the debt service is equal to the principal payment plus the interest on the unpaid balance. This can be expressed by the following formula:

$$D_{t+k}^{Bm} = \frac{B_t^m [1 + r(m - k)]}{m - 1}$$

which defines the debt service ($D$) in year $t + k$ for a bond issued in year $t$ of size $B$ and maturity $m$, with an interest rate of $r$.

Perhaps an example will help to clarify this formula. Assume that in 1965 (year $t$), a community issued a bond for $200,000 ($B$), with a 20-year maturity ($m$) and a five percent interest rate ($r$) on the unpaid principal. In 1966 the debt service charge would be $20,526.32 (i.e., $10,526.32 as a principal payment—1/19th of the total principal—and $10,000 as an interest payment—0.05 times $200,000). In 1967 the principal has been reduced to $189,473.68, and, therefore, the interest payment would be $9,473.68 and the principal payment $10,526.32, for a total debt service charge of $20,000. Using the previous formula, the debt service charges for 1975 ($t + k$) can be calculated as follows:

$$\frac{\$200{,}000 \, (1 + 0.05 \, (20-10))}{19} = \$15{,}789.47$$

The formula can be simplified by assuming that both an interest and principal payment are made in the first year of the bond issue (within 12 months after

# FORECASTING EXPENDITURES AND RESOURCES

the bonds are marketed); thereby, the principal is paid off in $m$ equal payments (20 in the above example) and the divisor in the formula become $m$. In the example above, the debt service charge for 1975 (i.e., 10 years into the bond issue) under these assumptions would be $15,000.

Normally, bonds are issued with maturities of 5, 10, and 20 years; the same formula applies, however, whatever the maturity of an issue. The level of debt payments in a given year in the future ($k$), therefore, is equal to the sum of all debt payments due in year $k$ on bonds issued during or before year $t$ (the base year) *plus* the debt service on all bonds anticipated to be issued in years $t + 1, t + 2, \ldots, t + k$. However, budget statements outlining anticipated dollar expenditures for capital improvements over some future period must be viewed as statements of *desired* rather than *actual* expenditures, that is, when finances are tight, it is far easier to cut the capital budget request than to make substantial cuts in operating expenditures. Therefore, the size of the capital budget ($K$) for some point in the future ($t + k$) must be modified by some factor ($a$) that represents the percentage of the total capital expenditure requests that can be expected to be approved in the years $t + 1, \ldots, t + k$; the factor (or factors) designated as ($a$) can be viewed as policy variables or as trend variables.

Again an example may help to clarify the preceding discussion. The data presented in Table 5-2 represent the bonds issued by a hypothetical community of Homeville over the period from 1965 to 1974, plus the anticipated issues for the following five years (1975 through 1979). These issues carry varying interest rates and maturities. The task in developing a forecast of the debt service charges in some future year, say 1980, is to first calculate the debt

Table 5-2
Level of Indebtedness of Homeville, 1965-79

| Date of Issue | Amount | Interest | Maturity | k | a |
|---|---|---|---|---|---|
| 1965 | $200,000 | 5% | 20 | 15 | |
| 1966 | 300,000 | 6% | 15 | 14 | |
| 1967 | 200,000 | 6% | 15 | 13 | |
| 1968 | 200,000 | 5.5% | 20 | 12 | |
| 1969 | 300,000 | 6% | 10 | 11 | |
| 1970 | 400,000 | 5.5% | 20 | 10 | |
| 1971 | 400,000 | 6.5% | 5 | 9 | |
| 1972 | 200,000 | 6% | 10 | 8 | |
| 1973 | 250,000 | 6% | 20 | 7 | |
| 1974 | 300,000 | 6.5% | 20 | 6 | |
| 1975 | 200,000 | 6.5% | 20 | 5 | 0.8 |
| 1976 | 100,000 | 6.5% | 15 | 4 | 0.7 |
| 1977 | 200,000 | 6.5% | 15 | 3 | 0.7 |
| 1978 | 100,000 | 7% | 20 | 2 | 0.6 |
| 1979 | 300,000 | 7% | 10 | 1 | 0.6 |

service on each bond issue prior to and including the base year 1974 that will be due in 1980 ($t + k$). In examining Table 5-2 it may be noted that the bond issue marketed in 1969 will be paid off by 1979 (i.e., has a 10-year maturity) and the issue in 1971 will be paid off by 1976 and therefore will not figure into the calculations for 1980. Completing these calculations results in a projected debt expenditure for 1980, based on bonds issued in 1974 or prior to that year, of approximately $178,130. In other words, if no further bonds are issued after 1974, the community of Homeville in the year 1980 will be expected to pay out $178,130 in interest and principal on the bonds outstanding. Table 5-2 shows a tentative capital improvements program in which additional issues will be made during the ensuing five years, however. For each of these issues a "probability of issue" has been assigned (factor $a$). Adding these data to the previous calculations, results in a total projected level of expenditure of $260,873 for debt service charges in 1980.

## Estimates of Financial Resources

The financial pressures that many local governments must face result from some sort of mismatch between receipts (revenues) and expenditures. These fiscal discrepancies have an important bearing on the ability and capacity of local governments to finance capital facilities, since a community's ability to accumulate capital reserves or to borrow to finance long-term capital investments is conditioned, in large measure, by its overall "financial solvency." Any capital improvements program must be formulated within the financial capacity of government to pay for its needs and desires. A community that cannot meet its short-term public expenditure demands from existing (and projected) sources of revenue will find difficulty in securing willing investors for its long-term bonds and may be in a position to do so only at a high cost (i.e., a high interest rate will be demanded to offset the risk). To propose improvements that the government cannot afford, or to propose improvements without some firm idea of how they will be paid for, is to invite unrealistic programs that, from the beginning, are destined to prove unsuccessful.

### Local Government Revenue

Apart from borrowing, local government receipts consist of local taxes, user charges, income from utilities and other public enterprises, and aid through intergovernmental (state and federal) programs of assistance. The yield from each of these sources is shown for selected years in Table 5-3.

During most of the history of this nation the property tax has been the most important tax revenue source by a wide margin. As late as 1940 the

## Table 5-3
## Local Government Revenues

| Revenue Category | Millions of Dollars, Fiscal Years | | | Compound Annual Rate of Growth | | Distribution by Source, 1970-71 | |
|---|---|---|---|---|---|---|---|
| | 1949-50 | 1959-60 | 1970-71 | 1950-60 | 1970-71 | Total General Revenue | Tax Revenue |
| Total general revenue[a] | $14,014 | $33,026 | $91,964 | 8.9% | 9.7% | 100.0% | |
| Tax revenue | 7,984 | 18,081 | 43,434 | 8.5 | 8.3 | 47.2 | 100.0% |
| Property tax | 7,042 | 15,798 | 36,726 | 8.4 | 8.0 | 39.9 | 84.5 |
| Sales & gross receipts taxes | 484 | 1,339 | 3,662 | 10.7 | 9.6 | 4.0 | 8.4 |
| Income tax | 64 | 254 | 1,747 | 14.8 | 15.6 | 1.9 | 4.0 |
| Licenses and other taxes | 394 | 692 | 1,289 | 5.8 | 5.8 | 1.4 | 3.0 |
| Charges & miscellaneous revenues | 1,602 | 4,831 | 14,058 | 11.7 | 10.2 | 15.3 | |
| Intergovernmental revenue | 4,428 | 10,114 | 34,473 | 8.6 | 11.8 | 37.5 | |
| Federal sources | 211 | 592 | 3,391 | 10.8 | 17.2 | 3.7 | |
| State sources | 4,217 | 9,522 | 31,081 | 8.5 | 11.3 | 33.8 | |

[a]Excludes revenues from utilities, liquor stores, and insurance trust funds.
Sources: U.S. Bureau of the Census, *Census of Governments, 1962*, and *Governmental Finances in 1970-71*.

property tax provided nearly 35 percent of all federal, state, and local taxes; the second ranking tax, on corporate income, provided only 10 percent. With World War II, however, the property tax lost ground, and by 1944 it provided only 9.4 percent of total collections, outranked by the revenue from taxes on individual and corporate income. The reason for the shift, of course, was the vast expansion of federal tax collections to which the property tax made no contribution, since it was, and always had been, wholly a source of state and local funds. Property taxes still account for about 85 percent of local tax revenue. While efforts of local governments during the past 30 years to develop other tax sources have borne fruit only in large cities, additional nontax revenues have been found, notably state and federal aid and collection of charges.

The near total dependence of local governments on the property tax stems from one inescapable fact—the lack of viable options. No other tax is available for productive use at the local level. Unilateral taxation of income, sales, or business by local governments tends to induce shrinkage in the tax base, that is, if one municipality in a region introduces such taxes, economic activities tend to locate beyond its taxing jurisdiction.[d] Therefore, the adoption of such nonproperty taxes may prove dysfunctional rather than beneficial to the financial well-being of such municipalities. Real property, however, is quite immobile; differential taxes seldom induces migration out of a local geographic area. Workers must reside close to their work; retail outlets tend to locate close to consumers; manufacturing establishments, once committed, tend to stay put, since property taxes are a modest part of their total costs (although such taxes may play an important role in their initial location decision). In short, real property offers a base upon which local governments can safely levy taxes.

The yield from the property tax in postwar years has been fairly elastic, responding well in the aggregate to increases in gross national product, as well as to increases of population. Thus, Jesse Burkhead concludes that: "... the property tax is a far better fiscal instrument than most of its critics have allowed. There is every reason to believe that it will continue to hold its relative fiscal importance in state-local public finance structures."[6] It is in the administration of the property tax, however, that significant reforms are required. The most serious administrative fault of the general property tax is inaccurate assessment, in terms of: (a) underassessment, and (b) deviation of individual property values from the general assessment ratio of the taxing jurisdiction.[7] Serious problems also exist with the equity of incidence of local property taxes. Although the property tax is levied in part in accordance with the *benefit principle,* the use of revenues generated by this form of taxation to support many local services that are not based on user-benefits results

---

[d]This consequence is most apparent in suburban areas of larger metropolitan regions, where major shopping facilities will locate just outside the taxing jurisdictions of cities that have been granted the power to levy local sales taxes by the state legislature.

in a regressive impact with respect to income. Attention to reforms in these two areas is required if local governments are to continue to use property taxes as their major source of revenue.

The general sales tax is by far the most productive of local nonproperty taxes. Such taxes are now permitted in about one-third of the states, and approximately 3,000 localities exercise the right. Selective sales taxes are next in importance, the most significant being the gross receipts tax levied on public utilities by local governments in most states under their regulatory powers. Income and wage taxes, while contributing only a small portion to total local revenues, are increasing in importance with recent additions to the number of taxing jurisdictions. As a consequence of the spotty distribution of nonproperty taxes, aggregate figures of collections for all governments tend to obscure their importance for some local governments. In the city of Columbus, Ohio, for example, local nonproperty taxes account for over 75 percent of all local tax collections, while in the cities of Birmingham, Toledo, St. Louis, Kansas City, and Louisville, they account for 60 percent of more.

Each source of local revenue has its own base, that is, the financial aggregate to which the rate of yield is applied. In the case of the property tax the base is the assessed value of taxable local property; for a retail sales tax the base is the annual value of taxable retail sales. The yield of any revenue source is the product of the base times the rate. Since an understanding of these base data is conditioned by an understanding of the total local economy, the need for a sound, continuous analysis of the structure and processes of local economic activities should be readily apparent.

*Financial Analysis: Estimating*
*Local Revenues*

The fundamental purpose of a financial analysis was stated succinctly some years ago in a report of the National Resources Planning Board.

> ... (to) determine approximately the present and future ability ... to pay for the construction and maintenance of public improvements, by estimating the present availability of funds, by research into the probable future trends of municipal revenue and expenditure, by appraisal of all factors related to the administration and operation of the program, and by determining what limitations are imposed, by statutes or prior commitments, upon the freedom of the municipality to act.[8]

Although the National Resources Planning Board reference is to municipal programming activities, the procedures outlined are equally applicable to any level of government. Thus, the financial analysis that must be undertaken as part of a capital improvements program is a three-step process that involves:

1. An estimate of available revenues under existing fiscal policies
2. An exploration of alternative fiscal policies
3. The selection of a general fiscal policy that will best fit the future public service and capital expenditure needs in light of the limitations placed on the jurisdiction's financial capacity

The first step in analyzing the "supply side" of local revenue-expenditure patterns is to determine whether any modifications in existing policies will be required to finance the desired service programs and related capital expenditures. An analysis of available revenues under existing fiscal policies will provide a basis for determining the most advantageous and realistic means by which revenues and expenditures can be brought into equilibrium, that is, by increasing the former or reducing the latter.

The probable amounts to be received from present rates of taxes and miscellaneous charges must be estimated after thorough analysis of collection trends and conditions affecting the yield from each source. The rates of all service charges must be compared to changes anticipated in the cost of rendering services at the same level and/or increasing the level of service, and consideration must be given to possible adjustments in the rate schedules. In order to accomplish these objectives a sound basis of *unit cost data* must be available through cost accounting procedures.

Each source of revenue may require a different formula in order to forecast a reliable figure to include in the budget. Each source should be tabulated over a sufficiently long period to establish valid trend lines that take into account both boom and recession periods. At the same time it is necessary to develop and project appropriate indices against which the various sources of revenue can be matched in order to make future estimations. Some revenues may produce practically the same yield from year to year (or proportionately the same yield as a consequence of increases or decreases in their base resulting from population and/or economic growth or decline). For example, revenues derived from an income or sales tax are a function of population and the level of personal income; motor vehicle license fees are dependent upon the relationship between future population and projected car registration trends; use taxes are a function of population, the level of the economy, and the level of personal income. Other revenues fluctuate violently and cannot be relied upon to produce the same amount from one year to the next. Several sources of revenue are more difficult to project than others (e.g., inheritance and gift taxes often result in windfalls and therefore must be projected on the basis of past trends leveled out over time). Some sources are dependent upon the fiscal policies of other levels of government (e.g., federal aid programs), while other sources are directly or indirectly related to the level of service and capital expenditures provided by government. Since many of these estimates require accurate projections of future populations and anticipated levels of economic activity, financial planners and development planners must work closely with one another in the preparation of this phase of the analysis.

For each revenue source, there is a rate of charge and an item subject to levy of tax, licence, or charge. The yield must be estimated by determining how frequently the item subject to tax (or charge) will occur. No source of revenue should be estimated solely on collections of the previous year. Some revenue sources are more stable than others; however, a high level of stability should not lull the administrator into the pitfall of routine estimating.

The following procedural steps are suggested as a basis for sound revenue estimates:

1. An analysis file should be prepared and kept up-to-date for each source of revenue, containing the following information:
    a) Summary of legal background, including date of adoption and reference to ordinances or legislation establishing the charges
    b) Summary schedule of rates or charges on items to which applied
    c) List of those factors that influence the revenue yield
2. A data sheet on each revenue source should be set up, showing information on collection by months and totals by years.
3. The percentages collected each month should be calculated as compared to annual totals for the past three to five years. This information will indicate seasonal influences and will provide information for establishing monthly or quarterly revenue anticipation for budget control purposes and for estimating receipts for the balance of any given period based on trends to date for the period.
4. Up-to-date tabulations should be kept on data indicating local economic conditions and trends. Data of particular value include information on building construction activity, real estate turnover, retail sales, employment and payrolls, and other common indices of business activities.
5. The advice of department heads administering public services for which special charges are made should be sought.
6. A preliminary revenue prediction should be prepared based on trend factors before the budget process is started for any given fiscal period so as to serve as a guide to the determination of fiscal policy. The final estimates—based on trends, economic projections, department estimates, and other related factors—should be prepared immediately prior to the transmission of the budget document to the council.

In developing this analysis all assumptions concerning methodology and current fiscal policies, as they might be extended into the future, should be carefully recorded. Three basic methods are generally used in forecasting: extrapolation, correlation, and some form of mathematical technique for curve fitting. Too heavy a reliance should not be placed upon statistical formula for computing future trends, however; rather, a careful analysis should be made of the various possible factors that may alter past trends or establish new ones.

*Alternative Fiscal Policies*

The second step in the financial analysis is to explore the ramifications of alternative fiscal policies. This should include an analysis of ways by which the income derived from existing revenue sources might be increased or decreased; the availability and/or feasibility of new sources of revenue; and the effect of varying borrowing policies on available resources. The analysis of the likely changes in existing sources of revenue and the availability of new sources must be a continuous process, particulary in light of the ever increasing demands being placed on local governments for services and facilities. This analysis, of course, relates not only to revenues for capital expenditures but for operating programs as well. Alternative methods for financing capital facilities are discussed in detail in the next chapter.

*Determination of Fiscal Policies*

Having ascertained the availability of revenues under existing fiscal policies and having explored alternative methods of financing, these two areas must be brought together to focus on recommendations regarding future fiscal policies. A key function of planners and programmers, therefore, is to advise the chief executive and the legislative body in the formulation of a clear, explicit and definitive series of policy statements to serve as guidelines for the programming of capital improvements.

The following points are illustrative of the items that should be covered in these statements of fiscal policy.[9]

1. The total amount of funds to be expended annually for capital improvements in order to achieve and maintain some desirable level of public service
2. The ratio to be applied among the various methods of financing capital improvements, that is, what portion of the required allocation will be available from annual revenues and how much must be financed through borrowing or other methods of financing
3. The types and maturities of bonds to be issued for the financing of capital improvements expenditures
4. The relationship between self-supporting and tax-supported public improvements and the terms and conditions under which self-liquidating facilities are feasible
5. The ceiling on annual debt service charges deemed desirable

# FORECASTING EXPENDITURES AND RESOURCES

6. The role of outside (federal and state) assistance in the financing of capital improvements
7. Fiscal policies with regards to current outstanding debt
8. The relationship between the capital and operating budgets
9. Policies with regards to new sources of revenues
10. The feasibility of maintaining and increasing the borrowing reserve of government

Several of these points warrant further discussion.

(1) Having compiled and catalogued the various projects or improvements as submitted by the operating agencies, it is a relatively straight forward procedure to put a "price tag" on the total program that would be required to meet these projects requests. This figure, coupled with the financial analyses, can provide a rough guide to the establishment of a realistic range within which the capital improvements program can be carried out.

(2) In terms of the ratio among the various methods of financing capital improvements, it may be suggested from experience that at least 20 percent of capital improvements should be financed from current revenues. While this will vary from area to area and from year to year, as a matter of fiscal policy an effort should be made to establish a clearly defined range within which these adjustments can be made.

(3) To the extent possible, bond issues should have a limited life period so as to minimize the debt service charges. Where possible, bond issues should be of the serial type and should be assumed as general governmental obligations rather than as specific agency obligations. General obligation bonds normally carry a lower interest rate because they are based on the "full faith and credit" of local government. In connection with particulary long-term programs it may be necessary to create special authorities with powers to issue bonds. Bond issues made in connection with self-supporting projections may be permitted to have a longer maximum maturity than those issued for tax-supported loans. However, in general, maximum maturity periods should not exceed 30 years.

(4) All projects financed by self-supporting loans must clearly demonstrate an ability to produce sufficient revenue to repay their cost. In this regard there must be a careful analysis of proposed projects as to justification, scheduling, cost estimates, and impact on the operating budget.

(5) In accordance with recognized finance principles, annual debt service charges payable from general revenues should not exceed 20 percent of the total available funds. Here again, a close analysis and coordination with the operating budget is essential.

(6) Continual analyses must be made of the likelihood of new or sustained federal and state programs that might assist in the financing of capital improvements. At times it may be necessary to adjust or modify the capital improvements program in order to take full advantage of these assistance programs.

(7) Every effort should be made to level off and reduce the outstanding

debt of government at the earliest possible date. Capital expenditures under the six-year program must be scheduled carefully to ensure a reasonable outstanding debt-structure in relation to the general level of the economy, the sources of revenue available, and the overall ability to pay for these improvements.

(8) The need to relate the capital budget with the operating budget has been stressed previously. The amortization of the capital improvements approved in any given year becomes a charge against the operating budget in many future years. The administration and maintenance of new capital improvements generally require additional manpower, equipment, and supplies that will also affect future operating budgets. To provide a complete picture of their impact, estimates of annual operating costs relating to scheduled improvements should be clearly noted. In order to demonstrate how the individual programs may be consumated and what affect they will have on the fiscal affairs of government, financial data should be projected forward on the basis of the existing considerations, as well as the judgment of those officials responsible for operating public programs. This requires a close working relationship among the various operating agencies, the development planners, and the capital improvement programmers.

Items (9) and (10) were discussed at length in other sections of this chapter.

*Summary*

In summary, it should again be stressed that financial analysis and planning serve as the necessary foundation for intelligent capital improvements programming. Three elements are fundamental to the development of a financial framework for capital expenditures: first, an analysis must be made of the sources of revenue currently available under existing fiscal policies, including an analysis of the revenue program and the operating budget; second, alternative fiscal policies and methods of financing should be explored to include an analysis of the current debt structure and the ability of government to incur new debt; and third, policy statements should be formulated which deal with revenues, operating expenditures, capital improvements, bonds, and the relationships among and between them.

# 6

## Methods of Financing Capital Facilities and Choice of Debt Form

**Methods of Financing**

Having estimated revenues to be derived from the maintenance of existing fiscal policies and from new sources or shifts in yields from current sources under alternative policies, the final step in the formulation of a long-range revenue program involves the selection of a general fiscal policy from among the alternatives. A sound revenue policy can only be formulated at the same time that the public service and capital facility needs are being determined. The two go hand in hand, and it is not sound procedure to settle just one and then adjust the other to it. In financing capital facilities, as with the purchases of individuals, it is possible for a municipality to: (a) pay cash, (b) save money for future acquisitions, or (c) borrow on anticipated earning power. A sound long-range revenue program will seek to develop the appropriate mix among these three methods of financing.

*Pay-As-You-Go*

For many years state and local officials held that the only appropriate method of financing was to pay for capital facilities (and all other governmental costs) out of current revenues—to "pay-as-you-go" as contrasted to the "go-now-and-pay-later" scheme promoted by personal finance companies and various travel agencies. A capital budget may be formulated on a pay-as-you-go basis, or a city may adopt such a program without a formal capital budget. The goal is to finance 100 percent of the city's capital improvements out of the current budget. Few governments have been able to operate successfully (i.e., meet the needs of their citizens) strictly on a pay-as-you-go basis, however.

The feasibility of a complete or partial pay-as-you-go approach (the latter being adopted by many governments) largely depends upon two factors: the nature of the community and the character of the anticipated expenditures. Older, more established communities are in a better position to adopt a pay-as-you-go approach than are newer communities or communities continuing to experience rapid growth. Once the infrastructure of an older community has been established it may be easier to finance required municipal improvements out of increased taxes. As to character of expenditures, capital facility needs may be recurrent or nonrecurrent. A pay-as-you-go approach is more feasible when capital expenditures are recurrent, either as to purpose or as to amount, as for example, the paving of streets, the acquisition of neighborhood recreational areas, and so forth. While the main advantage of the pay-as-you-go approach is that it is cheaper in the long run, since the cost of borrowed money is eliminated, a second advantage is often cited in justification of this technique: Many public economists hold that the planning of improvements and the actual expenditure of public revenues will be handled more efficiently when the taxpayers feel the cost immediately. In the pursuit of efficiency, however, many public officials have foregone the objective of effectiveness, that is, providing public improvements when needed.

Several procedures may be applied in shifting to a partial or complete pay-as-you-go basis.[1] One approach is to gradually shorten the term of all new borrowing; each new bond issue is given a slightly shorter maturity period than the preceding one. A second approach, one which may be very difficult to achieve, is to declare a moratorium on new capital construction until a substantial portion of the outstanding debt has been reduced. A third approach is to require a down payment for each new facility from current revenues, gradually increasing the portion of capital outlays to be met from current revenues, and thereby slowly arriving at the desired goal. It is easier, of course, in periods of relative prosperity to increase taxes or to increase revenues by raising assessed valuations in order to finance capital facilities within the current budget. Alternative sources of current revenues may be adopted to support a pay-as-you-go approach, including nonproperty taxes such as an income tax or sales tax, nontax revenues such as licenses, fees, and fines, special assessments (when paid in advance), service charges such as sewer rentals, and state and federal grants-in-aid. In adopting any of these procedures, singly or in combination, the formulation of a capital budget and capital improvements program is a vital first step.

*Special Benefit Assessments and*
*Excess Condemnation*

*Special benefit assessments* place a major share of the burden of financing on those individuals, groups, or properties receiving the greatest benefit from the improvement. These levies may be made directly as assessments, such as in the case of an extension of a municipal sewer system whereby the properties served are taxed (or charged a special fee) to pay for the improvement, or as indirect levies, such as hunting and fishing license fees or park visitation stickers (where the fees collected are applied toward the acquisition of additional facilities).

*Excess condemnation* is the policy, on the part of a state or city, of taking by right of eminent domain more property than is actually necessary for the creation of a public improvement, and of subsequently selling or leasing this surplus. On the theory that, at the completion of the project, the value of the excess lands will have increased by virtue of their proximity to the project, it is held to be within the power of government to sell these properties at the increased value to some appropriate user. While it has been argued that excess condemnation places government "in the real estate business" and, therefore, is an infringement on private enterprises, in those states in which such practices have been authorized (about one-fourth of the states), it has been upheld by the courts as a valid exercise of government powers, being in the interest of public welfare. Excess condemnation has not been widely used, and where applied, the returns from the sale of excess land have not greatly exceeded the cost of acquisition, administration, and resale.[a] Government bodies are rarely so alert as to condemn all the property they intend to acquire before some part of the anticipated increase of value is worked into the price of the condemned parcels.

*Reserve Funds*

Financing capital facilities through the accumulation of a reserve fund (sometimes called a "capital reserve") can be thought of as the opposite of borrowing in that the timetable is reversed. A portion of current revenues is set aside each year and usually is invested in order to accumulate sufficient funds to initiate some particular capital project or to finance capital improvements in general. The amount ($S$) of a reserve fund created by a fixed investment ($N$) placed annually at compound interest ($r$) for a term of $n$ years, the first investment being made at the end of the first year, can be expressed by the following formula:

$$S = N \cdot \frac{(1 + r)^n - 1}{r}$$

Thus, an investment of $1000 a year for ten years at six percent will yield a

---

[a] While only of limited application as a revenue producing method, excess condemnation can serve as an effective devise to safeguard against improper use of abutting land that may impair the usefulness of a major public improvement. This application is particularly appropriate in connection with parks and recreational areas as a means of minimizing the garish and unplanned "strip development" that detracts from the approaches to such facilities. Another related opportunity—of an expenditure rather than a revenue nature—is the purchase of *development rights.* Any low-density form of land use often benefits the general public. The sale of such properties for more intensive use can create a collective loss. It might be appropriate, therefore, for the local government, or perhaps the state, to buy the legal right to the *change* in the land use and thus keep the change from taking place. This concept is particularly appropriate for such semipublic uses as a golf course or in connection with large private estates.

reserve fund of $13,180. Conversely, the amount ($N$) that must be placed annually (at the end of the year) at compound interest ($r$) for a term of $n$ years to create a reserve fund ($S$) may be calculated by the following formula:

$$N = S \cdot \frac{r}{(1+r)^n - 1}$$

Should the objective be to develop a reserve fund of $20,000 at the end of ten years, the community would be required to invest $1517.36 per year at six percent.

Another useful formula applicable to reserve fund calculations is the so-called "present value of an annuity" formula. This formula is used to calculate the amount that would have to be invested ($P$) at a given rate of interest ($r$) in order to provide a fixed annual payment of $N$ dollars for a period of $n$ years, and can be expressed as follows:

$$P = N \cdot \frac{(1+r)^n - 1}{r(1+r)^n}$$

Thus, if a municipality wanted to set aside a sum of money, invested at six percent, to meet annual debt service charges of $10,000 for 20 years, it would be necessary to establish a reserve fund of $114,700.

Reserve funds are particularly effective in smaller communities where certain capital improvements are not recurrent, for example, school construction. Using a combination of reserve funds and borrowing, the community can accumulate the necessary funds to make a substantial down payment on the facility and then finance the remainder of the cost through borrowing, thus spreading the total cost and achieving at least partial user-benefit equity.

Many cities accumulated substantial reserve funds during World War II, when capital construction of public facilities was held to a minimum by the shortage of materials, labor, and the overall defense effort. In 30 states legislation was passed to enable cities to build up funds for financing postwar construction. Such legislation was encouraged by the federal government, whose economic advisors foresaw the possibility of a major recession at the end of the war and sought to develop a backlog or "shelf" of public works projects to facilitate the conversion from a wartime to peacetime economy. However, for a number of years after the war, construction costs increased so rapidly that many local governments continued to postpone capital construction on all but the most necessary projects. Inflation rather than recession followed the war, causing many cities to use their accumulated reserves to meet rising current operating costs. This practice caused some authorities on public finance to look with disfavor upon the accumulation of reserve funds unless adequate safeguards are installed to ensure that the tax money will go for the planned capital improvements.

Various methods have been developed to provide the safeguards called for by these public finance experts. One approach requires that reserve fund allocations be deposited by municipalities with the state treasurer or other appropriate state finance officer, to be invested and held until time for construction of the local improvements. This approach is particularly beneficial to smaller units of government, since the state can usually invest the total funds of all depositing municipalities at a higher rate of return than could be obtained by any one municipality.

A second approach is to create a reserve fund, financed by a regular tax levy or by a stipulated amount set aside from the general fund, earmarked for a specific project that has been approved by a local referendum. Thus, expenditures from the fund would be limited solely to the purpose approved by the electorate when the fund was established, and approval to use the special fund for any other purpose could be obtained only by another local referendum. This approach ties the reserve fund to a specific project (and may result in the creation of a number of reserve funds, each tied to a particular capital improvement), the cost of which may be uncertain, thereby making it difficult to project the exact level of "set aside" necessary from annual tax revenues to ensure an adequate reserve some years hence to finance the project. To provide a greater degree of flexibility, some cities have adopted a basic tax for the financing of public improvements, the revenues from which are assigned to a capital reserve that cannot be used for current operating purposes. Part of the capital reserve can be used to finance improvements on a pay-as-you-go basis for equipment and low-cost construction, such as streets and additions to public buildings; another portion of the fund can be used as down payments for major capital expenditures; and the balance can be used for debt service. Since the rate of the capital improvements tax is set by the overall tax rate of the community, this approach provides an even level of revenue each year.

The same objective can be achieved without the enactment of a special capital improvements tax if a stipulated proportion of the total budget is set aside for capital improvements. Based on long-range planning of the community's capital facility needs, for example, it may be deemed desirable to set aside 25 percent of the regular annual budget for capital purposes. To the extent that this 25 percent set aside is not required for debt retirement, the balance could be assigned to new capital construction on a pay-as-you-go basis or could form the basis of a reserve fund to be invested and accumulated for some future purpose. For most municipalities a 25 percent allocation from the total annual budget would seem to be an appropriate level to achieve good financial planning for capital improvements.

*Borrowing*

Government loans are marketed with maturities ranging from a few days to several decades. For purposes of discussion it is possible to divide government borrowing practices into three categories: (1) short-term loans with maturities of a year or less, (2) intermediate loans with maturities over one year but not more than five years, and (3) long-term loans with maturities of over five years. While it is this latter category that is most commonly associated with long-range financing of capital projects, each may have a role in the financial planning of a municipality.

Short-term government borrowing takes various forms—bills, certificates, or notes sold to banks or other investors, bank loans, warrants paid out in place of cash,[b] and unpaid bills and claims. Short-term borrowing is most frequently used to smooth out irregularities between expenditure and income flows and to finance governmental operations temporarily during periods when tax receipts fall off unexpectedly. Some cities have found it convenient to finance the construction of a series of improvements initially through short-term borrowing rather than to float a separate long-term issue to finance each individual improvement. These projects then may be refunded or refinanced into a consolidated long-term debt.

Intermediate government borrowing, with maturities from one to five years, has limited but definite uses. A city whose outstanding debt is in the form of callable-term bonds (bonds that may be called in and the principal paid in full after a specified period) may discover a favorable opportunity to convert a portion of such debt by floating a new intermediate loan at a lower rate of interest. Cities operating largely on a pay-as-you-go basis may resort to loans of intermediate maturities when exceptional expenditures cannot be met from current revenues.

Most state and local governments, at one time or another, find it necessary to issue long-term bonds to finance capital projects. A *bond* is the promise of the issuer to pay a specified amount of money (principal) at a specified future date (maturity) and to pay periodically a specified rate of interest. *Municipal bonds* are those issued by local governmental units to finance the construction, repair, or improvement of local public facilities, interest on which is exempt

---

[b] A warrant is an administrative order to a governmental disbursing officer to pay the holder, usually a private firm or individual with whom the government regularly does business, a specified sum on demand. Finding themselves pressed for cash, local governments may make their warrants payable in three or six months or payable out of some subsequent tax receipt rather than on demand. In effect, holders of such warrants are compelled to extend credit to the government for the term of the warrant. Warrants may be discounted at local banks, but usually at a cost. All parties having business dealings with such governments, except their salaried employees, usually take this "cost" into account and make a corresponding addition to their charges. The practice of permitting bills to go unpaid leads to similar excess charges.

from all present federal income taxes. Although referred to as "municipal bonds," this broad category of investment opportunity includes bonds issued by a state, territory, or possession of the United States, or by any municipality, political subdivision (including cities, counties, school districts, and special purpose districts), or public agency or instrumentality (such as an authority or commission) of one or more of the foregoing.

In addition to the tax exempt feature, municipal bonds possess three significant investment features, as follows:

1. The *security* of municipal bonds is generally considered to be second only to federal government bonds.[c]
2. Municipal bonds have a high *marketability,* assuring that an investor can always sell them if he wishes to do so.
3. The *diversity* of municipal bonds enables an investor to obtain bonds in a geographical area and at a maturity of his preference.

In addition to the exemption from all present federal income taxes, the interest on municipal bonds usually is exempt from state income taxes in the state where the issuer is located.

In general, long-term borrowing is appropriate under the following conditions: (1) where the project is of a type that will not require replacement for many years, such as a city hall, auditorium, major health facility, or sewage disposal plant; (2) where the project can be financed by service charges to pay off revenue bonds; (3) where needs are urgent for public health and safety purposes or other emergency reasons; (4) where special assessment bonds are the only feasible means of financing improvements in the absence of subdivision regulations or other controls; (5) where intergovernmental revenues may be available on a continuous basis to guarantee the security of the bonds, as in the case of public housing; and (6) for financing projects in newly annexed areas or areas of rapid expansion where the demands on municipal resources are comparatively large and unforeseen.

A widely accepted principle is that the proper maturity for a given debt should be determined by the anticipated life of the improvement. Since future generations, as well as the present, will benefit from the improvement, it is deemed appropriate that the payment be spread among all who benefit. Under this approach, however, long-term debt may pile up until it reaches the legal limit imposed by state legislation. At that point further public improvements cannot be constructed no matter how pressing the need. Therefore, although

---

[c]While municipal bonds are generally considered second only to federal bonds in security, there are variations in the security behind municipal bonds dependent upon many factors. Therefore, a sound fundamental rule for an investor to follow is to consult a reliable broker for advice as to what municipal bonds are best suited to particular investment needs.

the life of an improvement may be properly viewed as setting a *maximum* maturity for a loan, shorter maturity is often preferable.

Another approach to long-term borrowing involves the financing of only the excess of a year's capital expenditures over and above that covered by annual revenues. Excess-capital-expenditure loans do not apply to any particular improvement; such indebtedness covers that portion of total capital construction in a given year that cannot be met on a pay-as-you-go basis or out of capital reserves. Since there is no particular improvement to whose life the maturity of such loans can be related, the "expected life" principle cannot be applied, for example, the costs of paving streets, building schools, constructing parks, and so forth are lumped together, with each having a different life expectancy. The maturities of such loans must be determined by such factors as the maturities of the government's outstanding loans, expected developments in the local economy, changes in the size and composition of the community's population, and the possibility of future shifts in interest rates.

There are several practices followed by some municipalities in long-term borrowing that should be discussed although they can not be recommended as sound practices. One approach, known as "debt equalization," involves the levelling off of peak-year maturities by refunding outstanding issues so that, roughly, an equal annual debt service load over a period of 15 or 20 years is attained. While possessing a certain basic appeal of a "balanced" approach to debt financing, the danger of debt equalization lies in the fact that little or no room is left in the maturity schedule for the debt service burden of new issues. Another practice, the so-called "gross bonding plan," involves a one-time authorization of a large bond issue to cover planned capital improvements over a relatively long period. The bonds are not issued, however, until needed. This approach has the advantage of reducing preliminary costs of financing, such as the cost of bond referenda, and assuring the financing of planned programs for the period covered. Gross bonding, however, tends to overemphasize long-term borrowing as the sole means of financing capital imporvements, that is, given the authorization, governmental officials may tend to use up the bonding capacity rather than seek other methods of financing capital projects. A gross bonding plan can be made acceptable if a balanced financing program is adopted by the municipality in which long-term borrowing forms only a part.

*Summary*

Given the intensity of demands for new public facilities that face most municipalities today, relatively few communities are in a position to finance capital projects strictly on a pay-as-you-go basis. By the same token, cities that finance practically all capital improvements out of borrowed money—an "all-loan policy"—fail to recognize the basic principles of long-range financial planning. The foundation for a sound capital improvements program must be built upon an appropriate mix of pay-as-you-go financing, an accumulation of reserve funds, and a debt policy that is based upon a maturity schedule reflecting the municipality's ability to bear certain levels of debt burden.[2] The formulation of an appropriate debt policy and the range of bonds that can be issued are the subjects of subsequent sections in this chapter.

**Choice of Debt Form**

Municipal bonds can be categorized according to several distinct criteria, as follows: (a) the security that stands behind the bonds, (b) the method of redemption, (c) the callable provision, and (d) the method by which title can be transferred. A given bond issue should be described in terms of each of these criteria, and the choice of debt form should reflect the nature of the project to be funded and the overall debt planning of the community or authority.

*Types of Security*

There are four general types of municipal bonds according to the security that stands behind them: (1) general obligation bonds, (2) special tax or special assessment bonds, (3) revenue bonds, and (4) new housing authority bonds. As the Advisory Commission on Intergovernmental relations pointed out in the early sixties:

> By far the most striking change in the composition of local debt during recent years (and which has also involved State Government debt) concerns the *type of liability incurred.* There is an increased proportion of nonguaranteed bonds, as distinguished from bonds backed by full faith and credit of the issuing governments.[3]

Nonguaranteed debt, as defined by the Census Bureau reports on governmental finances, is debt "payable solely from pledged specific sources—e.g., from earnings of revenue producing activities . . . , from special assessments, or from specific nonproperty taxes." With the exception of general obligation bonds, each of the basic types listed above would be considered as "nonguaranteed bonds."

*General obligation bonds* are secured by a pledge of the full faith, credit, and taxing power of the issuing authority. If bonds are so secured but the taxing power of the issuing authority is limited to a specified maximum tax rate, the bonds are still "general obligation," but they are *limited tax bonds* and purchasers should be informed of the limitations on the taxing authority of the issuer. For many investors general obligation bonds are seen as the most "secure" of municipal issues, since the issuing authority has the power to levy taxes at the level necessary to meet debt service requirements. There are, however, practical limits beyond which taxes cannot be successfully collected. Therefore, the security of general obligation bonds, of necessity, is based upon the economic resources of the taxpayers in the issuing governmental unit.[4]

*Special tax* or *special assessment bonds* are payable only from the proceeds derived from a special tax (such as highway bonds payable from a gasoline tax) or from a special assessment levied against those who benefit from the facilities constructed with the funds acquired through the sale of the bonds (e.g., special assessments for curbs and gutters in certain residential areas). The rising costs of special assessment bonds in recent years has resulted in the great majority being additionally secured by a pledge of full faith and credit, making them general obligation bonds.

*Revenue bonds* are payable solely from revenue derived from the operation of the facilities constructed with the proceeds from such bonds (such as tolls, rental charges, fees, etc.). Such bonds do not carry the "full faith and credit" pledge. Municipal bonds that are payable from a limited or special tax or from specified rents, leases, or appropriations are also classified by some analysts as municipal revenue bonds. The security for revenue bonds is based primarily upon the specific revenue producing activity, special tax, or special fund, rather than upon the economic resources of the taxpayers of the issuing jurisdiction.[d]

*New housing authority bonds* are issued by local public housing authorities and secured by an Annual Contributions Contract, obligating the United States Public Housing Administration (PHA) unconditionally to make annual payments that, together with other funds of the local public housing authority available for such purposes (net rental revenues), will be sufficient to cover the principal and interest on the bonds when due. Since the annual contribution obligation of the PHA is unconditional, the faith of the United States government, and not the local issuing unit, is pledged to the payment of such bonds.

In the early seventies several hybrid types of municipal bonds have emerged in which debt service charges are payable primarily from pledged revenues or from limited or special taxes, but for which the issuing unit also pledges its full faith, credit, and taxing power if these limited sources fall short. In discussing such "hybrids," most analysts have tended to group them with general obligation bonds.

Nonguaranteed debt was originally developed to finance utility-type operations of local government, such as water supply and sewer treatment

---

[d]There is considerable controversy as to whether or not an issuing or benefiting government unit has a "moral" obligation to implement its revenue bonds by providing temporary or permanent financial assistance in the face of possible default. Some jurisdictions have aided their revenue bonds in this fashion, while others have openly refused to do so (e.g., the state of West Virginia refused to aid the defaulting West Virginia Turnpike). For a further discussion of this issue see: Hempel, *Measures of Municipal Bond Quality*, pt. 3.

facilities. Later, under federal sponsorship, such debt was broadened to provide for local public housing projects. As recently as 1957 the bulk of all local non-guaranteed debt outstanding had been incurred for these two purposes.[5] Beginning in the late fifties, however, there has been a rapid extension in the use of revenue bonds to finance types of project traditionally financed by full faith and credit borrowing, for example, public schools and office buildings, with debt service paid from "rentals" derived from taxes or other general government revenue, and various projects with debt service payable from the yield of earmarked nonproperty taxes or other specific revenue sources.[e]

### Method of Redemption

Bonds fall into two general types according to the method of redemption: (1) term or sinking fund bonds, and (2) serial bonds. *Term bonds* become due in a lump sum at the end of the term of the loan (all bonds in the issue mature at the same time) and are met by making annual payments to a *sinking fund* that, when invested at compound interest, will produce the amount of principal required at the time it comes due. An issue of *serial bonds,* on the other hand, is retired by annual installments directly from appropriations or from earned income in the case of revenue bonds.

As a consequence of the difficulties in maintaining the integrity of a sinking fund, serial bonds have largely replaced term bonds (bonds the principal for which is funded solely through a sinking fund are not legal in some states). Sinking fund bonds require expert investment of funds and frequent actuarial computations to determine the adequacy of funds to be applied to the principal payment as maturity. They also lack the flexibility in maturity possessed by serial bonds, which often adds to the marketability of the latter form of issue. Term bonds do have some advantages, however. The accumulations in the sinking fund may afford a means of disposing of new bond issues when the general market is unsatisfactory, that is, a municipality may "buy" all or a portion of its own general obligation bonds in a new issue. Sinking funds also afford an opportunity for short-term borrowing when banking accommodations are not readily available, providing that proper safeguards are installed to ensure prompt repayment. When long-term bonds are at a premium, it may be possible to market term bonds to the particular advantage of the issuing unit. Finally, used in combination with serial bonds, term bonds may serve to finance utilities and other enterprises that do not have established earning records.

For most cities, particularly smaller communities, and for most purposes, *serial bonds* are preferable, both because of simpler retirement requirements and greater flexibility in marketing the bond issue and in arranging the debt

---

[e]Due to the special character of revenue bonds, this form of long-term financing is discussed in greater detail in a subsequent chapter.

structure of the community. With a serial bond issue, some of the bonds mature each year beginning after the date of issue through a maximum period of 10, 20, or 30 years or longer. There are two types of serial bonds: annuity serials and straight serials.

With *annuity serials,* the annual debt service payment, covering interest and principal during each year that the bonds are outstanding, is approximately the same (like a home mortgage). The portion of the annual payment that covers interest is higher in the early years of the issue but declines as payments toward principal are made. When bonds are issued for the construction of a self-liquidating enterprise, conditions may exist that make the use of serial annuity bonds highly desirable or essential. Thus, in financing projects where earning power will expand gradually or where the facility must have a reserve capacity for future expansion, revenue bonds frequently are issued as annuity serials to avoid a peak level of debt service charges in the early years of operation. Serial annuity bonds provide a more equitable and manageable distribution of costs that may be of particular importance to special districts or small school districts that infrequently market a large issue of bonds. However, serial annuities tend to carry a more complex maturity schedule and, therefore, are not favored by investment bankers.

*Straight serial bonds* (or declining principal bonds) require annual payments of principal of approximately equal amount;[f] interest payments are large in early years and decline gradually as bonds approach maturity. Table 6–1 illustrates an approximate payment schedule for straight serial bonds, where interest (at six percent) is calculated over ten years on a declining principal, and for serial annuity bonds, with interest calculated at six percent on the outstanding principal for the life of the loan.

Straight serials have the general advantage of lowering the total cost of borrowing and of progressively lowering the annual debt service charge, thereby freeing the municipality's debt margin for new borrowing without increasing the general level of debt service. While debt service requirements are higher in early years, total interest cost is lower because the principal is paid off more rapidly. Provision can also be made for offsetting increasing maintenance costs as the improvement ages, that is, as the level of debt service declines, a portion of the funds annually allocated in support of the project (or a portion of the revenues derived from the project if self-supporting) can be assigned to a reserve fund to cover future maintenance.

The status of the money market may be a significant factor in determining which of the two types of serial bonds is to be preferred. The interest rate on serial bonds may vary with the term of the maturity, that is, bonds with

---

[f] As will be illustrated in a subsequent discussion of serial bonds, straight serials are not always redeemed in equal installments, particularly when they are used to finance projects with high start-up costs.

## Table 6-1
### Debt Service Charges on $1 Million for Ten Years Under Straight Serial and Annuity Serial Bonding

| | Straight Serial Bonds | | | | Annuity Serial Bonds | | | |
|---|---|---|---|---|---|---|---|---|
| Year | Outstanding Principal | Principal Payment | Interest Payment[a] | Total Debt Service | Outstanding Principal | Principal Payment | Interest Payment[b] | Total Debt Service[c] |
| 1st  | $1,000,000 | $100,000 | $60,000 | $160,000 | $1,000,000 | $ 75,868 | $60,000 | $135,868 |
| 2nd  | 900,000    | 100,000  | 54,000  | 154,000  | 924,132    | 80,420   | 55,448  | 135,868  |
| 3rd  | 800,000    | 100,000  | 48,000  | 148,000  | 843,712    | 85,245   | 50,623  | 135,868  |
| 4th  | 700,000    | 100,000  | 42,000  | 142,000  | 758,467    | 90,360   | 45,508  | 135,868  |
| 5th  | 600,000    | 100,000  | 36,000  | 136,000  | 668,107    | 95,782   | 40,086  | 135,868  |
| 6th  | 500,000    | 100,000  | 30,000  | 130,000  | 572,325    | 101,528  | 34,340  | 135,868  |
| 7th  | 400,000    | 100,000  | 24,000  | 124,000  | 470,797    | 107,620  | 28,248  | 135,868  |
| 8th  | 300,000    | 100,000  | 18,000  | 118,000  | 363,177    | 114,077  | 21,791  | 135,868  |
| 9th  | 200,000    | 100,000  | 12,000  | 112,000  | 249,100    | 120,922  | 14,946  | 135,868  |
| 10th | 100,000    | 100,000  | 6,000   | 106,000  | 128,178    | 128,178  | 7,690   | 135,868  |
| Total |           | $1,000,000 | $330,000 | $1,330,000 |          | $1,000,000 | $358,680 | $1,358,680 |

[a] Calculated at 6 percent on the decling principal.
[b] Calculated at 6 percent on the outstanding principal.
[c] Total Debt Service = Principal $\cdot \dfrac{(r)(1+r)^n}{(1+r)^n - 1}$

longer terms may have a higher or lower rate of interest, depending on the money market. If the established rate for short-term borrowing is very low and the rate for long-term maturities significantly higher, the issuance of straight serial bonds affords a means of lowering total debt costs by bringing a larger proportion of the principal within range of the lower interest rate. When the demand for short-term money is abnormally heavy, however, there is no advantage in competing for it in the money market. When investors are seeking long-term, annuity serials are preferable and term bonds have special advantages. Annuity serials also appeal to investors who are seeking a fairly constant return on their investment, whereas term bonds provide certain additional tax benefits for the investor.

There are certain additional modifications to the serial form of debt retirement, including: (a) deferred serial bonds, and (b) irregular serial bonds. With *deferred serial bonds,* the first annual payment on principal is postponed for several years from the data of issue; this method of financing is only justified for self-liquidating projects and is a very unsound practice in the case of tax-supported debt. Deferred serials may be appropriate in situations where an existing debt is scheduled for rapid retirement and the deferment of the new debt for a few years may provide a better "fit" with the municipality's general retirement schedule.

*Irregular serial bonds* involve a "balloon maturity," usually in the final year, that is, a relative significant portion of the principal is postponed until the full term of the issue is reached. Such bonds are frequently used to finance projects for which there is no previous record of earning capacity or where there is some uncertainty as to the amounts that will be available for debt service after operating and maintenance costs are met. Irregular serial bonds almost always carry a provision for early redemption, an action that may take place after reserves have been established. With the proper convenants in the bond ordinance or resolution to prevent the misuse of surplus net income, this method may provide a relatively orderly means of refinancing some of a municipality's debt or for adjusting the overall debt schedule to a more workable program.

### *"Callable Term" Provision*

Some municipal bonds are *callable,* which means that the issuer may pay off the bonds before the maturity date.[g] If bonds are called in before maturity,

---

[g]Government bonds have been issued in several European countries without definite maturities but with a "call" provision effective after a stated period. Such issues need not be redeemed unless and until the government wishes. The individual bond holder is able

however, it usually is provided that the issuer will pay the holder a specified "premium," which is an amount in addition to the face amount of the bond.

A "call" provision makes it easier for a government to convert old debt into new, to smooth out retirement operations, or to save interest. Even where no conversion intervenes, callable-term issues make debt retirement easier than with fixed-term issues, because the government has an optional period during which to redeem or not, according to its financial circumstances. The investment market, however, dislikes the element of uncertainty that is introduced by callable bonds. This dislike is often translated into an insistence upon slightly higher yields for such bonds, a cost consideration that has discouraged state and local governments from issuing callable bonds as often as they might otherwise.

*Form of Bond Title Transfer*

The final characteristic of municipal bonds relates to the method by which the title of a bond can be transferred. In this connection, there are two forms: coupon bonds and registered bonds. A *coupon bond* is transferable by the bearer's delivery of the bond to the perspective investor, whereas a *register bond* is recorded on the books of the municipality and title can be transferred only by endorsement of the registered owner. Therefore, one of the advantages of registered bonds is that in the event they are lost or stolen, there is a certain protection for the registered owner. On the other hand, the advantage of the coupon bond is that it is more marketable and easier to use for collateral. Some bonds are interchangeable between registered and coupon form, with the conversion usually made at the expense of the holder.

In many instances coupon bonds have the privilege of registration, either as to principal only, or as to principal and interest. If a bond is registered as to principal only, the coupons are left on the bond and are cashed to collect the interest, that is, the investor holds the bond and detaches and presents the coupons for interest payment as with a regular coupon bond. At maturity, however, the registered owner is the only person who can be paid the principal on the bond. If registered as the principal and interest, the coupons are detached, the name of the owner is recorded on the books of the municipality, and interest payments are sent to the registered owner by check, that is, it is a fully registered bond.

---

to sell the bond in the security market, at a price determined by prevailing interest rates and other conditions. A government with a debt of this kind is not compelled to make an appropriation for debt retirement, and, yet, it can never technically be in default as to the principal. Since the government is under no pressure to redeem such loans, it is unlikely to do so. As a consequence, the debt tends to become permanent.

*Duration of Loans*

It is axiomatic that borrowings for public improvements should be retired within the period of the useful life of the facility. The theoretical "useful life" of a facility may be shortened by factors of obsolescence other than actual wear and tear, and as the facility ages, maintenance costs tend to increase significantly. Therefore, the total "life cycle costs" of a facility—cost of construction, operations, maintenance, and repair—must be considered in determining the period of usefulness.

In only exceptional cases should a capital project be financed for more than 30 years. Borrowing for a longer period may be justified for more permanent facilities, such as a water system designed with a large future capacity for expansion, whereas projects of a more temporary nature, such as street paving, call for a relatively short-term (e.g., five to ten years) form of borrowing. As a general rule, the debt retirement of a municipality should be scheduled so that at least 25 percent of the outstanding principal is always due for amortization within a five-year period. In this way if a municipality incurred no new debts, it could liquidate the outstanding principal in a 20-year period.

*Face Amount, Maturity, Interest Rate,
and Yield*

Until recently, practically all municipal bonds were issued with a face amount (or denomination) of $1,000, which the issuer promised to pay at a specified date known as the "maturity" date. Now, however, bonds in many larger issues are in $5,000 denominations at the request of the underwriters (financial agents who purchase bonds from an issuer and distribute them to investors), because many institutions that purchase large amounts of bonds prefer the $5,000 denominations to reduce the number of bonds to be handled and to save storage space.

Several factors must be taken into account in determining the *maturity* of bond issues. First, there is the usual legal requirement that the bonds be retired within the useful life of the improvement to be financed; some state laws specify the maximum life of an issue in general terms without regard to the purpose. Second, the sooner the bonds are paid off, the lower will be the total interest cost. For example, a 20-year, five percent serial bond will aggregate interest equal to 52.5 percent of the principal, whereas the same bond issued with a 15-year maturity would accrue interest equal to only 40 percent of the principal. Third, for tax-supported bond issues, the total debt charges must clearly reflect the municipality's ability to pay. Experience indicates that declining debt charges for combined principal and interest are looked upon more favorably than constant debt charges. Fourth, the maturities for any new issue must be planned in such a way that the maturity schedule for all outstanding debts represents a reasonable and economic plan for debt retirement. Fifth, payment of the bonds should usually start one year from the date of issue, with provision made for interest to be paid on a semiannual basis.

The *interest* that the issuer agrees to pay on a municipal bond is shown (a) in coupons attached to the bonds if the bonds are coupon bonds or (b) in the bond itself if the bond is a registered bond. With coupon bonds the holder detaches and presents the coupon for payment of the interest, whereas with registered bonds the interest payment is sent directly to the registered holder by the paying agent.

As noted previously, while some municipal bonds are issued on a term basis, whereby all bonds mature at the same time, the more general practice is to issue general obligation bonds on a serial basis. The interest rate on term bonds is fixed at the time of the issue and is uniform for all bonds in the issue. The interest rate on serial bonds, however, may vary considerably, as shown in Table 6–2, which represents a general obligation bond issue of $70 million by the San Francisco Bay Area Rapid Transit District (BART) in 1967.

As may be seen from this table, initial maturities were relatively small (less than seven percent of the total issue was scheduled for retirement in the first five years) due to the high start-up costs of such a project and the gradual

Table 6–2
$70 Million San Francisco Bay Area Rapid Transit District General Obligation Bonds, Series G, Issued June 1967, Due Serially June 15, 1972 to 1999, Inclusive

| Amount | Maturity | Rate | Yield or Price |
|---|---|---|---|
| $ 675,000 | 1972 | 6% | 3.60% |
| 800,000 | 1973 | 6 | 3.65% |
| 925,000 | 1974 | 6 | 3.70% |
| 1,050,000 | 1975 | 6 | 3.75% |
| 1,200,000 | 1976 | 6 | 3.80% |
| 1,325,000 | 1977 | 6 | 3.85% |
| 1,475,000 | 1978 | 6 | 3.90% |
| 3,400,000 | 1979–80 | 6 | 3.95% |
| 1,925,000 | 1981 | 4 | 3.95% |
| 2,050,000 | 1982 | 3.95 | 100 |
| 9,475,000 | 1983–86 | 4 | 100 |
| 11,750,000 | 1987–90 | 4.05 | 100 |
| 10,200,000 | 1991–93 | 4.10 | 100 |
| 11,400,000 | 1994–96 | 4.15 | 100 |
| 8,350,000 | 1997–98 | 4.20 | 100 |
| 4,000,000 | 1999 | 3 | 4.50% |

Source: Newspaper announcement by winning syndicate, as reproduced in Alan Rabinowitz, *Municipal Bond Finance and Administration* (New York: Wiley–Interscience, 1969).

build-up of earning power. These early bonds, however, carry a higher interest rate than bonds with longer maturities so as to make them more attractive to investors seeking relatively short-term commitments.

The "profit" that bond buyers receive for lending to a government—the "price" that the borrowing government must pay for a loan—is generally expressed on a *yield basis,* meaning that the selling price is stated as a percentage of the yield or return on investment that will be obtained if the bond is held to maturity.[h] Yield takes into account three factors: (a) the "face" rate of interest, (b) calculated against the bond's selling price, which may involve either a discount or a premium on par value,[i] (c) with an allowance for annual amortization of the discount or premium. As shown in Table 6-2, bonds with longer maturities generally provide a higher yield (the bonds issued with maturities between 1982 and 1998, as shown in the table, carry a par value price, that is, the yield equals the interest rate established for these bonds). The yield on government securities also reflects: (1) the credit standing of the borrowing government, (2) maturity and redemption terms, (3) the trading market that will exist for the issue after its flotation and (4) the current level and pattern of interest rates.

Changes in the value of money in the general money market produce changes in the investment yield that a bond purchaser may demand for his money. Since the face amount to be paid at maturity and the rate of interest to be paid on the bond are fixed, adjustment in the yield can only be made in the price of the bond. Assume, for example, that a $1,000 bond is issued with a 4.0 percent interest coupon, maturing in ten years. If interest rates in the general money market are rising so that a purchaser can expect to obtain a greater yield on his investment (say, 4.2%), he will be willing to pay less than the face amount in order to obtain the desired return if the bond is held to maturity. In short, the bond would have to be sold at a discount in order to attract buyers (a $1,000 bond at 4.0% discounted to $983.80 would yield a 4.20% return in ten years). Conversely, if money rates in the general money market are on the decline, so that 3.7% would be an appropriate investment yield on the bond, a purchaser might be willing to pay a premium for the bond (a $1,000 bond purchased at $1024.90, with a coupon rate of 4.0%, held for ten years will yield a 3.7 return on the investment).

Yields on government debt issues marketed within the past 40 years have ranged from a fraction on one percent to over eight percent. Since complicated mathematical computations are required to determine the dollar price of a bond at a specified yield basis, "basic books" are available, containing tables that show the dollar price for bonds in the usual range of interest coupon rates,

---

[h]If the bond is callable the yield basis stated should be the minimum yield to the purchases under any of the possible options.

[i]When a bond is priced at its face amount, it is said to be offered at "par," that is, no discounts or premiums are involved.

maturities, and yields. A typical quotation of a bond price would be: "City of Richmond, Virginia, 4% of 1982 at 3.8%," which means that bonds issued by the city of Richmond, carrying 4 percent interest coupons, maturing in 1982, were offered at a price to yield 3.8 percent. If issued in 1972 these bonds would have been priced at $1016.50, that is, would have carried a $16.50 premium.

The *credit standing* of a government is the investment market's estimate of the probability that the specified interest will be paid in full and that the debt will ultimately be redeemed in accordance with the specified terms. The higher a government's credit standing, the lower is the yield its bonds must carry.[j] A major consideration in the credit standing of a borrowing government is the economic resources of its jurisdiction relative to its outstanding debt. Many investors prefer bonds of a government whose economy is diversified rather than dependent upon a single industry.[k] Obviously, a wealthy community has greater leeway in imposing debt service taxes, and thus in avoiding default, so that its bonds carry lower yields than those of a community whose inhabitants have low-average incomes. All other things being equal, a community with a small debt is better able to service it (and therefore has a better credit standing) than one with a large debt. Another consideration affecting a community's credit standing is its prior debt record: If a community has once defaulted, with or without justification, its issues may be stricken from the "approved" lists, and subsequent issues must bear higher yield rates.

The *maturity term* of a debt issue also affects its yield. The longer the term, the greater is the possibility that intervening events may interfere with eventual redemption (i.e., the greater the uncertainty); hence, the risk is greater, and the expected yield tends to be higher. Moreover, the longer the period to maturity, the greater the chance that better investment opportunities will subsequently appear. On the other hand, institutional investors, such as life insurance companies and pension funds, dislike the trouble, expense, and risk involved in frequent turnover of their investment portfolios, and therefore, may be willing to take a slightly lower yield for a long-term issue.

The *timing of the issue* in combination with the maturity period may also affect the yield that investors demand. When market interest rates are high, the longer the term of the issue—and therefore, the longer the continuation of its high yield through later years when interest rates may fall—the more willing are investors to take a yield somewhat below the current market rates. On the other hand, issues floated in periods of low interest rates will face demands from investors for somewhat higher yields than the market levels to assure a reasonable average return over the entire life of the issue.

---

[j]The form and methods of "bond ratings" are discussed in a subsequent chapter.

[k]The federal government enjoys an unparalleled advantage in this respect; consequently, its issues bear relatively low interest rates (although not the lowest, since interest on federal debt is not exempt from federal income tax); state governments are generally better off than their local units.

If there is a *continuous trading market* in a government's securities after they have been issued, they gain an element of "liquidity," highly valued by many investors who, consequently, may be willing to accept a lower yield. Although the holder is not required to release his bonds until their maturity or call date, he knows that he can sell them at any time. Constant over-the-counter trading of many state and local bonds give them relative liquidity.[1]

*The Money Market*

Underlying all individual variations in yield on government securities is the common fact of *current interest rates* in the money market. Like any other borrower, governments must pay more for their borrowings when money is "expensive," that is, when alternative investments are attractive, then when money is "cheap."

The term "money market" is something of a misnomer, since the "merchandise" being bought and sold is not money but the short-term debt of various issuers, public and private. The financial assets traded in these markets, however, are relatively free of risk and standardized to a degree that they can be converted into money without difficulty or undue delay—thus, the designation as money markets. As a consequence of the greater risk involved, transactions that produce a debt extending over more than one year, are classified as capital market rather than money market instruments. The functioning of the money market, however, has an important bearing on the operations of the capital market in terms of alternative investment opportunities. Therefore, it is important to briefly review this relationship.

Successful operation of a money market requires: (1) a substantial supply of "near money" instruments, (2) adequate demand in the form of generally acceptable currency and bank deposits, and (3) a substantial degree of financial sophistication. Since these conditions are not frequently present, money markets of any size and importance have been relatively rare. Currently, New York City is the chief money market of the world as a consequence of its unparalleled communication facilities, enormous financial capital, and large number of financial institutions located there.

The cost of money in relation to the riskless financial assets dealt in the money market is calculated and very often expressed in terms of interest rates. If paid in advance, that is, deducted from the principal, this is referred to as a discount rate. Short-term interest rates are normally, but not necessarily, lower than long-term rates that prevail in the capital market. This difference

---

[1] Only federal issues are listed on the stock exchange; however, there is a significant secondary or "trading" market for the larger municipal bond issues. No organized trading market exists, however, for the small issues of many minor communities whose bonds often become "frozen" investments almost immediately after initial placement.

in rates arises from the fact that individuals committing their capital for a longer period expect a higher return and because the debtor securing a long-term lease on capital is usually more able to pay higher rates for use of the money than the borrower who receives only transitory use of it. In times of stress or temporary disequilibrium in the money markets, however, short-term rates, which by their nature are more volatile, will occasionally rise over the long-term rates.

While the interrelationship of short- and long-term interest rates has been the subject of much economic research, conclusive findings have not yet been achieved.[m] It has been established that the more consistent a short-term rate, that is, the longer it prevails, the more profound its effects on long-term yields. This relationship is known as the interest rate curve. A steady short-term interest rate tends to attract investment away from the long-term return of fixed interest rates to the more speculative short-term money market. Conversely, when the short-term interest rate is fluctuating widely, many investors tend to prefer the relative security of a fixed interest (long-term) investment.

The transmission of money market influence on interest rates to capital assets of all kinds is fundamental to the whole structure of the economy. It is through this medium that one of the main governmental interventions in economic life—monetary policy—takes place. Thus, the operations of the money market and governmental efforts to guide these operations through monetary policy exercises a primary and profound influence on the prices of bonds, whether public, corporate, or municipal.

*Net Interest Cost*

When preparing to make a bond issue, a municipality must be cognizant of the general money market and the investment yield sought by potential purchasers. Failure to do so may result in an offering unattractive to potential investors, that is, carrying an insufficient yield to compete successfully with other investment opportunities. Anticipated changes in the general money market must also be taken into account in the case of bonds with longer maturity periods.

Underwriters of municipal bonds must also be cognizant of the general money market and the desired investment yield of potential buyers; here, failure to take proper account of these factors will result in a smaller "spread" or gross profit for the underwriters. Underwriters of municipal bonds must make several calculations on the stated interest rate in order to determine a *net*

---

[m]Until the early fifties yields on short-term investments were below that on long-term issues, in line with general market conditions; the gap was significantly reduced, but not eliminated in the sixties. Like many aspects of the current investment market, these relationships have been very instable and unpredictable in the first half of the seventies.

*interest cost* (i.e., the bid that they will make on the bonds) and the *production* of the bonds at the posted prices (i.e., the anticipated return on the sale of the bonds by the underwriters). The net interest cost is equal to the gross interest cost over the life of the bond issue less any premiums that must be paid, divided by the total number of "bond years." The total number of "bond years" is the sum of separate calculations for each of the years in which bonds mature.

The nature of these calculations can be illustrated by returning to the data in Table 6-2, reflecting the 1967 bond issue by the San Francisco Bay Area Rapid Transit District. The number of "bond years" represented by the 675 BART bonds (each $1,000 face amount) issued in 1967 and maturing in 1972 can be calculated by multiplying 5 (years to maturity) by 675 (bonds). This process is repeated for each of the years of maturity; the total number of "bond years" for the BART issue shown in Table 6-2 is 1,541,000. By multiplying the coupon rate (interest rate) times the "bond years" for each maturity period and summing across all maturity periods, a total interest cost can be obtained. This figure for the data in Table 6-2 is $6,388,333.75. Since only a $7,000 premium was established for the BART bonds, the net interest cost can be calculated as follows:

$$\text{Net Interest Cost} = \frac{\text{Gross Interest Cost less Premium}}{\text{Total ``Bond Years''}}$$

$$\text{NIC} = \frac{\$6,388,344 - \$7,000}{1,541,000} = 4.14103 \text{ (which is expressed as a percent)}$$

The net interest cost included in the winning bid by the underwriting syndicate that purchased the BART bonds, that is, the real "cost" to the BART authority in terms of interest payments, for borrowing $70 million was 4.14128 percent.

The "production" of a given issue may be calculated by first multiplying the reoffering price (yield or par value) times the face amount for each maturity date. This figure is then multiplied times the amount being offered with a given maturity date, and these calculations are then summed for all maturity periods in the issue. For example, in Table 6-2 the yield for bonds maturing in 1972 (i.e., five years after issue) is 3.60 percent, times the face amount ($1,000) equals $1108.90, which is the reoffering price per bond. In other words, an investor would be expected to pay the underwriter $108.90 over the par value ($1,000) to secure a bond with a five-year maturity period. When multiplied times the amount being offered ($675,000), a production of $748,507.50 results, that is, the amount the underwriters would expect to "earn" on the first segment of the bond issue. The "production" of the $2,050,000 bonds issued with a 1982 maturity, on the other hand, is $2,050,000 since these bonds are issued at par value (i.e., at the face amount). The $4,000,000 issued with a

1999 maturity date are at "below par," with a reoffering price per bond of $743.30 and a "production" of $2,973,600.

Carrying out all of the appropriate calcuations on the data presented in Table 6-2 results in a maximum "production" of $70,842,377.50. Since the par amount of the issue plus premium equaled $70,007,000 (i.e., the amount paid by the underwriters to the BART District), the amount available as "spread" or gross profit to the underwriters before expenses was calculated to be $835,377.50.

## Summary

The foundation for sound capital facilities planning must be built upon an appropriate mix of the various methods of financing available to local jurisdications and a debt policy that reflects the municipality's ability to bear certain levels of debt burden. While relatively few communities are able to finance capital projects strictly on a pay-as-you-go basis, this method of financing, along with the creation of a capital reserve fund, must be used in concert with long-term borrowing. In choosing an appropriate debt form, municipal officials must examine the characteristics of projects to be funded, their earning capacity if self-supporting, the methods of redemption for bonds to be issued, the duration of loans to be secured, and the net interest cost arising from various maturities and interest rates. They also must be cognizant of the general money market and the investment yield sought by potential purchasers. These factors affecting the cost of borrowing are not to be approached lightly, and since most jurisdictions enter the municipal bond market only on an infrequent basis, local officials would be well advised to secure the professional services of a recognized financial consultant as they undertake this important phase of capital facilities planning.

# 7 Marketing Municipal Bonds

**Issuance of Municipal Bonds**

Since the authorization and issuance of bonds are regulated by various constitutional provisions, general statutes, special acts, and local charters that vary from state to state, only general procedures can be described. Controlling laws are not always conveniently codified, and as a consequence, the procedural steps necessary to secure the authorization of bonds often are confusing to local elected officials and administrators. Thus, expert legal advice is essential to ensure that the process leading up to the issuance of bonds is in compliance with all applicable legal requirements. Even minor errors may result in annoying delays, expensive litigation, and possible invalidation of issues or sales.

*Preliminaries to Marketing*

In most states some form of popular referendum is required for the authorization of most types of bonds.[a] Depending upon the prevailing law, a majority vote may be sufficient or a two-thirds vote may be necessary. In other cases the governing body may have the power to issue bonds without any vote of the electorate. At times an issue represents the unsold portion of a larger issue that had been previously authorized, to be issued over a period of years. If any question as to the need for a public referendum should exist, as in the case of a revenue bond issue, legal advice from a qualified municipal bond attorney may obviate complications.

It is important in marketing municipal bonds that they be *negotiable instruments,* that is, that they contain an unconditional promise or order to pay. Since revenue bonds contain only a promise to pay from special funds, they may not meet this requirement unless state legislation has been enacted to establish that municipal revenue bonds are negotiable instruments. The Investment Bankers Association has urged the adoption of such legislation by all states to ensure the negotiability of revenue bonds. In marketing revenue bonds a careful examination of their negotiable status should be made, and if

---

[a]In a few states there are optional provisions under which local legislative bodies may authorize bonds, within certain limits, without popular vote. Experience has shown that this optional privilege should be used sparingly and held in reserve for emergencies.

state legislation does not exist, special legal provisions should be made to increase the marketability of the issue.

Each municipal bond issue must be approved by an attorney whose legal opinions satisfy the market where the bonds are to be sold. Usually the city attorney or corporation counsel is not a bond specialist. Therefore, it is generally the practice for the issuing municipality to secure the services of a firm of bond attorneys whose opinion is marketable and to specify in the announcement of the issue (the official notice of sale) that the unqualified approving legal opinion of that firm will be furnished to the buyer. Legal opinions may be furnished at the expense of the issuer or the buyer. Since bids will reflect the additional expense when the buyer must pay for the legal opinion, it is usually at the expense of the issuer. There are a number of firms of bond attorneys in the United States that specialize in municipal law exclusively or have a department that does so.

The bond ordinance or resolution should be drawn with precision, setting forth, among other things, the nature and limits of the security offered. It is customary to submit such resolutions or ordinances to the bond attorney so that his preliminary approval can be secured in advance. While final approval cannot be given until the sale is completed, the preliminary approval before bidding assures prospective buyers that the legal opinion can and will be furnished without delay. The ability of an underwriter to reoffer bonds immediately after the sale, without concern regarding a legal opinion, may be a material factor in obtaining the lowest interest rate possible.

*Notice of Sale*

As a municipality nears the date when a bond issue is to be opened to competitive bidding, it must publish an "official notice of sale," usually in *The Daily Bond Buyer,*[b] and perhaps in regional bond publications; in some states, notices of bond issues must also be placed in the official state newspaper. While these notices vary in content, generally the following information is included:

1. The correct legal name of the issuing body, the special law (if any) under which it was organized, and the authority for the sale
2. Type of bonds to be issued (revenue, general obligation, special assessment, etc.)
3. The amount and purpose of the issue, the maturity schedule, and call feature (if any)
4. Date, time, and place of sale (i.e., when and where bids will be opened)

---

[b]*The Daily Bond Buyer* is generally considered to be the industry's trade paper.

5. Manner in which the bid is to be made (sealed or oral)
6. Limitations as to interest rate, payment dates of interest, and when and where principal will be paid
7. Denomination and registration privileges
8. Basis for bidding (e.g., at par or better or discount allowed, whether "split-rate" bids will be permitted, any statutory regulations governing the sale, etc.)
9. Amount of good faith check required (usually ranging in amount from one to five percent of par value of issue)
10. Bid form and basis for award
11. Name of approving attorneys and a statement to the effect that these attorneys will furnish an unqualified opinion approving the legality of the bonds and also a certification that no litigation is pending affecting the issuance of the bonds
12. Provisions made for the payment of principal and interest, that is, are debt charges payable from unlimited ad valorem taxes, from special improvement taxes, or from revenues of a particular enterprise
13. Total tax rate in the governmental unit, rate for each levying body, and constitutional or statutory limits restricting debts or the taxes levied for their payment
14. Method and place for settlement and delivery of the bonds
15. The right to reject any or all bids

Since the market for the bonds and the price they will bring, to a considerable extent, will depend upon the publicity given to the offering, the notice of sale should be published at least two weeks in advance of the date set for opening bids. This permits the news to circulate and gives propsective bidders the opportunity to form their bidding accounts and to secure and study information regarding the offering. Such advance publicity also eliminates any suspicion of collusion and demonstrates to the prospective buyer that the municipality is willing to submit its financial condition to careful inspection.

Unless required by law, the municipality accomplishes very little by setting a maximum interest rate on the issue in its official notice. If the rate named is too low, no bids will be received; if too high, the bonds will bring less favorable prices. The best practice, if the enabling legislation permits, is to let the bidding underwriters fix the rates or rate of interest.[c] The purchaser can make a bid that best fits his own market when he can determine the coupon rate (interest rate). If within the provisions of controlling state regulations, bidders should be permitted to bid different rates on various maturities or groups of bonds (known as "split-rate bids") in order to gain the most favorable overall net

---

[c]The procedures applied by underwriters in determining an appropriate rate or rates of interest are discussed further in a subsequent section.

interest cost for the municipality. In some states, of course, a maximum coupon rate has been established, and in such cases, it must be stated in the notice of sale.

Complications arise, however, when bond laws allow too little flexibility in determining the coupon rate or prohibit sale below par. The price of an issue and the interest rate or rates are significant only in that they determine the net cost to the community—these are the variables that the dealer should be permitted to work with in order to determine a marketing "fit" that best reflects the character of the issue.[d] A price slightly below par is likely to appeal to the bidder, as it will enable him to sell the bonds to individual investors without charging a premium. A price much above par not only hinders the disposal of the bonds by the underwriter but also creates for the municipal officials the problem of proper disposal of the premium. When a municipality is bound by legal requirements to secure par for its bonds (i.e., must sell them at the face value), sufficient flexibility should be afforded in the bidding to allow the underwriter to keep the premium he must pass on to individual investors at a minimum. This may be accomplished by permitting the bidder to name the rate in fractions of a percent (quarters, tenths, etc.) and by accepting split rate bids.

In some instances, supplemental coupons have been used as a means of attracting dealers when restrictions limit the flexibility of bidding. *Supplemental coupons* are additional coupons attached to a municipal bond and covering the same interest period as one or more of the regular coupons (i.e., when a supplemental coupon is in force, the municipality is required to make two interest payments for that period). Supplemental coupons are usually detached by the underwriter at the time of original delivery from the issuer and may be held until the payment date or sold by the dealer at a discount. There are four general situations that give rise to the use of supplemental coupons:

1. Where mandatory state requirements provide that municipal bonds must be sold at par and callable bonds must be called for at par. Should such bonds be salable only at a discount, no profit margin would exist for the dealer unless some device such as a supplemental coupon were used.
2. Where states require that the bonds be sold at par and that the coupon carry a specified rate of interest. If the market rate for such bonds at the time of sale is higher than the statutory coupon rate, the bonds would have

---

[d] A $1,000 bond with a ten-year maturity and an interest rate of 3.80 percent, selling at a $16.50 discount (i.e., at $983.50) will yield approximately the same rate of return to the investor as a bond of similar maturity with a 4.0 percent interest rate, selling at par, that is, at $1,000. The implications for the issuing municipality are that in the first case fewer dollars are available at the outset to cover the cost of the capital project but the interest payments through the life of the issue are lower, whereas in the second case, a higher interest payment must be made to ensure the par value of the bonds. In both cases, the principal payment on the bond is the same, that is, $1,000.

# MARKETING MUNICIPAL BONDS

to be sold at a discount to the individual investors. Without the use of a supplemental coupon, not only would the dealer have no margin of profit but he would lose money on the transaction.

3. Where a governmental unit, typically a school district, may receive reimbursement from the state for a portion of its capital expenditures, such reimbursement may not apply to bonds that have been discounted but may be allowed for the amount of the supplemental coupons.
4. An apparent lower net interest cost may occur where supplemental coupons are used to cover the early maturities and where a relatively low coupon rate may be applied for the longer maturities. Such an approach, however, does not take into account the "present value" of the larger interest payments on early maturities.

Since confusion can arise as to whether a supplemental coupon will be accepted, the request for bids should clearly stipulate either that: (a) only one coupon will be attached to each bond for each installment of interest and that bids providing for supplemental coupons will not be accepted; or (b) bids may specify that the interest payable for any period prior to maturity will be represented in part by separate coupons designated as supplemental coupons.

### *Timing of an Issue*

In deciding when to offer a major bond issue, the condition of the market should be studied to determine the proper timing so as to secure the most favorable bids. The bond market experience minor fluctuations within the course of every few months, brought on by an excess of supply over demand, as well as economic and political trends. By following municipal bond publications and consulting with investment bankers, the municipal finance officer can often apply these fluctuations to a municipality's advantage. By reviewing these publications the municipality can avoid setting the date of sale in the midst of a general rush of new offerings (many large school bond issues, for example, reach the market in late spring or early summer), or immediately following large sales by other municipalities. It is also unwise to set the sale date for the day before or after a holiday or on Mondays or Saturdays. It is unwise to enter the market too frequently (thus, the advantage of a consolidated issue for general obligation bonds rather than separate issues for individual projects), and if dealers have not completed the distribution of a previous issue from the municipality, a less satisfactory price on a new issue may be anticipated.

Since in most cases the month of maturity is determined by the date on which the bond is sold (e.g., if bonds are sold on April 12, they probably would be dated May 1st or April 1st and the maturities would be the same month), this factor must be taken into account in planning the sale. The time of the year when the revenues of a municipality are collected varies. In some states taxes are collected only once a year; in others they may be collected semiannually or quarterly. As a consequence there are certain times of the year for each municipality when its funds are low, and, therefore, the maturity date should be scheduled so that the municipality will not be faced with a large account of bonds coming due each year at a time when funds are not on hand to pay them.

## Miscellaneous Requirements

The largest buyers of municipal bonds are financial institutions that are exacting in their requirements. Failure to comply with their "rules of the game" tends to narrow the market and is reflected in the interest cost to the municipality. Some of the more important requirements are as follows:

1. Bonds should be dated as near as possible to the delivery date; if the date is too early the amount of accrued interest is excessive.
2. Bonds should be issued in denominations of $1,000 or $5,000, except for odd amounts that should be retired the first year if possible. Odd denominations and small bonds are not readily salable.
3. Interest should be payable semiannually.
4. The bond owner should have the privilege of registering his bonds as to principal only or as to both principal and interest, provided the municipality has proper registration facilities.
5. Where the bonds have a wide market, principal and interest should be payable in a large financial center, preferably at a bank located in a city where there is a Federal Reserve Bank or branch. Most large investors prefer to avoid the expense and inconvenience involved in collection of principal and interest payments outside such centers.
6. Funds should be on deposit at the paying agent several days before the payments are due to ensure adequate time for the agent to prepare checks or bank drafts for payment when coupons are presented. In the case of registered bonds, interest checks should reach the holder on the day the interest is due.
7. To safeguard against counterfeiting and forgery of bonds, they should be printed by a firm that specializes in such work. In this way the complicated procedures for numbering bonds and coupons will be accurate, printing employees will be supervised, and duplicate or illegal bonds eliminated.

## Bond Prospectus

Fully as important as any other factor in the successful marketing of municipal bonds is the provision for the publication of all essential facts concerning the financial condition of the municipality. While in the past a perfunctory statement of assessed valuation, tax rate, and bonded debt may have been sufficient, today's investors seek and are entitled to the basic facts regarding the security offered. The inability or unwillingness to provide such data may be viewed as an admission of inferior administration.

With the exception of large revenue bond issues, no elaborate prospectus is necessary. The four-page statistical form, approved jointly by the Investment Bankers Association and the Municipal Finance Officers Association, usually is adequate and provides the information that most investors seek regarding debt and provisions for payment, the adequacy of the community's revenue system and the effectiveness of its administration, and the recent and present state of financial operations in the municipality. Investors want to know the provisions that have been made for the payment of principal and interest; that is, are debt charges payable from unlimited ad valorem property taxes, from limited ad valorem taxes, from special improvement taxes, or from the revenues of a particular enterprise. Where bonds are payable primarily from special assessments or utility revenues but also from ad valorem taxes, the fact should be stated.

Revenue bonds payable solely from the earning of a particular enterprise require extensive data to substantiate the earnings and such facts are usually given in a special prospectus. Unless the facility has a well established record of earnings, the investor will usually require the opinion of qualified engineers or other consultant experienced with the operations of such facilities who can project the future earnings record with some degree of accuracy. This study, usually known as the feasibility report, together with the copy of the bond ordinance or resolution setting forth protective covenants and other information, should be made a part of the official prospectus.[e] It is not uncommon to engage a qualified consultant for even well-established operations as a further aid to improve the price of the bonds being offered.

Other items of information to be included in the prospectus are as follows:

1. Total tax rate in the governmental unit, the rate for each levying body, and constitutional or statutory limits restricting debts or the taxes levied for their payment
2. Any previous defaults by the municipality on the principal or interest of its debts and the actions to remedy such defaults
3. Population according to latest census data, and a reliable estimate of present population

The financial information required in the prospectus for general obligation bonds should include those items covered in Appendix 7A. Financial information required for revenue bonds is covered in more detail in chapter 8.

---

[e]Protective covenants required for revenue bonds and other matters associated with self-supporting debt are discussed in detail in a subsequent chapter.

The bond prospectus should be printed and ready for distribution at the time of notice of sale. It should be sent, without request, to investment bankers and other institutions interested in the municipality's securities and to a select list of large investors. Financial papers that publish the paid notice about the sale will usually carry a news story about the community and therefore should also receive copies of the prospectus. Rating and information agencies should be given these data as well. In both the official notice of sale and in the prospectus the name of a contact person in the community should be provided in the event further information about the municipality or the bond sale is required by prospective investors.

### Costs Involved in Marketing Municipal Bonds

The cost of borrowing not only involves the interest payable over the term of the bonds, but also includes costs incurred in readying bonds for market and their actual delivery to the initial investment firms. Such costs reflect the expense of conducting an election to obtain approval to incur debt for the purpose intended, fees for various legal and financial advisors, and a variety of "miscellaneous" costs, including: preparation and publication of bond notices and the bond prospectus; printing the bonds; obtaining a bond rating; costs of renting a signature machine used in signing bonds; filing fees; court fees; registration or recording fees; certification costs; and costs of delivering the bonds.

In a survey by the Municipal Finance Officers Association of 481 governmental units in the United States and Canada regarding municipal bond issues, it was found that the average cost for marketing general obligation bonds amounted to $1.98 per $1,000, as compared with $3.84 per $1,000 for revenue bonds, and $5.13 for special assessment bonds (see Table 7-1). As would be expected, the cost per $1,000 declines steadily as the size of the issue increases; the average size of the 267 general obligation bonds issued was approximately $7.55 million, whereas the average size of the 154 revenue bonds was approximately $6.44 million and for 75 special assessment bonds, approximately $1.116 million.

Variations in costs also occurred with respect to particular expenditure categories (see Table 7-2). As could be anticipated, special election costs occur more frequently for general obligation bonds than for the other two types. Costs for this purpose amounted to 12.7 percent of total costs for marketing general obligation bonds but only 1.1 percent for revenue bonds and 0.1 percent for special assessment bonds. Legal and financial counsel account for the major portion of the costs incurred. These are less, in total, for general obligation bonds than for revenue or special assessment bonds (see Table 7-2). That revenue bonds may require particular attention for fiscal advice is illustrated in the total

### Table 7-1
### Cost per $1,000 for Marketing Municipal Bonds

| Size of Issue | General Obligation Bonds | | Revenue Bonds | | Special Assessment Bonds | |
|---|---|---|---|---|---|---|
| 0–$499,999 | $10.66 | (33) | $13.90 | (29) | $15.12 | (40) |
| $500,000–$999,999 | 8.69 | (42) | 12.87 | (28) | 9.90 | ( 9) |
| $1,000,000–$1,999,999 | 6.98 | (49) | 9.98 | (25) | 5.38 | ( 9) |
| $2,000,000–$2,999,999 | 5.48 | (32) | 7.50 | (18) | 3.50 | ( 8) |
| $3,000,000–$4,999,999 | 4.00 | (30) | 5.98 | (19) | 3.83 | ( 6) |
| $5,000,000–$9,999,999 | 3.32 | (31) | 5.44 | (18) | 3.14 | ( 3) |
| $10,000,000–$24,999,999 | 1.99 | (31) | 2.94 | ( 9) | – | |
| $25,000,000 and over | .80 | (19) | 2.34 | ( 8) | – | |
| All issues | $ 1.98 | (267) | $ 3.84 | (154) | $ 5.13 | (75) |

### Table 7-2
### Percentage Distribution of Total Costs for Marketing Municipal Bonds

| Cost Category | General Obligation Bonds | Revenue Bonds | Special Assessment Bonds |
|---|---|---|---|
| Special election costs | 12.7% | 1.1% | 0.1% |
| Legal & financial fees | 62.7% | 81.0% | 78.5% |
| Fiscal advisor | (31.5%) | (50.1%) | (40.4%) |
| Bond notice | 2.5% | 1.8% | 3.7% |
| Prospectus | 3.3% | 4.6% | 2.7% |
| Printing of bonds | 8.5% | 3.6% | 6.8% |
| Bond rating | 2.7% | 1.7% | 2.0% |
| Other costs | 2.7% | 1.4% | 2.7% |

costs incurred for revenue bonds, 50.1 percent went for a fiscal advisor. Cost per $1,000 of issue for each of these cost categories are shown in Table 7-3.

The survey conducted by the Municipal Finance Officers Association reveals that, while no single cost incurred in the marketing procedure is large, in the aggregate these costs can amount to a considerable sum. In some instances total marketing costs amounted to 5.5 percent of the value of bonds marketed. These costs usually can be paid from the bond proceeds, but this then reduces the amount available for the project, or requires an increase in the amount borrowed to meet capital costs. In either case interest costs would also attach to that portion of the proceeds used to meet marketing costs.

Some approaches to reducing costs of marketing bonds are apparent. If approval of the electorate is required, such approval should be obtained, if possible, at a general or primary election rather than through a special election.[f]

---

[f]There are two schools of thought on the nonfinancial aspects of this recommendation. There are those who suggest that the inclusion of a bond referendum as part of a general election ballot can help its passage since the referendum tends to become "lost" on

### Table 7-3
### Costs per $1,000 for Marketing Municipal Bonds: Specific Cost Categories

| Cost category | General Obligation Bonds | Revenue Bonds | Special Assessment Bonds |
|---|---|---|---|
| Election costs | $1.25 | $0.36 | $0.15 |
| Legal & financial fees | 2.02 | 2.21 | 3.88 |
| Bond notice | 0.06 | 0.09 | 0.25 |
| Prospectus | 0.10 | 0.25 | 0.34 |
| Printing of bonds | 0.20 | 0.19 | 0.49 |
| Bond rating | 0.09 | 0.24 | 0.48 |
| Other costs | 0.08 | 0.11 | 0.26 |

Approval should be obtained for a total program, rather than for single issues, thus avoiding the need of hold several separate elections. When sales are offered an attempt should be made to combine smaller issues into a single issue or to explore the possibilities of conducting a combined sale with an overlapping governmental unit. Where possible local governments should utilize technical assistance available from the state. This may reduce the need for special advisory services or, as a minimum, can indicate those particular instances where such services may be essential.

A careful review of miscellaneous costs should be made and cost control procedures established wherever possible. Public finance officers should review all bond marketing costs, not only with an eye toward cost savings, but also in terms of the extent to which they may enhance the sale of the bond issue. The incurrence of some expenditures may actually result in a broader sale, culminating in a lower interest cost than otherwise might have been obtained; but other expenses may add little to the marketability of a bond issue.

### *Ratings for Municipal Bonds*

Ratings have assumed considerable significance in determining interest rates and the eligibility of bonds for purchase by certain types of investors.[g] Municipal bonds are rated only in terms of credit risk and not in terms of their investment

---

the ballot. Others contend that the larger turn-out for a general election and possibility of the referendum becoming a local election issue supports the notion of a separate election for capital expenditure needs. The counterargument is that only those opposed to the referendum are likely to turn out in force for a special election. Unfortunately, much of this argument is based on speculation and little empirical data. Therefore, local officials must use their own judgment as to the sensitivity of the issue and should endeavor to inform the electorate as to the purpose of the referendum regardless to the type of election used to gain approval.

[g]Generally speaking, municipal bonds carrying a Standard & Poor's rating of "BBB" or higher are considered investment quality, and thus are eligible for investment by banks. Tax-exempt bond funds contain only BBB or higher rated bonds.

merits. Bond ratings appraise two basic risk factors: (1) the risk that bond quality will be diluted by an inordinate increase in debt, and (2) the risk that ability to meet maturing bond principal and interest may be impaired under depressed business conditions.[1] The first risk involves activities within the control of the issuing government, whereas the second risk is related to the impact of general economic conditions on a given locality.

The two major rating services—Moody's Investors Service, Incorporated, and Standard and Poor's Corporation—classify into broad quality gradation slightly over 40 percent of the total number of municipal bonds issued, constituting approximately three-fourths of the total dollar amount issued. These rating services use symbols, arranged in order from municipal bonds with the least credit risk to those with the greatest risk, as shown in Table 7-4. Some issues rated by one service are not rated by the other service, and the opinions

Table 7-4
Comparison of Municipal Bond Rating Systems

| Moody's Investors Service | Symbol | Symbol | Standard and Poor's Corporation |
|---|---|---|---|
| Best quality, carrying smallest degree of investment risk; referred to as "gilt edge" | Aaa | AAA | Prime: obligation of highest quality and lowest probability of default; quality management and low debt structure |
| High quality; rated lower than Aaa because margins of protection not as large | Aa | AA | High grade: only slightly less secure than prime; second lowest probability of default |
| Higher medium grade, many favorable investment attributes; some element of future risk evident | A | A | Upper medium grade: safe investment; weakness in local economic base, debt burden, or fiscal balance |
| Lower medium grade; neither highly protected nor poorly secured; may be unreliable over any great length of time | Baa | BBB | Medium grade: lowest investment security rating; may show more than one fundamental weakness; higher default probability |
| Judged to have speculative elements; not well safeguarded as to interest and principal | Ba | BB | Lower medium grade; speculative noninvestment grade obligation; relatively high risk and uncertainty. |
| Lacks characterists of desirable investment | B | B | Low grade; investment characteristics virtually nonexistent |
| Poor standing; issues may be in default | Caa | CCC | Defaults |
| Speculative in high degree; marked shortcomings | Ca | CC | |
| Lowest rated class; extremely poor prospects of ever attaining any real investment standing | C | C | |

of the two rating services may differ slightly on specific issues. However, the overall rating distributions appear to be quite similar. Moody's rates bonds of most issuers that have $600,000 or more of debt, except projects under construction, enterprises without established earning records, and situations where current financial data are lacking. Standard and Poor's will rate governmental bodies upon request and payment of a fee, to be paid either by the issuer or the underwriter. A third service, Fitch's Investors Service, rates some municipal bonds, using rating symbols similar to Moody's except that Fitch's symbols are all capital letters (thus Aaa becomes AAA).

The ratings published by the bond rating services are based upon periodic evaluations by a relatively small team of analysts. These analysts supplement their examination of secondary data with occasional site visits. The relatively small number of analysts available to prepare ratings has been a subject of criticism, as has the practice of rating only the larger issues. These criticisms, in part, contributed to the decision of Standard & Poor's in the late sixties to provide confidential rating reports under contract to any person or firm willing to pay a fee (ranging from several hundred to several thousand dollars). In this way Standard & Poor's has been able to expand its staff and make a profit on rating services. Such ratings are considered valid for one year or until the same issuer comes into the market again, whichever time is shorter.

Generally speaking, there is only one rating for all of the general obligation bonds of a particular governmental unit and for all the municipal bond issues of a specific revenue project. Some governmental units or revenue projects have more than one rating because special security has been pledged for some of the bonds. New issues of a previously rated governmental unit or revenue project usually are assigned the same rating as the outstanding bonds unless there have been material changes in the credit situation. Therefore, new issues of a previously rated governmental unit or revenue project usually increase the dollar value outstanding in a rating category but rarely affect the number of municipal credits in a rating category. Similarly, the serial retirement of bonds is reflected by a decline in the dollar value of municipal bonds outstanding in a particular category, but it does not affect the number of municipal credits outstanding.

It must be emphasized that ratings are very general and are not absolute standards of quality. While undergoing continual improvements particularly since the advent of high-speed data analysis equipment, existing rating systems are not without deficiencies, as summarized by the Joint Economic Committee:

1. The undue dependence by financial institutions upon ratings in determining municipal bond investments
2. The higher interest cost to borrowing municipalities because of a lower rating or the absence of a rating
3. The lack of verified information to support ratings (resulting from a lack of a uniform financial reporting system among the States, reliance upon the

issuers to supply their periodic financial data, and inadequate staff to ascertain completeness or biases)
4. Possible conflicts of interest wherein the bond rating services also function as advisors to investors and as consultants to governmental bodies [2]

As Alan Rabinowitz has observed:

> The problems facing the bond analyst . . . suggests how little is truly known by state officials, credit analysts, budgetmakers, politicians, political scientists, economists, and planners about our complex urbanizing environment and the conditions under which local government can best be operated. What is known is rarely subject to administrative control and, in all cases, is subject to revision in an era of rapid change in many dimensions. It has also become clear that a rating system designed to advise a few investors concerning major bond issues is ill adapted to serve the needs of local government generally. . . . [3]

Thus, Rabinowitz raises the question of a nationalized and/or standardized rating system to not only help local governments secure long term funds from investors at lower interest rates (rather than maintaining high interest rates that are of primary advantage for the relatively few investors who pay high taxes and therefore seek the shelter of tax-exempt income), but also protect ". . . the widows, orphans, depositors, policy-holders, and stockholders of insurance companies, banks, trusts, and other repositories of individual savings." [4] Rabinowitz's suggestions for improvements in the current rating systems center on an expansion of the activities of the Census Bureau, as well as other federal data gathering agencies, to make available to municipal bond analysts more complete data regarding the relationship between fiscal, social, and economic trends at the local level, resulting in the compilation and publication for every issuer of a one-page abstract of the statistical data and relative standing of the issuer in terms of statistical norms developed by the researchers.[5] Rabinowitz concludes by observing:

> The more one considers the rating problem, the more one realizes how intimately connected it is with our inability to date as a nation to come to grips with the "urban problem" or to define adequately a "good city". Intervention by the federal government in the rating picture is not the answer, nor could any national organization do much better. Since nationalization of ratings is unwarranted, since ratings reflect more than create our concern, the solution may have to be found as the sum of all the small improvements that can be made at all levels of government and within all types of institutions concerned with the municipal performance.[6]
>
> Continuing efforts should be made to maintain and improve the credit

standing of a municipality. After bonds have been issued current financial reports should be sent regularly to investment bankers, financial newspapers, large investors and credit or rating agencies. The importance of providing such information is emphasized by the fact that national banks, which are large purchasers of municipal bonds, are required to keep their files current regarding supporting information and data that will enable bank management to exercise informed judgment in determining whether each issue should be purchased or retained in the investment portfolio and to permit examiners to determine that the investment securities meet the requirements specified in the Investment Securities Regulations. Since large institutional buyers are often limited by state law in the selection of their investments, it is very important for a city, if it is now on the legal investment lists of leading investor states, that nothing be done to imperil this favored position. Thus, when requested by state banking and insurance departments to file answers to questionnaires, municipal officials should do so promptly.

### Bond Sale and Delivery

All bids made on a particular issue should be on a basis that permits a comparison of total cost to the issuer. Officials should insist that all bids comply strictly with the terms of the sale. The governing body of the municipality should meet at the hour designated for the receiving of bids and should confirm in writing the award of the bonds to the successful bidder. All bids should be received and opened in public and the bonds awarded to the bidder on the basis of the lowest net interest cost.

After the sale and its confirmation has been completed, the good faith checks of all unsuccessful bidders should be returned promptly. All papers required to complete the bond transcript should be forwarded to the attorneys as soon as possible. Before the bonds are delivered the appropriate municipal official will record the information required for the establishment of the *bond register,* sometimes called the bond and interest record. The record of each bond issue should provide the following information: name of municipality, amount of issue, reference to resolution, ordinance, state law, or bylaw authorizing the bonds, reference to popular approval if voted bonds, name of purchaser of original issue, the price, coupon rates, net interest cost, date of bonds, interest dates, maturities, bond numbers, denominations, approving attorneys, and any callable or optional features. At the time a bond issue is sold the interest due on each date to maturity should be computed and recorded, as should the payments of principal or payments into a sinking fund. With such records a complete schedule of debt service requirements can be readily prepared for the current budget or for all outstanding bonds.

Bonds should be delivered at the earliest practical date after the sale (not later than 30 days after the award); the winning bidder usually has the option to cancel his obligation and to receive prompt refund of his good faith deposit check if delivery is not made on or before the date specified in the contract. The purchaser should be required to stipulate where the bonds should be delivered. Many municipalities prefer to have at least one official sign the bonds at point of delivery and to have the municipal seal imprinted at that time. Large bond issues are usually signed at the place of delivery because the travel expense of officials frequently is less than the insurance on the delivery of signed bonds.

*Summary*

It is critical that local officials be mindful of the procedures for marketing long-term bonds from the planning of the issue through the actual delivery of the bonds to the winning bidder. Failure to adhere to these procedures at any point can result in unnecessary delays, higher costs, and possible legal ramifications. As a practical matter almost any bond issue that is in proper technical form can be sold at any time. However, whether a particular offering meets favor with underwriters and investors at the date of sale depends on the congruence of the many factors outlined in this discussion. The coming to market of an issue of tax-exempt securities represents a midway point in the municipal bond cycle.[7] In the first half each municipality must appraise its position as a viable economic and social entity. The second half is then played out in various parts of the market itself. The municipal finance officer is caught in the middle, faced on the one hand by uncertainties as to the political and economic structure of his community and, on the other hand, by uncertainties of a marketplace that he cannot fully comprehand. Adherence to the procedures outlined in this discussion can go a long way to reducing the uncertainties that confront the municipal official from both sides. Foremost in these procedures is the fact that an underwriter does not expect to hold bonds for his own account; he is interested only in securing the appropriate guarantees that he can resell immediately to permanent investors.[8]

**Underwriting Municipal Bonds**

Municipalities seldom deal with the final investor in the issuance of bonds. Rather, municipal bonds are *underwritten* by large investment syndicates that provide the funds to the local issuing jurisdictions and, in turn, reoffer the bonds to individual investors, that is, the underwriter attempts to make a profit by selling the bonds to individual investors at a price higher than his purchase price. The mark-up in price by the underwriter, which is his compensation for distributing the bonds and for assuming the risk of a change in the market value of the bonds while they are being distributed, is known as the "spread." Unfortunately, underwriters do not always obtain a profit because in some cases they can sell the bonds only at a price lower than the price they paid and, therefore, must take a loss in the transaction. This may result from a general change in money rates and the market values of securities, from some adverse factors with respect to the particular issue, or from an overestimate of the market value of the particular security.

*Negotiated Sales Versus Competitive Bidding*

Municipal bonds may be purchased by underwriters in one of two ways: (a) in a private negotiated purchase, or (b) as the highest bidder at competitive bidding. In most states the law requires that issuers sell general obligation bonds by competitive bidding, usually by submission of sealed bids. Even when negotiated sales are permitted, many bonds are sold by competitive bidding. There are many negotiated sales of revenue bonds because in such situations it is often advantageous to the issuer to have the underwriter participate in setting up the issue from the outset.

Negotiated sales originate with a designated governmental official (comptroller, chief fiscal officer, etc.) seeking the assistance of an investment banker or with an investment banker seeking a contract with an issuer known to be contemplating the sale of bonds. For competitive bidding sales, underwriters use the publication *The Daily Bond Buyer* as a reference, as well as other publications that carry advertisements of municipal bond sales on a regional basis. While *The Daily Bond Buyer* contains many timely articles pertaining to the municipal bond market, of more essential interest to underwriters are the sections of the publication entitled "Proposed New Issues," "Invitation for Bids," "Official Municipal Bond Notices," and "Results of Bond Sales." The first three sections indicate what issues are proposed to be offered for sale, while the "Results of Bond Sales" provides a complete summary of the bids received for issues recently sold, along with the names of the accounts and their respective members who bid on the issue. *The Daily Bond Buyer* also has a service, known as the "New Issue Work Sheet and Record Service" (available on a subscription basis), used by many dealers to obtain notice of coming municipal bond sales and concise data, including a summary financial statement of the issuer and the bidding details. This service covers all issues of $1,000,000 or more and general market issues of $500,000 or more.

*Establishing the Investment Syndicate*

In formulating a bid the underwriter must decide whether the size of the contemplated financing is such that he requires partners or whether he is going to bid the issue alone. In the event that an underwriter has previously bid a syndicate (sometimes called a joint account) on a bond of the same municipality, that same account will generally function again. Changes in the make-up of the account, of course, may occur by firms going out of business or deciding that they do not want to handle a certain bond; however, once a firm is included in a joint account for any given issue, that firm usually will be given an opportunity to participate in the syndicate as new issues are selected for bidding. Should the size of the issue or market conditions warrant such action, the manager of a syndicate account may increase or decrease participation or may merge with other accounts to bid on an issue. A member of the syndicate may also request the manager for a larger or smaller participation in an account. In the case of a relatively small issue the manager may release some or all members from their historical commitment for the sale. If dissatisfied with conditions of the syndicate agreement, a member may withdraw from the account and join another. This action is taken only in extreme situations, however.

There are two principal forms of joint accounts in the municipal bond market: (1) the Eastern or undivided account, and (2) the Western or divided account. The Eastern account is said to be undivided as to selling and liability, that is, all of the bonds of the issue are placed under the control of the manager of the account. Usually municipal bonds are in serial form and to divide them would mean that, in some cases, the various members would have very few bonds from any maturity to work on; therefore, it is much more practical to keep all of the bonds together.[h] Undivided as to liability means that as long as any of the bonds in the account are still unsold, each member of the account is liable for his proportionate share of the unsold amount.

In the Western account members may purchase bonds from the account at the terms fixed in the initial syndicate agreement, but any resale of bonds so purchased by a member shall be solely for his own account and not as an agent for the managers or for the syndicate account. Purchases of bonds from the account by a member reduces his liability for any bonds remaining in the account at its termination.

Syndicate accounts are usually established to run for 30 days during which time the offering prices cannot be changed without consent of all (or at least a majority) of members. If, at the end of 30 days, the issue has not been sold in its entirety, the account may be renewed and extended by mutual agreement, or the remaining bonds (in an Eastern account) may be divided up among members in accordance with their pro-rata share based upon their original percentage, or (in a Western account) may be confirmed to the members having liability for the unsold bonds. Price restrictions binding members to syndicate reoffering terms are normally removed immediately after all the bonds are sold or the syndicate is disbanded on a particular issue.

---

[h]Occasionally there may be a demand for certain maturities and these will be divided and prorated among members of the account; all other bonds are held together, and any member may obtain confirmation of those bonds as long as they are available.

In the past most investment banking firms sent out elaborate questionnaires to localities contemplating bond issues, soliciting a considerable amount of statistical information concerning the issue and the community or governmental unit. More recently many investment bankers have come to rely on the reports of Dun and Bradstreet and the New Issue Worksheet Service of *The Daily Bond Buyer*. While in some unusual cases it may be necessary to send someone to the municipality to interview officials and obtain more detailed information, contact with officials of the issuing jurisdiction is generally confined to requests for the notice of sale.

A day or two before the sale it is necessary for members of the syndicate to decide preliminarily on the price at which the bonds will be offered to the public. The account manager calls a meeting and representatives from the account membership offer their ideas as to the price at which the bonds should sell. Assembling these estimates and any other pertinent information concerning the market, the manager will suggest a bid scale and profit margin that he believes can be underwritten by the account (see Table 7-5). Those members unwilling to make this bid may withdraw from the account and their share must be divided among the remaining members who have indicated a willingness to accept the increase.[i] If the remaining account members are unwilling to increase their participation, a lower bid may be agreed upon to attract back some of the members who had declined to make the original bid.

After the price has been set the next step is to submit the bid to the issuing jurisdiction. There is very strict observance of the deadline in municipal sales. On the date of the sale officials of the issuing jurisdiction usually meet in a body at the stipulated time and receive the bids from the bidders in person or through the mail. With small issues bids may be mailed. However, on more important sales the bidder will either send one of his own representatives to attend the sale or will arrange to have a local dealer or a local bank submit the bid. It is customary to require from each bidder a "good faith check," ranging in amount from one to five percent of the par value of the bonds being sold; this check is held by the issuing jurisdiction as liquidating damages in case the successful bidder does not take up and pay for the bonds on the settlement date in accordance with the terms of the Official Notice of Sale.

It is customary to receive sealed bids at the vast majority of municipal bond sales. There are occasions, however, when a municipality requests auction bids, in the hopes of getting a better price due to the various bidders forcing each other up.[j] If all bids are on the basis of one coupon rate for the entire issue,

---

[i] Of the original 178 firms invited to participate in the syndicate account that produced the winning bid on the BART bond issue, 72, or 40 percent, declined to underwrite about $28 million of the $70 million required, because they disliked the price scale, profit spread, or the amount of unsold bonds in the market in other accounts.

[j] There is some risk in this practice in that a bidder may go to a sale with a limit of, say, 106.5 for an issue that is being sold and find that his competition is prepared to go only to 103, in which case he can secure the issue for 103.01, or nearly 3 ½ points under what he was willing to pay.

### Table 7-5
### Underwriters' Calculation of "Production" for $70 Million BART Bond Issue

| Year Due | Amount Offered ($000) | Coupon Rate (%) | Reoffering Price (Yield) (%) or (100 = PAR) | Reoffering Price per Bond ($) | Production (Col. 2 × Col. 5) ($) |
|---|---|---|---|---|---|
| 1972 | 675 | 6.00 | 3.60 | 1,108.90 | 748,507.50 |
| 1973 | 800 | 6.00 | 3.65 | 1,125.60 | 900,480.00 |
| 1974 | 925 | 6.00 | 3.70 | 1,140.70 | 1,055,147.50 |
| 1975 | 1050 | 6.00 | 3.75 | 1,154.30 | 1,212,015.00 |
| 1976 | 1200 | 6.00 | 3.80 | 1,166.40 | 1,399,680.00 |
| 1977 | 1325 | 6.00 | 3.85 | 1,177.10 | 1,559,657.50 |
| 1978 | 1475 | 6.00 | 3.90 | 1,186.40 | 1,749,940.00 |
| 1979 | 1625 | 6.00 | 3.95 | 1,194.40 | 1,940,900.00 |
| 1980 | 1775 | 6.00 | 3.95 | 1,206.90 | 2,142,247.50 |
| 1981 | 1925 | 4.00 | 3.95 | 1,005.30 | 1,935,202.50 |
| 1982 | 2050 | 3.95 | 100 | 1,000.00 | 2,050,000.00 |
| 1983–86 | 9475 | 4.00 | 100 | 1,000.00 | 9,475,000.00 |
| 1987–90 | 11750 | 4.05 | 100 | 1,000.00 | 11,750,000.00 |
| 1991–93 | 10200 | 4.10 | 100 | 1,000.00 | 10,200,000.00 |
| 1994–96 | 11400 | 4.15 | 100 | 1,000.00 | 11,400,000.00 |
| 1997–98 | 8350 | 4.20 | 100 | 1,000.00 | 8,350,000.00 |
| 1999 | 4000 | 3.00 | 4.50 | 743.40 | 2,973,600.00 |
| Maximum production at posted prices | | | | | $70,842,377.50 |

Note: The data in Table 6-2 was used to arrive at the above calculation, illustrating the approach applied by the winning syndicate in developing its bid on the BART bond issue. It will be noted that for the first eight maturities (1972–79), a 6 percent coupon rate was established, producing a gradually increasing yield (from 3.60 to 3.95). For 1980 the coupon rate was set at 6 percent but the yield was held to 3.95 percent; in 1981 a lower coupon rate was selected (4.00 percent– but the yield was still 3.95 percent. For the next 17 maturities (1982–98) the yield was held at PAR, while the coupon rate was gradually increased from 3.95 to 4.20. For the final maturity a coupon rate of 3.00 percent and a yield of 4.50 percent was established, forcing the sale at a substantial discount. The second lowest bidder used a combination of 6, 5, 3.90, 4, 4.10, 4.20, and 3 percent coupons to come within $5,950 of the winning bid.

the bidder naming the lowest rate receives the award. If the bid entails more than one rate of interest, the award is determined by the lowest average cost (net interest cost). If more than one bidder names the same rate, then whoever bids the highest premium and lowest rate gets the award. When the sale is concluded the good faith checks of the unsuccessful bidders are returned and the successful bidder's check is retained by the municipality until the contract is completed.

For the bidder who purchases the bonds the next step is to reoffer them, usually at the scale that had been decided upon prior to the bidding. Although it may take up to four weeks for the actual delivery of the bonds (to allow for printing, etc.), the bonds will be sold on a "when, as and if issued" basis.

*Investment Banker's Profits*

The previous discussion of the 1967 Bay Area Rapid Transit District bond issue illustrates how municipal bonds are brought into the investment market through the activities of underwriters acting independently or in syndicates. During the week that the BART general obligation bonds were first offered, a total of almost $400 million in municipal bonds were listed in *The Bond Buyer's* Calendar of Sealed Bid Openings, representing 64 issues, three-quarters of which had face values less than $5 million.[k] With this volume of sales in a "typical" week, it is often assumed by the layman that tremendous profits are made by investment bankers dealing in municipal bonds. Therefore, people are surprised by the relative small margin of profit sought by investment bankers in the sale of new issues of municipal bonds.

As a rule investment bankers (underwriters) do not charge a commission when they sell municipal bonds, since they are acting as principals, rather than as agents. Therefore, they make their profit by selling bonds at a price higher than they paid to secure the bonds from the issuing jurisdiction, that is, the profit of the investment banker is included in the price that the purchaser pays for the bonds. The profit of an investment banker is the "spread" (the difference) between the purchase price paid to the issuer and the sale price to investors. The expected profit varies considerably with different issues, depending on the maturity of the bonds, the size of the issue, the type of issuer, the nature of the credit behind the bonds, and the stability of the money market, all of which affect the difficulty in marketing the bonds and the risk that the investment banker must assume. In general, the expected profit of the investment banker (before deduction of expenses) on a $1,000 bond will vary from around $2.50 to $20 (0.25 to 2.0 percent of face amount). Under unusual circumstances or faced with a difficult marketing problem, the expected profit may exceed 2 percent. On the other hand, in some cases where the market drops significantly while bonds are being offered, or where there is an adverse development with respect to the issuer of the bonds, the underwriter may sell the bonds for substantially less than the price paid for them, suffering a loss.

With few exceptions, bonds are offered at basis prices, that is, on a yield basis (longer maturities may be offered at a dollar price). Bonds may be sold to individual investors in one of three ways: (1) by the syndicate acting for the mutual benefit of all members, (2) by individual account members, or (3)

---

[k]Of these 64 issues, 33 were education related, 18 represented local government general obligation bonds, 1 was a state issue of general obligation bonds, and the remaining 12 were made up of revenue bonds, mostly for community facilities such as sewer and water systems. Since *The Bond Buyer's* Calendar lists only issues with face amount of at least $750,000, there must have been several other smaller issues for sale in regional markets for every one being offered in the national market. The other major issues of that week were by the Georgia Education Authority ($32 million), the Los Angeles Unified School District ($30 million), and the Dallas Independent School District ($20 million).

through other dealers outside the syndicate. When outside dealers are permitted to buy bonds from the syndicate for resale, they usually do so at the offering price less some agreed upon "dealer's concession," which may range from ¼ to ½ point or more on longer term bonds.[1] The dealer then sells the bonds to his customers at the offering price, his profit being the amount of the concession. Individual members of the account, on the other hand, secure bonds from the manager at the offering price less what is called the "take-down," that is, the discount from the list price allowed to a member of an underwriting account on any bond he sells. The take-down generally includes any subsequent dealer's concessions. For example, if the take-down on particular maturities is ½ point and the dealer's concession is ¼ point, a member of the account takes down bonds at the offering price less ½ and may sell them to a nonmember dealer at the offering price less ¼, thereby making a ¼ of a point on the transaction. The net profit over and above the take-down that participating dealers receive goes into the account and is divided among the various members at the termination of the account.

When the bonds have been printed and recorded and the municipal bond attorneys are ready to render their final approving opinion, the executed bonds are delivered to the underwriters by the issuing jurisdiction, along with the usual closing papers (such as a treasurer's receipt and nonlitigation certificate). The underwriters then make payment to the issuer.[m] If the bonds were sold to investors during the period between the award and the time of delivery, they are then redelivered by the underwriters to the individual investors (or dealers) along with a copy of the legal opinion (a copy of the complete final legal opinion may be printed on the back of the bonds).

Bonds are sold on a "plus accrued interest" basis from the date of issue or from the last interest payment date if one has passed, that is, the purchaser is only entitled to interest from the time he makes payment, and the previous owner is entitled to it up to the time payment is received. In the case of a municipality selling an issue, the bonds might be dated July 1, and the purchaser may receive delivery and make payment on August 1. The municipality has not had the use of that money for one month after the date of the issue and, therefore, is paid accrued interest for that period. The underwriter of the bonds

---

[1]A point on a municipal bond, in reference to the dollar price, the take-down, or dealer's concession, is $10 per $1,000, so that ¼ of a point is $2.50 on a $1,000 bond. This differs from a basis point, in reference to the percentage of yield, which is 1/100th of the percentage point, for example, an increase of three basis points on a bond yielding 3.05 percent would provide a yield of 3.08 percent.

[m]If there is a dealer bank heading the issue the bank puts up the money for the syndicate. If no bank is involved in the syndicate the manager will arrange for a loan at one of the banks, simply putting up whatever margin is required, usually five or ten percent, depending on the type of issue. By carrying the bonds at a bank the dealer has to put up a comparatively small amount and is able to handle considerably more issues. As the bonds are sold the loan is paid down until it is eventually liquidated by the ultimate sale of the entire issue.

collects accrued interest from the parties to whom he sells them. The investor, in turn, receives the full amount of the interest payment on the date it becomes due. He, in turn, had previously paid the interest accruing up to the date of delivery to him.

### Termination of a Syndicate Account

The bond issue of the San Francisco Bay Area Rapid Transit District, previously cited, provides a good illustration of the activities of an investment syndicate leading up to its termination. The syndicate that was organized and successfully bid on the BART bonds was composed of 106 underwriters.[n] On the first day following the award of the issue about $30 million of the $70 million bonds were sold and another $3.7 million were sold on the second day, leaving $36.9 million in the account for subsequent disposal. After 21 days of posting at the original prices, during which time other issues were being sold at relatively higher and more attractive yields, the syndicate account was "broken up," and the bonds remaining unsold were distributed to the members in proportion ot their share of the underwriting liability. With the syndicate restrictions removed individual underwriters were free to offer their share of the remaining bonds at below-list (and perhaps below-cost) prices. During the first few days of the free market dealers and brokers engaged in a flurry of transactions to clear the market. Some of syndicate members took losses, while other dealers (including some members of the former syndicate) stockpiled blocks of bonds at the lower price level. Moreover, various investors seeking a bargain entered the market at this point and were rewarded for having foregone the opportunity to buy on the first day of sale at the posted price level. Within a few months most of the bonds ended up in institutional or bank portfolios, although on almost any day, for such a large issue, some of the BART bonds may be found in the offerings of the secondary market.

### Secondary or Trading Market

After the initial issuance and distribution of a municipal bond, it is vital to the industry that a free market be maintained for subsequent disposal or reinvestment. Like any other security, municipal bonds often are disposed of before maturity. Heirs sell, institutions acquire different tax-exempt needs, commercial banks see deposits rise or fall cyclically, and so on. A change in money rates may influence a syndicate to break up and divide the unsold bonds

---

[n] The winning bid was only 0.0085 percent or $5950 below the second lowest bid, producing a sale with a "close cover," that is, with the second responsible bid very close to the winning bid, considered a good omen in the market (Alan Rabinowitz, *Municipal Bond Finance and Administration* (New York: Wiley-Interscience, 1969), pp. 13–14).

among its members. At other times dealers may acquire larger holdings of bonds in anticipation of a possible price appreciation. Whatever the reason, bonds return to the market to be offered to the investing public for a second time; hence, the term "secondary market." The volume of transactions, in terms of par value of bonds traded, in the secondary market far exceeds that of the "new issue" (or primary) market on any given day. Since transactions in the secondary market are often held in secrecy, the size and character of this market is known only in fragmentary fashion. Daily volume of secondary offerings, as shown in *The Blue List*,[o] together with estimated unadvertised blocks, would suggest an *annual secondary to primary market* ratio of 20 to 1.

There are two types of trading markets: (1) auction markets and (2) negotiated trade (over-the-counter) markets. Municipal bonds are seldom traded in auction markets, generally reserved for listed securities on the national exchanges, in which a broker competes in open auction for the best possible execution of a transaction. Rather, municipal bonds are most often traded in over-the-counter markets (markets other than the recognized stock exchange), in which any individual may go for his own account or may arrange for a recognized dealer to act as his agent to negotiate the best bid or offering available for which he has knowledge at the time of execution. Over-the-counter trading markets encompasses generally all types of securities, including United States government, foreign bonds, corporates, railroad stocks, common and preferred stocks, script, rights, warrants, as well as municipal bonds.

There are many highly competitive trading departments in bond houses throughout major cities. Therefore, the field is very competitive with spreads ranging from ¼ of a point ($2.50 per bond) to two points ($20.00) in the case of obscure issues or odd lots. The average spread is $10.00 per $1,000 bond.

Municipal bonds are traded with accrued interest to date of delivery added to the cost price,[p] delivery and payment to be made on the fifth full business day after the trade date. Trades initially are made verbally and are confirmed by a written statement, mailed on the day of the trade so that statements can be compared the following morning.

### Tax Treatment of Discount

When an investor purchases a municipal bond at a discount, so that the yield is higher than the specified rate of interest, and subsequently sells or

---

[o]*The Blue List,* a daily listing of offerings of bonds by dealers in and out of syndicate, emerged out of the practice in the thirties of dealers collecting and tabulating offering sheets from competing houses in order to compile an "available list" that was then distributed to the dealer's customers and sales department. The "available lists" became so popular it was inevitable that a commercial enterprise organized the available bonds of the entire industry into one huge "available list."

[p]Each person who owns a bond for any period between interest payment dates is

redeems the bond for a price in excess of the purchase price, only the interest is exempt from federal income tax; the additional yield is taxable as a capital gain when realized. Thus, if a $1,000 bond with 3.25 percent interest coupons, maturing in 10 years, was purchased for $958.60 to secure a 3.75 percent yield, the semiannual interest payments of $16.25 would be exempt from federal income tax but, when the bond is redeemed by the investor at the maturity date for $1,000, the appreciation of $41.40 would be capital gain for federal income tax purposes.

When municipal bonds are issued at discount, however, the discount is considered to constitute compensation which the obligor has contracted to pay for the use of the money loaned and, therefore, is equivalent to interest for federal tax purposes. Most sales at a substantial discount result from authorizations at a fixed coupon rate at a time of lower money rates than those prevailing at the time of sale. That is to say, a municipality receiving authorization, through referendum, to issue a number of bonds over a period of years may find at the time of a desired issue that the money market has become less favorable (to sellers). Therefore, to achieve a successful issue, the bonds may have to be offered below par, that is, at a discount. Issue discount is recognized as being interest in substance, and as "interest" on a tax-exempt bond, such issue discount is tax exempt. This is true only where the bond is issued at a discount and does not apply where bonds, originally sold at par or at a premium, are subsequently reoffered at a discount. When an issue of serial bonds is purchased from the issuer by an underwriter at a single unallocated price of not less than their total par value (face amount), and some of them are reoffered by the underwriter at a discount, such bonds are not *issued* at a discount.

### Tax Exempt Bond Funds

First established in 1961, Tax Exempt Bond Funds have grown rapidly in investment popularity. These funds are registered investment companies, the assets of which are invested in a diversified portfolio of tax-exempt bonds. Each fund is a closed-end trust created under the terms of a trust indenture by an investment banking firm (or firms) that acts as "sponsor," depositing selected securities with a trustee bank (or trust compnay), and receiving in return certificates, or units, each representing a fractional, undivided interest in the principal and net income of the trust. These certificates are then distributed to individual investors, either by the sponsor or by a group of investment firms forming an underwriting syndicate.

---

entitled to the interest for the period during which he owned the bond. Therefore, each purchaser of a tax-exempt bond must pay the seller the accrued interest from the last interest payment date up to the date of delivery and payment.

These funds have the objective of providing tax-free income consistent with preservation of capital and diversification of risk. Substantially, all fund units have been purchased by private investors, rather than institutional investors. The vast majority of bonds used to create these funds were revenue secured bonds (over 80%) with the remainder being in general obligation bonds. Some funds include in the portfolio only bonds issued within a particular state, thereby gaining exemption from state income taxes as well as federal income taxes; other funds include so-called "businessman's risk" type of bonds, which provide a higher rate of return.[9]

## Summary

The marketing of municipal bonds is a complicated process, the mysteries of which, insofar as the uninitiated is concerned, are comparable to that of the stock market. While local officials are concerned primarily with the initial sale of bonds and must take appropriate steps to ensure their marketability and delivery, the transactions that follow—the reoffering by the investment syndicates and the trading in the secondary market—are equally important. The interest of the underwriting syndicate in securing appropriate guarantees that a given bond issue can be resold to permanent investors dictates that municipal officials closely adhere to the procedures outlined in this discussion. The success of a given issue, however, may be determined by forces in the marketplace beyond the direct control of local officials, although an awareness of these factors can provide important insights in the overall planning of long-term bonds for capital facility.

## Appendix 7A
## Financial Information Required in Municipal Bond Prospectus for General Obligation and Special Tax Bonds

The Investment Bankers Association of America recommends that the following financial information be included in any municipal bond prospectus covering general obligation bonds or special tax (assessment) bonds.

1. Assessed valuation and basis of assessment in relation to actual value, for both real and personal property (separately, if available). Actual valuation may also be included if an official estimate is obtainable (in such cases the date and source of such statement should be given).
2. Total bonded debt, including present issue, payable from general taxes and other bonded indebtedness for which the municipality is either primarily or ultimately liable.
3. Self-supporting debt and sinking funds for other than self-supporting debt.
4. Debt payable primarily from special assessments, but ultimately from general taxation, should be included in the total bonded debt, but may be shown by appropriate footnote as representing only contingent liability of the municipality.
5. Net Direct Bonded Debt—total bonded debt less self-supporting debt and sinking funds for other than self-supporting debt and less debt payable from special assessments.
6. Per capita net direct bonded debt and ratio of net direct bonded debt to assessed valuation.
7. Notes or other evidences of indebtedness issued in anticipation of later funding into bonds.
8. Debts of any other political subdivision having the power to levy taxes upon the taxable property of the issuing municipality (i.e., overlapping debt).
9. Record of tax collection over the past five years, showing actual tax levy and amount collected.

In addition, the prospectus should include a general description of the municipality's economic base, major employers (e.g., ten largest firms), total employment and level of unemployment, transportation facilities (airport, railroads, bus service, highways), and overall economic outlook.

# 8 Revenue Bonds

## Security of Revenue Bonds

A revenue bond is an obligation issued fo finance a revenue-producing enterprise; both the principal and interest of such bonds are paid exclusively from the earnings of the enterprise. While laws and practices vary, the fundamental characteristic of revenue bonds, as distinguished from other forms of long-term municipal financing, is the reliance on the income generated by the project to cover the attendant debt service charges. Such issues are not ordinarily guaranteed, that is, they have no claim on the general credit or taxing power of the governmental unit that issues them. To assure investors that the financial affairs of the project will be maintained in good order and all commitments honored, however, a system of sinking funds and operating controls is typically established.

There are two principal reasons for the issuance of revenue bonds, rather than general obligation bonds: (1) Revenue bonds are based on the concept that only the users of a facility financed by the sale of bonds should pay for that facility; and (2) revenue bonds are not ordinarily subject to statutory or constitutional debt limitations. While it is sometimes said that municipal revenue bonds are not a debt of the municipality, such bonds do constitute an obligation of the issuing jurisdiction; however, the obligations of the municipality extend only to the payment of the bonds from a special source of revenue.

## Historical Background

While revenue bonds were used in England over 200 years ago for the financing of toll bridges, turnpikes, and canals, the first revenue bond law in the United States was not enacted until 1897, when provision was made in the state of Washington for the issuance of $350,000 in bonds by the city of Spokane, secured solely by a pledge of revenue of its waterworks systems. It is interesting to note that Spokane adopted this then novel borrowing mechanism for the same reason that influenced subsequent expansion of its use—state restrictions on general borrowing and taxing powers of municipalities that limit the use of general obligation bonds.

Other states were slow to pass similar provisions, however, and where such laws were enacted, they received rather conservative interpretations by the courts. Consequently, revenue bonding found application in only a few areas and for only a limited range of purposes, mainly water systems and toll bridges. The concept of a *commission* or *authority* (i.e., a municipal corporation formed for the purpose of operating certain facilities that may or may not be confined within a given municipality) became a part of the revenue bonding process in this country from its earliest applications. Water districts, without the power to tax but with the right to sell revenue bonds, date back to 1899 in Maine.

While the creation of the Port of New York Authority[a] in 1921 directed widespread attention to the possibilities of this method of borrowing, it was the depression of the early thirties that was most instrumental in the significant expansion of revenue bonding to provide needed capital funds to hard-pressed municipalities. During this period the federal government sought to promote local public works, particularly those of a self-liquidating nature, through grants and loans to shore up the declining general borrowing power of states and municipalities.

Many new state statutes were enacted and many projects were financed by revenue bonds under the pressures of fiscal emergencies. As pointed out previously, this also was a period of rapid expansion in the concepts of long-range capital improvements programming and budgeting at the local level.

As urban communities began to invest in new facilities following the hiatus of World War II, the proportion of revenue bonds came to represent at least a third and sometimes as much as 45 percent of all tax-exempt bonds issued in a given year. By the mid-fifties, almost all states had some sort of enabling legislation for revenue bonding, and an estimated $9.5 billion of revenue bonds were outstanding, utilized to finance revenue-producing projects by over 1,000 municipalities, counties, special districts, states, and state agencies. The list of varied and diverse projects financed by revenue bonds included: water, sewer, electric, and gas systems; bridges, tunnels, turnpikes, parkways, and expressways; dock and harbor facilities; airports, parking facilities, mass transit; stadiums, arenas, and auditoriums; hospitals, sanitariums, and college dormitories; public housing projects; swimming pools, golf courses, and other public recreation facilities; hydroelectric power projects; and even municipal cemeteries.

With the creation of the Port of New York Authority and the Triborough Bridge Authority in early forties, it was clearly established that not only were political subdivisions entitled to exemption from federal income taxation on bond interest, but also special district governments with wide functional and territorial jurisdictions. Such special districts have played a vital role in the development of intermunicipal and intrametropolitan facilities required in

---

[a]The Port of New York Authority is the prime example of a large-scale authority created by a compact between the participating states and ratified by congressional action. The annual budget of the Port Authority exceeds that of most states, as does its indebtedness.

contemporary urban society. Thus, the courts began to accept arguments, legal and economic, justifying these revenue-financed enterprises. The technical features of sinking funds, reserves, and the entire financial structure of such authorities had been improved to make the bonds acceptable to investors and the markets. At the same time tax rates remained high, inducing continued investor interest in the purchase of substantial quantities of tax-exempt bonds, particularly since revenue bonds are generally sold at slightly higher yields than general obligation bonds. From the point of view of the municipal administrator, revenue bonded projects often enable the bypassing of both the requirement of voter authorization and the debt limits of the issuing community. In addition, it is often possible to finance construction without raising taxes, even though in some cases the bonds of the authority carry a contingent guarantee from the local government served.

Revenue bond financing and the use of special districts, however, have raised a number of philosophical questions that have yet to be fully resolved. There are differing opinions as to the extent to which an authority or special district should be responsive to the electorate, as well as the range of activities appropriate to such public enterprises that can be held to be in the public interest. Some political scientists argue that the widespread use of special districts has severely inhibited the creation of multipurpose agencies and metrogovernments that might be more effective in the solution of complex urban service delivery problems. Economists also have argued that these special districts, through their revenue bonding powers, have distorted the municipal bond market by offerring the investor a higher yield than general obligation bonds can produce.

### Appropriate Uses of Revenue Bonds

While revenue bonds have certain advantages and tend to encourage the businesslike management of public enterprises, their legal availability does not justify indiscriminate use. Revenue bonds should not be issued to pursue speculative projects or merely to evade sound and reasonable debt limtis. When a jurisdiction has an adequate borrowing capacity at its disposal, the primary consideration should be which type of bond can be sold at the lowest cost. In general, the types of projects suitable for revenue bond financing include: (1) those that can be readily operated on a service charge or user-fee basis; (2) those for which experience, either under public or private operation, has demonstrated the potentialities for self-support; and (3) those that can produce sufficient revenue without jeopardizing other important economic or social objectives of the community.[1]

While revenue bond financing forces the project to be strictly self-supporting, there are instances when this requirement may seriously limit the adaptability of the project to the general benefit of all persons in the community. Problems of equity may arise when traditionally tax-supported functions are placed on a service charge basis. Facilities supported by service charges also frequently produce benefits to individuals who do not pay for them, for example, an enhancement in land value that may accrue to the speculative holder of unimproved real estate.

For these reasons significant questions have been raised regarding the validity of funding certain public service delivery systems, such as water supply and sewage disposal systems, as self-supporting utilities, to be financed totally through the issuance of revenue bonds. The counterargument can be made, however, that by placing such facilities under the more rigid financial arrangements required by revenue bonds, proper attention can be given to operating appropriations that sometimes are inadequately covered in tax-financed systems. The potential inequities of service charges, in turn, can be minimized by placing "readiness-to-serve" charges on unimproved properties having access to such facilities and thereby benefiting from their development.

### Revenue Bond Laws

While nearly all states now have some type of enabling legislation or constitutional provision authorizing the issuance of revenue bonds, these provisions vary considerably in their application and coverage. Some apply to all political subdivisions, while others apply only to certain classes of municipalities; some are limited to a few types of public improvements, while others include broadly all publicly owned utilities and related public service delivery systems. Similarly, the creation of special authorities or districts may be prohibited, optional, or mandatory and/or may be limited to only certain classes of enterprises. In short, revenue bond laws throughout the United States are far from uniform in scope and content.

In spite of this lack of uniformity, a number of general characteristics of revenue bond laws can be enumerated, including the following:

1. Identification of the governmental units authorized to borrow and the types of utilities to which the enabling legislation applies
2. General grant of power to acquire, construct, improve, or extend the particular improvements, to issue revenue bonds, and to pledge revenues to the payment of these bonds
3. Requirements that the issuing body establish sufficient charges or rates to operate and maintain the project and to meet principal and interest requirements
4. Guarantees that revenue bonds have all the qualities of negotiable instruments under the appropriate laws of the state

# REVENUE BONDS

5. Provisions governing the authorization and sale of revenue bonds (including regulations relating to public referenda)
6. Provisions designed to secure the successful operation of the project
7. Remedies to be initiated in the event of default

Since some state laws are very general in their provisions, carrying no specific requirements regarding fiscal management of the enterprise, it is important that covenants be made between the borrower and the bondholders regarding such matters as the use and disposition of funds generated by the project, development of adequate reserves, proper upkeep and repairs, provisions of insurance, and maintenance of adequate records for account audits. Such covenants are necessitated by the fact that the security offered the investor is not the full faith, credit, and taxing power of the municipality, but only the earning power of the project. These covenants are incorporated in the bond ordinance or resolution and made a part of the bond contract. They can protect the project from political interference, as well as save money and help to assure its success.

### Sources of Revenue

While the purposes for which revenue bonds are issued are many and varied, the sources of revenue in support of these bonds can be classified in five general categories: (1) user charges for utilities, (2) tolls, fees, and concessions, (3) special taxes, (4) rental payments under lease-backs, and (5) industrial revenue bonds.

*User charges,* including projects such as water, sewer, electrical and gas systems, are one of the oldest and most common sources of revenue. In financing utility systems many municipalities issue bonds payable solely from such revenues, while other municipalities guarantee debt service payments in the event these revenues are insufficient. This latter form of bonds, which are really general obligation bonds, is sometimes referred to as a "double barreled" security.

Following World War II significant capital construction was initiated in the development of turnpikes, toll bridges, docks, warehouses, airports, and rapid transit systems. For the most part these projects were financed by commissions and authorities, with the bonds payable solely from the revenues collected (*tolls* and *fees*) and from the marginal income of *concessions* (e.g., automobile service facilities and restaurants along turnpikes, space lessees and parking lots at airports, etc.). Bonds issued for such purposes generally require a margin of protection considerably higher than those issued for water systems or other strictly municipal purposes, since they are projects with no earning history. Therefore, anticipated revenues are based solely upon engineering estimates.

*Special taxes* are those derived from an additional levy on such items as tobacco, alcoholic beverages, and other goods and services considered semi-luxuries. This form of support for revenue bonds has been attaining more prominence in recent years.

Such bonds have been issued by states to finance expressways, veterans' bonus issues, and other projects. Florida municipalities for some time have been levying special taxes to subsidize the issuance of revenue bonds for water, sewer, and electric service purposes. Such special taxes are particularly appropriate in resort communities where considerable transient population places demands on public facilities and services.

Under the *lease-back arrangement,* bonds are usually issued by an authority to finance construction of a given facility, which is then leased to the state, school district, or city concerned at a rental level calculated to be sufficient to pay interest and retire the indebtedness. The funds for the rental payments are obtained by the lessee from various sources, including legislative appropriations, special taxes, and direct taxes. One of the advantages of this approach is that the financing authority may be able to secure more favorable interest rates by offering a larger bond issue than the lessee could obtain. The lease-back arrangement has been widely used in several states, including Kentucky, Indiana, and Pennsylvania, which has three statewide authorities for this purpose.

Since 1936 nearly 300 cities, counties, and other local units (mostly in the South) have borrowed over $1 billion to provide industrial plant facilities for private use through the issuance of *industrial revenue bonds.* Such local governments have floated loans to (a) construct factories or other business facilities that are then leased to private businesses, or (b) purchase factories or other facilities from private businesses that are then leased back to the sellers. The security behind such loans is a net lease entered into between the issuer and the private corporation, with the rentals designed to cover the debt service on the public bond issue. Private enterprises with insufficient equity capital to borrow the amount required for capital construction or expansion obviously benefit from such arrangements. Furthermore, since state or local bonds are tax exempt, the interest charges included in the rental is lower than could be possible if the company borrowed the equivalent sum in the normal capital market.

While the "buying" of new business location through property-tax exemptions or the use of public credit for private purposes has been strongly opposed by many financial organizations, including the Investment Bankers Association, legislatures in a growing number of states have authorized this type of debt as a means of enticing new industry; half of the states have authorized their local governments to enter into such "industrial development" programs and a quarter of the states have developed programs of their own. The use of general obligation credit for this purpose may seriously impair the margin of debt required at some future time for appropriate public facilities. Moreover, revenue financing of this type of debt is more difficult to obtain and requires more protective covenants than most revenue debt supported from public service enterprises. In their haste to find a lessee of the property, municipal officials may not take the necessary precautions to investigate the financial stability of the enterprise or to safeguard the investment by insisting that the lease extend over the life of the bonds. As a consequence the community or state runs the risk of having a contingent liability become an actual one, or of finding itself saddled with debt for special facilities for which another lessee cannot be found. This danger is particularly acute in those instances where a municipality issues bonds to finance the construction of a "shell-type" facility prior to securing an industrial tenant or invests in public improvements for an "industrial park" before the acreage is marketed.

Industrial bonds represent a gross abuse of the tax-exemption privilege of public securities. Here is one area where restrictions on state-local borrowing need to be tightened rather than eased. Alternatively, federal tax exemption of the interest on such state-local debt should be eliminated or severely limited.

Communities unable to finance industrial projects by means of revenue or general obligation bonds issued by the municipality or by a local public authority may achieve such projects by use of nonprofit corporations. A group of citizens may form a corporation, issue corporation bonds, construct or otherwise acquire the project, lease the project to a private firm (or possibly to the local government if the intent is to circumvent existing debt limitations), and pay the bond debt service from the rentals received under the lease. If the Internal Revenue Service determines that the corporation is truly nonprofit and, among other things, that the project reverts to municipal or other local governmental ownership after the bonds are retired or at a stated definite time, then as a rule, the interest on the bonds is free from federal income taxation under present regulations and laws. Such bonds must be issued under state enabling legislation.

In some states an authority or commission can be created to issue bonds to finance projects and receive legislative appropriations to pay debt service on the outstanding bonds for the fiscal period preceding the next regular legislative session. The Pennsylvania General State Authority is representative of this type of financing. The primary objection to this approach is that one legislature cannot bind succeeding legislatures; accordingly, there is no assurance of continued appropriations.

### Planning the Sale of Revenue Bonds

The success of revenue bonding requires systematic project planning, proper promotion and management of the bond sale, and businesslike administration of the project, including development and adherence to the protective covenants relating to the debt. While on the whole revenue bonds have a good credit rating, defaults that have occurred can invariably be traced to mistakes in planning and management, such as: (a) failure to adhere to appropriate state enabling legislation; (b) underestimation of operating costs of overestimation of anticipated revenues, (c) excessive expenditures for property acquisition, (d) failure to segregate and safeguard project revenues in accordance with the covenants of the bond ordinance or resolution, (e) insufficient care in engineering studies, and/or (f) failure to allow sufficient time for project completion before bond payments begin to come due.[2]

Since the revenue is the security for the payment of principal and interest, a primary factors is whether the earnings of the enterprise, as judged by past operating results (if any) or by projections by competent analysts, will provide adequate coverage for debt service with a margin for unforeseen contingencies. A municipality can find a satisfactory market for its revenue bonds only by demonstrating the economic and financial soundness of the project. No matter how experienced a municipality's engineering staff may be, it is necessary to secure the independent analysis and advice of a competent outside consulting engineer, for it is largely through his reports that a favorable market can be found for the bonds. Reputable investment bankers and conservative investors are not likely to buy an issue of revenue bonds solely on the representations of the seller.

Bonds should be planned as to their terms, conditions, and safeguards with two objectives in mind—to suit the nature of the project and to attract the investor. Principles to be observed in planning bonds may be outlined as follows:[3]

1. Bonds should be scheduled for retirement well within the useful life of the project, that is, the rate of amortization of the bonds should at least equal an adequate rate of depreciation on the facility.
2. The retirement of bonds, however, should be distributed in such a way as to allow a comfortable margin of revenue coverage for debt service without the need to charge abnormal rates or fees.
3. The amount of combined annual interest and amortization should follow an even or possibly slightly rising trend in order to coincide with the prospective pattern of revenues, that is, through the use of serial bonds, the maturity pattern should be established to reflect the anticipated income pattern.
4. The first payment on principal should be deferred until the operations of the facility have become well established.
5. Assurances must be evident to the investor from the outset (through the willingness of the issuer to grant reasonable covenants) that: (a) the project will receive businesslike management, (b) bond funds will be properly expended, (c) construction will be carefully inspected, (d) the plant and equipment will be properly maintained after the project is operational,

(e) the rate structure or fee schedule is designed to keep the project self-supporting, and (f) adequate financial safeguards are met to assure the maintenance of adequate working capital and reserves.

Thus, in planning the debt structure of a project to harmonize with its physical and financial characteristics, the borrower goes a long way toward making the bonds attractive to the prospective investor. However, in addition, the investor wants assurances that the project will be managed carefully both during construction and under operation, since his security lies in the financial success of the undertaking. A potential investor may be suspect of a project that promises an early high return on his investment, since such practices may jeopardize the long-term success of the project by unduly limiting the reserve margin for operations and maintenance.

Expert advisers are just as necessary in planning the bonds, therefore, as they are in planning the project. Bond houses with experience in "setting up" revenue bonds and a few firms of municipal finance consultants are available to provide these services. Since in a number of states revenue bond issues can be established through negotiated sales, financial advisors may be drawn from the special experience of bond house personnel or from associated financial consulting organizations. It is also important to recognize that the services of a firm of attorneys specializing in the laws and regulations pertaining to municipal bonds will be required to work with the fiscal advisors in presenting a bond proposal to the investing public. Avoiding the use of qualified fiscal and legal advisors is false economy and will usually result in higher interest costs many times over the fee for expert advice. Moreover, it is rare that bonds can be delivered to the investor without the opinion of a recognized qualified attorney.

### Maturity Provisions

In any type of financing it is unsound to have bonds run beyond the expected life of the improvement for which they were issued; this is particularly true in the case of revenue bonds where the only source of payment is the revenue of the project. While maturity schedules for revenue bonds vary from issue to issue, there are three general types: (1) serial maturities, (2) term bonds, and (3) serial and balloon maturities.

*Serial maturities* are commonly found when financing facilities that have a fairly stable revenue pattern, as for example in water revenue bonds. Serial maturities consist of annual principal payments, calculated to retire the amount of bonds outstanding by the final maturity date. The life of maturities may range from 1 to 40 years; however, with a going concern such as water, sewer, or electric system a range of 1 to 25 years is more common. The pattern of maturities may be tailored on a level debt service basis, whereby the combined annual payments of interest and principal are approximately equal throughout the maturity range, or they may be scheduled so as to produce maximum payments in anticipated peak income years (with perhaps substantially lower payments during the early years of the project to reflect the start-up period).

*Term bonds* frequently are issued when a project is being financed principally on the basis of estimated revenues, that is, where a reliable income pattern has not been established but can only be projected based on "demand" studies. The most outstanding examples of term bonds are those issued to finance toll roads, turnpikes, and bridges. Under term bonds pay-back of principal is deferred until the project is well-established; in many cases the principal is not paid until the full maturity of the bonds. Interest payments are made from current revenues, with funds being set aside in a sinking fund to meet the scheduled principal payment(s). If revenues derived from the operation of the facility exceed the projections, then the money is used, in most cases, to retire bonds prior to maturity.

The use of *balloon maturities,* as part of a serial bond offering, may be preferable to a straight serial issue where the revenues supporting the bonds tend to fluctuate or in cases where it is expected that considerable time will elapse before optimum earnings will be realized. A margin of safety for periods of uncertain earnings can be provided, therefore, by issuing a certain amount of serial bonds with a "balloon," that is, a large amount of principal maturing on the ultimate maturity date. While balloon maturities usually have a callable feature, if revenues are not sufficient, default may be avoided by omitting the call. With a straight serial issue, there is no alternative except to pay the principal that is due or default if revenues are insufficient to cover debt service charges.

In almost all cases revenue bonds are callable prior to maturity through the utilization of surplus funds or a mandatory sinking fund. This callable provision may apply to all or a portion of the outstanding bonds and usually carries some penalty charge for early payment of principal. Nevertheless, the callable feature of revenue bonds is a sound fiscal device to be used when revenues build up beyond initial estimates (which are generally conservative). In the case of serial maturities the call is usually in inverse numerical order, although at times it may be by maturity. Term bonds are called by lot in most instances.

### Covenants on Revenue Bonds

Certain covenants for the protection of the investor are spelled out in all bond resolutions or trust indentures. These covenants, among other things, establish appropriate and clearly defined fiscal policies that, in turn, are protected against political tampering. No covenants should be entered into that involve unfair demands or in any way hamper the progress of the project. There should be no hesitancy, however, in the making of pledges that commit management to the observance of sound fiscal policies. It has been said that "covenants which protect the bondholder have equal protection to the bond issuer." While revenue bonds are not considered to be a direct debt of the municipality, they are issued by and usually carry the name of the municipality. Therefore, a default in payment of either principal or interest on this debt will impair the general credit of the municipality. While covenants vary from indenture to indenture, certain basic provisions that bondholders have come to expect are listed below. Failure to incorporate these provisions into the basic instrument generally results in higher interest rates.

**Rate Covenant.** One of the more important covenants is that which pledges the issuing body to fix rates, with revision when necessary, sufficient to meet operation and maintenance charges, as well as annual debt service requirements, and to provide for certain reserves (see below). In general, this covenant requires that rates be maintained sufficient to provide some minimum margin of safety over one times the foregoing charges, for example, for toll facilities, the covenant has been approximately 120 percent of the foregoing charges. If, upon periodic review of the rate or fee schedule, it is found that annual revenues will not cover this margin of safety, then the municipality is expected to revise its schedule accordingly.

**Maintenance and Insurance.** The issuing body must covenant to maintain the properties in good repair and working condition at all times. In order to assure the bondholder of continuity of operation of the facility, the issuing body also attempts to carry insurance on the facility, corresponding in amount and in kind to that which is normally carried under private enterprise.

**Records and Financial Reports.** Most issuing bodies covenant that gross revenues will be deposited in a special fund and kept separate from all other funds of the city; proper books and accounts will be kept, to be audited annually by independent certified public accountants of recognized standing; and certified financial statements will be made available periodically. The Investment Bankers Association recommends that this financial information be filed at least annually with the principal underwriter and principal financial reporting agencies.

**Consulting Engineer.** With the advent of toll road financing, the practice has been to create a covenant whereby a consulting engineer will be placed on a retainer by the municipality to perform certain "watchdog" duties over the facility's operations. This practice is now extended to other municipal facilities such as water and sewer systems.

**Nondiscrimination Covenant.** The practice has been adopted of including a covenant to guarantee that neither preferential treatment nor discrimination shall be applied to any groups in the matter of payment of rates for services, that is, that charges will be equitable for all users. The only departures from this provision might be to certain essential municipal agencies in the performance of their duties, such as fire protection, police protection, etc.

**Application of Revenues.** A series of covenants are usually included in the basic agreement relating to the disposition of funds according to certain specified priorities. A typical arrangement would be: (1) operations and maintenance; (2) interest and principal on bonds; (3) renewal and replacement fund; (4) working capital fund; (5) interest on future bonds, tax equivalent, or other return to the municipality. These covenants, discussed further in the next section, should always be defined clearly to secure satisfactory administration. Other contractual agreements relate to such items as the sale of future bonds, possible sale of the facility, and remedies in the event of default.

### Distribution of Revenues

The order in which revenues generated by self-supporting projects shall be applied, sometimes referred to as the "flow of funds," is set forth in the bond resolution or trust indenture, the basic instruments of security for revenue bonds. Although these procedures may vary in some respects, a basic pattern has developed with regards to the handling of income and revenues. In most cases a basic fund, known as the *reserve fund,* is established, into which all receipts and income derived from the operation of the project are deposited. Monies in the reserve fund are then distributed monthly by the trustee or other handler of funds in the order cited above.

The first claim on the reserve fund is usually a pro-rated amount to meet the cost of operation and maintenance, as set forth in the annual budget. Since, without proper operation and maintenance, a facility or project may experience severe loss of income, revenue bonds are most commonly payable from net revenues, that is, gross receipts less operating and maintenance costs. There are issues, however, where principal and interest requirements constitute a first lien on all revenues derived from the project prior to any payment of operating and maintenance charges. These are known as gross lien or gross income bonds.

The *bond service account* constitutes an amount that, with other such monthly payments, will be sufficient to pay the next semiannual interest payment, as well as the principal next serially maturing. In the case of term bonds a *mandatory sinking fund* is sometimes required in lieu of principal payments on serial bonds.

Payments into a *debt service reserve fund,* in the case of serial bonds, are usually accumulated and maintained equivalent to one year's maximum principal and interest requirements, that is, this fund is gradually built up to equal a full year's debt service. In the case of term bonds the normal requirement is two years' interest. For preferred issues, such as water bonds, one year of interest on term bonds may be acceptable.

A *renewal and replacement fund,* sometimes called a *replacement reserve,* is established to replace equipment or provide necessary repairs beyond normal maintenance. Funds are paid into the account in an amount recommended by the consulting engineer and may be cumulative.

Payments are also made into a *reserve maintenance fund* to meet unusual or extraordinary maintenance charges that have not been budgeted. As a matter of practice deposits to this fund are sometimes payable prior to deposit in the debt service reserve fund on the premise that it is essential to keep the facility in good operating condition. Some municipalities combine the reserve maintenance and renewal and replacement funds. In other cases an effort is made to establish a *working capital fund* equivalent to about one-tenth of a year's gross revenues to cover such unforeseen contingencies.

Monies remaining in the reserve fund after the foregoing distributions are made may be placed in the *surplus fund,* to be divided into various categories, such as the following:

1. *Redemption account.* monies used to retire bonds in advance of maturity.
2. *Payment in lieu of taxes.* when an authority or agency purchases a going operation that had been a corporate unit, either by legislative requirement or to create good will, payments may be made in lieu of taxes.
3. *Other lawful purposes.* including improvements and extension of the facility, support of other bond interest, etc.

### Issuance of Additional Bonds

An important requirement in long-range debt planning is the reservation of the right to issue future bonds with a claim on earnings equal to those outstanding. When a facility is being constructed it is not always possible to foresee just what the future may hold. It may become necessary to increase the size of the facility or to make other improvements that will require additional financing. Therefore, there should be sufficient leeway in the indenture or resolution to permit the issuance of additional bonds. However, this is one of the more controversial features of revenue bonding, the controversy centering on the issue as to whether the additional bonds should rank equally with the outstanding bonds or should constitute a second lien, ranking junior to those outstanding.

If bonds of equal rank are permitted, safeguards must be set up against the undue dilution of the security of the original bonds and provisions made that earnings be at a certain level before additional bonds can be issued. There are two basic types of trust indentures: (1) the *closed end indenture,* which means that no parity bonds may be issued, other than those necessary to complete the project where initial financing proves insufficient—additional bonds must be junior in lien to the then outstanding bonds; and (2) the *open end indenture,* which permits the issuance of additional bonds but provides a formula prescribing the conditions to be met. The services provided by the facility usually determine the stringency of such a formula. In the case of basic municipal services, such as water and sewer, normally it is required that net revenues for the year prior to the issuance of additional bonds be not less than 120 percent of the maximum annual debt service on all bonds then outstanding and to be issued. In the case of other facilities the historical earnings may be combined with estimates as to future earning power to determine an appropriate point at which additional bonds may be established. While most indentures permit the issuance of additional bonds to complete the project, financing extensions or additional facilities may be permitted only under the most carefully considered provisions.

### Summary

Accounting for over one-third of all municipal bonds issued annually, revenue bonds have continued to grow in significance during the past several decades as a means of financing vital public service facilities that evidence the potential of self-support. Revenue bonds can play an important role in a municipality's long-range capital facilities planning. However, before a project is financed by revenue bonds, certain specific requirements, more precise than if the project could rely on tax support, must be fulfilled in keeping with well-defined fiscal policies. It must be clearly established that revenues generated by the proposed project are sufficient to: (1) cover the cost of operation, maintenance, and debt service; (2) provide a comfortable margin of working capital; and (3) create a reserve fund for emergencies and to cover possible declines in income. In addition, project revenues must be controlled carefully to avoid reckless diversion to other purposes. In short, while revenue bonding offers considerable potential in the arsenal of long-term financial planning mechanisms of local government, it must be approached with the principles of sound management and debt administration firmly in mind.

# 9  Debt Administration

When long-term debt was a small part of the total fiscal commitments of local government and consisted primarily of general obligation bond issues, debt administration was a relatively simple and routine task for local officials. The basic requirement was to ensure that a sufficient amount was set aside each year from general revenue sources to cover annual debt service charges, or, in the case of term bonds, to cover annual interest charges with an additional sum sufficient to build an adequate sinking fund that would produce the requisite principal payments at maturity. The decade of the fifties, however, witnessed an unprecedented growth in general obligation debt, coupled with revenue bond financing, which previously had not been used extensively by local governments. These trends were further accelerated in the sixties, with substantial new offerings of municipal bonds coming to the market. Unfortunately, many governing bodies and even chief administrative officials have failed to recognize their increased responsibilities resulting from the growth of long-term debt and the significant aspects of administration peculiar to revenue bond financing. It is the purpose of this chapter to examine these responsibilities.[a]

## Debt Records and Reporting

Adequate bond records must be maintained in local government for two general purposes. First, accurate record keeping, including maintenance of auditable ledgers as to the identity, purpose, and amount of all bonds, and the principal and interest payments made, is vital to the short-term fiscal operations of government, particularly so if the bonds are registered. The second purpose is that of financial planning. Bond records should be kept in such a form that at any time the principal and interest requirements on the total debt over the full maturity of all issues can be determined quickly and accurately. Such computations must be consulted to ascertain financial capacity to meet future capital construction requirements and in planning the retirement schedule for any new borrowing.

---

[a]The author is indebted to the earlier work of the Municipal Finance Officers Association in establishing the framework for much of this discussion through its publication, *Municipal Finance Administration* (Chicago: International City Managers' Association, 1962).

*The Bond and Interest Register*

The above requirements can best be met through the creation of a *bond and interest register* (Table 9-1), which provides entries that trace the complete history of each bond issue. The purposes of such a register are to collect in one place all pertinent information regarding individual bond issues, to assist in setting up a schedule of debt service requirements, and to collect information for posting to the bonded debt and interest payable ledgers.

Bonds and interest payable from general revenue sources must be distinguished from special assessment and revenue bonds payable from specific funding sources. The amount of unmatured bonded debt payable from general revenues and the amount of unmatured interest thereon should be carried in a separate self-balancing group of accounts independent of any municipal funds, since no present assets of these funds will be used to retire these bonds. In short, general obligation bonds are totally dependent on annual revenue collections (except where a sinking fund has been created).

A separate sheet is provided in the register for each bond issue. Information is provided at the top of each sheet as to the project title, purpose, and amount of interest; date of bonds, interest rates, price paid by underwriters, and where and when principal and interest are to be paid; and if the bond is registered, the date of registration, and the registered holder. Each register sheet is subdivided into several parts, showing the amount of interest due semiannually during the life of the bond, the amount of bonds to be retired each year (or the amount of the annual sinking fund contribution in the case of term bonds), and the total interest and principal due on each payment date.

Statistical data on interest and principal requirements at each payment date and on the outstanding balance should be computed for the entire life of the issue and entered in tabular form, with a separate line for each payment date. From such a record, an overall schedule of debt service requirements can be readily computed, and a *maturity and interest calendar* for all debt can be compiled as a means of checking revenue needs for debt service on a month-to-month basis. As new issues are marketed, the calendar must be adjusted and updated.

The *bonded debt ledger* (Table 9-2) contains a sheet for each bond issue, showing the amount of bonds originally outstanding, the amount retired to date, and the balance outstanding. A separate sheet is similarly maintained for each bond issue in the *interest payable ledger* (Table 9-3). As interest payments come due, they are entered in the "credit" and "balance" columns, and as payments are made the amount is entered in the "debit" column and the balance payable is reduced by a corresponding sum.

## Table 9-1
## Bond and Interest Register

City of _____

Bond and Interest Register

Title _____ (1)        Amount of issue _____ (6)
Authorized by _____ (2)    Purpose _____ (7)
Sold to _____ (3)       Coupon rate _____ (8) Payable _____ (9)
Price _____ (4)        Payable at _____ (10)
Bonds dated _____ (5)   Bonds payable at _____

| Date of Maturity | | | Interest Due | | Principal Due (11) | | Principal & Interest Due | Remarks |
|---|---|---|---|---|---|---|---|---|
| Month | Day | Year | Coupon Nos. | Bond Nos. | Amount | Bond Nos. | Amount | |
| | | | | | | | | |

(1) The title of the project should be fairly descriptive and, if possible, include location.
(2) The specific ordinance or referendum that authorized the issue should be recorded.
(3) Name of underwriting syndicate or holding company that purchased issue.
(4) The actual price paid, which may be lower or higher than amount of issue.
(5) With serial bonds the specific maturity date for each portion of the issue; for term bonds, the overall maturity date.
(6) The face value of the issue, that is, the total principal to be paid.
(7) The functional category in which the project can be associated.
(8) The interest rate.
(9) Usually semiannual, but occasionally on an annual basis.
(10) The specific location where interest and principal are to be paid.
(11) In the case of term bonds these two columns would be replaced by a column entitled "Sinking Fund Contribution."

**Table 9-2**
**Bonded Debt Ledger**

City of _____

Bonded Debt Ledger

Title of issue _____

Control account _____

Bond and interest record page no. _____

Fund _____

| Date | Explanation | Debit | Credit | Balance |
|------|-------------|-------|--------|---------|
|      |             |       |        |         |

## Table 9-3
## Interest Payable Ledger

City of _____ Interest Payable Ledger

Bond and interest record page no. _____ Title of issue _____
Fund _____ Control account _____

| Date | Explanation | Debit | Credit | Balance |
|------|-------------|-------|--------|---------|
|      |             |       |        |         |
|      |             |       |        |         |

## Accountability of Funds

Municipal accounting systems should be organized to ensure complete accountability of funds. A *fund* is a sum of money or other resources that is established to carry out specific governmental activities or to attain certain public objectives in accordance with specific regulations, restrictions, or limitations. Several such funds are tied directly to the responsibilities of debt administration. Each fund represents an independent fiscal and accounting entity. Municipal accounting systems must be organized so that at any time it is possible to determine the total resources, obligations, reserves, and surplus of each fund, as well as its current revenue, expenditures, receipts, and disbursements.

All revenues not accounted for in some special fund, and the activities financed by them, are covered by the *general fund.* Among the revenues usually included in this fund are general property taxes, licenses and fees, permits, fines, and penalties. All expenditures from this fund must be authorized in the general budget. It is this fund that provides the source of interest and principal payments for most general obligation bonds. Exceptions are found in those communities that have enacted a capital facilities tax or similar levy as an add-on to the general property tax. Such taxes and other revenues that are set aside by law for designated purposes are accounted for in *special revenue funds.*

*Special assessment funds* account for levies to finance specific public improvements or to provide services deemed to benefit properties against which such assessments are made. If such improvements are financed through bond issues, the special assessment fund must account both for the bond proceeds and for the special assessment revenue required to retire such bonds and to pay the requisite interest. *Bond funds,* on the other hand, account for only the receipt and disbursement of proceeds from the sale of general obligation bonds; such accounts are not involved with the repayment of the bonds which is accounted for through either the general fund or special revenue funds.

*Sinking funds* are used to account for the accumulation of periodic contributions and the earnings resulting from investments necessary to retire term bonds at their maturity. Sinking funds are used only to retire principal; interest payments are usually accounted for by the general fund. Individual sinking fund accounts should be established for each issue of term bonds. *Reserve funds* (or capital reserves) are similar to sinking fund accounts except that the contributions are accumulated in anticipation of capital expenditures, invested at some appropriate interest rate, and applied as needed to finance some capital project.

Finally, *revenue funds* (sometimes called utility or enterprise funds) are established to account for the financing of facilities and services that are self-supporting, that is, for which fees are collected or other charges made to the general public. Revenue funds may be subdivided into several different accounts (see chapter 7).

Two other fund categories have an indirect relationship to debt administration. *Working capital funds* are established to account for the financing of activities carried out by one agency for the benefit of other agencies in the same jurisdiction; examples include central shops, garages and motor pools, central stores, and other auxiliary activities internal to local government. Frequently, in revenue bonding a working capital fund equivalent to about one-tenth of a year's gross revenues is established. *Trust funds* account for assets held by a municipality as trustee; these funds are of two types—expendable and nonexpendable. Expendable trust funds are those that may be spent providing expenditures are in accordance with trust indentures and other governing regulations, for example, employee pension funds. Nonexpendable trust funds are those in which the principal (but not necessarily income) must be kept intact. Where state enabling legislation permits, trust funds may be invested in municipal bonds of either the controlling municipality or other municipalities.

*Financial Reporting*

One of the weakest points in municipal reporting relates to the development of annual financial reports concerning public debt. This shortcoming is unfortunate and unnecessary—unfortunate because such reports are critical to the basic credit rating of the municipality and are of interest not only to local officials and citizens but also to the holders of the municipality's bonds; and unnecessary because adequate debt records, as outlined above, facilitate the preparation of such reports, reducing this task to a relatively simple procedure.

Annual financial reports, as a minimum, should cover three categories of information regarding debt (see Table 9-4).[1] First, there should be a listing of all outstanding debt by type of issue broadly grouped according to purpose, that is, general obligation, special assessment, revenue, etc. For each bond issue the following information should be provided: date of issue, original amount, date of maturity, coupon rate, total interest, amount presently outstanding, and amount carried in sinking funds. All of this information can be taken directly from the bond and interest register. For each broad classification of debt, information should be presented as to the annual schedule of debt service, including interest, amortization requirements, and total debt service requirements. This statement should also include data as to the level of unfunded debt, that is, short-term borrowing that constitutes an obligation payable out of current revenues. The second information category deals with the overlapping debt of the community, that is, that portion of the debt of schools, counties, townships, and special districts payable from taxes levied by the reporting jurisdiction. The third entry should be a computation showing the status of the jurisdiction's legal borrowing capacity. If term bonds are outstanding there also

## Table 9-4
## Debt Statement

### Part 1

City of _____ County _____ State _____

Debt Statement as of _____ 19___

#### Direct Debt

| Purpose and Type of Debt | Original Amount | Date of Maturity | Coupon Rate | Total Interest | Amount Outstanding | Sinking Fund |
|---|---|---|---|---|---|---|
| *Bonded Debt* | | | | | | |
| General obligation bonds | $ _____ | _____ | _____ % | $ _____ | $ _____ | $ _____ |
| Special assessment bonds secured by general taxes | $ _____ | _____ | _____ % | $ _____ | | $ _____ |
| Secured by assessments only | | | | | | |
| Utility & public enterprise debt secured by general tax | $ _____ | _____ | _____ % | | $ _____ | $ _____ |
| (a) Water[a] | | | | | | |
| (b) Sewer[a] | | | | | | |
| (c) Other (specify) | | | | | | |
| Secured by enterprise revenue only | $ _____ | _____ | _____ % | $ _____ | $ _____ | $ _____ |
| (a) Water[a] | | | | | | |
| (b) Other (specify) | | | | | | |
| Bonds to fund deficit or floating debt[a] | $ _____ | _____ | _____ % | | $ _____ | $ _____ |
| Total direct bonded debt | | | | | $ _____ | $ _____ |

*Unfunded Debt*
  Tax anticipation notes    $ \_\_\_\_\_
  Delinquent tax notes        \_\_\_\_\_
  Bond anticipation notes    \_\_\_\_\_
  Bank loans                  \_\_\_\_\_
  Warrants                    \_\_\_\_\_
  Other (specify)            \_\_\_\_\_

Total unfunded debt          $ \_\_\_\_\_

Total direct debt             $ \_\_\_\_\_

## Part 2

### Overlapping Debt

| *Name of Overlapping Entity* | *Debt Limit* | *Gross Debt Less Sinking Fund* | *Reporting Jurisdiction's Share of Debt* |
|---|---|---|---|
| School districts | \_\_\_\_\_ % | $ \_\_\_\_\_ | $ \_\_\_\_\_ |
| County | \_\_\_\_\_ % | \_\_\_\_\_ | \_\_\_\_\_ |
| Township | \_\_\_\_\_ % | \_\_\_\_\_ | \_\_\_\_\_ |
| Other districts (list separately) | \_\_\_\_\_ % | \_\_\_\_\_ | \_\_\_\_\_ |
| Reporting jurisdiction | \_\_\_\_\_ % | \_\_\_\_\_ | \_\_\_\_\_ |

[a] Additional entries as necessary.

**Table 9–4 (continued)**

Part 3

## Debt Limit – Reporting Jurisdiction

| | |
|---|---|
| Assessed valuation | $ _____ |
| Debt limit – percent of assessed valuation | _____ % |
| Debt limit – amount | $ _____ |
| Total direct debt (as shown above) | $ _____ |
| Less: utility debt (not included in debt limit) | _____ |
| Special assessment debt (not included in debt limit) | _____ |
| Total debt to which debt limit is applicable | $ _____ |
| Legal debt margin | $ _____ |

## Composition of Sinking Funds

| | |
|---|---|
| Cash on hand or in banks | $ _____ |
| Federal securities | _____ |
| Bonds of reporting jurisdiction | _____ |
| Other municipal bonds | _____ |
| Other investments (specify nature) | _____ |
| Total | $ _____ |
| Amount of term bonds for which sinking funds are required | $ _____ |

# DEBT ADMINISTRATION

should be a sinking fund balance sheet, including the relation of sinking funds to actuarial requirements and a listing of current holdings.

If debt arising from the issuance of revenue bonds exists, the reporting process must also include complete and factual information covering the facilities that support such debt. In addition to the general information illustrated in Table 9-5, the report should include, as appropriate, the names of the corporate trustee, consulting engineers, and attorneys approving the legality of the issue. Most revenue bond ordinances also require that a report be prepared annually by an independent certified public accountant, including a current balance sheet and a statement of any contingent liabilities not shown in the balance sheet. Particular types of revenue bonds, such as those for water or sewer facilities, often require supplemental information, such as average daily supply and consumption, storage capacity, number of customers, consumption per customer, method of billing, legal provisions, etc.

Accurate and complete financial reporting is essential to the development of confidence on the part of investors and the general public as to the management of a municipality's financial affairs. The returns will more than repay the relatively small amount of time and expense involved in the preparation of such reports. In addition to the annual report an interim report covering much of the same information should be prepared midway in each fiscal year for distribution to those interested in the financial status of the municipality, that is, nonresident investors as well as local citizens.

## Short-term Borrowing

As shown in Table 9-4 the annual debt statement must record the status of the municipality's short-term debt. Short-term borrowing falls into three general categories—borrowing in anticipation of taxes, borrowing for operating emergencies not anticipated in the annual budget, and borrowing for capital purposes in advance of long-term bonds issues. Short-term borrowing takes various forms—bills, certificates, or notes sold to banks or other investors, bank loans, warrants paid out in lieu of cash, and unpaid bills and claims.

### Tax Anticipation Borrowing

Short-term borrowing in anticipation of current taxes and other revenues has become a routine procedure in all too many local governments. Such borrowing could and should be eliminated, resulting in the saving of interest costs, which are particularly heavy when short-term money rates one high, and in freedom from dependence on credit that is not always readily available. Tax anticipation borrowing can be held to a minimum if the due date for

## Table 9-5
### Financial Statement for Revenue Bonds

Name of issuer _____
Type of facility _____

### Part I. General Information & Protective Features

Amount of bonds authorized $ _____ Amount issued $ _____
Date of issue _____
Purpose of issue _____

#### Maturities

| Amount | Rate | Date | Amount | Rate | Date | Amount | Rate | Date |
|--------|------|------|--------|------|------|--------|------|------|
| $ ____ | ____ | ____ | $ ____ | ____ | ____ | $ ____ | ____ | ____ |
| ____   | ____ | ____ | ____   | ____ | ____ | ____   | ____ | ____ |
| ____   | ____ | ____ | ____   | ____ | ____ | ____   | ____ | ____ |
| ____   | ____ | ____ | ____   | ____ | ____ | ____   | ____ | ____ |
| ____   | ____ | ____ | ____   | ____ | ____ | ____   | ____ | ____ |

Call provisions (if any) _____

Estimate of gross and net revenues over next five years _____ (Date)
Gross $ ____ $ ____ $ ____ $ ____ $ ____
Net   $ ____ $ ____ $ ____ $ ____ $ ____
Peak requirement for interest and principal (or sinking fund) _____
Securities having prior claim to issue: amount _____
    Maturity _____ Peak requirements $ _____
Securities having equal claim to issue: amount _____
    Maturity _____ Peak requirements $ _____

# DEBT ADMINISTRATION

Securities having junior claim to issue: amount $ _____
Maturity _____ Peak requirements $ _____
Total additional claims against issue $ _____
Schedule & date of rates or charges for services of facility _____
  (Give particulars in a separate statement)
Controlling covenants of bond indenture & authorizing resolution _____
  (attach separate statement, if necessary)
Order of revenue disposition (flow of funds) _____
_____

## Reserve Fund Requirements

| Name of Reserve Fund | Requirements | Present Amount |
|---|---|---|
| _____ | _____ | $ _____ |
| _____ | _____ | _____ |
| _____ | _____ | _____ |
| _____ | _____ | _____ |

Method of investment of reserves _____

Covenants or legal requirements regarding rates to be charged _____
  (attach separate statement, if necessary)
Provisions for issuance of additional bonds _____
_____

Type and amount of insurance required _____ Amount $ _____

## Part II. Current Data on Revenues, Expenditures, and Financial Condition

|  | Fiscal Year 19__ | Previous Year | Two Years Previous |
|---|---|---|---|
| Operating revenues | $ _____ | $ _____ | $ _____ |
| Nonoperating revenues | _____ | _____ | _____ |
| Total gross revenues | $ _____ | $ _____ | $ _____ |

## Table 9-5 (continued)

| | | | |
|---|---|---|---|
| Expenditures: | | | |
|   Operations | | | $ _____ |
|   Maintenance | | | |
|   Other charges (if any) | $ _____ | $ _____ | $ _____ |
| Net income available for debt service | $ _____ | $ _____ | $ _____ |
| Interest paid on bonded debt | $ _____ | $ _____ | $ _____ |
| Principal paid | $ _____ | $ _____ | $ _____ |
|   Matured | | | |
|   Called | | | |
| Other charges against net income (specify) | $ _____ | $ _____ | $ _____ |
| Amount available for retirement of debt by call | $ _____ | $ _____ | $ _____ |
| Surplus (purpose applied) | | | |
| Total amount of bonds issued | $ _____ | | |
| Bonded debt at end of period | $ _____ | | |
| Bank loans at end of period | | | |
| Other unfunded debt | | | |
| Principal & interest on bonded debt in next fiscal year | $ _____ | | |
| Present book value of facility equipment & fixed assets | $ _____ | | |
| Method of depreciation _____ | | | |

initial property tax payments is set to coincide with the beginning of the fiscal years, and if a quarterly or semiannual installment method of tax payments is adopted. In addition to providing for greater harmony between tax collections and fiscal obligations, this approach generates a revolving fund to finance operations until taxes become due. Many large cities operating under this approach have not had to borrow or issue warrants in anticipation of taxes for several decades.

Should a municipality find it necessary to borrow in anticipation of taxes, the loans sought should be of no longer duration than the period in which current taxes are to be collected, usually corresponding closely to the delinquency date or some equivalent date for other revenues. If taxes are collected in installments, the loans should be for each period, or for such portion as necessary. The maximum amount of the loan should be governed by the amount of revenue anticipated. Sound management dictates that allowance be made for tax delinquency and that the level of borrowing be reduced accordingly. Unless the delinquency is abnormally high there is no justification for borrowing against delinquent taxes.

Budgetary estimates of revenue receipts in line with reasonable expectations, coupled with careful budget execution that makes allowances for delinquency, can enable a municipality to operate on a cash basis—whereby budgets are balanced not merely on the basis of revenues and expenditures but on the basis of actual cash receipts and expenses. This is a worthwhile objective for most municipalities to seek, since it not only eliminates the high cost of short-term borrowing, but also improves the general credit position of the city. Heavy reliance on short-term borrowing in periods of relatively easy credit may make a municipality highly vulnerable to financial difficulties in periods of restricted credit. It is difficult to shift to a cash basis operation under such conditions since tight money markets impact the private sector as well, resulting in reductions in investments that generate new tax revenues and increases in tax delinquency. The community that has operated on a cash basis, however, is in a much better position in terms of its options when economic conditions produce credit strictures. Thus, municipalities should avoid large accumulations of cash deficits and corresponding accumulations of delinquent tax borrowings, and thereby demonstrate fiscal solvency to obtain the most favorable rates should short-term loans become necessary.

Three administrative conditions must be maintained if a municipality is to operate successfully on a cash basis.[2] First, the administration of the tax system must be such that delinquent taxes are held to a minimum and those that do arise are collected without delay or undue expense. Second, estimates of annual receipts must be in line with reasonable expectations.[b] And third,

---

[b]In some states cities operate under a general budget law that requires current and delinquent tax receipts to be estimated each year on the basis of the percentage collected the previous year, with miscellaneous revenue estimates not exceeding the actual receipts of the previous year.

any budget deficits that arise must be eliminated as quickly as possible in succeeding budgets. In short, municipal officials must be willing to take a hard line on delinquent tax penalties, tax sales, and tax lien enforcement; they must base annual budgets on realistic estimates of receipts that reflect past experiences; and they must exercise fiscal sagacity should deficits arise.

### *Emergency Borrowing*

Nearly every municipality is faced periodically with the need to borrow on a short-term basis to meet unforeseen emergencies. The need to repair damage to public facilities resulting from storms, floods, or other natural catastrophies, unusually heavy demands for snow removal or "pot hole" repairs resulting from a severe winter, sudden, unanticipated shifts in particular operating expenses, or the award of a judgment against the city are all examples of such emergency expenses. Emergency borrowing supplies the needed funds that should then be provided for in the next budget unless the amount is so large as to require longer term financing.

While it is common practice for a municipality to deal with one lending institution, both in a fiscal advisory capacity and as the source of short-term funds, the rates paid for short-term loans by other municipalities should be reviewed carefully by following such financial publications as the *Financial Reporter* and the *Bond Buyer*. In this way municipal officials may be assured that rates required by local banks are not out of line with the general market.

### *Bond Anticipation Borrowing*

If used with discretion, short-term borrowing in anticipation of the issuance of bonds may be a fiscally sound strategy in terms of a municipality's overall debt administration. Certain public improvements may be undertaken in stages and bond anticipation notes may be issued as required to finance construction as the project progresses. When the improvement nears completion, or, if a sizeable project, when temporary borrowing reaches some predetermined level, permanent long-term bonds then may be issued and the temporary obligations retired. This procedure has the advantages of avoiding interest payments on the full amount of funding until it is actually required, of avoiding the accumulation of idle funds, and of greater flexibility in choosing the most advantageous time to market long-term bonds. When used as a means of financing the cost of planning, engineering, and other preliminary studies, it may even obviate the need for the long-term bond issue when a project is delayed or abandoned.

Bond anticipation borrowing, at times, may be used inappropriately as a means of evading prompt debt retirement.[c] Under normal conditions bond anticipation notes should not extend for more than one year; occasionally, however, borrowing for intermediate terms—three to five years—may be justified, particularly when interest rates for near-term maturities are abnormally low. Under such circumstances, it may be good fiscal management to spread moderate-sized improvements and replacements, unusual equipment purchases, and the cost of emergency items over several years.

*Deficiency Financing*

When a jurisdiction, either because its financial administrative procedures have been inadequate or its economic resources have temporarily declined to abnormally low levels, has accumulated a substantial cash deficiency that threatens a total breakdown in public operations, the only solution may be to spread normal current operating costs over future years. Fortunately, this rather unorthodox form of borrowing has been applied sparingly, except during the depression years of the thirties. Local conditions, however, may create financial situations that defy any immediate prospect of resolution except by this approach. Two principles should govern such deficiency financing, however. It should be for as short a period as possible, and it should be part of a definite plan to restore the jurisdiction to a firm basis of balanced fiscal operations.

One method of deficiency financing is to issue bonds secured by a pledge of back taxes. This approach provides the double security of a specific commitment of realizable assets as well as the city's full faith and credit; its drawback is that pledged back taxes are no longer available to help offset current tax delinquency or to balance the current budget. A second approach is to issue funding bonds to be retired exclusively from future budget appropriations without the specific pledge of uncollected revenues, thus freeing back taxes from any encumbrance of temporary debt and thereby creating a revenue base that may assist in balancing future budgets. It should be reserved, however, for those situations when there is no prospect of eliminating the financial stringency for some period.

**Debt Service and Retirement**

Prompt payment of all principal and interest requirements is the most direct evidence of sound debt administration and, consequently, the way in

---

[c]This may be undertaken as a political expediency, as when incumbent officials standing for reelection avoid long-term borrowing to keep the level of debt down during an election year by financing projects through short-term loans.

which a municipality administers its debt service is one of the most important factors in determining its credit standing for future borrowing. Even temporary defaults may adversely affect the municipality's ability to borrow at optimal interest rates. Therefore, well-defined administrative procedures, including advanced planning regarding the payment calendar and sound management of sinking funds and/or capital reserves, are essential to ensure regularity in the payment of interest and redemption of principal.

## *Establishing the Payment Calendar*

The first step in this phase of debt administration is to establish an information system regarding interest and redemption requirements over the life of the issue. For this purpose the bond and interest register and the parallel ledgers for bonded debt and interest form a ready basis for the development of a payment calendar. These records furnish the information necessary to identify total debt service requirements in the annual budget of the municipality, as well as the cash requirements and timing of individual issues. Whenever a new issue is marketed a schedule should be prepared showing the amount due on each principal and interest date and this schedule should be incorporated into the consolidated payment calendar to show the timing of total cash requirements. If sinking funds or other debt service funds are involved, these considerations must also be taken into account in the annual budgetary process.

It is not enough, however, merely to make the appropriate allocations for principal and interest payments in the annual budget; the allotment of funds must be so timed as to provide cash when it is needed. Thus, budget officials must plan ahead to ensure that early payments required in the following year can be met, that is, that a sufficient fund balance is carried over from the previous fiscal year and/or provision is made in the tax collection system to generate an adequate level of funds in the early part of the new fiscal year.

It is preferable that payment of all principal and interest requirements be made through a single agency of the city, that is, the city treasurer's office or some other designated fiscal agent. In many cities such payments also require authorization by the director of finance or the controller. It is usually a good administrative practice to appoint a bank or trust company in the financial center in which a municipality's bonds are marketed to serve as its paying agent. Funds are deposited with the paying agent in advance of interest (and principal) due dates, and the agent oversees the payment of coupons and matured bonds as they are submitted. This arrangement is preferred by investors; it saves the municipality considerable routine work; and the paying agent is equipped to handle this function at a relatively low cost.

## Management of Sinking Funds

A *sinking fund* is the mechanism for accumulating funds for the payment of term debt at maturity. Such funds should not be confused with other debt funds sometimes required by law for interest payment or payment of principal and interest of serial bonds.[d] Sinking funds are for the payment of principal of term bonds or of deferred or irregular serials that require similar treatment.

The management of a sinking fund requires that annual contributions be made to a segregated account that, when combined with the return from the investment of these account funds, will provide an amount sufficient to cover the required principal payments when the bonds reach maturity. A sinking fund, therefore, provides the mechanism for spreading the cost of repayment over the life of the bond issue so that large, irregular demands will not be made on the municipality's annual budget. The amount earmarked each year for the sinking fund should be determined by: (a) the dollar value of bonds to be retired, (b) the number of payments to be made into the account, and (c) the anticipated rate of earnings on the invested funds. Given these three factors, the annual amount ($N$) that must be placed (generally at the end of the year) at compound interest ($r$) for a term of $n$ years to create a sinking fund ($S$) can be computed by applying the following formula:

$$N = S \cdot \frac{r}{(1 + r)^n - 1}$$

For example, a municipality seeking a fund of $200,000 at the end of 10 years, with funds invested at six percent compound interest, would be required to make 10 annual payments of $15,173.60 to a sinking fund. Early payments or payments in semiannual or quarterly installments, of course, would increase sinking fund earnings and reduce the total requirements to be raised from taxes.

In some states municipalities are required to establish a fixed tax rate for sinking fund purposes. This requirement has been criticized by some municipal finance experts on the grounds that over the life of such bonds the tax base will be subject to wide variations, and as a consequence, the accumulated funds may be inadequate to meet the principal requirements. Others have argued that a "sinking fund tax" (or even better, a capital facilities tax) is sound in principle, but what is needed is greater flexibility in the administration of such a tax.

Sinking fund requirements should be recomputed on an annual basis. It

---

[d] Many of the same principles outlined in this section, however, also apply to the management of so-called "capital reserves" or reserve funds, the basic difference being that such reserve funds are built up prior to capital investment.

may be possible to lower future requirements should a surplus in excess of actuarial requirements develop. It is sound debt management practice, however, to absorb any significant surplus gradually over several tax periods rather than effecting a large reduction in payments in a single year. Should a deficit arise in the sinking fund (i.e., should it fall behind actuarial requirements), adjustments should be made as soon as feasible by increasing the level of payment into the fund and/or seeking new investment opportunities that will produce a greater rate of return. While the requirements for each issue of term bonds must be computed separately, in many states it is permissible to use a surplus in one tax-supported issue to offset a deficit in another. When a substantial deficit develops, there is a temptation to refund (refinance) the entire issue; this approach violates sound principles of debt administration, however, and should be used only as a last resort. The practice of refunding is discussed further in a subsequent section.

A major problem in the use of sinking funds (and one contributing to the severe restrictions on this method of bond financing in many states) lies with the technical difficulties of managing the trust accounts. This is particularly true in smaller communities where few persons possess the specialized knowledge required to oversee such investments. Two general principles should govern the administration of sinking funds: (1) investments should be sound, and (2) funds should have adequate liquidity.

In most states municipalities are restricted by law to the types of sinking fund investments that can be made, usually being limited to federal, state, and municipal bonds.[e] Within these categories, investments should be limited to high-grade issues and should exclude special assessment bonds and revenue bonds on projects within unproven earning power. The same type of analyses should be made of another municipality's offerings as investors made of the investing community's issue. Bonds with equal security at times vary in terms of their yield, and the relationship of maturity to yield tends to vary with changes in market conditions. Study of the municipal bond market, therefore, is essential to secure the maximum earnings for sinking funds compatible with the safety of investment.

While there is some controversy surrounding the practice, investment of sinking funds by a municipality in its own securities has certain advantages. It avoids the complex analysis required when selecting bonds of other municipalities, it simplifies the administration of the sinking fund and lowers costs, and it affords a ready market for a municipality's borrowing that may be particularly important when the general market is uncertain. The principal argument against this practice is that the sinking fund may become a dumping ground for excessive amounts of tax notes issued to offset inadequate administration; under

---

[e]In the past, municipal sinking funds have encountered difficulties by investing in real mortgages, railroad stock, and other private corporate obligations.

such conditions the security for payment is little more than a collection of IOUs.[f] With proper safeguards, however, this investment practice remains a viable alternative to other forms of sinking fund investments. When a municipality invests in its own new bonds, it does not increase its net debt any more than if it sold these bonds to outside investors, and when it buys in its outstanding bonds, it decreases its net debt just as much as if it invested in other municipals. In either case the taxpaying capacity in relation to net debt is not affected.

In addition to security, sinking fund investments must have liquidity—the maturities of the various investments must be so timed that funds will be readily available to retire the municipality's term bonds when they come due. Without careful investment planning it may be necessary to sell the holdings of the sinking fund in the open market, with the possibility of taking a loss. Greater flexibility often can be attained by investing in several different types and sizes of offerings, rather than a single set of securities.

To the extent permitted by state law, sinking funds should be consolidated to simplify transactions, to save time in putting funds to work, and to secure a better investment position. Separate fund accounts should be maintained, however, for administrative purposes in calculating annual contributions. Securities purchased from sinking funds should be kept in a safe deposit box, covered by fire and theft insurance, and with limited access by responsible officials. Many municipalities require that safe deposit boxes be opened only in presence of two designated officials. Whenever possible, sinking fund investments should be registered.

An independent audit of the sinking fund should be made annually in addition to regular auditing by the comptroller of all sinking transactions. The par value of securities normally is used in determining the asset value of such investments. The annual report of sinking fund investments should show the purchase price as well as the par value, with premiums and discounts amortized over the term of the fund.

It should be evident from this discussion that the management of sinking funds is a complex and difficult task—one that should not be undertaken without adequately trained personnel and proper safeguards to protect the integrity of the funds. As has been noted, many states have legislated against term bonds secured by sinking funds insofar as general obligation borrowing is concerned. However, such funds remain as a viable means of financing many revenue-producing projects, whereby annual contributions to the funds are generated by the self-supporting facilities. In such cases adherence to the guidelines outlined above is especially important since such debts often are

---

[f]This approach has also been used as a means of distributing securities to some favored investor without provision for competitive bids—a very questionable, and in some state, illegal practice.

outside the protection of the full faith, credit, and taxing power of the municipality.

### *Recording and Cancellation of Coupons and Bonds*

The final step in servicing a municipal debt involves the recording and cancellation of coupons and bonds that have been paid. Following each scheduled payment, coupons and bonds must be checked to determine if any have not been redeemed; some will always be slow in coming in, and occasionally, some may be missing permanently. Records must be maintained for several years after the final maturity date in most cases. Cancelled bonds and coupons must be filed carefully, with bonds arranged by issue and number and coupons filed in serial order, with a separate bundle for each bond issue maturity date. Cancelled coupons and bonds are usually kept for several years, after which they are destroyed by shredding or burning. Many commerical banks and trust companies that serve as paying agents for municipal bonds include as a part of their services all phases of recording and cancellation. These banks and trust companies provide the municipality with a certified list of the cancelled and destroyed bonds and coupons. Many municipalities mandate that the disposition of these documents take place in the presence of the director of finance or the comptroller and at least one other municipal official. The "mortgage burning" ceremony is one that still has considerable significance for many small communities.

### *Callable Bonds*

At times municipal bonds are issued with the provision that they may be "called" for payment prior to their maturity date. Use of the call feature, of course, depends on the availability of specific legal authorization, and the provision for call must be incorporated in the original bond contract. While most readily applicable to term bonds, callable bonds may be used in conjunction with serial issues without undue complications in the marketing process if they are applied to bonds outstanding after the issue has run for several years.

The call provision may take a wide variety of forms. Bonds may be made callable at any time after the date of issue; in practice, however, the privilege is normally exercised with appropriate notice only on interest payment dates. A bond issue may be made part callable and part noncallable. Bonds may be made callable at par or at a premium.

While callable bonds usually carry slightly higher coupon rates, there are conditions under which the call feature has important advantages. During periods of high interest rates there is always the possibility that bonds can be

DEBT ADMINISTRATION 191

called and refunded at lower rates at some time during their term, either because the market has changed or because the municipality has improved its credit standing. Conversely, there is little advantage, and possible disadvantages, to insist on the callable feature during periods of low interest rates. Callable bonds may afford greater flexibility in the municipality's debt structure. If the initial retirement schedule proves to be too rapid, or a period of declining revenues is encountered, bonds may be recalled and refunded at the most favorable time. There is also the opportunity for the acceleration of debt retirement. Callable bonds are especially appropriate when the earning capacity of a revenue producing enterprise is uncertain. The callable feature can be used to avoid overly rigid fiscal responsibilities, while at the same time, permitting more rapid retirement if the project's revenue capacity expands.

While callable bonds offer an additional dimension of flexibility in debt administration, they also carry additional responsibilities for the administrator in terms of the decisions required to determine if and when such provisions shall be required and if and when the call option will be exercised. Since most investors insist on a premium for callable bonds, the resultant net savings must be carefully considered, for example, a one percent premium on a callable bond placed at seven percent interest would wipe out any net savings if the bonds were refunded at six percent. Factors such as the additional flexibility of debt structure, however, may outweigh the factor of relative cost.

### Refunding, Conversion, and Defaults

The final points to be covered in this discussion of debt administrative responsibilities relate to the issues of refunding, and particularly forced refunding, and default on debt service. The process of refunding applies to callable bonds, as outlined above, to bonds at maturity, which should be avoided under sound principles of debt administration, and to bonds in default, which may be necessary to avert fiscal catastrophe. Defaults fall into three general classifications—minor defaults of a temporary nature, more extensive defaults that are not the result of any fundamental weakness in credit structure, and serious defaults that necessitate the complete revision of outstanding debt obligations.

#### *Refunding of Mature Bonds*

The practice of refunding mature or maturing bonds should be avoided if at all possible, and if necessary, should be undertaken with great discretion.[g]

---

[g]Refunding normal serial maturities merely for the purpose of effecting a temporary tax reduction has no justification; the motivation is usually political. There have been some flagrant cases in which bonds have been refunded just prior to elections to "improve" the record of the incumbent office holders even though there was every indication that

The time-honored rule in municipal finance is that the terms of bonds should correspond with the useful life of the financed project, and, therefore, bonds should be paid off at maturity. At times, however, conditions arise that may force the refunding of debts to eliminate irregularities in the existing debt schedule arising from overly optimistic retirement schedules or from sudden shifts in economic conditions beyond local control that lead to changes in the municipality's revenue system. Refunding may also be a preferable alternative to emergency borrowing, particularly when a good credit relationship has been established in connection with outstanding bonds and significantly higher costs would be incurred by new borrowing.

Should the refunding of a maturing issue become necessary, the refunded bonds must be scheduled into the debt retirement program as soon as possible within the fiscal capacity of the municipality. This is necessary to avoid an excessively long retirement period for the refunded debt that would seriously limit future borrowing. On the other hand, the retirement period of the refunded bonds should be of sufficient duration to avoid the need for further refunding.

### Forced Refunding

Faced with the prospect of default on bonds or serious disruption of governmental operations, by reason of a sudden shift in fiscal resources beyond local control, a municipality may find it absolutely necessary to refund outstanding debts to avoid financial disaster. Unfortunately, such forced refunding to avoid default frequently encounters unfavorable market conditions, since the economic factors that give rise to the need for refunding may be widespread, as was the situation confronting many cities during the depression years of the thirties. Under such circumstances a municipality may be unable to sell refunded bonds to new investors but instead be forced to negotiate with existing bondholders for the exchange of their holdings for new maturities. Since bonds may be widely held and bondholders difficult to locate, this can be a most cumbersome undertaking, particularly if the issue has undergone several transactions in the secondary trading market.

Forced refunding should never be unduly postponed; it is a matter of good fiscal administration to anticipate such emergencies and to take the necessary steps with sufficient lead time to resolve the problem in an orderly and businesslike manner. A frank and open presentation of the municipality's fiscal problems is likely to secure understanding and cooperation from major bondholders.

---

the existing debt could be carried out according to the established schedule without undue strain on the community's resources. Such practices result in unstable fluctuations in the tax levy, rising debt trends, and serious disruptions of the debt structure of the community.

## Defaults

Defaults on debt service, no matter how satisfactorily resolved, are likely to result in a sharp decline in a municipality's credit standing, producing skepticism among lenders and major difficulties in negotiating favorable interest rates on future issues. Even temporary defaults, if allowed to extend beyond the normal 90-day grace period, may result in the removal of a city from the listing of securities approved for fiduciary investments.

By far the largest number and most severe municipal defaults took place during the depression era from 1929 through 1938 (see Table 9-6). The total debt of all governmental units whose defaults were recorded during this period was approximately $5.5 billion, or approximately 30 percent of the average net municipal debt outstanding.[3] This figure includes some large defaults that lasted for a relatively short period or were of a technical nature, the most prominent of which was that of New York City, with total indebtedness of slightly over $2.5 billion. The default of New York City lasted for only a few days and involved some general obligation notes issued in anticipation of delinquent tax collections. The $5.5 billion figure also included approximately $160 million of indebtedness in default by the state of Arkansas, $2.1 billion in default by local governmental units with governmental units of less than 5,000 or more, $190 million in default by local government units of less than 5,000 population, and $400 million in default by special purpose and special assessment districts.[4]

Prior to the depression, municipal debt had increased at a very significant rate. The two most apparent reasons for this rapid growth were the speculative overdevelopment of real estate that took place in the twenties and the lack of realistic debt limitations. In some cases the officers of real estate companies became officials of municipal units and promoted bond issues to develop their real estate holdings. Special assessment or local improvement districts often were created to permit the improvement of undeveloped and speculative areas. Debt limits in most cases were expressed in terms of certain ratios of debt to assessed valuation; changes in assessed values or the issuance of debt in the name of an overlapping unit made these limits ineffective.[5]

The rapid expansion of municipal debt in the years prior to the depression, however, was not necessarily the cause of default in most cases. A more direct cause was the fact that local government's ability to pay these debts did not increase nearly as rapidly as the debts themselves. As wealth, income, and assessed values plunged downward in the early years of the depression, municipal revenues also declined rapidly. The decrease in tax revenues, for which there were no adequate substitutes, was not accompanied by commensurate declines in expenditures. Many governmental units were confronted with rising debt service charges, the results of unwieldy debt structures contracted in the past, and with increased demands for unemployment relief payments.

Table 9-6
Number of Recorded Defaults on Municipal Bonds, Selected Dates, 1933–38

| Date | States | Counties | Cities & Town | School Districts | Other Districts | Special Purpose Districts | Total Political Subdivisions |
|---|---|---|---|---|---|---|---|
| Jan. 1, 1933 | 1 | 172 | 309 | 135 | 28 | — | 645 |
| Jan. 1, 1934 | 1 | 324 | 669 | 343 | 60 | 369 | 1,766 |
| July 1, 1934 | 1 | 359 | 758 | 562 | 168 | 537 | 2,385 |
| Jan. 1, 1935 | 1 | 349 | 851 | 623 | 209 | 683 | 2,716 |
| Aug. 1, 1935 | 1 | 337 | 843 | 882 | 283 | 906 | 3,252 |
| Jan. 1, 1936 | 0 | 309 | 816 | 840 | 272 | 922 | 3,159 |
| July 1, 1936 | 0 | 274 | 767 | 831 | 245 | 1,054 | 3,171 |
| Jan. 1, 1937 | 0 | 258 | 735 | 806 | 238 | 1,014 | 3,051 |
| Jan. 1, 1938 | 0 | 186 | 755 | 732 | 245 | 1,164 | 3,082 |

Note: As this table indicates, the total number of recorded defaults more than trebled between 1932 and 1936. The number of units recorded as being in default reached a peak of 3,252 on August 1, 1935. It may be noted that counties peaked somewhat earlier, followed by cities and towns, school districts, other districts, and special-purpose and special-assessment districts that did not peak until May 1, 1938. In 1935 the number of recorded defaults represented less than two percent of 175, 417 governmental units in the United States. Allowing for the fact that some very small defaults were undoubtedly not reported and that not every eligible governmental unit had issued debt, it seems apparent that a relatively small proportion of the United States municipal units with debt outstanding in the early 1930s defaulted during this period. For those that did, however, the experience was quite traumatic.

Source: Adapted from George H. Hempel, *Measures of Municipal Bond Quality* (Ann Arbor, Mich.: Bureau of Business Research, University of Michigan, 1967), table 3, p. 53.

While most municipalities with unbalanced budgets were able to borrow enough to cover their operating deficits, this borrowing added to the already large fixed charges of many communities, and was actually encouraged by the availability of capital at fairly low interest rates in the late twenties. In 1932 and 1933, however, municipal borrowing was greatly curtailed as a consequence of rapidly rising interest costs, bank failures, and loss of public confidence in municipal bonds. Therefore, many municipalities with deficit budgets were forced to default.

*Types of Default*

Minor and temporary defaults, involving failure to meet the maturity payment of a single security or temporary postponement of interest payments, may be the result of unanticipated declines in revenue collections, the shutting off of normal lines of bank credit, and/or a temporary inability to market refunding bonds. Such minor defaults can usually be corrected by various means without disturbing the general debt structure or further interrupting debt service. Adjustment strategies include: (a) payment during the grace period from belated tax receipts, (b) short-term bank loans, (c) small issues of refunded bonds, or (d) exchanges of securities.[6] This latter strategy is particularly effective for relatively recent bond issues; bondholders are contacted and negotiations are conducted to effect an exchange of outstanding bonds for new securities that more closely fit the community's long-term ability to pay.

A second, more serious class of defaults involves municipalities that have encountered such fiscal problems as peak debt service in period of low-paying capacity, serious breakdowns in the local economic base, and/or abnormally high tax delinquency. Under such circumstances the municipality may experience difficulties in meeting current accounts as well as long-term obligations. Adjustments usually are effected by refunding or partial refunding a few years' obligations in order to free up some fiscal resources to meet current operating costs. This may be accomplished without a major disturbance of the general debt structure and without any scaling of debt. Once current obligations are returned to a more balanced basis attention can be redirected toward long-term obligations that may require further readjustments to reflect sound principles of debt administration.

The third class of defaults, which fortunately has occurred infrequently since the thirties, involves situations in which the municipality is confronted by abnormally high debt, severely curtailed revenues, and significant accumulations of operating deficits, with little or no prospect for correction except through a comprehensive refunding plan. Such a plan usually involves not only a complete reconstruction of the entire debt retirement schedule but also a scaling down of interest and even principal payments. The scaling of debt, that is, actual reduction in the municipality's commitments, becomes necessary when the total obligation is clearly beyond the local government's capacity to pay. Investors are naturally reluctant to forego any portion of their contractual rights and particularly so with regards to principal. Unless the situation is hopeless, they tend to prefer extensive postponements, with the expectation that subsequent community growth and development will eventually bring protection to their investment. Thus, when necessary, scaling can be more readily accomplished through a reduction in interest rates.

*Steps in Readjustment*

Insofar as possible a municipality should take the initiative in readjustment and in planning and implementing the refunding plan. While serious defaults require time for careful investigation and deliberation before commitments are made, immediate and continuing action indicates both competence and good faith and may gain for the municipality the necessary cooperation from investors to successfully resolve the pending financial crisis. Putting off the necessary readjustment or attempting to cover up the fiscal state of the municipality merely exacerbates the uncertainty, increases expenses, and ultimately may result in the municipality being placed in receivership, whereby local officials no longer can control the readjustment process. When it is evident that readjustment is unavoidable, an official statement should be issued to the municipality's creditors, giving notice of its inability to meet its obligations and identifying the causes, probable duration, and steps contemplated to correct the situation as expeditiously as possible.

If uncertainty and obscurity clouds a defaulted debt, bondholders are likely to become suspicious and distrustful. The municipality should open its records to bondholders and their representatives and should distribute a summary analysis of its financial status and capacity to pay, followed by frequent factual reports of financial and economic trends. Only by such means can the municipality retain the initiative and assure the most constructive negotiations with its creditors.

Should the magnitude of default dictate extensive readjustments, a complete investigation of all relevant factors—financial, administrative, and economic—is a prerequisite to the planning of corrective action.[7] Reliable experts in the field of municipal administration and finance should be consulted and a competent adviser retained. The relationship between outstanding obligations and normal capacity to pay must be ascertained, and operating costs should be examined to determine if they afford a basis for appropriate adjustments. The municipality must evaluate its financial status and relation to resources and liabilities, both immediate and future. In short, the municipality should approach its creditors with full knowledge of where it stands and of the reasonable expectations regarding its capacity to recover from its financial difficulties.

To be successful the refunding plan must first provide mechanisms to release current accounts from all accumulated deficiencies, as well as financing procedures that will assure the maintenance of balanced operations. While a brief hiatus from full debt service obligations may be necessary, such postponement is valid only if it is used as a means of systematically adjusting current accounts. Such refunding as is necessary should postpone the retirement of as little debt service as possible; the replanning of the debt structure should not trade a difficult immediate situation for an impossible future one. Callable bonds should be used in the refunding plan to the extent possible, as they permit a re-refunding at lower interest rates if justified by market conditions, as well as the potential of accelerating the retirement process when conditions improve.

Adjustments of serious defaults, at best, involve a process of compromise, in which there is little opportunity for impartial settlement. Furthermore, refunding arrangements may contain the potentialities for recurring financial difficulties for several decades in the future. The experiences of many communities in the thirties offer ample support for the necessity of sound debt policies. Traces of the consequences of default are still evident in some of these communities even today.

## Summary

Debt administration is one of the most significant responsibilities of local government officials. It requires that comprehensive and systematic procedures be established for the maintenance of records, for annual financial reporting, and for the accountability of funds. Such procedures are essential to development confidence on the part of investors and the general public as to the overall management of a municipality's financial affairs.

Recognition of the pitfalls and potentialities of short-term borrowing forms an important part of debt administration, as does the desirability of cash basis operations. A careful examination and, if necessary, readjustment of a municipality's tax collection system may obviate the need for short-term borrowing except for emergency purposes. The use of bond anticipation borrowing, however, may provide a fiscally sound strategy if applied with discretion.

Prompt payment of all debt service charges is the most direct evidence of sound debt administration. To achieve this objective it is necessary to establish an information system regarding interest and redemption requirement over the life of all outstanding issues. The management of sinking funds or other debt service funds may form a critical part of the debt administrator's responsibilities.

Recording and cancellation of coupons and retired bonds must be undertaken in an orderly manner to insure the proper closing out of debt obligations.

Finally, the procedures of refunding and the safeguards against defaults should be clearly understood by local officials. While most states have adopted legislative measures to circumvent the financial catastrophe faced by many governments in the thirties, ultimate responsibility still rests with officials of local government to adopt debt administrative procedures that will protect their community from "mortgaging its future."

# 10 Cost-Benefit and Cost-Effectiveness Analysis

**Cost-Benefit Analysis**

The resource allocation problem is as old as mankind. Ever since the Garden of Eden, man has been concerned with the allocation of scarce resources to achieve certain specified objectives. Then, it was the problem of allocating four fig leaves between two people. Today, it is the question of how to spend billions of dollars to satisfy the needs of millions of people.

In theory the problem is quite simple; it is difficult only in practice. In theory one merely must decide what is wanted (specification of ends), measure these wants (quantification of benefits sought), and then apply the limited means available to achieve the greatest possible value of the identified wants (maximize benefits). In contemporary society the *means* become public budgets, and, therefore, the problem is one of maximizing benefits (once specified and quantified) for any given set of fiscal inputs (i.e., specified and quantified costs).[1]

In the late sixties, concurrent with the development of program budgeting and PPBS systems, more systematic analyses of benefits and costs associated with public programs became an increasingly important part of the budget makers responsibilities. While it may be assumed that governments have always considered both the benefits and costs associated with various programs requiring the allocation of limited fiscal resources, these examinations often have been haphazard, with little systematic effort to quantify benefits or to include all costs and benefits appropriate to particular alternatives under consideration. Too often, the public decision-making process has been dominated by a "money first" approach, whereby only a certain amount of revenue is available and therefore expenditures are limited to this amount, or has manifested an "absolute needs" approach, whereby a given set of expenditures is deemed so essential that it must be undertaken regardless of cost.[2] However, due partly to the increasing scope of governmental activities and expanding interest in more systematic budgeting and partly to the development of improved techniques and computational capacity that permit more thorough evaluations, there has been a significant increase in emphasis on various cost-benefit forms of analysis.

*Elements of Cost-Benefit Analysis*

Cost-benefit analysis can be defined as a systematic approach to the examination of benefits and costs of a particular public program, setting forth those critical factors that should enter into the evaluation of the desirability of the program, and frequently involving the analysis of several alternatives for the attainment of public objectives. Cost-benefit analysis seeks to determine whether or not a particular program or proposal is justified, to rank various program alternatives appropriate to a given set of objectives, and to ascertain the optimal course of action to attain such objectives. In contrast to more traditional forms of evaluation that tend to be short-range and narrow in scope, cost-benefit analysis operated within an extended time horizon and, in so far as possible, considers both the direct and indirect factors involved in the allocation of resources.

Cost-benefit studies may be undertaken as a preliminary to budget preparations or as a continuing program to ascertain optimal expenditure patterns and budget recommendations. In general there are two principal approaches to cost-benefit analysis: (1) the *fixed cost* or *fixed budget approach,* where the objective is to maximize benefits for an established level of costs or a predetermined budget allocation; and (2) the *fixed benefits approach,* where the objective is to ascertain the minimum level of expenditures necessary to achieve some specified level of benefits. As discussed in a subsequent section, this second approach is sometimes called "cost-effectiveness analysis." The fixed level of benefits or budget may be specified by someone "outside" the analysis, that is, it may be a "given," and may be treated as such by the analyst. Very often, however, a major part of the analysis will center upon a determination of this constraint. Either (or both) of these approaches may be used, depending on the context of the allocation problem. In any event, the objective is to facilitate comparisons among alternatives, and for this purpose it generally is necessary to hold something constant.

The problem becomes much more complex when both benefits and costs vary. One approach to this type of problem is to solve for the optimal size of the public sector (this is the approach advocated by Paul Samuelson), which reverts the original problem back to a fixed budget form. Given the widest possible range of production possibilities, the allocation problem still focuses upon a scarce supply of resources. A second approach for less than universal solutions permits the decision maker to see how sensitive outputs are to marginal changes in inputs and vice versa. Thus, the analyst may use several levels of costs and benefits (e.g., high, medium, and low) to investigate the sensitivity of the rankings of alternatives.

The crux of cost-benefit analysis lies in a statement of the problem, for if the problem is explicitly known, one already has a basis for its solution. As Anatol Rapoport has observed, the first step in solving a problem is to state it.

The statement usually involves a description of an existing state and a desirable state of affairs where the factors involved in the discrepancy are explicitly pointed out. The success with which any problem is solved depends to a great extent on the clarity with which it is stated. In fact, the solution of the problem is, in a sense, a clarification (or concretization) of the objectives.[3]

Vague statements of the problem lead to value methods, where success is doubtful or at best, erratic. The more a given situation is extensionalized, the better the classification of the problem, and the greater the promise of a successful solution. A common source of error in allocation decisions, however, arises from a traditional emphasis on finding the *right answer* rather than on asking the *right question.* As Peter F. Drucker has observed: ". . . the important and difficult job is never to find the right answer, it is to find the right question. For there is few things as useless—if not as dangerous—as the right answer to the wrong question."[4]

In the traditional formulation of the cost-benefit approach, as first outlined by Otto Eckstein,[5] the allocation problem is clarified through the identification of: (1) an objective function, (2) constraints, (3) externalities, (4) time dimensions, and (5) risk and uncertainty. Roland N. McKean has restated these components of the cost-benefit approach in systems analysis terms as follows:[6]

1. Definition of program objectives, that is, what achievements need to be made in order to yield the desired benefits
2. Identification of alternative courses of action (policies and programs) to achieve stated objectives
3. Estimation of costs associated with each alternative
4. Construction of mathematical models to assist in the estimation of benefits and costs and the subsequent choice between alternative policies, programs, or systems
5. Development of a *criterion of preferredness* or *social discount rate* to assist in the selection of the "best" alternative

Selecting an *objective function* involves the identification and quantification (in dollar terms, to the extent possible) of the benefits and costs associated with each alternative under consideration. In this way various alternatives can be compared with each other and against the cost of attaining the desired benefits. The question of what constitutes an objective function and how the first three items in McKean's process definition are obtained is discussed in further detail in a subsequent section.

*Constraints* specify the "rules of the game," that is, the limitations within which a solution must be sought. Frequently, solutions that are otherwise optimal must be discarded because they violate these imposed rules. Constraints are incorporated into mathematical models as parameters or boundary conditions.

*Externalities* are those factors—inputs (costs), outputs (benefits), and constraints—that initially are excluded from the statement of the problem in order to make it more manageable. Ultimately, the long-range effects of these phenomena must be considered. This step is usually undertaken after the objective function or model has been tested carefully and the range of feasible and acceptable alternatives has been narrowed.

In examining the time dimensions of various alternatives, it is necessary to delineate life-cycle costs and benefits. *Life-cycle costs* can be grouped as follows: (1) research and development—costs associated primarily with the development of new programs or capabilities to the point where they are ready for operational use; (2) investment—costs beyond the "start-up" development phase, frequently in the form of capital construction or capital equipment costs; and (3) operations—recurring costs of operating, supporting, and maintaining a program or capability. Economists often look beyond these fundamental cost concepts to opportunity costs, associated costs, and social costs. *Opportunity costs* are the value of lost chances to do other things, that is, spending money one way preempts the opportunity to spend it another way. *Associated costs* are "any costs involved in utilizing project services in the process of converting them into a form suitable for use or sale at the stage benefits are evaluated."[7] Associated costs are incurred by beneficiaries as they avail themselves of the services of a particular project. *Social costs* may be visualized as "subsidies" to those persons impacted by a particular project.[8] Similarly, direct and indirect benefits to be derived from a new program or expanded capacity under an existing program or project must be delineated carefully over the expected life of the proposed undertaking.

To evaluate costs to benefits it is necessary to predict the future—and in so doing the analyst encounters the problems of risk and uncertainty. Estimating benefits associated with long-lived assets requries that future socioeconomic settings and tastes of people be predicted, a difficult task at best. While future costs may appear to be relatively easier to estimate, they are not if past experience is any indication. *Risk* can be associated with situations in which a probability distribution can be assigned to the various outcomes, that is, all possible outcomes can be enumerated or described and a likelihood of occurrence can be assigned to each one. The term *uncertainty* can be associated with those situations in which, while the possible outcomes may be known, there is no good way to estimate the probabilities of their occurrence. One of the objectives of cost-benefit analysis is to reduce uncertainty by providing more information concerning the consequences of various alternative courses of action and to bring risk into some range of tolerance.

Having examined these component elements of cost-benefit analysis in a definitional context, it is necessary to explore some of the issues pertinent to each of them. In so doing it is necessary to sojourn briefly in the realm of welfare economics as a prerequisite to understanding the various criteria that have been developed for cost-benefit analysis.

## The Objective Function

The goals of any public program must be defined clearly if any systematic form of analysis is to be applied. What does the program seek to attain? What is it that we wish to maximize in terms of benefits? In theory the answer is simple: to maximize welfare, happiness, ultimate satisfaction, the "good life," and so forth. These are very broad objectives and are difficult to quantify. Therefore, many analysts prefer to choose very specific objectives, such as, to bring 2,000 acres under cultivation by providing adequate water supply through an irrigation project. The more sharply an objective can be defined, the greater the contribution that cost-benefit analysis can make in the public decision-making process. However, it must be recognized that many programs and projects have multiple objectives, that, at times, may even be contradictory. Furthermore, long-range programs and projects may involve goals and objectives that are much less well defined than those programs focusing on immediate objectives. In such cases the analyst may be confronted with four choices.[9]

1. He could put aside the needs of the broader society and assign value only to the needs of individuals or relatively small groups, maximizing the benefits to be gained by these individuals or groups.

This is frequently the approach when, in the interest of formulating a manageable cost-benefit analysis, the goals and objectives of a particular public program or project are narrowly defined, for example, the irrigation project. The objective is to optimize for some relatively specific project objectives; but in so doing, a suboptimal solution may result in so far as the broader society (community or region) is concerned.

Even if this approach is followed, however, three other choices remain:

2. The analyst could play the game "everybody wins," that is, he could manipulate the pieces in the game so that all individuals gain in terms of social or economic welfare.
3. He could play the game "someone wins, and no one loses," that is, move the pieces so that at least one individual gains and no one is worse off (this approximates the concept of Pareto Optimality).[a]
4. He could play the game so that "the winners outweigh the losers," that is, move the pieces so that there is a net gain, the gains outweighing the losses (this approximates the Kaldor-Hicks Criterion).

The approach that most economists and policymakers seem to prefer is game 4.

---

[a]Near the turn of the century Vilfredo Pareto set forth a principle of welfare economics that was to guide the field for nearly four decades. He asserted that an economic policy is desirable if it makes some persons better off (in their own judgment) while making no one worse off (in his own judgment). Conversely, a policy is undesirable if it makes some persons feel worse off and no one feel better off. A policy makes some better off and some worse off is not evaluated by the Pareto criterion.

Since the Kaldor-Hicks Criterion is basic to this fourth approach, it may be useful to review this concept.

In 1939 Roy Harrod, using the repeal of British laws pertaining to restrictions on the import of grains to illustrate his position, asserted that the gain to the whole society could be considered to be alike. In response Nicholas Kaldor denied the need for such interpersonal comparison, saying:

> Where a certain policy leads to an increase in physical productivity, and thus of aggregate real income . . . it is *possible* to make everybody better off than before. . . . There is no need [that] nobody in the community is going to suffer. [It] is quite sufficient to show that even if all those who suffer . . . are fully compensated for their loss, the rest of the community will still be better off then before.[10]

Kaldor's proposition received prompt support from J. R. Hicks,[11] and in a subsequent paper, Hicks presented his own statement of what is now generally referred to as the Kaldor-Hicks criterion: "If A made so much better off by a change that he could compensate B for his loss and still have something left over, then the change is an unequivocal improvement."[12]

The Kaldor-Hicks criterion is important because it is essentially the same as the criterion used in cost-benefit analysis. If benefits exceed costs on a given project, the project would be deemed desirable according to the Kaldor-Hicks criterion, that is, by proceeding with the project and then having the gainers compensate the losers, a position that is Pareto-better than the initial position could be attained. Whether or not the compensation actually takes place, according to Kaldor, is a political and not an economic question; the economist is satisfied if the compensation *could* take place. In short, public policy issues can be measured according to the Kaldor-Hicks criterion, but may require other policies in order to ensure economic and/or social equity.

A further modification to the Kaldor-Hicks criterion (and thus to the concept of Pareto Optimality) should be noted. Shortly after the criterion was proposed, Tibor Scitovsky pointed out that situations can arise in which the gainers from an economic change are able to compensate the losers and still be better off, and yet the losers also could profitably "bribe" the gainers to return to the initial position.[13] This observation suggests that the Kaldor-Hicks criterion can produce contradictory evaluations, the contradiction arising when there is more than one source of "gain" (e.g., short-run versus long-run) to be derived from a particular decision. For example, in negotiating a new labor contract, management offers the union representatives a long-range profit sharing plan as a trade-off for a substantially higher immediate increase in wage levels. The union representatives would be faced with the question of giving up more immediate returns (and thereby becoming "losers" in the short run if inflation erases the proposed increases in wage levels) in order to obtain a greater share of the returns of long-run productivity. The negotiations that might transpire to arrive at a mutually agreeable settlement would depend on the level of risk taking that both management and the union was willing to accept with regards to the long-range payoffs of the profit-sharing plan.

The contradiction in the Kaldor-Hicks criterion led to a further modification by I.M.D. Little, who suggested that: "An economic change is desirable (and increases welfare) if it causes a good redistribution of wealth, and if the potential losers could not profitably bribe the potential gainers to oppose it."[14] Thus, the Little criterion suggests that an economic change is desirable (and therefore should be supported by public policy) if: (1) the person(s) passing judgment on the change approves of the gains and losses that people would receive, *and* either (2a) the change is desirable according to the Pareto criterion *or* (2b) a position cannot be achieved that is Pareto-superior to that caused by the change by having the losers (resulting from the change) give something to the gainers in order to dissuade them from supporting the change.[15] Part 2b of the Little criterion (sometimes called the Little efficiency criterion) resembles the second part of the Kaldor-Hicks criterion. The two criterion, however, are not the same, as they require significantly different information to evaluate a given change. Even with full information they may produce quite different answers. Essential to the Scitovsky-Little criterion is the requirement that the gains and losses be examined both before and after a sequence of moves or changes in positions.

The Little efficiency criterion, however, is only part of the Little criterion. Part 1 suggests that an economic change would be deemed desirable only if the person passing judgment regards the gains and losses as *fair* and *just.* The Kaldor-Hicks criterion does not even raise the issue of fairness; it only asks whether the gainers are able to compensate the losers. And herein lies a crucial defect in welfare economic decisions (and cost-benefit decisions) that are based strictly on the Kaldor-Hicks approach. The mere possibility of compensation may be insufficient to assuage the losers, particularly when the hope of compensation lies in the rather distant future (as when politicians and economists assert that wage-earners should willing accept higher taxes as a curb to inflation, while encouraging big businesses to expand their profits, justifying their actions on the grounds that the "losers" will eventually benefit from the long-run increases in productivity and economic expansion). It is little consolation for those evicted from their homes by urban renewal to know that the persons who moved into the renewed area would still be in a preferred position even if they had to pay enough extra rent to provide "compensation" to the former residents. Furthermore, if the former residents are poor and the new residents prosperous, the sum of money that would be transferred if compensation was to be made, in some relevant sense, is worth considerably less to the new residents than it is to the former residents.[16] Therefore, without further, often complex analysis, it cannot be inferred that the change is worth more to the new residents.

There seems to be general consensus among welfare theorists that part 1 of the Little criterion is a very significant addition to the principles of economic/social welfare. Even if the Kaldor-Hicks criterion (like the Pareto criterion) provides answers that, in principle, can be verified, it ignores the issues of fairness and equity, and, therefore, it is ethically inappropriate.

What does all this economic/social welfare theory have to do with cost-benefit analysis, particularly as it might be applied to the allocation of public resources for long-term capital investment? It is simply to make the point that the goals and objectives of public programs and projects seldom can be viewed in terms of maximizing the "goodies" or minimizing the "baddies". Uncertainties, incommensurables, issues of social and economic equity, and other factors may prevail, thereby leading to quite different objective functions and/or criteria than those suggested by classical welfare economics. In a series of possible outcomes the public decision maker may be faced with the need to: (1) maximize the minimum possible gains or benefits to be derived from a resource allocation decision (the maximum criterion), or (2) to minimize the maximum possible regrets (i.e., losses) that are likely to arise from such a decision (the minimax criterion). Either of these situations may arise in the course of deciding how scarce public resources are to be allocated among competing social and economic needs. And there are a host of other possible objective functions or criterion that could be applied to such decisions. The significant point is that the critical first step in knowing what must be done is knowing what is wanted.

### Further Pitfalls in Setting Objectives

Aside from the issue of what criteria to apply in ordering a public decision (resource allocation) problem, there are many other pitfalls in establishing objectives. Among these, four are worth noting:[17]

1. Regarding means as ends
2. Not regarding means as ends
3. Improper quantification—to measure is to know, but not necessarily the right thing
4. The objective of not revealing objectives

Decision making frequently involves a process of choosing a prior end that is one of many means to a further end. As Herbert A. Simon has observed:

> In the process of decision those alternatives are chosen which are considered to be appropriate means for reaching desired ends. Ends themselves, however, are often merely instrumental to more final objectives. We are thus led to the conception of a series, or hierarchy, of ends. Rationality has to do with the construction of means-ends chains of this kind.[18]

In developing a cost-benefit analysis, the issue often is how far back along a means-ends chain the analyst should go in selecting ends or objectives as they relate to a particular area of concern. Not going back far enough may result in "suboptimization," involving attempts to achieve inputs or means that may or may not be correct or most efficient (or effective) in achieving specified ends or outputs. Failure to pursue the means-ends chain with sufficient vigor or to give adequate consideration to appropriate alternative ends may result in an incomplete or incorrect statement of the objectives to be attained through the choice of a particular alternative course of action. As Simon has observed: "Rational decision-making always requires the comparison of alternative means in terms of the respective ends to which they will lead."[19] Although analysts may attempt to isolate alternative courses of action as distinct means, in actual situations a complete separation of means is usually impossible, for alternative means seldom are "value neutral," that is, they imply some ends. Particular means used to attain particular ends may also have consequences other than the specific objectives being sought, and these other "unsought ends" or "spillover effects" must be given their proper weight in considering the desirability of the selected means. The choice of ends in a means-ends chain also involves the element of time, which, in turn, imposes two problems:(1) the realization of a particular end at a given time may result in the need to relinquish other alternative ends for that time period; and (2) may result in limitations being placed on the ends that may be achieved at some other times.

Paradoxically, the second classic mistake or oversight in identifying objectives is not to consider a means an end when indeed it is.[20] In many areas of life *process* is highly valued, in and of itself, over any set of finite objectives that might be articulated. In a democracy, for example, effective justice is not a legal system that fills the jails or maximizes convictions per dollar of expenditure for law enforcement. It is, instead, a system that guarantees *due process,* wherein the rights of the individual are preserved. Similarly, in the political arena the means toward reaching group decisions through democratic processes—freedoms of speech and assembly, the right to vote, etc.— may be valued more than the actual outcome of these processes. While policy analysts and decision makers may be accused of not seeing the forest for the trees (for assuming means to be ends), they also may be guilty of sacrificing the trees to preserve what they believe to be the forest.

While quantification is at the very core of science, the improper use of quantification may lead to distorted results in the art and science of governmental decision making. If critical means or ends are unquantifiable, then superficial precision with numbers within the analysis may be irrelevant, and even harmful, to the solution. Indeed, many ends may be obscured by a myopic fetish-like preoccupation with numbers.[21] The techniques of cost-benefit analysis seeks to select that alternative which involves the lowest total cost at the highest ratio of user benefits to total costs. An inability to quantify more fundamental measures of systems effectiveness, however, has lead to the identification of cost minimization as the most important goal in many such analyses. The application of cost-benefit techniques to many complex public decision situations cannot be accomplished successfully until there is full recognition that human values are as much an interacting component of such decision processes as economic considerations, fiscal constraints of budgeting, and factors of physical development. As Simon Ramo has observed, the critical task of analysis "is the handling of the 'unknown' factors . . . weighing the importance of human reactions, for example, or guessing political influences, or generally dealing with technological issues that lend themselves little to measurement and quantification."[22] Whereas the method of evaluating alternatives by focusing on measurable costs and benefits may be applicable to some decision situations, in many areas of public management, alternatives must be evaluated by somewhat more subjective considerations, careful "guesstimations," and even "gut feelings."

There are situations, times, and places in which it may be inappropriate to try to achieve agreement on objectives or even to spell out precisely the objectives sought. This is frequently the situation facing political coalitions or ideologically fragmented groups—to gain total clarity of objectives would likely result in the breakdown of a tenuous unity. Thus, it should not be assumed that obscure and obfuscated objectives are always totally lacking in function. Many times, objectives are uncertain, conflicting, and subject to significant changes as the decision process unfolds. The premature establishment of objectives in such situations may result in a decision inertia of dysfunctional proportions. Thus, it may be more appropriate to formulate objectives based on a feedback process as the situation unfolds.

*Criteria for Analysis*

Cost-benefit analysis seeks to rank alternatives regarding the utilization of scarce resources. In the typical situation several projects are competing for limited funds, with each project pursuable at one or more scales or levels of funding. The problem may be to choose which of several projects to pursue and then to choose the optimal level or scale from among several alternatives available. Another approach may be to choose the best scale for each project and then to choose the best alternative among the several projects, each taken at its optimal scale. Under either of these approaches, a ranking function is sought whereby alternatives can be identified and compared. Frequently, particular predesigned projects are examined, and the only decision to make is "Go" or "No Go." While such situations do not allow the freedom to choose an optimum, the ranking function may still assist in making such decisions.

The first step, therefore, in cost-benefit analysis is to select an indicator of "success," that is, a numerical index that will yield a higher value for more desirable alternatives and lower values for less desirable ones.[23] Conceptually, such an indicator involves the "maximization" of something. For example, businessmen are reputed to maximize profits. Such an indicator is maximized indirectly by adopting the alternative course of action for which the selected index has the highest value. At times the maximization problem can be dealt with more effectively by minimizing something, for example, costs. Frequently, the goal of cost-benefit analysis is stated as the maximization of benefits and the minimization of costs; in reality, however, both cannot be done simultaneously.[24] Cost can be minimized by spending nothing and doing nothing, but in that case no benefits result. Benefits can be maximized within a particular project by spending until marginal benefits are zero, but such action may require much more money than is available. Therefore, some composite criterion is needed. Three obvious choices are:

1. Maximize benefits for given costs
2. Minimize costs while achieving a fixed level of benefits
3. Maximize net benefits (benefits minus costs)

The first cost-benefit criterion to be used in the quantitative evaluation of alternatives was the *benefit/cost ratio,* introduced by the Flood Control Act of 1936.[b] This act established the requirement that water-resource development projects could not be initiated unless the evaluation showed that a project's expected "benefits to whomsoever they may accrue [are] in excess of the estimated costs." From this initial application, benefit-cost ratios have been used extensively in evaluations of not only water resource programs but also human resource (training and education), urban renewal, transportation, and health programs.[25] A second criterion, well established in the business world and reflecting a legacy of prominent economists such as John Maynard Keynes and Kenneth Boulding, is the *internal rate of return.* A third, and more recently developed indicator is *net benefits,* that is, benefits minus costs, which purports to summarize all relevant factors and therefore, is intuitively appealing. Before discussing each of these criteria in more detail, however, it is necessary to examine the concepts of life-cycle costs and benefits, present value as applied in cost-benefit analysis, and the techniques of discounting.

### Life Cycle Costs and Benefits

Cost-benefit analyses are usually undertaken in connection with investment projects of relatively long duration or life. Such projects typically have a sizable

---

[b]Methods of quantitative evaluation were advocated and explored in theory for over a century before practical applications were developed. One of the earliest and still one of the more sophisticated methods was devised by the Frenchman, Jules Depuit, in 1844 (reprinted as "On the Measurement of the Utility of Public Works," in *Readings in Welfare*

planning or development cost, followed by larger construction or procurement costs, and by a stream of relatively smaller costs of operation, maintenance, and repair. Such projects, therefore, must be examined in terms of *life-cycle costs,* as previously enumerated. Life cycle costing stems from the concept that the funds necessary to undertake a program or project initially should not be the primary consideration, nor should the funds required in any particular time period dominate the decision. Rather, the decision to undertake a particular course of action should take into account the total cost impact over time.

*Research and development (or planning) costs* are one-time costs and, in effect, are a function of the nature of the project or program. Such costs are essentially insensitive to the number of units that will be made operational once the project is initiated or the length of time the project will be in operation. *Investment costs,* on the other hand, are a function of the number of units planned; the greater the number, the higher the investment costs. Such costs generally are one-time costs per unit. *Operating costs* depend on both the number of units in the project or program and the length of time that such units must be operated, supported, and maintained. In short, R & D costs are concerned with development decisions and the choice among feasible alternatives; investment costs concern the extensiveness of the project's employment or the relative importance that the project will occupy in some larger system; and operating costs concern the manner and length of time that the project will be operated (this may be a function of effectiveness and thus in some cases a variable cost). Figure 10-1 depicts cost categories over the life cycle of any project or program.

Benefits may also vary widely over the life of a project or program. There may be a time lag between the initiation of a project and the realization of the first increment of benefits. Benefits may build gradually or may accumulate rapidly; they may reach a peak and decline rapidly or may taper off slowly. In short, the timing of costs and benefits cannot be ignored. It is not sufficient merely to add the total benefits and subtract the total costs that are estimated for a given project or alternative. Rather, it is necessary to consider the "stream" or pattern of benefits and costs over time and to calculate a measure that can reflect the impact of deferred benefits or future costs.

### Present Value and Discounting

Benefits that accure in the present are "worth" more to their recipients than benefits that occur some time in the future. Similarly, funds that must be invested today "cost more" than funds that must be invested in the future,

---

*Economics,* ed. Kenneth Arrow and Tibor Scitovsky (Homewood, Ill.: Richard D. Irwin, Inc., 1969), pp. 225–83).

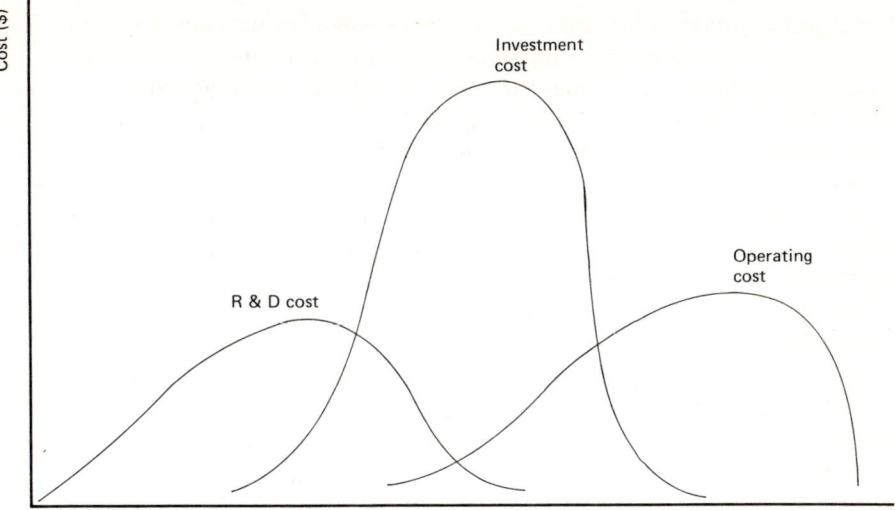

**Figure 10-1.** Life Cycle Costs Plotted Against Time

since presumably one alternative use of such funds would be to invest them at some rate of return that would increase their value. Therefore, it is necessary to calculate the *present value* of both costs and benefits by multiplying each stream by an appropriate discount factor. This factor gets smaller as the costs or benefits occur farther in the future. If the alternative is to invest available funds at some interest rate ($i$), then an appropriate discount factor can be expressed as:

$$\frac{1}{(1+i)^n}$$

where ($i$) is the relevant interest rate per period, and ($n$) is the number of periods into the future that the benefits or costs will accrue. If, as is the usual case, ($i$) is positive, the farther an event is in the future, the smaller is its present value. A high discount rate means that the present is valued considerably over the future; that is, there is significant time preference,[c] a higher regard for

---

[c]A.C. Pigou (*The Economics of Welfare,* first published in 1912) asserts that most people have a "defective telescopic faculty" when it comes to benefits, that is, they tend to prefer the present over the future more than they should. This leads to too much consumption and not enough investment (and therefore, saving) for the future. Eckstein (*Water Resource Development,* pp. 99ff) and William J. Baumol (*Welfare Economics and the Theory of the State* (Cambridge, Mass.: Harvard University Press, 1952), pp. 91-93) maintain that at least two time preferences exist: one for individuals acting on their own and one for individuals acting collectively. Both agree with Pigou that the benefits to future generations should be accorded more weight than the market gives them.

present benefits than for equal future benefits, and/or a willingness to trade some amount of future benefits for current benefits. The technique of discounting is illustrated for three different discount rates in Table 10-1.

Two reasons exist for discounting public projects: (1) to reflect a social preference for earlier over later benefits; and (2) to reflect the opportunity costs of public investment, that is, the cost of investing in project A now over investing in project B at some time in the future. S.A. Marglin has suggested that these factors can be combined into a "synthetic rate of discount" that reflects both social preferences and opportunity costs.[26] The following example may help to explain this concept, while illustrating some of the difficulties in identifying an appropriate discount rate for many public projects.

Assume that for a given society to sustain an optimal rate of growth, its Gross National Product must be maintained at an annual average increase of 6 percent. Further assume that in the private sector the current rate of return on marginal projects is 15 percent, that is, each additional $1,000 invested yields $150 each year. Capitalized at the rate of 6 percent (the social rate of discount), this $150 annual return has a present value of $2,500, that is, discounting the annual return of $150 over an extended time period and summing the discounted values yields $2,500. Therefore, the marginal benefit-cost ratio in the private sector is 2.5 (i.e., $2,500/$1,000). On this basis, in order to maximize present value of output in the economy, no public sector project should be undertaken unless it has a marginal benefit-cost ratio greater than 2.5; to do so would result in an opportunity cost in the private sector in excess of the benefits, that is, to invest a like amount in the private sector would yield a greater benefit.

To place this example in more generic terms, assume that private sector investment opportunities yield at the margin $a$ in present value per dollar invested (in the example $a$ equaled $2.50). The marginal dollar yields $r$ each year in perpetuity (e.g., $r$ equals 15% in the illustration). Therefore, the opportunity cost is the present value per dollar invested, or $a = r/i$, where $i$ is some social rate of discount.[d] If public projects yield $b$ per year for $n$ years, such projects should be undertaken only so long as:

$$\$b \left[ \frac{1 - (1+i)^{-n}}{i} \right] > \$a$$

that is, the present value of benefits arising from public projects must exceed the present value of opportunity costs in the private sector.[e] Substituting the

---

[d]This equation is simplified in two respects: it assumes that public investments displace private investments on a dollar for dollar basis and that all the benefits of public investment are consumed rather than reinvested.

[e]That portion of the equation within the square brackets represents the sum of the finite series, $(1+i)^{-1}, (1+i)^{-2}, \ldots, (1+i)^{-n}$. This can be verified by letting $i = 0.06$,

## Table 10-1
### Discounting $1,000 Over Ten Years

| Year | Discount Factor @ 4% | Value | Discount Factor @ 5% | Value | Discount Factor @ 6% | Value |
|---|---|---|---|---|---|---|
| 1 | 0.961538 | 961.54 | 0.952381 | $ 952.38 | 0.943396 | $ 943.40 |
| 2 | 0.924556 | 924.56 | 0.907029 | 907.03 | 0.889996 | 890.00 |
| 3 | 0.888996 | 889.00 | 0.863847 | 863.85 | 0.839619 | 839.62 |
| 4 | 0.854804 | 854.80 | 0.822702 | 822.70 | 0.792093 | 792.09 |
| 5 | 0.821927 | 821.93 | 0.783526 | 783.53 | 0.747258 | 747.26 |
| 6 | 0.790314 | 790.31 | 0.746215 | 746.22 | 0.704960 | 704.96 |
| 7 | 0.759917 | 759.92 | 0.710681 | 710.68 | 0.665057 | 665.06 |
| 8 | 0.730690 | 730.69 | 0.676839 | 676.84 | 0.627412 | 627.41 |
| 9 | 0.702586 | 702.59 | 0.644608 | 644.61 | 0.591898 | 591.90 |
| 10 | 0.675564 | 675.56 | 0.613913 | 613.91 | 0.558394 | 558.39 |
| Total | | $8,110.90 | | $7,721.75 | | $7,360.09 |

first equation for opportunity cost into the second, a necessary and sufficient condition for a public investment to be efficient becomes:

$$\$b \geq \frac{r}{1-(1+i)^{-n}}$$

Therefore, if, as in the example above, the marginal dollar yield ($r$) in the private sector is 15 percent and the social discount rate is 6 percent, $1,000 invested for 10 years in the public sector would have to yield approximately $340 in annual benefits to be considered an efficient investment[f], that is, an annual yield of $340, discounted at 6 percent and summed over 10 years produces a present value of $2,500, equaling the present value of $1,000 that produces an annual yield of 15 percent in the private sector.

Thus, a discount rate that synthesizes social time preference ($i$) and the rate of return lost in the private sector by undertaking a public activity may be defined as follows (this synthetic rate is $s$):

$$\frac{1-(1+s)^{-n}}{s} \equiv \frac{1-(1+i)^{-n}}{s}$$

Thus, the condition for an efficient public investment becomes:

$$b \cdot \frac{1-(1+s)^{-n}}{s} > 1$$

that is, every dollar invested in the public sector, when discounted at the synthetic rate, must yield more than one dollar of net benefits (total benefits less opportunity costs).

Public investment analysts argue that if a social rate of discount is used by government, then it should apply to private investment as well.[27] In this way all potential investments, public and private, that compete for the same funds would be considered on an equal basis with respect to time preference. In reality choices are never made regarding public and private investments in this fashion; furthermore, private firms do not use a social rate of discount but rather respond to market interest rates, calculated through various methods of *benefit investment analysis,* such as: (1) net cash proceeds, (2) cash payback period, (3) proceeds per dollar of outlay, (4) average annual proceeds per

---

$n = 10$, and $b = \$1,000$, solving the equation and comparing the results with the last column in Table 10–1.

[f]This figure is calculated as follows: $(1 + 0.06)^{-10} = 0.5583948$; $1 - 0.5583948 = 0.4416052$; 0.15 divided by 0.4416052 = 0.3396699; and 0.3396699 times $1,000 = \$339.67$.

dollar of outlay, or (5) average income on the book value of the investment. (Each of these methods of benefit investment analysis is examined briefly following the discussion of internal rate of return criterion.) Finally, a unique, universally accepted social rate of discount does not exist; the concept is controversial, and there is little consensus as to its numerical value (although there is a good deal of consensus as to its desirability). As a consequence most applications of cost-benefit analysis continue to apply a discount rate that reflects current market interest rates.

### Benefit-Cost Ratio

The gross benefit-cost ratio is defined as the present value of the benefits divided by the present value of the costs (or average annual benefits over average annual costs), which can be expressed mathematically as follows:

$$R = \frac{\sum_{n=0}^{N} B_n (1 + i)^{-n}}{\sum_{n=0}^{N} C_n (1 + i)^{-n}} = \frac{B}{C}$$

Thus, if the discounted stream of benefits over the life of the project equals $400,000 and the discounted stream of costs equals $320,000, the benefit/cost ratio is 1.25.

A variation of the basic benefit-cost ratio has been advanced, whereby operating costs are eliminated. This approach is summarized by the equation:

$$R_N = \frac{B - P}{K}$$

where all quantities are expressed in present value terms, $P$ represents operating costs, and $K$ represents capital costs. Returning to the previous example, assume that the present value of operating costs represents $80,000 of the total stream of costs; subtracting operating costs from both benefits and total costs results in a net benefit-cost ratio of 1.333. Thus it may be seen that the net benefit-cost approach tends to emphasize return on invested capital,[g] whereas the gross

---

[g]As operating costs account for an increasingly larger portion of total costs, discounted to present value, the net benefit-cost ratio becomes larger. In the above example, for instance, if operating costs account for half of the discounted total costs, the net benefit-cost ratio becomes 1.5.

benefit-cost ratio usually will lead to more capital-intensive projects because it emphasizes economizing on both capital and operating costs. Net benefit-cost ratios may be preferable for private enterprises in which capital is more constraining than operating expenses, especially when taxes are considered. Some economists argue for the use of gross ratios in the public sector on the basis that legislatures should consider operating costs ($P$) as well as capital costs ($K$) and give agencies credit for saving on $P$ by allowing them to spend more on $K$. [28]

### Internal Rate of Return

The internal rate of return ($r$) is defined by the following equation:

$$r: \sum_{n=0}^{N} \frac{B_n}{(1+r)^n} = \sum_{n=0}^{N} \frac{C_n}{(1+r)^n}$$

It should be noted that the internal rate of return is not set equal to anything: The right-hand side of the equation is the present value of costs and the left side is the present value of benefits. The internal rate of return is that interest rate ($r$) that makes the two sides of the equation equal; this interest rate is then compared with the cost of capital.

For favorable projects the undiscounted sum of benefits usually exceeds that of costs, since costs usually accrue first, and therefore, the sum of benefits must be considerably larger to equalize the present value. A numerically high $r$ means that even if the future benefits are discounted severely, the two sides of the equation are equal, whereas a lower $r$ would mean that the undiscounted benefits exceed costs by a lesser amount.

To illustrate the application of this criterion, assume that a firm is confronted with the decision whether or not to initiate a new product line that will require a first-year investment[h] in start-up costs of $100,000, with estimated annual operating costs of $40,000, and a shut-down cost of $70,000 in the fifth year of operations (at which time major modification in the product line dictate a new investment decision). It is estimated that the firm will have three years of operations in this product line during which time gross profits will average $100,000 annually. In short, for an investment of $290,000 over five years the firm will obtain a return of $300,000. The costs and benefits of this project are illustrated in Table 10-2.

---

[h]Some analyses set the base year at 0, and thereby do not discount initial investments (or benefits). Other analyses use the discount equation from the first year onward. As long as the technique is applied consistently, there is little difference in the comparative results, although present values will differ in numerical terms between these two approaches.

COST-BENEFIT AND COST-EFFECTIVENESS ANALYSIS 217

**Table 10-2**
**Internal Rate of Return Calculations on Five-year Project**

| Year | Benefits | Costs | Discount Rate @ 11.6% | Present Value Benefits | Present Value Costs |
|---|---|---|---|---|---|
| 1 | 0 | $100,000 | 0.89606 | 0 | $ 89,606 |
| 2 | $100,000 | 40,000 | 0.80292 | $ 80,292 | 32,117 |
| 3 | 100,000 | 40,000 | 0.71946 | 71,946 | 28,778 |
| 4 | 100,000 | 40,000 | 0.64468 | 64,468 | 25,787 |
| 5 | 0 | 70,000 | 0.57767 | | 40,437 |
| Total | $300,000 | $290,000 | | $216,706 | $216,725 |

As illustrated by the calculations on the right-hand side of Table 10-2, an internal rate of return of approximately 11.6 percent provides *one* solution to the equation. If capital "costs" less than 11.6 percent (in terms of the interest rate in the current market), the proposed project would be desirable (in practice, the firm would likely examine alternative investments and select that alternative that exhibits the greatest margin of return).

One problem with this approach is that $r$ is not necessarily unique, that is, more than one value may satisfy the equation. The equation for internal rate of return becomes a polynomial equation as soon as the project has more than two years of economic life (i.e., when $n$ is two or greater). An example may show this difficulty. Assume the benefits and costs of a three-year project are as follows:[29]

| Year | Benefits | Costs |
|---|---|---|
| 0 | 0 | $1,600 |
| 1 | $10,000 | 0 |
| 2 | 0 | 10,000 |

Perhaps the project is a farm labor camp or mining enterprise that has a relatively low set-up cost, is used for one year, and is levelled after a year of operations. To find $r$ the following equality must be solved:

$$0 + \frac{10,000}{(1+r)} + \frac{0}{(1+r)^2} = 1,600 + \frac{0}{(1+r)} + \frac{10,000}{(1+r)^2}$$

Multiplying through by $(1 + r)^2$ gives a quadratic equation, which when solved, yields two values for $r$, that is, $r = 0.25$ and $r = 4.00$. Thus an internal rate of return of 25 percent or 400 percent will bring the equation has two roots; higher degree equations, of course, will have still more. Reexamining the first example, however, there is one and only one solution to the equation. In the first example the sum of the undiscounted benefits is $300,000 and that of costs is $290,000, whereas in the second example, the sum of undiscounted benefits is $10,000 and that of costs is $11,600. Therefore, it may be concluded that a necessary and sufficient condition for the existence of a single positive internal rate of return is an excess of undiscounted benefits over costs.[30]

The usual case of a profitable investment is shown in Figure 10-2. The diagonal line in Figure 10-2 represents the net present value (benefits minus costs) at different rates of interest. At discount rates below $r$ a project has positive present value of net benefits; at discount rates above $r$ projects have negative present values. The rate that makes a present value zero is the internal rate of return $r$.

The internal rate of return provides a reasonably good measure of investment potential when all alternatives are of the same order of magnitude. When the alternatives are of different scales it is of lesser practical value, since very little is revealed about the absolute size of the net benefits in the application of this technique.

*Other Techniques of Benefit Investment Analysis*

Long-term investment decisions in the private sector focus on four basic areas:

1. Equipment replacement—techniques of operations research have made significant contributions in the determination of when it is more efficient (i.e., more profitable) to replace existing equipment rather than repair and maintain it.
2. Cost-saving investments—designed essentially to increase efficiency, to replace outmoded procedures, to modernize facilities, etc.; this form of investment often includes the acquisition of land for future expansion, options of new sites, etc.
3. Expansion investment—investments in internal and external diversification, new product lines, etc., often including investments in research and development operations.
4. Required capital investments—dictated by external forces such as competition or by law.

The principal objective of such investments is the maximization of profits, i.e., to obtain the maximum return on stockholder's investments. Industries frequently average as much as 50 percent of their total resources in long-term investment commitments. Much of this, of course, is involved in the development of an appropriate cash flow (annual profit margin) and in routine replacement. Factors affecting investment decisions include: (1) the overall philosophy

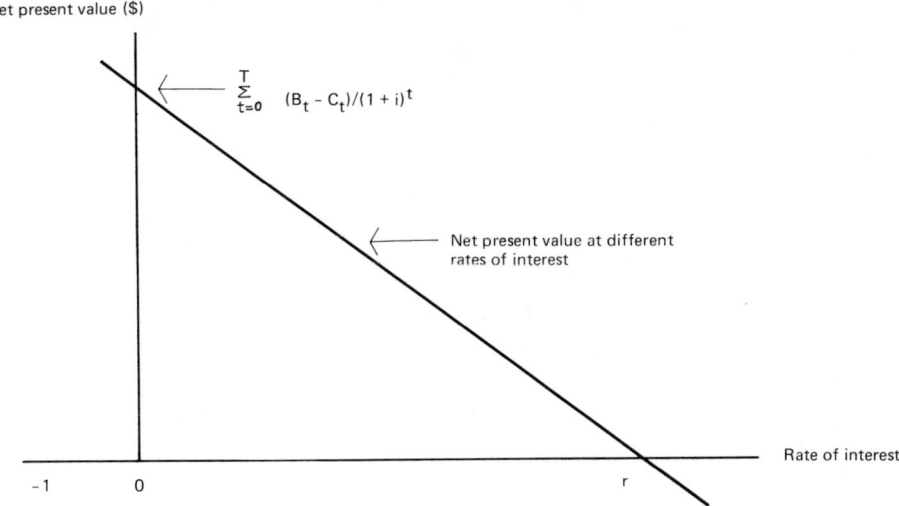

**Figure 10-2.** Solving for $r$: Benefits in Excess of Costs

of management (conservatism versus risk-taking), (2) market analysis and forecasting (many firms have a larger planning staff than many major cities), (3) the decisions of competition—there is a certain amount of "keeping up with the Jones," (4) sources of funding and the cost of capital, (5) the level of working capital available, (6) the effects of inflation, (7) the degree of risk and uncertainty perceived in the marketplace, and (8) governmental policies, particularly tax and depreciation allowances.

As noted previously, investment decisions in the private sector may be based on several different forms of analysis. Applying each of these different methods of investment analysis will yield different results (i.e., different rankings of alternative investments). To illustrate how each of these techniques operates, six alternative investments may be examined, as shown in Table 10-3. Each of these investment alternatives involves an initial commitment of $10,000; however, the *net cash proceeds* over a three-year period (i.e., the return on the investment) varies from $10,000 in the case of alternative A to $18,000 in the case of alternatives C and F. Alternatives D and A both yield $10,000 in the first year; however, alternative D has the potential (not a certainty) of additional yields of $3,000 in the second and third years. Therefore, D is superior to A. Alternatives B and E have a potential return of $15,000 over the three-year period (in addition to the return of the initial investment of $10,000); however, since the first year yield of E is $6,000 as compared with $5,000 for alternative

## Table 10-3
### Benefit Investment Analysis as Illustrated by Six Investment Alternatives

| Alter-natives | Initial Investment | Net Cash Proceeds | | | Annual Proceeds | Per $ Outlay | Average Depreciation | Average Income | P.V. of Return | Net Present Value |
|---|---|---|---|---|---|---|---|---|---|---|
| | | 1 Year | 2 Year | 3 Year | | | | | | |
| A | $10,000 | $10,000 | 0 | 0 | $10,000 | 1.00 | $10,000 | 0 | $ 9,434 | -$ 566 |
| B | 10,000 | 5,000 | $5,000 | $ 5,000 | 5,000 | 0.50 | 3,333 | $1,667 | 13,365 | 3,365 |
| C | 10,000 | 2,000 | 4,000 | 12,000 | 6,000 | 0.60 | 3,333 | 2,667 | 15,522 | 5,522 |
| D | 10,000 | 10,000 | 3,000 | 3,000 | 5,333 | 0.53 | 3,333 | 2,000 | 14,623 | 4,623 |
| E | 10,000 | 6,000 | 4,000 | 5,000 | 5,000 | 0.50 | 3,333 | 1,667 | 13,094 | 3,094 |
| F | 10,000 | 8,000 | 8,000 | 2,000 | 6,000 | 0.60 | 3,333 | 2,667 | 16.346 | 6,346 |

### Ranking of Alternative

| | | | | | | | | | | |
|---|---|---|---|---|---|---|---|---|---|---|
| A | | 6 | | | 1 | | | 6 | | 6 |
| B | | 5 | | | 5 | | | 4 | | 4 |
| C | | 2 | | | 2 | | | 1 | | 2 |
| D | | 3 | | | 4 | | | 3 | | 3 |
| E | | 4 | | | 5 | | | 4 | | 5 |
| F | | 1 | | | 2 | | | 1 | | 1 |

B, E is superior to B. Alternatives C and F both yield a net return over three years of $18,000; however, F has the larger first-year return and therefore is superior to C. Which of the six alternatives is the best investment depends on what can be done with the cash proceeds (how they can be reinvested). For example, even though alternative D yields $2,000 less than alternative F over the three-year period, if the initial return of $10,000 from F can be reinvested in, say, alternative A, which has a quick return of an additional $10,000 (assuming an investment of at least $10,000 must be made), then alternative D may be superior to alternative F.

A second approach to benefit investment analysis looks primarily at the *payback period,* that is, the length of time required to get back a return equal to the initial investment. This approach favors those alternatives with the shortest payback periods; therefore, among the six alternatives in Table 10-3, A and D (with one-year payback periods) would be the "preferred" investments. The payback period for alternative F is 1.25 years, for alternatives B and E, 2 years, and for alternative C, 2.33 years.

The *proceeds per dollar of outlay* approach examines the ratio between net cash proceeds and the initial investment. This approach is similar to the first technique except that it does not consider the rate of return. Under this approach, alternatives C and F rank first (with ratios of 1 : 1.8), followed by alternative D (1 : 1.6), alternatives B and E (1 : 1.5), and finally, A (1 : 1).

The *average annual proceeds per dollar of outlay* approach tends to be biased toward those investments that yield quick returns. As shown in Table 10-3, alternative A ranks first, although the returns from this project are for only one year (the presumption being that the monies can be reinvested). The *average income on book value* technique involves a calculation of the average depreciation on the initial investment (and assumes that the return of the initial investment in alternative A depreciates $10,000 in the first year, while each of the other investments depreciates at the average rate of $3,333 per year for three years. On this basis alternatives C and F rank first, since their average annual proceeds less depreciation (or average income) are $2,667. This approach, however, fails to take into account the timing of when these proceeds are actually received.

All of these methods have shortcomings and, therefore, are relatively limited in their application to the analysis of long-term public investments: (1) None of these methods takes proper account of the timing of proceeds; (2) unequal dollars are treated as equal; and (3) income received after the initial payback is largely ignored in these calculations. In spite of these shortcomings, however, it has been estimated that over 70 percent of the major firms in the country still use one or more (or some combination) of these techniques of benefit investment analysis, coupled with hunches and guesswork.

When it was found that intuitive models, developed in an era of easy profits through rapid industrial expansion, were no longer applicable, however, new tools and concepts began to be introduced in the private investment decision process in the mid-fifties. These new methods are generally classified as *discounted cash flow* techniques, since they apply the principles and concepts of compound interest in a way that takes into account the differences in the worth of money over time. Each method also uses as input data the future negative and positive cash flows of money required to produce the desired returns and those that are a consequence of the particular investment. These methods grew out of the efforts of management to get some measure of economic wisdom regarding capital investments in additional facilities, products, or processes, and the design engineer's desire for a technique of measuring the economy of his design in both construction and use.

Of the various more sophisticated methods used in investment decision analysis, two techniques—the equivalent uniform annual net return method and the net present value method—are of particular interest in connection with capital investment decisions in the public sector. The *equivalent uniform annual net return* method combines all investment costs and all annual expenses into one single annual sum that is equivalent to all disbursements during the analysis period if distributed uniformly over the period. This method also includes an income or benefit factor, the formula solution indicating the amount by which the equivalent uniform annual income (or benefits) exceeds (or is less than) the equivalent uniform annual cost. This formula can be represented as follows:

$$EUANR = -I\left[\frac{i(1+i)^n}{(1+i)^n - 1}\right] + T\left[\frac{i}{(1+i)^n - 1}\right] - K + R$$

whereby the initial investment ($I$) is multiplied times the capital recovery factor, the terminal value ($T$) at the end of the analysis period is multiplied by a sinking fund factor, with $K$ representing the total uniform annual expense of administration, operations and maintenance, and $R$ representing the uniform annual gross income from sales revenues, receipts, or their equivalent. $R$ is inclusive of return on investment (depreciation and net profit).

The *net present value* method gives the algebraic difference in the present worths of both outward cash flows and inward flows of income or benefits, including the factor of annual income. The formula for calculating net present value can be expressed as follows:

$$NPV = -I + \frac{T}{(1+i)^n} - K\left[\frac{(1+i)^n - 1}{i(1+i)^n}\right] + R\left[\frac{(1+i)^n - 1}{i(1+i)^n}\right]$$

whereby the present worth of the terminal value ($T$) is calculated, and $K$ and $R$ are multiplied by the present worth factor of a uniform series.

To illustrate the application of these two methods, assume that management is confronted with two alternative investment decisions. Alternative A involves an initial investment of $120,000 and has a terminal value at the end of 10 years of $10,000; the annual administrative, operations, and maintenance costs, including overhead, production and sales expenses, for this alternative is $500,000. Alternative B requires an initial investment of $200,000 and has a terminal value at the end of ten years of $18,000; the estimated annual administrative, operations, and maintenance costs are $485,500. Alternative A is projected to have an annual gross income from sales of $529,200, while alternative B is estimated to yield $550,000 in annual sales. The rate of interest on capital is 8 percent per annum.

Applying the formula for the equivalent uniform annual net return method, it may be shown that alternative A has a *EUANR* of $12,007, whereas alternative B had a *EUANR* of $35,937, and therefore is the better investment (all other things being equal). Similarly, alternative A has a net present value of $80, 566, while alternative B has a net present value of $241,137. It should be noted that the equivalent uniform annual net return for any project can be converted to the net present value by multiplying by the present worth factor of a uniform series (which in the case of the above example is 6.710081).

These two techniques of investment analysis applied in the private sector are significant in that they have counterparts in the analysis of public sector investments. The net present value method is similar in concept to the so-called net benefits criterion, while the equivalent uniform annual net return method has its counterpart in the annual net benefits approach.

## Net Benefits

Net benefits is the criterion recommended, if not used, most frequently in contemporary cost-benefit analysis in the public sector. The formula for calculating the present value of net benefits is:

$$N = -C_0 + \frac{(B_1 - C_1)}{(1 + i)} + \frac{(B_2 - C_2)}{(1 + i)^2} + \cdots + \frac{(B_n - C_n)}{(1 + i)^n}$$

Two projects of equal net benefits might not be regarded indifferently, however. Assume two projects offered net benefits of $1,000, but one involved a present value of benefits of $2 million and a present value of costs of $1.999 million, while the other had a present value of benefits of $10,000 and a present value of costs of $9,000. Suppose that something went wrong—perhaps the calculations of costs and benefits were off by ten percent; the first project might have negative net benefits of as much as $200,000, whereas the second would do no worse than break even.

The net benefit criterion has been criticized because it tends to favor large projects over small. While the benefit-cost ratio takes into account the size of the commitment, the criterion of net benefits does not. If used with budget constraints, however, this bias of the net benefits is most important. Using the data in Table 10-2, for example, it may be seen that the selection of a discount rate less than 11.6 percent will produce positive net benefits, whereas a discount rate greater than 11.6 will produce negative net benefits, as illustrated in Table 10-4.

*Annual Net Benefits*

A relatively recent criterion for public investment has been suggested that utilizes the concept of annualized benefits and costs. To find the equivalent annual cost or benefit it is first necessary to calculate the present value of the streams of costs and benefits over the life of the project. Having determined the duration of the project and the discount rate to be applied, a standard table that gives the size of an annuity whose present value is $1 can be consulted. The entry in the table for the appropriate discount rate (interest rate) and project duration is then multiplied by the present value to obtain equivalent annual benefits or costs.

Equivalent annual benefits and costs can be used exactly as present values of benefits and costs, that is, they may be subtracted to yield net benefits or divided to obtain a benefit-cost ratio. Since the use of these annual equivalents involves first calculating present values, however, there seems to be relatively little advantage to be gained by this approach over other present value methods. The annual net benefits criterion can be used to some advantage when comparing the present value of costs (investment plus operation costs) to the benefits in a "typical" year, although it tends to be bias in favor of the project because the "typical" year is usually one of full capacity of operation and tends to ignore the higher costs of early years of start-up in which net benefits may be substantially lower. Nevertheless, some analysts have applied this technique to evaluate investment alternatives, particularly of considerable duration.

Table 10-4
Calculations of Net Benefits Using Two Different Discount Rates

| Year | $(B_n - C_n)$ | Discount Rate @ 9% | P.V. of Net Benefits | Discount Rate @ 12% | P.V. of Net Benefits |
|---|---|---|---|---|---|
| 1 | -$100,000 | 0.91743 | -$91,743 | 0.89286 | -$89,286 |
| 2 | + 60,000 | 0.84168 | + 50,501 | 0.79719 | + 47,832 |
| 3 | + 60,000 | 0.77218 | + 46,331 | 0.71178 | + 42,707 |
| 4 | + 60,000 | 0.70843 | + 42,506 | 0.63552 | + 38,131 |
| 5 | - 70,000 | 0.64993 | - 45,495 | 0.56743 | - 39,720 |
| N | | | +$ 2,100 | | -$ 336 |

## Compariosn of Basic Cost-Benefit Criteria

It is sometimes fallaciously assumed that a project alternative ranked first in terms of net benefits will also rank first in terms of its benefit-cost ratio—that these techniques are readily interchangible. The fact that the net present value of alternative A is greater than the net present value of alternative B does not imply that the benefit-cost ratio of alternative A is greater than the benefit-cost ratio of alternative B—net present value measures *difference*, whereas benefit-cost calculations produce a *ratio*. To illustrate this point, assume the benefits in alternative A have a present value of $150,000 and costs have a present value of $50,000. The net present value of alternative A would be $100,000 and the benefit-cost ratio $150,000/$50,000 or 3.0. In alternative B let the present value of benefits be $100,000 and that of costs $20,000. Alternative B has a smaller net present value ($80,000), but a higher benefit-cost ratio ($100,000/$20,000 or 5.0). Knowing the benefit-cost ratio for a given alternative or project is not sufficient; it is also necessary to know the size of the project before as much information is available as is given in the present value of net benefits ($N$).

One of the central problems in cost-benefit analysis is the treatment of certain items that may be considered either as benefits or as cost savings. In dealing with this question the net benefits criterion has proven to be superior to the benefit-cost ratio method. For example, suppose that a project involving the construction of a new sewage treatment facility is estimated to cost $1,000,000 and have measurable benefits to the community of $1,200,000 (all figures in present value terms). In addition, it is estimated that this project will increase land values in some parts of the community by $400,000 due to increased service, while leading to a decrease in other land values of $200,000 (stemming in part from proximity to the project). If it could be determined that these changes in land values were not simply capitalization of otherwise measured benefits and costs so that their inclusion would result in double counting, it would be appropriate to incorporate them in the cost-benefit analysis.

How to treat these additional factors, however, remains the problem. Land value increases could be included as benefits, while decreases in land values could be considered as a cost, resulting in a benefit-cost ratio of 1.33 ($R_1$). Or the net change in land values (i.e., $400,000 - $200,000) could be included either as benefits ($R_2$) or as cost savings ($R_3$). In considering several alternative investments,

$$R_1 = \frac{\$1,200,000 - \$400,000}{\$1,000,000 - \$200,000} = 1.33 \ \phi \ R_2 = \frac{\$1,200,000 + \$200,000}{\$1,000,000} = 1.4$$

$$\phi \ R_3 = \frac{\$1,200,000}{\$1,000,000 - \$200,000} = 1.5$$

elaborate accounting rules and procedures must be devised to keep the analyses comparable. As long as the algebraic sign and time period in which benefits and costs accrue are known, such ambiguity does not exist in the application of the net benefits criterion.

A further problem is encountered when equal amounts of costs and benefits are added to initial estimates, for example, when a project is expanded to provide additional service on a one-to-one basis in terms of costs and benefits. Consider the two project alternatives shown in Table 10–5. Alternative A has a benefit-cost ratio of 1.385, and as such would be slightly favored over alternative B, which has a benefit-cost ratio of 1.333. If benefits and costs with present values of $80,000 were added to each of these alternatives, the new benefit-cost ratio for alternative B would be 1.250, shifting it to the "more desirable" position. The net benefits for project alternative A are $50,000, while the net benefits for alternative B are $80,000; the addition of equal amounts of benefits and costs (in present value terms) does nothing to alter these net benefits (since, in effect, they cancel out one another). Alternative B is an inferior opportunity unless investment funds are unlimited and there is no more profitable way to invest the additional $171,750 that is required to meet the total costs of alternative B over the cost of alternative A.

As the previous example illustrates, the net benefit criterion is indifferent to the effects of adding $80,000 in costs and $80,000 in benefits to either of the project alternatives. Benefit-cost ratios, however, point up the greater "desirability" of the two alternatives before the one-to-one costs and benefits are added, that is, in both cases, the ratios based on initial estimates are higher. Therefore, the net benefit criterion can be made more useful by stating the objective as: Maximize net benefits subject to a constraint on costs and to the constraint that total benefits exceed total costs. If the additional $80,000 required exceeds these constraints, the project would be infeasible.

The benefit-cost ratio similar to the reciprocal of an average cost figure; the latter has costs in the numerator and output in physical terms in the denominator, while the former has the value of output (benefits) in the numerator and costs in the denominator. The perfect analogue of average cost is the cost-effectiveness ratio. For example, assume a comparison of two program alternatives designed to encourage students to remain in high school and to stimulate their interests in vocational opportunities. Alternative A is estimated to cost $80,000 and is designed to reach 160 students, whereas the cost of alternative B is $120,000 and is designed to reach 200 students. The cost-effectiveness ratio of alternative A can be expressed as "$500 per dropout prevented," while alternative B's cost-effectiveness ratio is "$600 per dropout prevented."

The output level at which average cost is a minimum, however, is not necessarily the output at which "utility" (or benefits minus costs) is a maximum. Similarly, the scale of a project that maximizes the benefit-cost ratio is not

## Table 10-5
### Benefit/Cost Calculations for Two Alternatives

| Year | Discount Factor @ 25% | Alternative A | | | | | Alternative B | | | | | |
|---|---|---|---|---|---|---|---|---|---|---|---|---|
| | | Benefits | Costs | $PV_B$ | $PV_C$ | | Benefits | Costs | $PV_B$ | $PV_C$ | $PB_B$ | $PV_C$ |
| 0 | 1.0000 | 0 | $ 70,000 | 0 | $ 70,000 | | 0 | $100,000 | | | 0 | $100,000 |
| 1 | 0.8000 | $ 50,000 | 46,000 | $ 40,000 | 36,800 | | $100,000 | 75,000 | | | $ 80,000 | 60,000 |
| 2 | 0.6400 | 74,750 | 20,250 | 47,840 | 12,960 | | 127,000 | 53,000 | | | 81,280 | 33,920 |
| 3 | 0.5120 | 100,000 | 20,000 | 51,200 | 10,240 | | 150,000 | 50,000 | | | 76,800 | 25,600 |
| 4 | 0.4096 | 100,000 | 0 | 40,960 | 0 | | 200,000 | 50,000 | | | 81,920 | 20,480 |
| Totals | | $324,750 | $156,250 | $180,000 | $130,000 | | $577,000 | $328,000 | | | $320,000 | $240,000 |
| B/C | | | | 1.3846 | | | | | | | 1.3333 | |

| Year | Alternative A | | Alternative B | |
|---|---|---|---|---|
| | Net Benefits | Present Value | Net Benefits | Present Value |
| 0 | -$ 70,000 | -$70,000 | -$100,000 | -$100,000 |
| 1 | +$ 4,000 | +$ 3,200 | +$ 25,000 | +$ 20,000 |
| 2 | +$ 54,500 | +$34,880 | +$ 74,000 | +$ 47,360 |
| 3 | +$ 80,000 | +$40,960 | +$100,000 | +$ 51,200 |
| 4 | +$100,000 | +$40,960 | +$150,000 | +$ 61,440 |
| | | +$50,000 | | +$ 80,000 |

necessarily the scale that maximizes net benefits. Roy Radner's graph [32] (Figure 10–3) illustrates this point. This graph features a series of rays (D, E, and F), emanating from the origin, along which the benefit-cost ratio is constant. G, H, and I are a set of parallel lines with slope of one, along which net benefits are constant. The arc represents the set of feasible cost-benefit pairs dictated by the present state of technology. Starting from any point on this arc, to achieve more benefits, it is necessary to incur more costs. The highest benefit-cost ratio ($R$) shown is on ray D, the highest net benefits on line G. In the feasible set, neither D or G can be attained, however. The best benefit-cost ratio achievable in the feasible region is at the point where the arc intersects ray E. Highest net benefits can be attained at the point of intersection of the arc with line H. It can be readily seen that these two criteria are

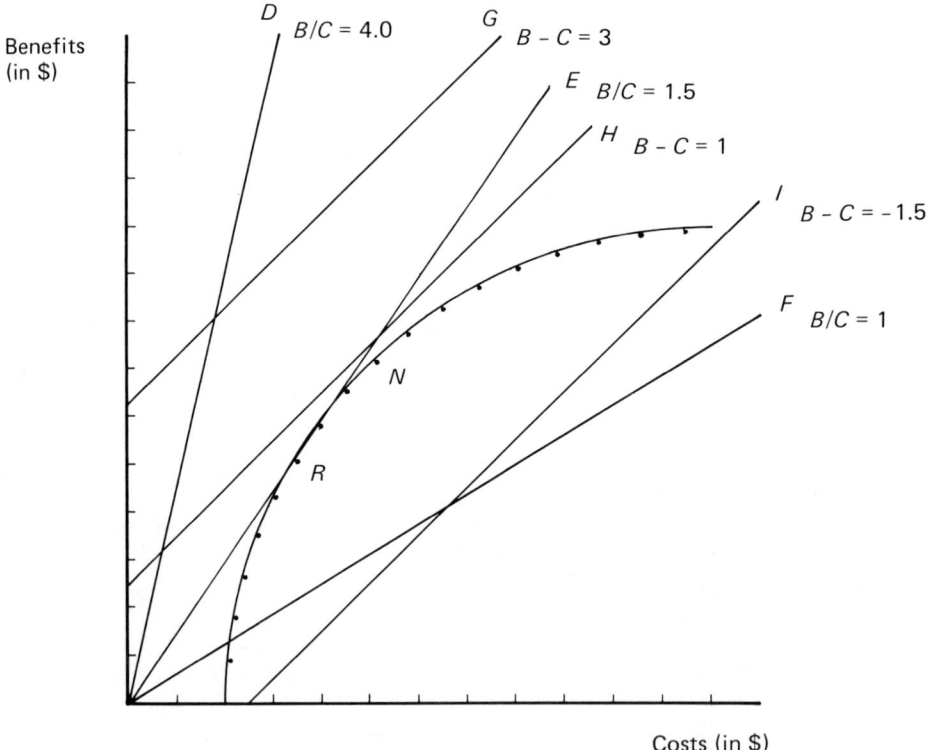

**Figure 10–3.** Radner's Graph of Optimal Scales

not maximized at the same point: R and N are distinct. Given the slope of the lines describing net benefits, the only case in which the two points coincide is where the benefit-cost ratio is one.

From this discussion it may be concluded that the basic objective of cost-benefit and analysis is not merely to maximize the ratio of benefits to costs.[33] While circumstances can exist where the "equalization" of benefit-cost ratios may serve as a necessary condition for achieving a desired "maximum" goal, other factors must be considered in selecting an appropriate cost-benefit criterion that can lead to the identification of the "best policy." These factors include: (1) the "time-stream" of costs and benefits and the time-preference of the society for present as opposed to future consumption of public and quasi-public goods; (2) the limitations imposed by budgetary (revenue) constraints; and (3) the issue as to whether benefits can be quantified or measured only in a "low-level optimization" or an "intermediate" sense, that is, whether goals and objectives can be specified in sufficient detail to permit a fuller identification of direct and indirect costs and benefits.

## Limitations of Cost-Benefit Analysis

There are several limitations to the application of cost-benefit analysis. Like program budgeting it does not purport to solve all problems relating to the allocation of scarce public resources. Cost-benefit analysis is of limited usefulness in the evaluation of programs of relatively broad scope or in the comparison of programs with widely differing objectives. It provides only limited assistance in establishing priorities for various goals. Problems associated with the measurement of benefits and the uncertainties encountered with many programs makes quantification a most difficult task. Many public programs have redistributive effects, whereby some persons benefit at the expense of others; cost-benefit analysis contributes relatively little toward the establishment of a social welfare function that might provide an answer regarding the relative merit of various patterns of income distribution.

It is virtually impossible to eliminate the need for subjective judgments in the public decision-making process. Nonetheless, a more "systematic" approach to cost and benefit comparisons, as provided by cost-benefit analysis, and the consideration of time-preference and marginal productivity of capital investments, can contribute significantly to more rational bases for governmental budgetary decisions, particularly when compared with the uncoordinated, haphazard, and intuitive approaches that characterize many more traditional methods. Examining expenditures in terms of programs or objectives instead of merely by spending agencies, and the consideration of total benefits of expenditures for alternative programs alongside of total costs of the inputs are in themselves important contributions of cost-benefit related techniques.

The more significant applications of cost-benefit analysis are to be found at lower levels of governmental decision making processes, that is, in the selection among alternative means of accomplishing rather specific objectives, and with programs and projects in which benefits can be quantified on some reasonably reliable basis. With clearly defined procedures and measurable costs and benefits, the cost-benefit approach provides specific assistance in arriving at decisions that are most appropriate in terms of agreed-upon objectives. Even with broader questions, cost-benefit approaches emphasize the importance of quantification whenever possible, of making implicit judgmental inputs more explicit, of minimizing the influence of prejudgments and biases, and of at least eliminating the worst projects.[34] Within these limitations, cost-benefit analysis can make, and is making, important contributions to the field of public decision making.

**Cost-Effectiveness Analysis**

The most significant decision problem confronting local government involves the allocation of fiscal resources, in an optimal fashion, to meet long-range physical, economic, social, and political needs and demands. The tendency of local governments to react rather than to plan and to approach their fiscal responsibilities in a crisis-oriented mode of action has led to extensive waste, inefficiencies, and duplication of efforts and a growing dependency on the state and federal governments to provide financial relief. While concepts of goal-oriented decision making have been described in some detail, attempts to apply such techniques in the assessment of the long–range resource allocation problems of local government have been relatively limited. Although efforts to translate current public decisions and programs into more systems-like frameworks continue to be made, proposed changes in governmental processes of resource allocation must be evaluated in view of the ambiguities and conflicts that, in a very real sense, represent the nature of contemporary government.[35] Attempts to being greater rationality and goal-directedness to public decision making must be based on the assumptions, concepts, and criteria that represent the current state of local government.

*Inputs (Resources) Versus*
*Outputs (Performance)*

In government resources are allocated through the budgetary process, which basically involves an adversary-type relationship among public agencies. The significant criteria and controls employed in the budgetary process traditionally have been of a financial nature, focusing on the expenditure of money (the fixed budget approach). Under such conditions public decision making frequently becomes *input-oriented,* that is, the analysis of objectives and alternative methods of achieving these objectives is based on money-related rather than policy-related issues. If there are sufficient funds to pay for the "inputs"— the resources requested by the various agencies—there is no major budget problem in government. Seldom are projections or estimates made of the effectiveness of these inputs in terms of meeting public needs and demands or the performance of public services. As a consequence there is no guarantee that the public decision process will be coherently responsive to comprehensive objectives.

Traditional decision making and analytical mechanisms (including cost-benefit analysis in many forms of its application) are designed to pursue *efficiency,* often at the expense of *effectiveness.* This characteristic of public decision making can be observed in the continual emphasis on the achievement of economies without decreasing service, that is, the focus is on the elimination of waste: with fixed resources, to produce more of A without decreasing the production of B. Questions of efficiency generally are defined and answered strictly in economic terms, with minimum consideration given to priorities and/or relative worth of the programs pursued.

It must be recognized, however, that many (if not most) governmental activities must produce and be responsive to noneconomic returns. The effects of analyses that consider economic variables while ignoring noneconomic factors may be seen today in irrelevant public school systems, environmentally destructive highway and freeway systems, and irrational public health and correctional programs. Further effects are seen in the analytical pretense that treats governmental program as mutually exclusive entities. There is no purely technical basis for deciding the relative importance or merit of an Upward Bound program versus an on-the-job training program for adults. By pretending that technical analyses—analyses that focus on efficiency—are sufficient for political decisions, decision makers often lose the very information necessary to determine effectiveness. It is possible, for example, to have an efficient transportation link that moves traffic from Point A to Point B with little or no waste. Such a link, however, is irrelevant if the need is to go to Point C. Effectiveness considers the relative worth of Point B versus Point C with reference to specific values (goals and objectives) and variables (fiscal and policy constraints). Consideration of this relative worth—the actual impact of resource expenditures in terms of program performance—represents effectiveness.

These indictments of current public decision making and budgetary practices point up the critical need for new techniques for optimizing the allocation of public resources. One such technique that holds considerable promise in this connection is cost-effectiveness analysis.

*Role and Attributes of
Cost-Effectiveness Analysis*

Cost-effectiveness is an analytical technique employed in the process of program budgeting. Although not restricted in application to long-range planning problems, cost-effectiveness analysis is a most useful tool for such planning, particularly when a wide range of alternative future courses of action must be examined in a broad context. A.R. Prest and Ralph Turvey define cost-effectiveness analysis as ". . . a practical way of assessing the desirability of projects, where it is important to take a long view (in the sense of looking at repercussions in the further, as well as the nearer, future) and a wide view (in the sense of allowing for side-effects of many kinds of many persons, industries, regions, etc.) i.e., it implies the enumeration and evaluation of all the relevant costs and benefits."[36]

Cost-effectiveness analysis provides the basis for the development of a decision-making process that is output-oriented, one that considers the impact of resource expenditures rather than the resources themselves. Under this approach, a distinction is made between efficiency and effectiveness in an attempt to discard strictly financial controls in favor of nonpecuniary accounting techniques to measure the output of public programs. This output or performance orientation of cost-effectiveness is its most notable attribute. A number of other characteristics, however, set this approach apart from other types of budget analysis techniques, including: (1) end-product orientation; (2) extended time horizon; (3) life-cycle costing; (4) examination of total systems costs and benefits; (5) measurement of goal achievement through the application of effectiveness measures; (6) development of a management information system; and (7) performance analysis techniques.[37]

A basic modus operandi of cost-effectiveness analysis involves the identification and analysis of alternative "systems" to achieve some agreed-upon end objectives.[38] In program budgeting the selected system becomes a *program element*—an integrated activity that combines personnel, services, equipment, and facilities.[39] The end-product orientation of cost-effectiveness analysis is thus reflected in this systems approach, that is, it is a basic principle that requirements for diverse resources be identified and associated with the achievement of a particular level of performance that defines the desired state of the system at some future point in time. The cost of a system should reflect the total resource impact of the decision relating to that system, identifying the magnitude of all relevant costs necessary to achieve a particular alternative course of action.

The span of time covered in cost-effectiveness analysis must be sufficiently long to take cognizance of such lead time as may be required to develop the system's capabilities and to cover the full period of the system's operations and its benefits. This extended time horizon has important implications for the development of cost estimates and estimates of program performance in terms of accrued benefits. A good deal of uncertainty surrounds such long-range analysis, and the farther out in time the analysis is extended, the greater the uncertainty. Such analyses may involve new materials and equipment never before produced, operations never before attempted, new processes, and new training concepts—all of which make their costing difficult and the estimates of benefits uncertain. Thus, emphasis must be placed on the comparability of estimates rather than on their absolute values.

While resource requirements must be stated in terms of personnel, equipment, real facilities, supplies, and so forth, total systems costs cannot be developed by merely summing over such a heterogeneity of resource needs. Nor is it possible to make meaningful comparisons between systems if their costs are expressed solely in terms of a wide variety of real resources. In estimating the cost of a system it is important to spell out the quantities of critical resources, the supplies of which are quite limited (e.g., technical personnel). It is also important to note that constant dollars are nearly always used in cost estimating.[40] Rarely is an attempt made to predict future price-level changes in evaluating alternatives, since such predictions are extremely difficult to make and many problems regarding methodology remain to be solved.

In the context of cost-effectiveness analysis, *goals* may be defined as codifications of desired (and desirable) patterns of performance, as exhibited by individuals and institutions, or by physical, social, economic, and political variables. Goals describe the desired state of any system. The public planning and decision-making process must be capable of manipulating and controlling system variables in order to achieve this desired state. The decision-making process is complicated by the fact that goals are not mutually exclusive. A single set of variables may be common to a number of goals; the primary variables may be common to a number of goals; the primary variables of a low-priority goal may be secondary variables of a high-priority goal.

Effectiveness measures must be devleoped and applied to determine the level of goal achievement. *Effectiveness measures* are defined as indicators that measure the direct and indirect impacts of resource allocations. They involve a basic scoring technique for determining the state of a given system at any point in time. Careful selection and application of effectiveness measures can go a long way in overcoming some of the difficulties and ambiguities of public decision making.

The first step in the application of effectiveness measures is the development of a *management information and program evaluation system* (MIPES). The emphasis of such an information system is on the identification, definition, isolation, and manipulation of specific variables as they relate to public goals. These variables can be used as effectiveness measures if consideration is given to the effects that resource allocations will have upon them.

The MIPES must be based on an examination of the structural and operational characteristics of the agency or agencies in question. For purposes of analysis, a series of discrete program categories must be defined in terms of agency goals and objectives. For example, a law enforcement agency, broadly speaking, is organized to achieve two general goals: the control of criminal behavior; and the control of noncriminal behavior. A health agency may be seen as having two broad goals: a remedial health mission; and a preventative health mission. These broad categories of activity, of course, must eventually be further subdivided, Initially, however, it may be feasible to establish only rather broad program categories.

In cost-effectiveness analysis it is assumed that normative statements of performance (goals) can be derived, or inferred, from current conditions. Thus, current operations and their effects must be under continuous surveillance, that is, continuous program evaluation is the most effective means available for initiating a goal-oriented decision-making system in an existing governmental structure. In this manner goals are defined by: (1) establishing current levels and types of performance in each discrete program category; (2) estimating the current impacts of agency resources on that performance; and (3) delimiting desired levels and types of performance. The development of positive statements of performance provides a base from which to define and evaluate change. This approach, based on the concept of marginal change from the system's current state,[41] yields normative statements of performance—goals— that can be defined as positive deviations from the current level of operation. A thorough analysis of the nature and extent of program output (performance) to formulate practical effectiveness measures and organizational and operational criteria serves three important functions: (1) the identification of desired ends, that is, desired levels and patterns of performance; (2) the establishment of a structure that will facilitate the evaluation of alternative methods of resource allocation; and (3) the creation of a planning and management framework that permits reevaluation and modification of criteria and measures, as well as program structure.

*Defining Positive-Normative Performance:*
*An Analytical Framework*

With the specification of policy and program variables, an analytical framework for goal definition and analysis can be structured. The use of policy and program variables to describe performance is necessary if an output-oriented decision process is desired. These variables do not consider directly agency activities or inputs, but rather focus on the effects (outputs) of these activities in the achievement of established goals.

Program performance can be classified by a number of factors. Agency programs involve identifiable persons (clientele) and/or events, and while programs often are considered to be continuous, certain milestones, or occurrences, can be identified. Therefore, the broad categories of information required to define patterns of performance might include the following items of data:

1. Number and frequency of occurrences—the number of reported and estimates of the number of unreported occurrences in a given period for a particular event toward which a given program is directed
2. Characteristics of persons or events involved in each occurrence
3. Relationships among persons or events involved
4. Circumstances surrounding the occurrence of events

One useful approach to the analysis of these characteristics is through the development of a matrix for each major subcategory of performance in which all of the pertinent variables are listed.[42] If the program under analysis deals with water pollution, for example, "characteristics" might refer to the types and sources of pollution, "relationships" might encompass the geographic location of the pollution sources or outflows, levels and types of pollutants, current levels of treatment given to the effluent, and so forth, while "circumstances" might pertain to weather conditions, stream flow, calendar period of pollution, and so on. The more extensive the listing of these factors, the more complete the analysis possible.

The next step in establishing the basis for analysis is to divide each cell of the matrix into four sectors, as shown in Figure 10-4. One sector of each cell is devoted to a record of the *reported* association between the two variables that form the coordinates of that cell. A second sector is used to identify the *estimated* (reported plus unreported) associations among variables. The third sector is used to identify the desired or acceptable levels of association. The

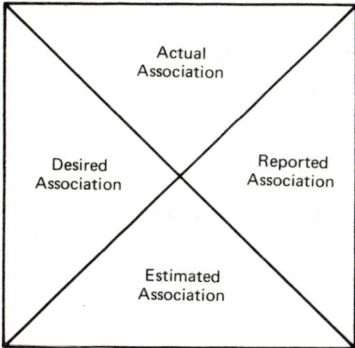

**Figure 10-4.** Sector Division of Each Cell in the Matrix

fourth sector can be applied to record the *actual* association between two variables after a period of time has elapsed. This last sector is for purposes of evaluation of program performance, once a new program is initiated.

Normative definitions mean, simply, that choices are to be made in concert with "desired," or perhaps acceptable, levels of performance. It should be clear that some forms of dysfunctional performance cannot be eliminated totally through the actions of governmental agencies. Therefore, in such cases, it is necessary that agencies recognize the limits of their resources and responsibilities and be prepared to accept levels of performance that may not be totally functional under all circumstances.

Initial statements of goals are not fixed or static. Goals must be continually evaluated and revised according to the outcomes available through various allocations or resources. At this stage problems or feasibility are confronted. It may be necessary to make rather drastic modifications of the initial goal statements after the potential of available resources is understood thoroughly.

*Types of Program Analysis Under Cost-Effectiveness*

Program analysis is concerned with the determination of programs and program levels that are most effective in achieving specific goals. It involves an evaluation of total program costs and anticipated program effects. Both costs and effectiveness are measured and analyzed in quantitative terms. While costs usually are expressed in dollar terms, the unit of measurement for effectiveness is that of the goal, that is, it may be pecuniary or nonmonetary. Policy and program variables represent the nonmonetary units of measure. The use of these variables should not be confused with the more typical forms of cost-benefit analysis—methods for determining whether a program is *economically* worthwhile by comparing costs and benefits, both of which are measured and analyzed in monetary terms. The development of many public programs, clearly, must be based upon more than monetary terms.

Under the cost-effectiveness approach program analysis requires three types of decisions and supporting studies:

1. Cost-goal analysis is concerned with the identification of feasible goals.
2. Cost-effectiveness analysis assists in the identification of the most effective program alternative.
3. Cost-constraint analysis determines the cost of employing less than optimal programs.

Ideally, program analysis should be an iterative process. In the early development of a goal-oriented budget structure, however, it probably will be desirable

COST-BENEFIT AND COST-EFFECTIVENESS ANALYSIS 237

(and necessary) to make these analyses more or less independently. With additional sophistication in data and techniques, iterative refinements can be made in the analysis.

## Cost-Goal Analysis

*Cost-goal analysis* assists in establishing program goals and program levels by determining the shape of program cost curves through the specification of input-output relationships. This analysis indicates the likely changes in program costs as program goals are changed. This technique has immediate use, since it usually requires an analysis and assessment of existing programs. Once the program cost curve is determined for each existing program, alternative programs can be considered and their impacts assessed. Figure 10-5 presents this type of analysis graphically. $O_1$, $O_2$, and $O_3$ represent goals (outputs) and $C_1$, $C_2$, and $C_3$ represent program costs.

The program cost curve represents the sensitivity of cost (input) to changes in the program's desired level of effectiveness (output). Unless program cost relationships are understood, it is not possible to know what would happen as the desired level of effectiveness—the goal—is raised or lowered. Costs may change more or less proportionately. However, if costs do not increase as rapidly as effectiveness, then the program is operating at a level of increasing returns (represented by a positively sloped curve accelerating at an accelerating

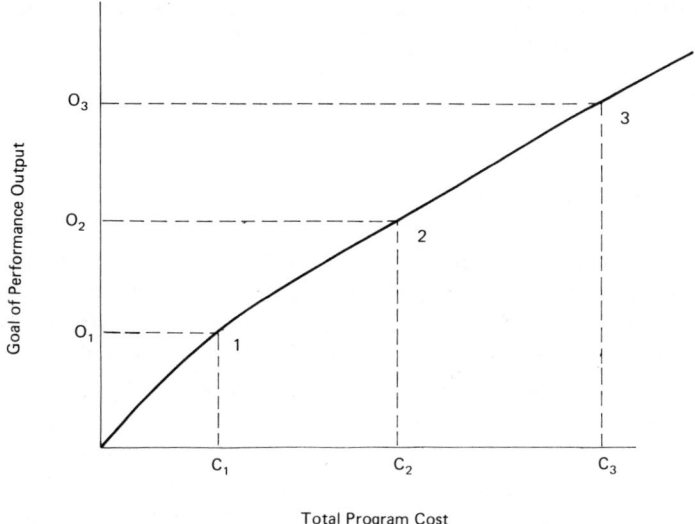

**Figure 10-5.** Cost-Goal Analysis in Graphic Form

rate). If costs increase more rapidly than effectiveness, the program is operating in an area of diminishing returns.

Increasing returns do not mean that a program should be expanded or, conversely, that it should be contracted if operating in an area of diminishing returns. A public program can be of such importance that it should be expanded even though it is operating with diminishing returns. However, it is useful to know, for example, that an additional commitment of $200,000 to one program will carry it 20 percent toward its goal, while the same resources added to another program would carry it only five percent closer to its goals.

Determining what might happen to program costs if the characteristics of the goal are changed is not an easy task. Frequently, only one point is known—that which relates the current cost to the current level of effectiveness. Cost-goal analysis requires the construction of a model that can relate incremental costs to increments in effectiveness. The problems of incremental costing are discussed further in a subsequent section. Construction of program cost curves should become increasingly more sophisticated as these relationships are better understood. For some types of programs, it is probably that practical models can be developed immediately. For others, program cost curves can be approximated from historical data.

A very crude first approximation can be obtained by plotting program costs against achieved levels of effectiveness for the recent past. A curve can then be drawn through these points. The construction of an historical curve in this manner represents a simple correlation analysis of independent and dependent variables. While it is very crude, it may be sufficiently accurate to judge whether the program under analysis appears to be operating in an area of increasing or decreasing returns. In the future it undoubtedly will be necessary (and possible) to resort to multiple correlation analysis in order to substantiate fully the shape of program cost curves.

### Cost-Effectiveness Analysis

There usually is more than one way of achieving a goal or set of goals. The objective of *cost-effectiveness analysis,* therefore, is to determine the most effective program for achieving each identified goal or goal set. An analysis of alternative program curves, representing either single programs or set of programs, can reveal the preferred program for a given goal or set of goals.

This type of analysis is illustrated graphically in Figure 10-6. $P_A$ and $P_B$ represent alternative programs; $O_1$, $O_2$, and $O_3$ are three different goals; $C_{1-B}$ and $C_{1-A}$ are program costs associated with the goal $O_1$; $C_2$ is the program cost associated with goal $O_2$; and $C_{3-A}$ and $C_{3-B}$ are program costs associated with the goal $O_3$. For the goal $O_1$, $P_A$ represents the most efficient and effective program since $C_{1-A}$ is the least cost. On the other hand, if the "higher" goal

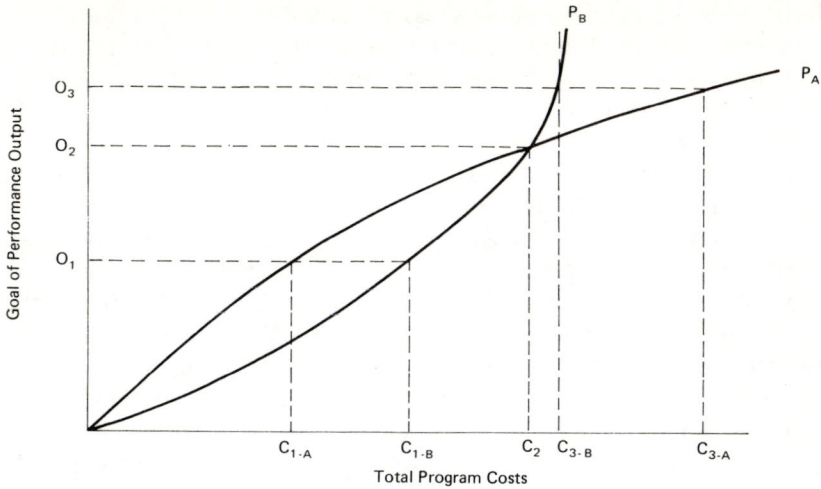

**Figure 10-6.** Cost-Effectiveness Analysis in Graphic Form

of $O_3$ is desired, $P_B$ is the most effective program at cost $C_{3-B}$. If goal $O_2$ were selected, the analyst would be indifferent among the two programs, since both have the same cost, $C_2$.

Normally, comparison of alternative program is made between an existing program and a proposed alternative. As it is difficult enough to construct the cost curve for the existing program, it frequently is impossible to develop detailed cost curves for largely theoretical alternatives. Initially, therefore, it may be useful to undertake only a partial comparison. Based on an established goal, it is necessary to know only which program would achieve that goal most effectively; it is not necessary to know the actual shape of the alternative program curve but rather, only the *tendency* of the curve. Consider, for example, that in Figure 10-6, $P_A$ represents an existing program and $P_B$ an alternative. If $O_1$ is the current goal and $O_3$ is selected as the new goal, the $C_{3-B}$ and $C_{3-A}$ need to be compared to determine the most effective program. Noting that $O_3$ can be achieved with fewer resources under the new program is illustrative of the dangers of assuming that one program, based on its superiority at one point, is the most effective program at all levels.

### Cost-Constraint Analysis

In practice governmental programs may be adopted that do not represent the most effective programs technically available. Legislative constraints, intergovernmental relations, union rules, employer rights, community attitudes, and so forth are among the more obvious reasons for this fact. The purpose of *cost-constraint analysis* is to illustrate the cost of these constraints. This is accomplished by comparing the cost of the program that could be adopted if no constraints were present with the cost of the optimum program that can be employed given existing constraints. The analysis, shown graphically in Figure 10-7, starts with the expressed goal $O_1$ and two programs ($P$ constrained and $P$ not-constrained). *P not-constrained* represents the most effective program as determined by cost-effectiveness analysis. The other program may be constrained by some legal, political, economic, or social factor. The constrained program may be the only program available. The cost of the constraints to the agency is the difference between the program cost of $P$ not-constrained and $P$ constrained. Once this cost is identified, decisions as to the importance (and feasibility) of attempting to remove the constraints can be made. On the basis of this analysis public managers can confront policy makers with the facts on how much the relaxation of a given constraint would save the program. The cost of the constraint is also indicative of the amount of effort that might be made to overcome a constraint, if such effort were acceptable. In some cases supporting a constraint would be more valuable for social or political reasons than a more effective program.

*Maximizing Program Effectiveness:
Fixed Budget Approach*

To illustrate the potential applications of cost-effectiveness analysis, it seems appropriate to begin with the predominate approach to traditional budget

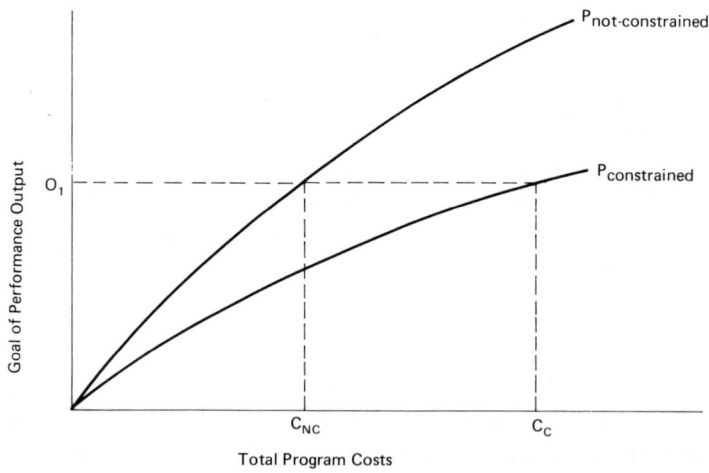

**Figure 10-7.** Cost-Constraint Analysis in Graphic Form

analysis—the fixed budget approach—which has also been adopted as the principal operational mode for cost-benefit studies. From this point it is possible to move to the greater complexities of a fixed benefits approach and to long-range applications of cost-effectiveness analysis.

Consider the following example adopted from the writings of Donald A. Krueckeberg and Arthur L. Silvers.[43] The health department in a middle-sized eastern city has traced the cause of a rash of hospital admissions of children with lead poisoning to a lead-based paint used many years ago to paint local housing. The paint is now peeling from the walls and is being ingested by young children. The goal of the department is to eliminate this potentially serious health hazard, and several programs are proposed for this purpose. The focus of this discussion will be on two quite distinct program alternatives:

Program A: Repaint local housing with nonlead-based paint

Program B: Educate parents and children to the hazards of eating the peeling paint.

Through an examination of hospital records it is determined that 80 percent of all children admitted with lead poisoning symptoms during the past year lived in housing that had been painted with lead-based paint. Therefore, an effectiveness measure for program A (to paint the lead-based painted buildings) would be to reduce the number of cases of lead poisoning by a factor of 3 (i.e., 80 percent minus 20 percent divided by 20 percent). It is estimated that the repainting will cost $1,000 per building.

To evaluate alternative B it is first necessary to determine the average number of children living in each building with lead-based paint so as to calculate the cost and effectiveness of the proposed educational program. From past child education studies it is ascertained that, by using a one-week program, teaching specialists can effectively educate small children to be aware of and to avoid dangerous situations with a probability of 25 percent. Thus, if 4 out of 5 children with lead poisoning symptoms come from housing with lead-based paint, the educational program has the potential of reducing the number of cases by a factor of 1 (i.e., 25 percent of 4). It is estimated to cost $200 to teach the children of each building.

From the foregoing it may be seen that if the decision can be based on the effectiveness per unit, alternative A is the preferred approach since it is three times as effective as alternative $B$. However, suppose that the budget for this program is set at $100,000 and there are 500 buildings in the community that have lead-based paint. Under this budget constraint alternative $A$ can be applied to no more than 100 buildings, at an effectiveness rate of three cases per buildings, whereas alternative $B$, at $200 per building, can be applied in all 500 buildings at an effectiveness rate of one per building. Therefore, under the budget constraint alternative $B$, with an overall program effectiveness rate of 500, is the preferred program when compared with alternative $A$, which has an overall effectiveness rate of only 300 (see Table 10–6). Setting up a linear programming problem as shown below indicates that there is no advantage in setting up a combined program using some of alternative A and some of alternative B, since as $P_A$ is increased, the level of effectiveness ($E$) will move downward from 500 toward the lower 300 level.

$$\text{(Objective Function)} \quad \text{Max } E = 3P_A + P_B$$
$$\text{Subject to: } \$1{,}000P_A + \$200P_B \leq \$100{,}000$$
$$P_A, P_B \geq 0$$

The same conclusions can be reached by calculating a cost-effectiveness ratio for each alternative: alternative A = \$1,000/3 = \$333; alternative B = \$200/1 = \$200.

### Cost-Effectiveness Analysis: Indivisible Projects

In the health problem described above, the units of analysis—buildings—were common to both alternative and could be reduced to a unit cost basis. In many problems, however, the units of alternative programs may consist of large projects that cannot be reduced to comparable unit cost figures. To illustrate this point, consider two alternatives designed to augment a statewide science museum program. Alternative A involves the construction of several regional museum facilities, each of which is estimated to serve 800,000 people per year at an annual cost of \$4,000,000 (construction and operational costs amortized over the life of the project and discounted to present value.) Alternative B involves the use of a number of mobile units designed to bring museum exhibits out to small communities, schools, etc. Each unit is estimated to cost \$40,000 annually (in present value terms) and is designed to serve 4,000 people each year.

As shown in Table 10–7, the cost-effectiveness ratio for alternative A is \$5 per user (\$4 million divided by 800,000), while the ratio for alternative

**Table 10–6**
**Cost–Effectiveness Analysis: Fixed Budget**

| Program Alternative | Effectiveness per Unit | Cost per Unit | Maximum Units within Budget | Program Effectiveness |
|---|---|---|---|---|
| A | 3 | \$1,000 | 100 | 300 |
| B | 1 | 200 | 500 | 500 |

### Table 10-7
### Cost–Effectiveness Analysis: Indivisible Projects

| Program Alternative | Effectiveness per Project | Cost per Project | Cost-Effectiveness Ratio | Program Effectiveness |
|---|---|---|---|---|
| Regional Facilities | 800,000 | $4 million | $5/user | 1,600,000 |
| Mobile Units | 4,000 | $40,000 | $10/user | 1,000,000 |

$B$ is $10 per user; therefore, alternative $A$ is the preferred approach, assuming no budget constraints.

Suppose that $10 million has been allocated to support his program on an annual basis. Given the annual cost of the regional facilities it would be possible to construct 2.5 facilities; however, since these facilities are indivisible (i.e., it is not feasible to construct 2.5 facilities), only two regional units can be built, resulting in an overall program effectiveness of 1.6 million users (as compared with a program effectiveness of 1 million users for alternative $B$). Thus, $2 million of the budgeted allocation is left unused. This $2 million surplus could be used to support the operation of 50 mobile units, which would have a program effectiveness of 200,000 users. Therefore, the optimal approach, assuming the availability of $10 million, is to construct and operate two regional facilities and to acquire and operate 50 mobile units, for an overall program effectiveness of 1.8 million users.

*Cost-Effectiveness Analysis:*
*Project Complementarities*

Many situations dictate the analysis of program alternatives that represent widely disparate approaches to achieve a common objective. Frequently these alternatives are difficult to compare on the basis of total costs and overall effectiveness because of the dissimilarities in cost components, impacted population, etc. Consider, for example, the problem facing an economically depressed rural region in which $1 million in funds have been made available for allocation among various projects designed to provide relief to the widespread poverty evident in the region. Four programs intended to increase incomes are proposed: a public recreational facility; a job training program; improved assembly, processing, and marketing facilities for agricultural products; and an industrial park. An analysis of the potential effectiveness of these four alternatives indicates that the public recreational facility has the potential of increasing the incomes of approximately 470 wage earners by 20 percent; the job training program has the potential of increasing incomes of approximately 920 wage earners by 25 percent; the agri-business improvement project would employ approximately 480 workers at wages 35 percent higher than the current annual family income of $3,000; and the industrial park project would employ approximately 850 workers at wages 40 percent higher than the current annual family incomes. The effectiveness measures and associated project costs are shown in Table 10–8.

Cursory review of these four alternatives might lead to the conclusion that the industrial park alternative is the most desirable project since it is projected to result in a 40 percent increase in the income levels of some 850 workers. However, if these four alternatives are evaluated on the basis of their cost-effectiveness ratios, the job training program, with a C/E ratio of 1.278, would be ranked first, the industrial park project (1.200) second, the agri-business project third, and the recreational facility a rather poor fourth (its C/E ratio is below 1). The job training project, however, utilizes only $540,000 of the funds available, whereas the industrial park project utilizes $850,000 of the budgeted monies. It would be feasible to initiate the job training project and either the agri-business project or the recreational project and still stay within the budgetary constraint of $1 million. The job training and recreational projects have a combined effectiveness of $972,000 at a cost of $890,000, for a cost-effectiveness ratio of 1.092, whereas the job training project in combination with the agri-business project would produce an overall effectiveness of $1,194,000 at a cost of $980,000, for a cost-effectiveness ratio of 1.218. Further these two projects in combination would affect some 1,400 workers, increasing their average annual income by 28.4 percent.

While cost-effectiveness analysis is useful in determining which project or program should be selected to maximize effectiveness subject to budgetary constraints, in fulfilling this objective it represents only a slight sophistication over the basic techniques of cost-benefit analysis. The more important contributions of cost-effectiveness analysis lie in the determination of most effective

### Table 10–8
### Cost–Effectiveness Analysis: Project Complementarities

| Program Alternative | Cost per Project | Current Income | Projected Increase | Workers Affected | Project Effectiveness | C/E Ratio |
|---|---|---|---|---|---|---|
| Recreation facility | $350,000 | $3,000 | 20% | 470 | $ 282,000 | 0.806 |
| Job Training | 540,000 | 3,000 | 25% | 920 | 690,000 | 1.278 |
| Agri-business | 440,000 | 3,000 | 35% | 480 | 504,000 | 1.145 |
| Industrial park | 850,000 | 3,000 | 40% | 850 | 1,020,000 | 1.200 |

alternatives under project interdependence, that is, when the effectiveness of one project or program is increased by the initiation of some other related project or program. This type of interdependence among projects that are intended to achieve a single goal is known as project complementarity.[44] For example, using the project alternatives in the previous illustration, the development of an industrial park and the initiation of a job training program, taken separately, each had a relatively high cost-effectiveness ratio. It is conceivable that these two alternatives, taken together, would have a cost-effectiveness impact even greater than that evidenced by their independent cost-effectiveness ratios. Thus, if two or more complementary projects are under consideration for inclusion in a single program package, the effectiveness measure for each alternative should be set aside in favor of an effectiveness measure for the alternatives taken in combination, that is, the effectiveness of the overall package should be examined, which included the effectiveness of each alternative separately plus their joint effectiveness.[45]

Returning to the example in Table 10-8, suppose that the job training program was designed specifically to complement the agri-business improvement project, such that the combined package would generate projected total effects of $1,295,000 or approximately $100,000 more than the two projects evaluated separately. Since the package would cost $980,000, the resulitng cost-effectiveness ratio would be 1.321, higher than any of the ratios taken separately. Even though the combination of a job training program and the development of an industrial park is outside the budgetary constraint of $1 million (costing $1.39 million to initiate), it would be useful to examine these two alternatives in combination as a final step in the evaluation. Suppose this program package also increases the level of effectiveness by $100,000 (from $1.710 to $1.810 million); given the total cost of $1.39, the resulting cost-effectiveness ratio of 1.302 would still be below the ratio of the previously examined program package. Assuming that there was no budgetary constraint, the increase in effectiveness of the job training program and the industrial park project would have to be $262,000 to be competitive with the program package of job training and agri-business improvements. One further program package alternative should be explored. Suppose that the development of the industrial park included provisions for job training, whereas the job training program assumed the need for some expenses in job placement. If the combination of these programs produced as small as a 1.5 percent reduction in the project costs, then the resulting cost-effectiveness ratio would be 1.322, making this package competitive with the job training–agri-business package (assuming no budgetary constraint).

One further supposition might be explored: The program package of job training and the industrial park development is approximately 39 percent over the budget limit of $1 million. Would it be possible to develop a smaller "package," bringing the combined program alternatives into the range of the budgetary constraint while reducing the overall effectiveness, by, say, only

25 percent? If this could be accomplished, then the cost-effectiveness ratio would be 1.358, making this modified package the most desirable alternative.

The point of this discussion is to illustrate the further analyses that are possible and should be carried out in the cost-effectiveness approach. The application of analytical techniques such as sensitivity analysis and contingency analysis plays an important role in these further explorations of program complementarities.[46]

### Incidence of Program Impacts

The effectiveness measure used in analyzing the several program alternatives in the proceeding example was the contribution that each might make to an increase in the aggregate regional income. For many purposes such aggregate measures are appropriate indicators of program effectiveness. Aggregate measures of effectiveness, however, do not reveal the composition of the impacted population; they do not answer the question of "who will benefit most directly from the program." For example, in Table 10-8 it was assumed that a 40 percent increase in income levels resulting from the development of an industrial park would impact some 850 workers with average current incomes of approximately $3,000. However, the same level of project effectiveness ($1,020,000) could be obtained by increasing by 30 percent the income level of 850 workers with average incomes of $4,000, or by increasing by 40 percent the income level of 638 workers with average incomes of $4,000. This information is not revealed by an aggregate income measure, and for many types of programs, such as in this example of a program to alleviate poverty in depressed rural regions, the use of an aggregate measure will not be very useful for program evaluation. What is required in such situation is: (1) sharper definitions of program goals; and (2) more detailed analyses to provide information on the incidence of program impacts.[47]

For example, a more explicit goal for the depressed rural region program might be "a reduction in the number or proportion of families located in the region that are poor," where the word "poor" is defined by some dollar income measure. Such a goal statement, in addition to requiring a measure of the increase in aggregate regional income, necessitates a breakdown of the aggregate measure generated by each program into component income groups to reflect the incidence of program impact. From this information it would be possible to determine the number of low-income families that would benefit from the program, and it is this measure, not the aggregate measure, that is more appropriate in determining the effectiveness of the various program alternatives.

Given data on the current state of the system, the projected change in this state arising from the adoption of each alternative, and an estimated number of persons impacted by a given alternative, however, aggregate effectiveness measures can be applied with validity. This can be proven by examining the data in Table 10-8. With an estimated 470 workers impacted by the adoption of the recreational facility project and a project cost of $350,000, the cost per worker is $744.68. By disaggregating these data into several income categories (assuming equal intervals from the mean), assigning weights to each category, and determining the distribution of workers that will meet the constraints assigned to each alternative, a new index can be computed. However, this index has a direct relationship to the aggregate data, as determined by the following formula: sum of the weighted values divided by the number of categories of disaggregation. This relationship is illustrated in Table 10-9 for various levels of disaggregation using the recreational facility alternative from Table 10-8. As may be seen from Table 10-9, when two categories are used, the weighted index

**Table 10-9**
**Cost–Effectiveness for Aggregate and Disaggregate Data**

|  |  |  |  |  |  | Totals |
|---|---|---|---|---|---|---|
| Income categories |  |  |  |  | $ 3,000 |  |
| Weights |  |  |  |  | 1 | 1 |
| Workers |  |  |  |  | 470 | 470 |
| Income increase |  |  |  |  | $282,000 | $282,000 |
| Cost/Worker Weight |  |  |  |  |  | $744.68 |
| Income categories |  |  |  | $ 2,500 | $ 3,500 |  |
| Weights |  |  |  | 2 | 1 | 1.5 |
| Workers |  |  |  | 235 | 235 | 470 |
| Income increase |  |  |  | $117,500 | $164,500 | $282,000 |
| Cost/Worker Weight |  |  |  |  |  | $ 496.45 |
| Income categories |  |  | $ 2,500 | $ 3,000 | $ 3,500 |  |
| Weights |  |  | 3 | 2 | 1 | 2 |
| Workers |  |  | 85 | 300 | 85 | 470 |
| Income increase |  |  | $42,500 | $180,000 | $ 59,500 | $282,000 |
| Cost/Worker Weight |  |  |  |  |  | $ 372.34 |
| Income categories | $ 2,000 | $ 2,500 | $ 3,000 | $ 3,500 | $ 4,000 |  |
| Weights | 5 | 4 | 3 | 2 | 1 | 3 |
| Workers | 75 | 95 | 125 | 105 | 70 | 470 |
| Income increase | $30,000 | $47,500 | $75,000 | $73,500 | $ 56,000 | $282,000 |
| Cost/Worker Weight |  |  |  |  |  | $ 248.23 |

(sum of the weighted values divided by the number of categories) is 1.5 and the cost per worker divided by this index is $496.45; when three categories are used, the weighted index is 2 (3 + 2 + 1 divided by 3) and the cost per worker divided by this index is $372.34; and when five categories are used the weighted index is 3 and the cost per worker divided by this index is $248.23. The five-category breakdown illustrates that there need not be an equal distribution of impacted subjects about the mean—the only stipulation is that the established constraints are met. Since each alternative, when disaggregated into a number of income categories, will evidence the same multipliers, it is just as valid to use the aggregate measures of effectiveness as it is to disaggregate the data, providing the appropriate parameters are described, as in Table 10-8.

The consequences for the cost-effectiveness analysis when such parameters are not initial specified, however, may be significant. To illustrate this point, suppose that, in the state museum program (the alternatives for which were described in Table 10-7), the objective was to reach all population groups, but that the impacts incident to certain groups were given greater weight, that is, service to residents with lower levels of education is particularly important to program administrators. To examine the implications of meeting this objective, the aggregate measure must be disaggregated to permit the identification of "low-education" users, Suppose that the program administrators were able to agree that service to "low-education" users is three times as important as service to all other users, and that it was found that 100,000 of the 800,000 users of the regional facilities and 3,000 of the 4,000 potential users of the mobile units were included in this category. It would be possible to transform the data in Table 10-7 to that shown in Table 10-10.

Using the assigned weights for the disaggregated data, each of the three alternatives has the same weighted cost-effectiveness ratio (i.e., $4 million divided by 1 million weighted users; $40,000 divided by 10,000 weighted users; and $10 million divided by 2.5 million weighted users). Given the budget constraint of $10 million, the program effectiveness of the regional facilities alternative is 2.0 million (1 million weighted users times 2 facilities), the program effectiveness of the mobile units is 2.5 million (10,000 times 250 units), and the program effectiveness of the combined solution is also 2.5 million. Therefore, the imposition of this additional objective reduces the relative effectiveness of the regional facilities alternative in serving the target population due to its characteristics of fixed location and indivisibility, while increasing the effectiveness of the mobile units precisely for the obverse reasons. Using the methods of contingency analysis it may be determined that, if only 2,000 of the 4,000 potential users of each mobile unit were in the low-education category, the weighted cost-effectiveness ratio for this alternative would be $5 per weighted user and the overall project effectiveness would be 2.0 million. Under this contingency the combined solution would have a weighted cost-effectiveness ratio of $4.17 per user and an overall program effectiveness of 2.4 million,

## Table 10-10
## Cost-Effectiveness Analysis with Incidence Considered

| Program Alternative | Effectiveness per Project Weight = 1 | 3 | Cost per Project | Weighted Cost-Effectiveness Ratio | Program Effectiveness |
|---|---|---|---|---|---|
| Regional facilities | 700,000 | 100,000 | $ 4 million | $4/user | 2.0 mil. |
| Mobile units | 1,000 | 3,000 | $40,000 | $4/user | 2.5 mil. |
| Combined solution | 1,450,000 | 350,000 | $10 million | $4/user | 2.5 mil. |

making it the more desirable approach. However, if the number of low-education users could be increased by only 1 user per mobile unit (i.e., to 3,001), the overall program effectiveness of the mobile unit alternative would be 2,500,500, as compared with 2,500,100 for the combined solution. Therefore, the choice between the mobile units alternative and the combined solution can be based on the confidence placed in the estimate of impacted low-education users.

*Optimum Envelope*

Frequently, in the formulation of program alternatives significant shifts in the configuration of the cost curves occur as additional levels of effectiveness are sought, that is, at one level of effectiveness (and cost) program A may provide the most desirable cost-effectiveness ratio, whereas at a higher level of effectiveness (and cost) some other program may provide the more desirable ratio.

This can be illustrated by a hypothetical case study. Assume that in Appalachia some 3,000 workers become unemployed each year due to technical obsolescence, that is, the job for which they are trained and skilled is eliminated through mechanization of industrial processes. The federal government has established an objective to retrain part or all of these workers to new skills by means of a one-year intensive training course. Through this program it is anticipated that the workers will be employable at a certain skill level ten years earlier than if they had to attain these skills on their own. Therefore, the benefits of this program will run for ten years. To provide this training it is necessary to develop regional training centers, build new facilities or significantly upgrade existing facilities, hire new instructional personnel, and so forth. It is anticipated that the program will continue to operate over a ten-year period.

After considerable study it is determined that there are two alternative means to achieve the program objectives—each of these alternatives can be

### Table 10-11
### Alternative Program Costs (In Thousands)

| Item of Cost | System A | System B |
|---|---|---|
| Development costs | $15,000 | $1,000 |
| Investment per training center | 500 | 400 |
| Operational costs per year per training center | 1,500 | 3,000 |

considered a "system". System A is an equipment-oriented approach, involving the extensive use of programmed learning techniques, tape libraries to upgrade basic skills in reading, use of computers, and so forth. It has only five instructors per training center and a trainee-instructor ratio of 60 to 1. System B is a teacher-oriented approach, involving team-teaching techniques. It requires 20 instructors per training center and has a 10 to 1 trainee-instructor ratio. The trainee capacity at training centers for System A is 300 and for System B, 200. The costs for each system are summarized in Table 10-11.

It now is possible to examine how costs and benefits (program effectiveness) are related in the tests for preferredness. First, assume that the benefits and costs cannot be measured in the same units, that is, they are incommensurable. In the case at hand gains are measured in terms of the number of workers retrained, and costs are measured in dollars. Since decision makers do not know the level of training they wish to support (or can afford to support given limited resources), it is necessary to develop a schedule of costs and benefits over the full range of workers to be trained (i.e., 0 to 3,000). For convenience it may be assumed that the costs are of a continuous nature, that is, training centers can be constructed and operated at various sizes.

The trainee load capability is charted on the top part of Figure 10-8. System A would require 10 training centers for 3,000 trainees and System B requires 15. The systems costs (development, investment, and ten years of operating costs) are charted on the bottom part of Figure 10-8, and are summarized in Table 10-12.

It is now possible to combine benefits (trainee capacity—assumed to be equal to workers trained) and costs into one chart (Figure 10-9) by eliminating the common denominator, number of training centers.

### Table 10-12
### Total Costs over Ten Years (In Thousands)

| | System A | | | System B | | |
|---|---|---|---|---|---|---|
| Centers | 0 | 10 | 15 | 0 | 10 | 15 |
| R & D | $15,000 | $15,000 | $15,000 | $1,000 | $ 1,000 | $ 1,000 |
| Inv. | – | 5,000 | 7,500 | – | 4,000 | 6,000 |
| Operation | – | 15,000 | 22,500 | – | 30,000 | 45,000 |
| Total | $15,000 | $35,000 | $45,000 | $1,000 | $35,000 | $52,000 |

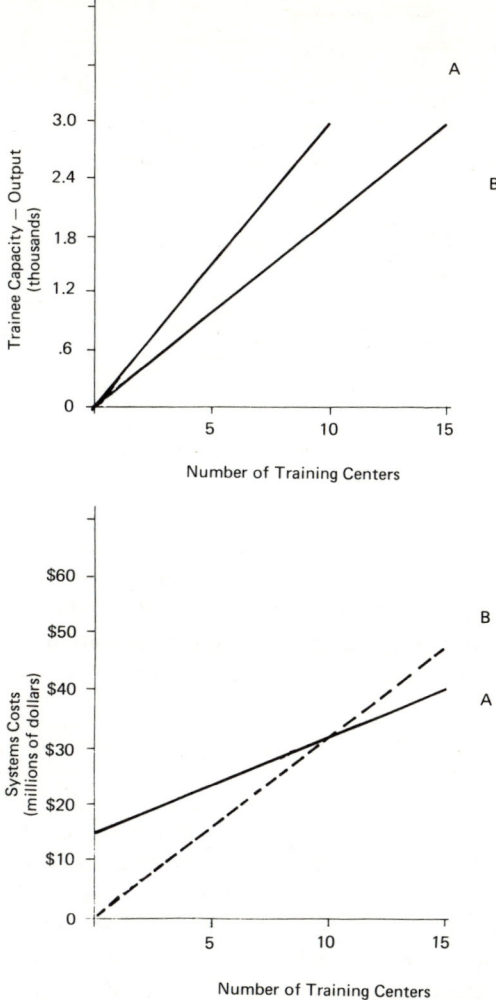

**Figure 10-8.** Trainee Capacity and Systems Costs Versus Number of Training Centers for Alternative Systems A and B

Recognizing that nonquantifiable factors may enter into the final decision—the discussion of which is omitted here for simplicity—it is possible to choose the best system given either a fixed budget or a specified level of benefits. The envelope of optimum costs to benefits is indicated on Figure 10-9: for all budgets under $24.2 million, System B is preferred because it will have a greater trainee capacity; conversely, for all trained loads less than 1,360, System B is preferred because it will cost less than System A. For budgets above $24.2 million or for trainee loads above 1,360, System A is preferred.

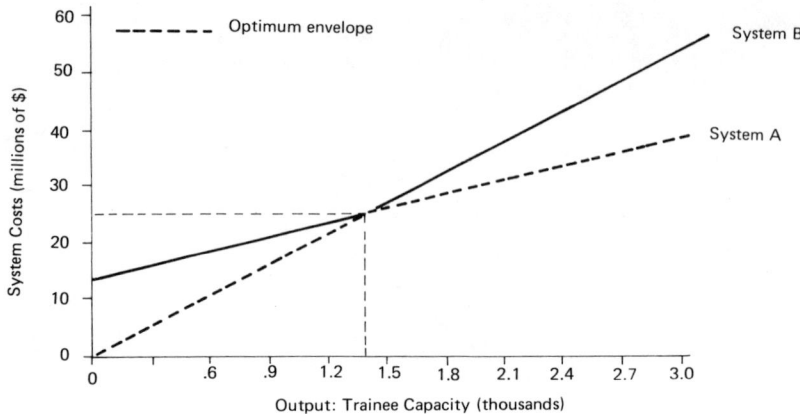

**Figure 10-9.** Trainee Capacity Versus System Costs for Alternative Systems A and B.

For example, at a $20 million budget System B has a capacity of about 1,100 trainees, while A has about 800 trainees. At a trainee load of 2,400, however, System A would cost $31 million whereas System B would cost $41.8 million. Although these illustration has been extremely simplified, it show how costs and benefits interact when they are incommensurable.

*Incremental Costing*

In cost-effectiveness analysis the cost analysis phase can be viewed as an application of the economic concept of marginal analysis. The analysis must always move from some base that represents existing capabilities (the present state of the system) and the existing resource base. The problem is to determine how much additional resources will be required to achieve some specified additional performance capability (the desired state of the system), or conversely, how much additional performance capability would result from some additional expenditure. Therefore, incremental costs are the most relevant factors in cost analysis. The economic concept of marginal analysis must be distinguished from the accounting concept of associating total costs, including an allocated share of indirect expense, to an end item. Ideally, the incremental cost of a system is the difference between two programs, one with the improved system and one without it.

In measuring incremental costs care must be taken to exclude *sunk costs*.[i]

---

[i] While sunk costs should be excluded from the cost analysis, they should form a part of the total program analysis in program budgeting, that is, in examining the program structure of an agency past costs levels should be evaluated in terms of effectiveness, as

Sunk costs or costs that have been expended in the past are not relevant to the question: "What will it cost in the future to acquire a future performance capability?" No matter how "unfair" it may seem, past costs, say for older systems, should not be included in the analysis regardless of how much money may be involved. This is not to say that the resources acquired by past expenditures should be excluded from the analysis, however. Should sunk costs result in *inheritable assets* (i.e., resources that will become available only to the system under analysis), the sunk costs of those assets should be excluded. Inheritable assets can result from sunk costs on many systems, not just the ones under obvious consideration. It is for this reason that explicitly costing a total program is best because all systems can be examined and a better picture of resources available for other systems can be revealed. Conversely, all the systems competing for these assets are revealed, and thus, a more accurate picture of net asset requirements can be shown.

These points can be illustrated by reference to the previous case study. It may be recalled that System A had an estimated development cost of $15 million for some complicated program learning equipment. If the study of this problem was delayed by two years, and in that period $3 million per year was invested in the program to further develop this capability, then, at the time of decision, the relevant costs would be $9 million ($15 million less $6 million) assuming no change in the total program estimates. The $6 million would be a "sunk" cost and irrelevant. Looking at this question from a more realistic viewpoint, it is possible that several millions of dollars already have been spent on the development of the program learning approach. If it is assumed that these expenditures amount to $20 million, then the $15 million represents "future costs" of a development program whose total cost will be $35 million. However, only the $15 million to achieve the new capability is relevant to the cost analysis; the previously expended $20 million is not.

## Dealing with Inheritable Assets

Regarding the question of inheritable assets, assume that a System C does now exist and has a capability of training 1,000 displaced workers, although it is not judged to be worthy of further expansion. This system has five teachers per training facility and a 20 to 1 trainee-instructor ratio. While the buildings and equipment of System C could be used by System B, the capacity of System C is only 100 students per facility. System A cannot use System C facilities because new facilities are needed for the advanced equipment of System A. If it is assumed that $0.3 million can be saved per training center if System B

---

well as the "new" costs to be incurred in seeking a more desirable level of performance. This is known as zero-base budgeting.

**Table 10-13**
**Alternative Program Costs (In Thousands)**

| Item of Cost | System A | System B | | System C |
| | | 1st 10 | Addition | (10 Centers) |
|---|---|---|---|---|
| Development | $15,000 | $1,000 | – | – |
| Investment/center | 500 | 100 | 400 | – |
| Operations/year/center | 1,500 | 3,000 | 3,000 | 1,000 |

utilizes the facilities of System C, the systems costs shown previously in Table 10-11 can be converted to the information shown in Table 10-13.

The data on System C could be added to the diagrams in Figure 10-8, resulting in the diagram shown in Figure 10-10. Unfortunately, the investment savings for System B are not very significant, so that the break in the system costs after the tenth training center is put into operation is not sharp. It should be noted that the cost curve for System C stops at 10 because it is not planned to expand the system. The cost curve for System A is unchanged from the previous situation because it cannot inherit any resources, and the cost curve of System B breaks after unit 10 when facilities can no longer be inherited. To complete the analysis the envelope of optimum cost to benefit for the three systems is shown in Figure 10-11. System C is preferred for all trainee loads up to 1,000, System B from 1,000 to 1,580, and System A from 1,580 to 3,000. Conversely, for budget levels of about $16.5 million or less, System C is preferred (even though only $10 million can be spent on C); System B is preferred from $16.5 million to about $25.5 million; and System A thereafter.

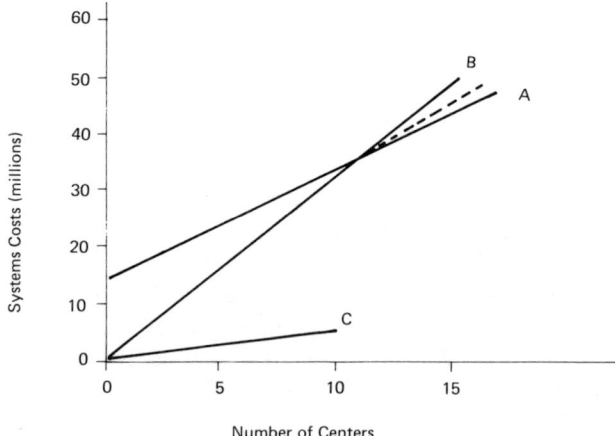

**Figure 10-10.** Systems Costs Versus Number of Centers for Alternative Systems A, B, and C.

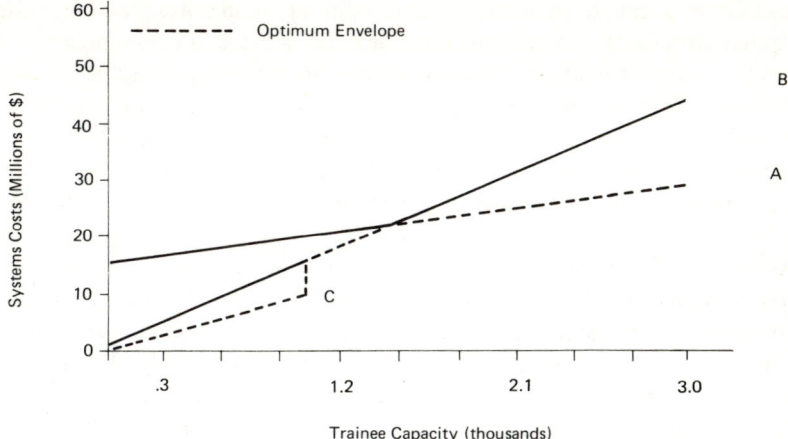

**Figure 10-11.** Trainee Capacity Versus System Costs for Alternative Systems A, B, and C.

*Externalities and Multigoal Programs*

In addition to having impacts on the intended goal, a program alternative typically will generate impacts incident to other goals. These impacts may be positive, as in the case of the antilead poisoning example (Table 10-6), wherein the repainting of houses with nonlead based paint not only contributes to the health goal but also contributes to the goal of housing improvement. Or these additional impacts may be negative, as in the case of an electric power program, wherein the air pollution produced by the power generating plant will negatively effect others goals, such as maintaining a clean environment. These additional program impacts are often referred to as *"externalities"* or *"spillovers."*[48]

The importance of including externalities in the decision-making process should be self-evident—programs that generate positive externalities should receive a more favorable evaluation when their externalities are included, whereas the reverse should be true of programs that generate negative externalities. The consequences of including both positive and negative externalities in the analysis are not necessarily a modification of choice among competing alternatives. The externalities that a program alternative generates may have little direct impact on the values assigned to costs and benefits, that is, there may be no "rewards" to the program alternative for generating positive externalities and no "penalties" for generating negative externalities.[49] Thus, faced with the situation where the cost-effectiveness ratio of alternative A exceeds that of alternative B only when the positive and negative externalities of both alternatives are included, the analyst is likely to recommend alternative B, unless a system of sanctions and rewards recognizes the importance of including these externalities (e.g., regulations requiring the consideration of such externalities, as in federal air pollution legislation, or transfer payments made between governments for services provided outside a given jurisdiction). A further problem arises from the fact that many externalities are difficult to measure.[50] In many cases, the problem of measurement is one of the reasons these factors have been categorized as exogenous and treated as externalities in the analysis.

As in the evaluation based on the incidence of impacts, the treatment of externalities requires that some consensus be reached as to the relative importance of each external goal or impact, and that this be expressed in terms of weight (economists often use prices to represent these weights).[51] These points can be illustrated by returning to the alternatives described in Table 10-8, relating to programs to alleviate conditions in an economically depressed rural region. Assume that, in addition to increasing employment opportunities, these various alternatives will produce positive externalities relating to improved highways, diversification of the economic base, expanded educational opportunities, as well as a negative externality regarding the cost of public service delivery (e.g., the industrial park project would require considerable expansion of public services in terms of water and sewer, etc.) Each of the alternatives would manifest these externalities to differing degrees and each externality might be assigned a different weight. Assume that some consensus can be reached on the relative importance of these externalities as shown in Table 10-14, and that the "pricing" of these externalities produces the array shown in each column (this approach assumes that the highest value for each externality equals the full weight assigned to that externality, with each lesser value rated proportionately). From Table 10-14 it may be seen that the diversification of the economic base is deemed to be half as important as the increase of employment, with aid to highways 30 percent as important, and increased educational opportunities 25 percent as important. The anticipated increases in public service delivery costs ( a negative externality) is rated as 20 percent as important as the central program goal of increasing employment. Within each goal category the job training alternative, which is estimated to produce 920 new jobs, is ranked first, with the other alternatives weighted proportionally; the industrial park is seen to have the greatest potential for an increase in highway funding and as a contributor to the diversification of the economic base; the agribusiness alternative has the highest potential for increased opportunities in educational programs; and the industrial park is seen to have the greatest impact on the cost of public service delivery. All other alternatives are rated proportionally.

As shown in Table 10-15, by multiplying the original project effectiveness for each alternative times the weighted effectiveness index, and dividing by the cost per project, a weighted cost-effectiveness ratio can be computed to reflect

### Table 10-14
### Cost-Effectiveness with Externalities Considered

| | Employment | Aid to Highways | Diversification of Economic Base | Increased Education Opportunities | Increased Public Service Costs | Weighted Effectiveness Index |
|---|---|---|---|---|---|---|
| Weight | 1 = 920 | 0.30 | 0.50 | 0.25 | -0.20 | |
| Recreation facility | 0.51 | 0.25 | 0.20 | 0.10 | -0.10 | 1.85 |
| Job training | 1.00 | 0.10 | 0.35 | 0.20 | -0.10 | 0.96 |
| Agri-business | 0.52 | 0.15 | 0.30 | 0.25 | -0.15 | 1.55 |
| Industrial park | 0.92 | 0.30 | 0.50 | 0.20 | -0.20 | 1.07 |
| | | | | | | 1.72 |

### Table 10-15
### Calculation of Weighted Cost-Effectiveness Ratios

| Project Alternative | Project Effectiveness | Weighted Effectiveness Index | Weighted Project Effectiveness | Cost per Project | Weighted C/E Ratio |
|---|---|---|---|---|---|
| Recreation facility | $ 282,000 | 0.96 | $ 270,720 | $350,000 | 0.773 |
| Job training | 690,000 | 1.55 | 1,069,500 | 540,000 | 1.981 |
| Agri-business | 504,000 | 1.07 | 539,280 | 440,000 | 1.226 |
| Industrial park | 1,020,000 | 1.72 | 1,754,400 | 850,000 | 2.064 |

the impact of these externalities. Through these calculations the industrial park alternative supplants the job training program as the "most desirable" course of action to pursue. Of course, such analyses may be subject to considerable criticism, depending upon the acceptance of the somewhat subjective weighings given to each externalities. Here the techniques of sensitivity and contingency analysis might be applied to provide further verification of the ranking of the various alternatives.

While the impact of externalities is most frequently disregarded, often with unfortunate consequences, the analyst should make every effort to identify and, if possible, quantify these factors to provide the decision makers with as complete a picture as possible of the implications surrounding the available choices. While the inclusion of externalities should never be used to "load" the analysis in favor of a particular alternative, their enumeration can help to clarify the choices that can and should be made.

*Summary and Conclusions*

The techniques of cost-effectiveness analysis are relatively new, having their origins in the early sixties, and consequently have not yet reached full maturity. Initially, cost-effectiveness analysis was developed for application when benefits could not be measured in units commensurable with costs. In these early cost-effectiveness analyses the output of level of effectiveness was usually taken as a given and several methods of achieving it were examined in the hope that one would have lower costs than others. These initial explorations revealed many important aspects of public decisions regarding the allocation of scarce resources, as outlined in the preceding discussion. Cost-effectiveness analysis provides an output-oriented focus for the evaluation of program alternatives through its emphasis on goals (the fixed benefits approach) and its application of effectiveness measures. The extended time horizon adopted in cost-effectiveness analysis leads to a fuller recognition of the need for life-cycle costing and benefits analysis and the importance of incremental costing, sunk costs, and inheritable assets. Cost-goal and cost-constraint analyses add important dimensions to the information available to the decision maker. Cost-effectiveness analysis is particularly applicable to indivisible projects, to an examination of complementarities under project interdependence—producing the concept of the "optimum envelope"—to an identification of the incidence of program impacts, and to an examination of externalities. While many of these analytical issues were implicit in cost-benefit analysis, they were made explicit through the development of cost-effectiveness techniques.

As with the other techniques of program analysis, the cost-effectiveness model need not be adopted "whole cloth." A number of subroutines of this approach may be introduced initially into ongoing procedures of analysis. Of particular importance would be considerations developed through the more narrowly defined technique of cost-effectiveness curve analysis. As the complexity of the resource allocation problem becomes more evident, other techniques then may be adopted, depending upon the availability of data and the needs and capabilities of the analyst.

# 11 The Role of Program Budgeting

While concepts of more rationalistic public budgeting, in the form of PPBS (planning-programming-budgeting-systems), burst on the scene in the early sixties amid general enthusiasm, heralded by many as the Holy Grail of over a half century of budget reform crusades, the future of these concepts in the seventies remains somewhat in doubt. As with many innovations introduced by dictum, inadequate groundwork was laid for the establishment of PPBS in the federal budgetary process and even less so in state and local governments.[1] What proved to be a highly successful technique in the Department of Defense for the evaluation of weaponry systems had only limited immediate application in other public agencies. Soon, proponents of PPBS were faced with strong arguments concerning its "failures" even in the Defense Department. Much heat but little light arose in the ensuing debates regarding PPBS that took place in legislative chambers, agency conference rooms, and college classrooms.

It is of no particular concern to this author whether the term PPBS survives this continuing controversy. What is important, however, is that the underlying framework—a more systemic and comprehensive approach to budget making—be further refined and perfected as an important mechanism of public management, particularly with reference to the process of capital facilities planning. With these objectives in mind, this discussion attempts to circumvent the PPBS debate by returning to the more basic concepts of program budgeting.

### Major Components of Program Budgeting

There are five major components to a program budget: The first involves an identification of major public goals and objectives in programmatic terms. This component is the essence of what has been labelled "strategic planning" by this author.[2] *Strategic planning* is the process of identifying public goals and objectives, determining needed changes in those objectives, and deciding on the resources to be used to attain them. It entails the evaluation of alternative courses of action and the formulation of policies that govern the acquisition, use, and disposition of public resources. Strategic planning is a dynamic process involving a systematic combining and extending of facts and possibilities to point out policy alternatives for long-range development. This evaluation must be undertaken in such a manner that deliberations may be subjected to constant correction and refinement in establishing a desirable range within which public choice can and should be made. The formulation of long-term public goals, therefore, serves as an integrative element in the preparation of a strategic plan. The theoretical basis for strategic planning represents a summary and coordination of these goals and consequent trends by which a given jurisdiction or area should develop. It thus serves as the basis for the transformation of such trends and goals into more definitive social, economic, and physical development plans. Much of the appeal of the strategic planning approach derives from the conscious inclusion of these elements as safeguards against the tendency to formulate future plans as mere extensions of the present or as extrapolations of the past. Strategic planning can mean the difference between success and failure in the delivery of vital public services and facilities. Unfortunately, the concepts of strategic planning are the least developed of the basic modes of public planning.

A second major component of program budgeting involves the structuring and analysis of public programs *across-the-board,* that is, without concern, initially, for the organizational prerogatives of agencies that might be involved in the processes of program implementation.[3] The across-the-board structuring of governmental programs is an ideal to strive toward—in reality such an objective should be considered long-range rather than immediate. Such a structure would focus the process of goal identification in terms of the total activities of government, regardless of where these activities may be carried out within the organizational structure. Some agencies simply cannot make the shift to such a program structure in the relatively short period mandated by many proponents of program budgeting. Indeed, this has been one of the major obstacles to effective implementation of the program budget concept, arising from the overzealous adherence to the across-the-board principle by advocates of the system. In most cases significant efforts must first be launched in the development of a management information and program evaluation system (MIPES) before the interdependencies of various public agencies can be examined and the goals of government programmed in a more comprehensive (and comprehensible) manner.

The third component of program budgeting involves an *extended time horizon* and multiyear program and financial plans. Program budgeting requires that public agencies incorporate program costs and budget constraints directly into the program evaluation and selection processes. The usual practice in public budgeting is to divide annual agency-wide or municipality-wide costs into a capital and an operating expense budget, showing cost totals on a "line item" or input basis (e.g., total salaries and wages, equipment rentals and purchases, repairs and maintenance, etc.). In contrast, program budgeting requires annual costs to be identified in terms of those programs, developed on a multiyear basis, that have been selected for inclusion in the current budget. Furthermore, these costs must be projected into the near future so that future cost implications of current programs can be known. This extended time horizon is necessary to establish a long-range process that can circumvent the "crisis programming" characteristic of many public activities, and thereby it serves to guide the total activities of government in a more coherent and comprehensive fashion. The *multiyear program plan* is needed to indicate the proposed outputs of public facilities and services according to the objectives outlined in the strategic planning stage. The magnitude of each program is determined through this phase of the budgetary process. Cost estimates, outlined in varying levels of detail according to the time span covered, must be matched with estimates of revenue sources required to support the proposed programs. Only through such an examination is it possible to determine the adequacy of current sources of revenue in the light of future demands. Once the budget is framed in program terms, the total costs of a given program can then be disaggregated by type of input (e.g., salaries and wages, materials and supplies, equipment, etc.). Through this process, the program costs within each category can be totaled to indicate the amount of the achievement of a given public goal. As Donald A. Krueckeberg and Arthur L. Silver have observed, however, this process requires that public agencies clearly articulate the goals they want to attain, "and this is often a novel activity in many governmental agencies."[4]

*Program analysis*—the fourth component—is the cornerstone of program budgeting; through this systematic analysis of alternatives, programs are selected from multiyear plans. While program analysis may take several forms, in essence it involves the reduction of complex problems into their component parts so that each can be studied in greater detail, followed by a synthesis of these parts back to the whole. To undertake such an analysis, explicit measures of program outputs must be quantified. The task of determining what these output or performance measures should be on a program-by-program basis, and of actually quantifying them, is frequently a difficult one, particularly for agency staff more accustomed to measuring program activity levels in terms of inputs rather than the outputs produced. As Krueckeberg and Silver have observed, agency personnel may offer considerable resistance to the formulation of new program output or performance measures.

> After all, it is not that difficult to spend budgeted money and, hence, his performance, when measured in terms of "numbers of new hospital beds installed" or "new teachers hired," is much easier to define than performance measures such as "number of low income persons made healthy" or "low income persons successfully trained."[5]

Program analysis recognizes the basic problems involved in the allocation of limited fiscal resources: (1) the problem of maximizing benefits given the costs involved; (2) the problem of minimizing costs to achieve a certain predetermined level of benefits; or (3) the combination of the above two problem types in which both costs and benefits may vary. The analytical task in program analysis involves the use of existing resources or the generation of new resources to create new means-ends patterns to resolve conflicts over the problem of choice. In general, this task involves: (1) identification of questions relevant to the inquiry; (2) operationalization of vaguely stated objectives; (3) elimination of imprecise factors; (4) ascertainment of quantifiable variables; (5) specification of assumptions; (6) selection of models and other tools of analysis; (7) specification of alternatives that meet the parameters of the selected models; and (8) selection of the "best" or "optimal" course of action or program.[6] The techniques of systems analysis, and in particular the procedures associated with cost-benefit and cost-effectiveness analysis (described in chapter 10), have formed the principal tools to accomplish this multistep task.

The final component in program budgeting involves *program monitoring and updating procedures.* Through such procedures the program analysis techniques are applied to determine needed program modifications and improvements once programs are implemented. Thus, the regular collection and systematic organization of performance (output) measures in a management information and program evaluation system (MIPES) can provide program managers and public officials with periodic reports by which to monitor ongoing programs and projects. Such information feedback provides managers with the mechanisms for program control and evaluation, for example, cost-effectiveness ratios, indicating the relationship between program cost and actual program output, can be calculated and, if properly defined, can be used as an effective tool for program evaluation.

The primary advantages of the program budget approach should be evident from the foregoing description of its basic components. By concentrating on end products instead of inputs and by providing better information on all costs and benefits, program budgeting offers a more useful basis for evaluation of agency requests by departments, the central budget agency, the chief executive, and the legislative branch. The stress on specific (measurable) end products, such as the reduction of poverty in the urban core by some definable percentage, rather than vague statements of program objectives couched in terms of various types of manpower and material inputs, affords a more effective basis for public evaluation of programs relative to the goals of governmental activities. The program budgeting approach is designed to consider the pursuit of public policy objectives in light of all economic costs and stresses the relationship between various outputs or programs and the inputs necessary to produce them. This emphasis, in turn, facilitates the use of more systematic techniques to analyze alternative programs directed to the attainment of public goals and various alternative means of implementation. The use of this approach forces agencies, in preparing budget requests, to stress product and input-to-output relationships and to give attention to a wider (and longer) range of costs and benefits.[7]

## Limitations to Implementation

The principal limitation to the implementation of program budgeting procedures is the difficulty in defining the output of many governmental activities, that is, of obtaining the necessary measures of program effectiveness against which alternative approaches can be tested. The aim of a public service activity such as police protection, for example, is not to arrest as many people as possible, but to deter crime—this is hard to measure. Thus, with many public activities, the ultimate "output" is not definable in a meaningful way and, as a consequence, secondary measures of performance must be used. Frequently, the problem centers on the procedures of data gathering and record keeping followed by public agencies. A city hospital keeps records on the number of patients admitted and the treatment administered, but seldom on the number of patients it successfully has made healthy. And even if such "output" records are maintained, they seldom are organized in terms of specific target populations that might be appropriate to the evaluation of various public health programs. The resistance of many public agency personnel to the identification and adoption of more meaningful performance measures has already been touched upon. In some situations the frequently heard argument that the cost of generating the necessary information is too great in light of the consequent limited improvement in program evaluation techniques or program performance may be valid. All too often, however, this argument is merely a smoke screen to hide organized bureaucratic resistance to change or general ineptness among agency personnel.

This is not to suggest that all defensive behavior regarding the application of program budgeting techniques is to be condemned as irresponsible. In some cases such behavior is well-founded, as when an overzealous analyst attempts to impose an inflexible and often arbitrarily defined format for the evaluation of complex activities for which he does not have a full understanding or appreciation. By the same token a costly data collection and computerization effort may yield vast quantities of computer printout, resulting in the institutionalization of the very bureaucratic inflexibilities that gave rise to the need for improved decision-making processes in the first place. Thus, care must be exercised to avoid, in the name of more rationale and "scientific" procedures of problem analysis, the substitution of one inflexible structure for another.

A more critical problem associated with the identification of effectiveness measures arises from the interrelatedness of public goals. Many public programs contribute directly to more than one goal and indirectly to many goals. While the procedures of analysis may be simplified by the use of effectiveness measures that suggest a given program contributes to the achievement of only one goal, such practices may be arbitrary and extremely limiting in terms of assessing actual program impacts relative to costs. If the total costs of a program are attributed to a single goal, the resulting evaluation may find the program to be ineffective, since important indirect contributions have been ignored. If, on the other hand, program costs are apportioned to each of the various goals that the program is purported to support, possible contradictions may arise, whereby the program contributes effectively to one set of public goals, while perhaps detracting from the achievement of another set. Such a situation may lead to the conclusion that the ineffective or detractive activities should be eliminated or at least cut back.[8] However, since programs that relate to multiple goals (so-called *joint production* programs) may yield results in unchangeable proportions that cannot be disassociated one from another, there may be no effective way to eliminate or even to cut back the impact of one or to increase the impact on another.[9] Thus, it may be necessary to measure, weigh, and sum multiple goal impacts, rather than merely devise a cost-effectiveness ratio for each goal. Total program costs must then be related to total program effectiveness, reflecting these multiple impacts.

To be applied properly in program evaluation, selected performance criteria (effectiveness measures) must be capable of identifying and measuring the actual change or impact experienced by the target population attributable to the initiation of the particular program under study, while isolating the changes arising from external factors. To achieve this level of "causality," however, in many instances may require an intensive and selective analytic effort beyond the capacity of many local governments. The more "tangible" the products of a particular program or project, however, the more accessible is the design of appropriate criteria. This is one of the important factors contributing to the conclusion that the application of program budgeting techniques in local government may well begin most effectively in the area of capital facilities planning, for it is here that public service objectives are (or should be) most straightforward and "tangible".

## Formulation of a Capital Facilities/Program Budget

It is not the purpose of this concluding section to suggest that local government efforts in program budgeting should be limited to the development of capital facilities plans. Rather, the premise is advanced that local governments, in adopting the procedures of capital facilities planning outlined in this book, can establish a firm basis upon which to gain experience in the procedures of program budgeting, experience that can be then carried over to other phases of budget preparation and fiscal administration. This examination of the application of program budgeting techniques in capital facilities planning will focus on the basic components of program budgeting, as outlined above.

### *Multiyear Plans*

Program budgeting seeks to produce a complete plan—one that projects for some reasonable period both a physical work program and an accompanying financial plan. As noted previously, multiyear program and financial plans serve as the critical link in program budgeting between the goals, objectives, impacts, and outputs, on the one hand, and resource inputs on the other. Such plans display or at least assert what accomplishments can be expected for a given commitment of resources.[10] Program budgeting, however, does not involve the establishment of a final plan for a fixed period. Rather, the multiyear plans "move," that is, each year the plans are revised and updated to include one additional future year and to omit the earliest year. Most commonly, multiyear plans in program budgeting cover seven years: the immediate past year, the current year, the budget year, and the four succeeding years. This format, of course, closely approximates that used in capital facilities planning for the formulation of a six-year capital improvements program. Thus, the framework for one of the more critical components of program budgeting is inherent in the practices of capital facilities planning. The adoption of the multiyear format for total budget analysis has mutually reinforcing potentialities. As S. Kenneth Howard has observed:

> PPB contemplates that projections of total program costs will cover a time span more in accord with the one typically used in capital budgeting. Increasing the time horizon used in projecting operating costs would reduce the difficulties that arise when operating costs are projected for one length of time but a program's capital aspects are estimated for another.[11]

A problem associated with the formulation of multiyear plans involves the establishment of realistic constraints to prevent resulting projections from making economically and politically impractical demands upon fiscal resources. Unless such constraints are imposed, program growth is likely to be projected beyond that which is feasible or practical. Such "pie-in-the-sky" proposals are precisely what began to emerge from the original PPBS efforts among federal civilian agencies in the sixties.[12] As program and financial plans became unrealistic "wish-lists," the Bureau of the Budget (BOB) in 1967 changed the ground rules to include the concept of *current commitments,* [13] defined by BOB *Bulletin No. 68-9* as those programs for which existing legislative authorization has been received, plus specific legislative proposals put forth by the president.[14] Programs that agencies wish to establish, but for which approval of the chief executive has not been received, are thus excluded from multiyear plans.

Here again, the concept of current commitments is readily adaptable to the procedures and practices of capital facilities planning at the local level. The most readily identifiable current commitments are those in which there is an obligation to service all claimants on the system. This category would include most public service programs involving substantial capital commitments, such as schools, health facilities, sewer and water systems, etc. The level of commitment, therefore, can be based on projections of potential users—projections that are a fundamental part of the capital facilities planning process. New project commitments must be analyzed and evaluated in terms of the long-term commitments already accepted as a responsibility of local government and in terms of projections of revenue expectations. Thus, considerable experience gained in the application of these constraints to a capital facilities/program budget can then be transferred to other facets of local budgetary practices.

Multiyear plans should project both program impacts (output data) and cost figures. Whereas a program structure only establishes what is to be measured, the multiyear plan must include the actual numbers. One of the main breakouts in cost data is that of investment or capital expenditures versus operating expenditures,[a] that is, for any given capital project, it is necessary to separate for purpose of analysis expenditures for items that have a relatively long life from those that are consumed in daily operations in support of such facilities. It is not apparent exactly how capital and operating costs should be linked within a common program framework, however. Since capital outlays require special processing and administration, they need to be singled out as identifiable parts of total program costs. Systematic analytical techniques mandate that program cost calculations reflect the expense of using existing as well as proposed capital assets, thus creating a further problem of identification in the development of multiyear plans.

*Problems of Program Analysis*

The application of program budgeting techniques to the planning of capital facilities presents some special problems in terms of program analysis. In budgeting terms programs consist of a number of complementary components, some of which may be effective without others and some of which are highly interdependent on the whole. Further, programs must be so structured as to reflect the time-span of expenditures. Capital investment decisions involved commitments that go beyond the expanded time horizons of program budgeting. Consequently the six-to-seven year time span of the multiyear financial and program plans represents only a segment of the total cost commitments for the capital components of any given program category. Furthermore, as in the private sector, the physical assets of governments must be maintained regularly and replaced periodically if the quality of services desired by the public is to be produced efficiently. As a general rule, however, governmental accounting

---

[a]The PPBS system developed in the Department of Defense utilized a three-way breakout of costs, including research, development, testing, and evaluation (RDT&E) costs, as well as investment and operation costs. The use of RDT&E costs, however, reflects the weaponry technology of the Defense Department, where research and development are essential features of total program costs. Since research in the civilian sector has not been of any significance, such a cost classification in multiyear plans is not particularly meaningful.

practices do not recognize *asset depreciation.* The International City Managers' Association (ICMA) text, *Municipal Finance Administration,* has the following to say about accounting for depreciation:

> General fixed assets are all fixed assets other than those carried in a working capital, trust, or utility fund. It has been pointed out that a city's general fixed properties should not be included as part of any fund or in the fund balance sheet. They should, however, be shown on the books and be made a part of the general accounting system as a self-balancing group of accounts. This is accomplished by offsetting the property accounts with accounts showing the sources from which the properties were acquired. . . .[15]

> With one exception, it is unnecessary to calculate depreciation on municipal properties, for property values are not the basis for a city's credit, and a depreciation reserve has no importance unless a cash fund of an equal amount is set aside to replace worn-out properties. This is usually impractical even if legal. The exception is for properties used to carry on an activity of a business characters. Depreciation must be computed on these because it forms a part of the cost of rendering service, and charges to consumers must include this element of cost.[16]

Consequently, unlike investment decision practices in the private sectors, depreciation is seldom considered in governmental decisions. Nonetheless, whether accounting records show it or not, governmental assets wear out, and if a community is to prosper and grow, it must maintain its asset base.

The failure of governments to keep detailed asset accounts and/or to calculate depreciation complicates efforts to determine and assign the costs of using existing capital facilities. Such costs, however, must be recongized and included in program analysis. A relatively simple device for resolving this problem would involve the assignment of debt-service costs to specific programs where the bond-financed facilities can be readily traced to such programs.[b] This approach could then be expanded, where necessary, by adopting record keeping systems similar to those required for revenue-bonded facilities. While there is no assurance that elaborate cost-accounting procedures will provide sufficiently useful information in public investment decision making to justify the cost of establishing such systems, some attention must be given to this problem, however, and appropriate techniques devised if existing capital assets are to be incorporated into program analysis on the same basis as proposed operating and capital outlays.

---

[b]This approach has been adopted by the state of Wisconsin in its program budgeting efforts. See: Roger Schrantz, "Planning-Budgeting Relationships: Wisconsin Case Study," in *Budgets for State Planning,* ed. James W. Martin (Chicago, Ill.: Council of State Governments, 1969).

Although little has been said in the literature concerning **PPBS** or program budgeting about the revenue or financial projections that should accompany cost estimates, it is reasonable to assume that any sound budget process will consider both aspects of the financial planning problem. However, the multiple sources of funding for capital investments create additional problems for program analysis. The extent to which any given program is dependent upon funds outside the immediate control of local government (e.g., revenue sharing or block grant programs) must be reflected in projections to indicate any anticipated changes in funding patterns. For example, some federal and state programs of local assistance begin with relatively large subsidies in the initial years and then in subsequent years the support is reduced significantly. While multiyear plans may allow for such reductions, the time span incorporated in such plans may be insufficient to take into account the impact on capital commitments of the pending shifts in funding sources. Such impacts, however, must be included in the program analysis. Where project funding comes from several sources or several jurisdictions, such funds must be prorated among all components of the program plan.

Additional problems in projecting costs involve assessments of systemwide changes. Inflation increases the costs of governmental operations, and many experts suggest that this must be taken into account in the formulation of multiyear plans.[17] Short-term affects of inflation on operating programs can be dealt with with relative ease, providing all agencies employ the same percentage basis for inflating costs. Determining the imapct of inflation on longer term investment decisions, however, is somewhat more problemmatic, that is, on the establishment of capital reserve funds to finance future capital projects. There is also the conflict between application of the techniques of cost-benefit and cost-effectiveness analysis, which tend to operate best when all future costs are expressed in constant dollars discounted to present values, and the realities of inflation as it effects operating costs, especially personnel costs, which often are the largest single item in operating and maintenance budgets.

The capital facilities aspects of programs will continue to have asset-maintenance, physical, and financial implications, and may therefore require special consideration in program analysis. In larger governments specialists or even specialized staffs that concentrate on in-depth appraisals of programs' capital aspects may have to be hired or trained. As renting, leasing, lease-purchase arrangements, and other similar techniques become more widespread as alternatives to outright ownership of facilities, staff specialization on capital outlay alternatives will become increasingly important.

The more specific techniques of program analysis have been discussed elsewhere in this book, with several illustrations as to their application in long-term capital investment decision making. The particular problems outlined above are not insurmountable. However, if an effective program budgeting system is to be devised for application in local government, considerable attention must be given to the development of program analysis procedures that offer solutions to these problems.

*Program Structure*

The structure developed for program budgeting should include all functions of government. This is a truism for all budgeting, regardless of the label applied, for example, line-item, performance, program, operating, or capital. It has been the frequent practice, however, to exempt certain programs or agencies from the regular capital budgeting process for various reasons. The wisdom of making such exceptions has long been questioned, and the more rationalistic emphasis of program budgeting has brought this issue into even sharper focus. The stress of program budgeting on comprehensiveness in terms of identifying and evaluating alternative solutions requires that program categories be designed to permit a thorough analysis of how effectively problems are being met, rather than designed to fit the existing organizational structure through which programs are to be carried out. To meet these objectives, all relevant functions of government must be included in the program structure and the subsequent program analyses that are undertaken based on this structure. Omissions and exemptions will be even less tolerable than they have been traditional capital budgeting procedures.[18]

The official terminology of the Office of Management and Budget, which has become standard throughout state and local government, is that program structure is divided into (a) program categories, (b) program subcategories, and (c) program elements. These are defined in *Bulletin No. 68-9* as follows:

> a. *Program categories.* The categories in a program structures should provide a suitable framework for considering and resolving major questions of mission and scale of operations which are a proper subject for decision at the higher levels of management—within the agency and within the Executive Office of the President. An agency generally should have between five and ten program categories.
>
> b. *Program subcategories.* Subcategories should provide a meaningful substantive breakdown of program categories, and should group program elements producing outputs which have a high degree of similarity.
>
> c. *Program elements.* A program element covers agency activities related directly to the production of a discrete agency output, or group of related outputs. Agency activities which contribute directly to the output should be included in the program element, even though they may be conducted with different organizations, or financed from different appropriations. Thus, program elements are the basic units of the program structure.[19]

From these definitions it may be concluded that a given capital facilities project may serve as a program element, a program subcategory, or even a program category in a local government's program structure.

Although *Bulletin No. 68-9* calls for program elements to "... produce clearly-definable outputs, which are quantified wherever possible ... .," [20] Aaron Wildavsky cautions against "mindless quantification," suggesting that: "The fixation on program structure is the most pernicious aspect of PPBS."[21] There are dangers inherent in quantification for its own sake and in the production of relatively meaningless data arising form an overly complex program structure. The objective of program structuring, however, should be to establish casual relationships among the more critical program components and to quantify these components to the extent necessary to permit decision makers to test the suggested relationships.[22] This must be an interative process by which rough, approximate data can become more refined, reliable, and valid.

Wildavsky also asserts that the program structure adopted for analysis frequently inhibits the examination of marginal change in terms of overall operations, for example, that a ten percent increase in $X$ will produce a ten percent increase in $Y$ impacts. This criticism of program structuring procedures introduces an interesting contradiction, since the amount of data required to achieve the level of analysis suggested by Wildavsky's assertion would far exceed the data gathering presently implied in these procedures that Wildavsky finds so offensive.

*Zero-base Budgeting and Program Updating Procedures*

The issue of marginal change analysis raises another important question regarding the application of program budgeting to capital investment decisions, however, that of the impact of zero-base budgeting, that is, the procedure of examining each program without regards, at least initially, to previous commitments. A distinguishing feature of PPBS is the defense and review of the *total* expenditures proposed for a given program, rather than merely the changes from its previous level of appropriations. As Harry P. Hatry puts it: "PPBS will ... tend to lessen the use of the current widespread practice ... of giving excessive attention to the changes from the preceding year's budget with too little attention to a review of an agency's budget as a whole in the sense of reconsidering the value of existing programs."[23]

Relatively little attention has been given in federal instructions concerning zero-base budgeting as to the treatment of the fixed assets inherent in agency programs or long-term commitments arising from debt financing. While the concept of zero-base budgeting arises from a commendable desire to curtail or terminate ineffective or obsolete programs,[24] the application of this concept to local decision-making processes concerning the allocation of resources to meet long-term capital commitments has yet to be developed fully. Since the zero-base budgeting has come under fire from many quarters and has been deemphasized in current discussions of program budgeting, it may be more appropriate to examine other program updating procedures that hold more promise.

One such procedure is introduced by Leonard Merewitz and Stephen H. Sosnick, building upon an earlier model by Verne B. Lewis.[25] Their approach is to formulate budget estimates and justifications for three levels of expenditures: (1) the same-dollar amount as the prior appropriation, (2) the same-performance amount, and (3) the recommended amount. The *same-dollar amount* is the sum last appropriated for the agency, whereas the *same-performance amount* is the sum that the agency would require in order to produce the same quantity and quality of output that the last appropriation achieved. The *recommended amount* represents the sum that the agency believes would be most appropriate to carry out its responsibilities. Relative to each of these estimates, an agency head would be expected to provide his superior with both numerical and supplementary information. Merewitz and Sosnick identify three kinds of numerical information and five kinds of supplementary information that would have to be supplied at each level in the administrative hierarchy as the budget was assembled. In providing numerical data the agency head would specify the appropriation that he thinks is needed to maintain his agency's level of output, together with the amount of money that would be saved if his agency's expenditures were enlarged as he recommends. In providing supplementary information he would explain why more money is needed in order to maintain the agency's level of output, what revision in activities are planned even if the same-performance appropriation is received, what result that appropriation would produce, what the sacrifice would be if the agency's appropriation were held to the previous year's level, and what would be gained if the expenditures of the agency were raised to the recommended level.

This approach has a certain basic appeal in that it allows for the explicit recognition of fixed assets and long-term commitments that must be assumed by an agency with extensive capital project responsibilities. If the program budgeting process is to be viable, such an approach should be provided for annual revisions and extensions so that program plans can be updated. Although certain phases of program budgeting, particularly program analysis, are designed to operate on a year-round basis, the entire process will likely continue to focus upon the requirement that a budget document be presented to the legislative body of government at some specified time. Nothing about program budgeting would suggest that this feature of public budgeting will change. As total estimates are revised and updated annually or biennially, the capital aspects of various programs will also have to be brought forward. At the same time financial plans covering anticipated revenues, changes in the tax rate, and bonding commitments and proposals must also be updated.

## Summary and Conclusions

As program budgeting systems mature and planning becomes a more inclusive activity of local government, all types of costs, both operating and capital, should be presented and evaluated in a common program framework. Under this emphasis the distinctions between operating and capital outlays may become less critical, since both are relevant in evaluation total program costs and results. This is not to imply, however, as the capital-operating dichotomy becomes less significant to budgeting procedures, that separate capital budget documents will no longer be prepared. Such presentations may be necessary to ensure the coordination of construction schedules; to adapt financial requirements to available revenues; to define better distributions, both geographic and programmatic, of needed capital facilities; and to achieve desired economies in the use of manpower and equipment.

When total program budgeting is implemented, however, the role of the capital budget as an intermediate instrument between the traditional, long-range, comprehensive development plan and the annual operating budget will probably be supplanted, since under this more rationalistic approach the entire budget system should provide such linkages. Thus, the observations of Vincent Moore at the end of the sixties regarding PPBS would seem to be equally, if not more appropriately, applied to the concepts of program budgeting as they have evolved in the seventies.

> The nice thing about PPBS is that it accommodates both theories [comprehensive, goal-directed planning and incrementalism], and one can plunge ahead knowing that even if the "middle-range bridge" turns out to be a one-way plank, one is at least introducing greater rationale into decision-making. The significance of PPBS to comprehensive planning is that it can serve truly comprehensive planning (including economic and social planning as well as physical planning) as capital programming has served our traditional physical development planning. The principles are essentially the same and PPBS incorporates the capital programming methodology, adding to it the other resource allocations required for government program service which do not require capital plant for operation (such as many welfare programs and economic development programs), but for which manpower and fiscal support and fiscal support allocations are required.[26]

As Howard has observed, the notion that quantitative techniques will provide a panacea in public budgeting is "a windmill with which even Don Quixote could tilt successfully!"[27] However, advances will continue to be made in the use of quantitative techniques for the analysis of fiscal resources and expenditures demands and in the establishment of priorities among resource allocation alternatives. Such techniques, whether undertaken as part of a full-blown program budgeting process, or introduced piecemeal, will have a significant impact on the future of capital facilities planning.

**Notes**

# Notes

## Chapter 1
## Capital Facilities Planning

1. For a further discussion of the evolution of modern public budgeting, see: Alan Walter Steiss, *Public Budgeting and Management* (Lexington, Mass.: Lexington Books, D.C. Heath and Company, 1972), chap. 7.
2. Joint Economic Committee, *State and Local Public Facility Needs and Financing,* vol. 1 (Washington, D.C.: U.S. Government Printing Office, December 1966).
3. Advisory Commission on Intergovernmental Relations, *State Technical Assistance to Local Debt Management,* Report M-26 (Washington, D.C., January 1965), p. 29.
4. Ibid., p. 29.
5. Robert E. Coughlin, "The Capital Programming Problem," *Journal of the American Institute of Planners* 26, no. 1 (February 1960). Reprinted by permission.
6. Ibid., p. 39.
7. Ibid., p. 39.
8. Ibid., p. 39.
9. Roscoe C. Martin et al., *Decisions in Syracuse* (Bloomington, Ind.: Indiana University Press, 1961), p. 15.

## Chapter 2
## Evaluation Criteria and Procedural Steps

1. Jackson M. McClain, *Capital Budgeting in Selected States* (Lexington, Ky.: Bureau of Business Research, University of Kentucky, 1966), pp. 10-19.
2. A.M. Hillhouse and S. Kenneth Howard, *State Capital Budgeting* (Chicago, Ill.: Council of State Governments, 1963), pp. 82-83.
3. *Municipal Finance Administration* (Chicago, Ill.: International City Managers' Association, 1962), pp. 350-51.
4. Hillhouse and Howard, *State Capital Budgeting,* p. 38.
5. McClain, *Capital Budgeting in Selected States,* p. 13.
6. Lennox L. Moak and Kathryn W. Killian, *A Manual of Suggested Practice for the Preparation and Adoption of Capital Programs and Capital Budgets by Local Governments* (Chicago, Ill.: Municipal Finance Officers Association, 1964), chap. 5.

7. McClain, *Capital Budgeting in Selected States*, p. 14; Moak and Killian, *A Manual of Suggested Practice*, pp. 2-3.
8. Chester I. Barnard, *The Functions of the Executive* (Cambridge, Mass.: Harvard University Press, 1956), p. 73.
9. Alex Bavelas and Dermot Barrett, "An Experimental Approach to Organization Communication," *Personnel* 27 (1951), p. 368.
10. Herbert A. Simon, *Administrative Behavior* (New York: Free Press, 1957).
11. For a further discussion of these points, see: Alan Walter Steiss, *Public Budgeting and Management* (Lexington, Mass.: Lexington Books, D.C. Heath and Company, 1972), chap. 5.
12. Frederick C. Mosher, *Program Budgeting* (Chicago: Public Administra-Service, 1954), p. 5.
13. Arthur Smithies, *The Budgetary Process in the United States* (New York: McGraw-Hill, 1955), p. 20.
14. Simon, *Administrative Behavior*. For a further discussion of this concept as applied in capital budgeting, see: Jesse Burkhead, *Government Budgeting* (New York: John Wiley & Sons, 1956).
15. McClain, *Capital Budgeting in Selected States*, p. 16.
16. Victor A. Thompson, *Modern Organizations* (New York: Alfred A. Knopf, 1963); Jerald Hage, "An Axiomatic Theory of Organization," *Administrative Science Quarterly* 10 (December 1965), pp. 289-320.
17. Hillhouse and Howard, *State Capital Budgeting*, p. 61; McClain, *Capital Budgeting in Selected States*, p. 17.
18. *State Capital Improvement Programming—An Outline of Practices and Procedures with Reference to Their Application in New Jersey* (Trenton, N.J.: New Jersey Division of State and Regional Planning, 1962).
19. Robert E. Coughlin, "The Capital Programming Problem," *Journal of the American Institute of Planners* 26 (February 1970).
20. Special Assistant to the President for Public Works Planning, *Planning for Public Works* (Washington, D.C.: U.S. Government Printing Office, 1957), p. 14.
21. Ibid., p. 15.
22. Ibid., pp. 15-16.
23. William B. Rogers, "Fiscal Planning and Capital Budgeting," *Planning 1954* (Chicago, Ill.: American Society of Planning Officials, 1954), p. 96.

## Chapter 3
## The Role of Economic Analysis

1. Council of Economic Advisors, *Economic Report of the President, January 1967* (Washington, D.C.: Superintendent of Documents, 1967), p. 157.
2. *Local Planning Administration* (Chicago, Ill.: International City Managers' Association, 1948), p. 6.
3. Alvin H. Hanson and Harvey S. Perloff, *State and Local Finance in the National Economy* (New York: W.W. Norton and Company, 1944), pp. 11-12.

4. Alan Rabinowitz, *Municipal Bond Finance and Administration* (New York: John Wiley & Sons, 1969), pp. 141–42.
5. John R. Meyer, "Regional Economics: A Survey," *American Economic Review* (March 1963), pp. 21–27.
6. Harvey S. Perloff, *Regional Studies at U.S. Universities* (Washington, D.C.: Resources for the Future, 1957).
7. Walter Isard et al., *Methods of Regional Analysis* (New York: John Wiley & Sons and the M.I.T. Press, 1960).
8. L. Lefeber, *Allocation in Space* (Amsterdam: North Holland Publishing Co., 1959); Martin Beckman, "Some Reflections on Losch's Theory of Location," *Papers and Proceedings of the Regional Science Association* 1 (1955).
9. G.H. Borts, "The Equalization of Returns and Regional Economic Growth," *American Economic Review* 50 (1960), pp. 319–47.
10. Vinod Dubey, "The Definition of Regional Economics," *Journal of Regional Science* 5, no. 2 (1964), p. 29.
11. Ibid., p. 26.
12. Michael B. Teitz, "Regional Theory and Regional Models," *Papers and Proceedings of the Regional Science Association* 9 (1962).
13. An excellent summary of location theory can be found in: Martin Beckman, *Location Theory* (New York: Random House, 1968).
14. For a further discussion of economic impact studies, see: Harvey S. Perloff, *How a Region Grows* (New York: Committee for Economic Development, 1963); and D.C. North, "Locational Theory and Regional Economic Growth," in *Regional Economics: Theory and Practice,* ed. D.L. McKee, R.D. Dean, and W.H. Leahy (New York: The Free Press, 1970).
15. Wilbur Thompson, *A Preface to Urban Economics* (Washington, D.C.: Resource for the Future, 1963).
16. Wassily W. Leontief, *The Structure of the American Economy, 1919–1939* (Oxford: Oxford University Press, 1951), p. 11.
17. Walter Isard, *Location and Space-Economy* (New York: John Wiley & Sons, 1956).
18. Walter Isard et al., *Methods of Regional Analysis* (Cambridge, Mass.: The Technology Press, 1960).
19. Thompson, *A Preface to Urban Economics.*
20. Eugene W. Schooler, "Industrial Complex Analysis," in Isard, *Methods of Regional Analysis,* p. 377.
21. Werner Hochwald, ed., *Design of Regional Accounts* (Baltimore, Md.: The John Hopkins Press, 1961), p. xvii. *Exogenous* refers to growth that originates outside, and *endogenous* to growth that develops from within.
22. For a further discussion of regional multipliers, see: Charles M. Tiebout, *The Community Economic Base Study* (New York: Committee for Economic Development, 1962); Ralph W. Pfouts, ed., *The Techniques of Urban Economic Analysis* (West Trenton, N.J.: Chandler-Davis Publishing Co., 1960); and Charles L. Leven, *Theory and Method of Income and Product Accounts* (Pittsburgh, Pa.: University of Pittsburgh Press, 1963).
23. Thompson, *A Preface to Urban Economics,* chap. 1.
24. Richard D. Andrews, "Mechanics of the Urban Economic Base," *Land*

*Economics* (November 1953), pp. 344–49; "Urban Economics: An Appraisal of Progress," *Land Economics* (August 1961), pp. 223–25; Economic Planning for Small Areas: An Analytical System," *Land Economics* (May 1963), pp. 143–55; "Economic Planning for Small Areas: The Planning Process," *Land Economics* (August 1963), pp. 253–64.

25. William J. Reilly, *The Law of Retail Gravitation* (New York: G.P. Putnam Sons, 1931), p. 9.
26. Charles M. Tiebout, *The Community Economic Base Study* (New York: Committee for Economic Development, 1962), p. 47.
27. Ralph W. Pfouts, "An Empirical Testing of the Economic Base Theory," *Journal of the American Institute of Planners* (Spring 1957).
28. Hans Blumenfeld, "The Economic Base of the Metropolis," *Journal of the American Institute of Planners* (Fall 1955).
29. Richard B. Andrews, "Economic Planning for Small Areas: An Analytical System," *Land Economics* 39 (May 1963), pp. 143–55.
30. Ibid., p. 151.
31. Richard B. Andrews, Discussion of the Economic Dominants Approach in application to areas within the state of Wisconsin, October 1965.

## Chapter 4
## Formulation of a Debt Policy

1. William J. Shultz and C. Lowell Harris, *American Public Finance* (Englewood Cliffs, N.J.: Prentice-Hall, 1965), p. 476.
2. Benjamin Chinitz, "Contrasts in Agglomeration: New York and Pittsburgh," *American Economic Review* (May 1961), p. 279.
3. Charles M. Tiebout, *The Community Economic Base Study* (New York: Committee for Economic Development, 1962), p. 18.
4. John F. Kain, "Review of Wilbur R. Thompson's *A Preface to Urban Economics,*" in *Journal of the American Institute of Planners* (May 1966), pp. 186–88.

## Chapter 5
## Forecasting Local Expenditures and
## Financial Resources

1. James Heilbrun, *Urban Economics and Public Policy* (New York: St. Martin's Press, 1974), pp. 324–30.
2. Heilbrun, *Urban Economics and Public Policy*.
3. Advisory Commission on Intergovernmental Relations, *State-Local Finances: Significant Features and Suggested Legislation, 1972 Edition*, Report No. M-74, table 134, p. 301.
4. Heilbrun, *Urban Economics and Public Policy*.

5. J. Richard Aronson and Eli Schwartz, "Forecasting Future Expenditures," *Management Information Service* 2, no. S-7 (Washington, D.C.: International City Management Association, July 1970).
6. Jesse Burkhead, *State and Local Taxes for Public Education* (Syracuse, N.Y.: Syracuse University Press, 1963), p. 70. Less Optimistic conclusions are reached by Benjamin Bridges, Jr., in "Past and Future Growth of the Property Tax," *Property Taxation–USA*, ed. Richard W. Lindholm (Madison, Wisc.: University of Wisconsin Press, 1967), pp. 31-27.
7. For a further discussion of these points, see: James A. Maxwell, *Financing State and Local Governments* (Washington, D.C.: The Brookings Institution, 1969), 137-46.
8. Public Works Committee, *Long-Range Programming of Municipal Public Works* (Washington, D.C.: National Resources Planning Board, 1941), p. 7.
9. ASPO Planning Advisory Service, "Capital Improvement Programming," Information Report No. 151 (Chicago, Ill.: American Society of Planning Officials, October 1961).

## Chapter 6
## Methods of Financing Capital Facilities and Choice of Debt Form

1. For a fuller discussion of these procedures, see: Elizabeth Y. Deran, *Financing Capital Improvements: The "Pay-As-You-Go" Approach* (Berkeley, Calif.: Bureau of Public Administration, University of California, 1961).
2. For a classic work on the determination of maximum debt and the nature of an ideal debt maturity schedule, see: Carl H. Chatters and Albert M. Hillhouse, *Local Government Debt Administration* (New York: Prentice-Hall, 1939).
3. Advisory Commission on Intergovernmental Relations, *State Constitutional and Statutory Restrictions on Local Governmental Debt*, Report A-10 (Washington, D.C., September 1961), p. 24.
4. George H. Hempel, *Measures of Municipal Bond Quality*, Michigan Business Reports Number 53 (Ann Arbor, Mich.: University of Michigan Bureau of Business Research, 1967), p. 21.
5. Advisory Commission on Intergovernmental Relations, *State Constitutional and Statutory Restrictions on Local Governmental Debt*, p. 25.

## Chapter 7
## Marketing Municipal Bonds

1. Alan Rabinowitz, *Municipal Bond Finance and Administration* (New York: Wiley-Interscience, 1969), p. 75.

2. Joint Economic Committee, *State and Local Public Facility Needs and Financing*, vol. II (Washington, D.C., U.S. Government Printing Office, December 1966), p. 11.
3. Rabinowitz, *Municipal Bond Finance and Administration*, p. 77.
4. Ibid., pp. 86–87.
5. Ibid., pp. 88–89.
6. Ibid., p. 89.
7. For a further discussion of this point, see: Rabinowitz, *Municipal Bond Finance and Administration*, chap. 4.
8. Ibid., p. 50.
9. For a further discussion of tax-exempt bond funds, see: Gordon L. Calvert, ed., *Fundamentals of Municipal Bonds* (Washington, D.C.: Investment Bankers Association of America, 1969).

## Chapter 8
## Revenue Bonds

1. *Municipal Finance Administration* (Chicago: International City Managers' Association, 1962), p. 315.
2. Ibid., p. 316.
3. Ibid., pp. 317–18.

## Chapter 9
## Debt Administration

1. *Municipal Finance Administration* (Chicago: International City Managers' Association, 1962), pp. 267, 326–27.
2. Ibid., pp. 319–20.
3. George H. Hempel, *Measures of Municipal Bond Quality* (Ann Arbor, Mich: Bureau of Business Research, University of Michigan, 1967), p. 52.
4. Ibid., p. 54.
5. Ibid., p. 59.
6, *Municipal Finance Administration*, p. 334.
7. Ibid., p. 335.

## Chapter 10
## Cost-Benefit and
## Cost-Effectiveness Analysis

1. Harley H. Hinrichs, "Government Decision Making and the Theory of Benefit-Cost Analysis: A Primer," in *Program Budgeting and Benefit-Cost Analysis*, ed., Harley H. Hinrichs and Graeme M. Taylor (Pacific Palisades, Calif.: Goodyear Publishing Co., 1969), p. 9.

2. John F. Due and Ann Friedlaender, *Government Finance—Economics of the Public Sector* (Homeville, Ill.: Richard D. Irwin, 1973), p. 62.
3. Anatol Rapoport, "What Is Information?" *ETC: A Review of General Semantics* 10 (Summer 1953), p. 252.
4. Peter F. Drucker, *The Practice of Management* (New York: Harper and Brothers, 1954), p. 353.
5. Otto Eckstein, *Water Resource Development* (Cambridge, Mass.: Harvard University Press, 1958).
6. Roland N. McKean, *Public Spending* (New York: McGraw-Hill, 1968), p. 136-38.
7. Subcommittee on Evaluation Standards, Report to the Interagency Committee on Water Resources, *Proposed Practices for Economic Analysis of River Basin Projects,* Washington, D.C. (May 1958), p. 9.
8. Leonard Merewitz and Stephen H. Sosnick, *The Budget's New Clothes* (Chicago, Ill.: Markham Publishing Company, 1971), p. 210.
9. Hinrichs, "Government Decision Making," p. 11.
10. Nicholas Kaldor, "Welfare Propositions of Economics and Interpersonal Comparisons of Utility," *Economic Journal* 49 (1939), p. 550.
11. J.R. Hicks, "The Foundations of Welfare Economics," *Economic Journal* 49 (1039), pp. 696-712.
12. J.R. Hicks, "The Rehabilitation of Consumer Surplus," *Review of Economic Studies* 8 (1940-41), p. 108.
13. Tibor Scitovsky, "A Note on Welfare Propositions in Economics," *Review of Economic Studies* 9 (1942), pp. 98-110.
14. I.M.D. Little, *A Critique of Welfare Economics* (Oxford: Clarendon Press, 1957), p. 109.
15. Merewitz and Sosnick, *The Budget's New Clothes,* p. 82.
16. Ibid., p. 85.
17. Hinrichs, "Government Decision Making," pp. 12-13.
18. Herbert A. Simon, *Administrative Behavior* (New York: The Free Press, 1957), p. 62. Talcott Parsons analyzes social action systems with the use of these same concepts in *The Structure of Social Action* (New York: McGraw-Hill, 1937), pp. 44, 49, 228-41.
19. Ibid., p. 65.
20. Hinrichs, "Government Decision Making," p. 13.
21. Ibid., p. 13.
22. Simon Ramo, *Cure for Chaos* (New York: David McKay Co., 1969), p. 109.
23. Merewitz and Sosnick, *The Budget's New Clothes,* p. 85.
24. Ibid., p. 86.
25. For discussions of benefit-cost studies, see: Robert Dorfman, ed., *Measuring Benefits of Government Investments* (Washington, D.C.: The Brookings Institution, 1965); A.R. Prest and Ralph Turvey, "Cost-Benefit Analysis: A Survey," *Economic Journal* (1965), pp. 683-735; Robert Haveman, *The Economics of the Public Sector* (New York: John Wiley & Sons, 1970); and Werner Hirsch, *The Economics of State and Local Government* (New York: McGraw-Hill, 1970).
26. S.A. Marglin, *Public Investment Criteria* (Cambridge, Mass.: M.I.T. Press, 1967), pp. 47-69.

27. Merewitz and Sosnick, *The Budget's New Clothes,* p. 116.
28. Joe S. Bain, "Criteria for Undertaking Water-Resource Development," *American Economic Review* 50 (May 1960), pp. 310–20.
29. Adopted from Merewitz and Sosnick, *The Budget's New Clothes,* pp. 88–89.
30. Jack Hirschleifer, "On the Theory of Optimal Investment Decisions," in *The Management of Corporate Capital,* ed. Ezra Solomon (New York: The Free Press, 1959), pp. 224ff.
31. Merewitz and Sosnick, *The Budget's New Clothes,* pp. 87–88.
32. Roy Radner, *Notes on the Theory of Economic Plannning* (Athens: Centre for Economic Research, 1963), pp. 74–82.
33. Roland N. McKean, *Public Spending* (New York: McGraw-Hill, 1968), pp. 136–38.
34. Due and Friedlaender, *Government Finance,* p. 69.
35. For a further discussion of this point, see: Don H. Overly, "Decision-Making in City Government," *Urban Affairs Quarterly* 3, no. 2 (December 1967).
36. A.R. Prest and Ralph Turvey, "Cost-Benefit Analysis: A Survey," *The Economic Journal* 74 (December 1965), p. 683.
37. For a further discussion of these characteristics, see: Alan Walter Steiss, *Public Budgeting and Management* (Lexington, Mass.: Lexington Books, D.C. Heath and Company, 1972), chap. 10.
38. E.S. Quade, ed., *Analysis for Military Decisions,* the RAND Corporation, R–387–PR (November 1964), p. 13.
39. Bureau of the Budget Circular 66-3, *Planning-Programming-Budgeting* (October 1965).
40. Prest and Turvey, "Cost-Benefit Analysis," p. 691.
41. Charles Kepner and Benjamin B. Tregoe, *The Rational Manager* (Princeton, N.J.: Princeton University Press, 1965).
42. For a further discussion of these matrices, see: Steiss, *Public Budgeting and Management,* pp. 234–37.
43. Donald A. Krueckeberg and Arthur L. Silvers, *Urban Planning Analysis: Methods and Models* (New York: John Wiley & Sons, 1974), pp. 201-3.
44. Krueckeberg and Silvers, *Urban Planning Analysis,* p. 207.
45. Russell Ackoff, "Toward Quantitative Evaluation of Urban Services," *Public Expenditure Decisions in the Urban Community,* ed. Howard G. Schaller (Washington, D.C.: Resources for the Future, 1963), pp. 91–117.
46. For a further discussion of these analytical techniques, see: Steiss, *Public Budgeting and Management,* chap. 6.
47. Krueckeberg and Silvers, *Urban Planning Analysis,* p. 208.
48. For a theoretical introduction to the economics of externalities, see: Robert Haveman, *The Economics of the Public Sector* (New York: John Wiley & Sons, 1970), pp. 35–43.
49. Krueckeberg and Silvers, *Urban Planning Analysis,* p. 211.
50. For a discussion of several indirect methods of measurement, see: Julius Margolis, "Shadow Prices for Incorrect or Non-Existent Market Prices," in *Public Expenditures and Policy Analysis,* ed. Robert Haveman and Julius Margolis (Chicago, Ill.: Markham Publishing Co., 1970), pp. 314–29.

51. Margolis, "Shadow Prices," provides a discussion of the rationale and calculations of these prices.

## Chapter 11
## The Role of Program Budgeting

1. An excellent introduction to PPBS at the local level is provided by Selma J. Mushkin, "PPB for the Cities: Problems and the Next Steps," in *Financing the Metropolis,* ed. John P. Crecine, *Urban Affairs Annual Reveiw,* vol. 4 (Beverly Hills: Sage Publications, 1970).
2. Alan Walter Steiss, *Public Budgeting and Management* (Lexington, Mass.: Lexington Books, D.C. Heath and Company, 1972), especially chap. 9.
3. For a discussion as to what constitutes a "program" for budgetary purposes, see: Steiss, *Public Budgeting and Management,* pp. 157–62.
4. Donald A. Krueckeberg and Arthur L. Silvers, *Urban Planning Analysis* (New York: John Wiley & Sons, 1974), p. 198.
5. Ibid., p. 198.
6. Steiss, *Public Budgeting and Management,* p. 157.
7. John F. Due and Ann Friedlaender, *Government Finance–Economics of the Public Sector* (Homeville, Ill.: Richard D. Irwin, 1973), pp. 59–60.
8. Krueckeberg and Silvers, *Urban Planning Analysis,* p. 199.
9. For a discussion of joint impacts, see: Russell Ackoff, "Toward Quantitative Evaluation of Urban Services," in *Public Expenditure Decisions in the Urban Community,* ed. Howard G. Schaller (Washington, D.C.: Resources for the Future, Johns Hopkins Press, 1963),
10. Robert D. Lee, Jr. and Ronald W. Johnson, *Public Budgeting Systems* (Baltimore, Md.: University Park Press, 1973), p. 168.
11. S. Kenneth Howard, *Changing State Budgeting* (Lexington, Ky.: Council of State Governments, 1973), p. 260.
12. Lee and Johnson, *Public Budgeting Systems,* p. 170.
13. Charles L. Schultze, *The Politics and Economics of Public Spending* Washington, D.C.: The Brookings Institution, 1968), pp. 26–27.
14. Bureau of the Budget, Executive Office of the President, "Planning-Programming-Budgeting (PPB) System," *Bulletin No. 68-9* (April 12, 1968), p. 4.
15. Institute for Training in Municipal Administration, *Municipal Finance Administration* (Chicago, Ill.: The International City Managers' Association, 1962), p. 229.
16. Ibid., p. 230.
17. Lee and Johnson, *Public Budgeting Systems,* p. 172.
18. Howard, *Changing State Budgeting,* p. 261.
19. Bureau of the Budget, "Planning-Program-Budgeting (PPB) System" p. 3.
20. Ibid,, p. 3.
21. Aaron Wildavsky, "Rescuing Policy Analysis from PPBS," *Public Administration Review* 29 (1969), p. 194.

22. Lee and Johnson, *Public Budgeting Systems,* p. 174.
23. Harry P. Hatry, "Consideration in Instituting a Planning-Programming-Budgeting System (PPBS) in State or Local Government," The George Washington University State and Local Finances Project, Washington, D.C. (October 1966), p. 21.
24. Leonard Merewitz and Stephen H. Sosnick, *The Budget's New Clothes* (Chicago, Ill.: Markham Publishing Co., 1971), p. 65.
25. Ibid., pp. 65–71; Verne B. Lewis, "Towards a Theory of Budgeting," in *Planning Programming Budgeting: A Systems Approach to Management,* ed. Fremont J. Lyden and Ernest G. Miller (Chicago, Ill.: Markham Publishing Co., 1968).
26. Vincent J. Moore, "Integrated Planning-Programming-Budgeting Systems: Breakthrough or Bureaucracy?" in *Planning-Programming-Budgeting Systems* (Chicago, Ill.: American Society of Planning Officials, 1969), p. 2.
27. Howard, *Changing State Budgeting,* p. 263.

# Glossary

**A Summary of Terms Used in the Programming of Capital Improvements**

*Accrued Interest:* interest earned on a bond since the last coupon payment.

*Ad Valorem Tax:* a tax based on the assessed value of real (land and improvements) and personal property.

*Amortization* (of bonds): a straight-line reduction of debt by means of periodic payments sufficient to meet current interest and to liquidate the debt (pay down the principal) at maturity.

*Assessed Valuation:* the valuation placed on property for the purpose of taxation; generally property is assessed at well below 100 percent of the market value.

*Assessment Ratio:* the ratio of the assessed value of property to the full or true property value; full value may be defined as fair market value at the bid side of the market less a reasonable allowance for sales and other expenses.

*Authority:* a quasi-public corporation created by one or more governmental bodies to carry out certain functions, either within a community or among several communities. These are often a "proprietary," revenue-producing nature, such as providing a water supply, sewage treatment facilities, or building and maintaining roads, bridges, or ports and air terminals, for which tolls, rents, or other user charges may be imposed.

*Basis Book:* a book of mathematical tables used to convert yield percentages to equivalent dollar prices.

*Basis Price:* the price expressed in yield or net return on the investment.

*Bear Market:* a period of generally pessimistic attitudes and declining market prices (compare: Bull Market).

*Bearer Bond:* a bond that has no identification as to owner; it is presumed to be owned, therefore, by the bearer or the person who holds it.

*Blighted Area:* an area in which a substantial proportion of the dwellings are unsafe, unsanitary, dilapidated, obsolescent, or so lacking in light, air, or space as to be conductive to unwholesome living; may include industrial buildings that are no longer used and have been allowed to fall into a state of disrepair, or residential districts where the structures for various reasons are detrimental to health, safety, morals, or welfare.

*Blue List:* a daily list of dealers' municipal bond offerings published by the Blue List Publishing Company.

*Bond:* an interest-bearing certificate of debt representing the obligation of a public body to repay a certain sum—usually issued in $1,000 units—on a specific date, with interest at a fixed rate to maturity.

*Bond Anticipation Notes (BAN):* short-term notes sold in anticipation of a bond issue and retired by proceeds from the sale of the bonds.

*Bond Buyer:* a daily trade paper of the municipal bond business; it also publishes *The Weekly Bond Buyer,* devoted to capital market news as well as providing a wrap-up of municipal news, and a monthly "pink sheet," listing all bond sales for a given month.

*Bond Discount:* the amount by which the face value of a bond exceeds the purchase price.

*Bond Issue:* generally a certain number of bonds marketed at one time by a municipality, school district, or other public organization.

*Bond Premium:* the amount by which the purchase of redemption price of a bond exceeds the face value.

*Bonds—General Obligation:* "tax supported" bonds for which the full faith and credit of the government issuing the bonds is pledged.

*Bonds—Maturity:* the date on which the principal amount of a bond becomes due, or the period intervening between the date of issue and the due date; a bond issued in 1961 and due in 1980 would have a 20-year maturity.

*Bonds—Retirement:* the payment of the principal of the bond or bonds at the maturity date, or by purchase or redemption.

*Bonds—Revenue:* bonds payable from revenues derived from the use of a facility, such as bridge tools, water rents, and the like; the credit and taxing capability of local government is not necessarily pledged in support of such bonds.

*Bonds—Serial:* bonds maturing in periodic, generally annual, installments as opposed to "term bonds."

*Broker:* middleman who brings buyers and sellers together and handles their orders, generally charging a commission for his services; in contrast to a principal or a dealer, the broker does not own or take a position in the security.

*Bull Market:* a period of generally optimistic attitudes and increasing market prices (Compare: Bear Market)

*Callable:* feature of a bond whereby it may be redeemed by the issuer prior to maturity under terms designated prior to issuance.

*Capital Budget:* a plan for the expenditure of public funds for capital purposes, showing as income the revenues, special assessments, free surplus, and down payment appropriations to be applied to the cost of a capital project or projects, expenses of issuance of obligation, engineering supervision, contracts, and any other related expenses.

*Capital Expenditures:* nonrecurring payments for capital improvements including construction, acquisition, site development and overhead costs. The fees for architects, engineers, lawyers, and other professional services plus the costs of financing, advance planning may be included.

*Capital Improvements:* acquisition, construction, replacement of, or major repairs to capital plant facilities, with a relatively long useful life.

*Capital Improvements Program:* a comprehensive schedule for staging the construction or acquisition of capital improvements and the allocation of costs by sources or revenue, in accordance with a system of priorities, usually covering a period of five or six years.

*Capital Plant:* buildings and other facilities needed for the operation of public services provided by local government, including schools, roads, water and sewer systems, street lights, parks and playgrounds, harbor improvements, police and fire department headquarters, administration buildings, and libraries and health centers, among other facilities.

*Capital Reserve Deposits or Capital Improvements Fund Deposits:* deposits by a municipality, county, or school district of current revenues in a special fund called a "building fund," capital reserve fund," or "capital improvement fund," which may be used for payments for capital improvements or debt service.

*Capitalization:* the translation of an annual revenue or expenditure into terms of capital value or capital cost, on the basis of a fixed ratio.

*Comprehensive Plan, Master Plan, or General Plan:* a long-range plan in graphic and written form for the coordinated, rational, future development of a community based upon past and present trends, existing conditions, as well as estimates and projections of future trends and conditions. It includes proposals for such improvements as schools, parks, roads, and sanitation facilities.

*Concession:* the allowance (or profit) that an underwriter permits a nonmember of the account; sometimes referred to as a dealer's reallowance.

*Coupon:* that part of a bond which evidences interest due. Coupons are detached from bonds by holders (usually semiannually) and presented to the issuer's designated paying agent, or deposited in his own bank for collection.

*Coupon or Interest Rate:* the annual rate of interest payable on a bond, note, or any other fixed income obligation, usually expressed as a percentage of the principal amount, which the borrower promises to pay to the bondholder.

*Coverage:* this term is usually associated with revenue bonds and indicates the margin of safety for payment of debt service, reflecting the number of times by which earnings for a given period exceed debt service payable in such period.

*Current Yield:* a relation stated as a percent of the annual interest to the actual market price of the bond.

*Debt Financing:* the financing of the cost of capital improvements by the creation of debt (usually done by the issuing of bonds).

*Debt Limit (or Debt Ceiling):* the maximum debt that may be incurred by a local government, school district, or state, usually expressed as a percentage of the net debt to the "equalized valuation basis."

*Debt Schedule:* a schedule showing annual payments for interest, principal, sinking funds, and other deposits to be used toward the payment of principal maturities.

*Debt Service—Aggregate:* total debt service over the life of a bond.

*Debt Service—Annual:* total debt service falling due in any one year.

*Debt Service—Level:* a bond issue where approximately the same amount is paid for total debt service during each year of the life of the bonds. Under this approach more bonds mature during the later years of the issue.

*Default:* failure to pay principal or interest promptly when due if caused by a minor omission that if remedied promptly is known as a technical default.

*Discount:* the difference between the cost price of a security and its value at maturity when quoted at lower than face value. A security selling below original offering price shortly after sale also is considered to be at a discount.

*Dollar Bond:* a bond that is quoted and traded in dollars rather than in yield.

*Down Payment:* payment for a capital improvement from current revenues or reserves, as opposed to borrowed funds.

*Face Value:* the par value of a bond that appears on the face; this is the amount that the issuer promises to pay at maturity, and also the amount on which interest is computed.

*Flat Scale:* little or no difference between short- and long-term yields over the maturity range of an issue.

*Floating Debt:* temporary or shifting short-term debt that has not been funded on a permanent basis into longer maturities.

*General Obligation:* a bond secured by pledge of the issuer's full faith, credit, and taxing power.

*Gross Debt:* the sum total of a debtor's obligations.

*Gross Yield:* the percentage return on a security that is determined by dividing the dollar price into the annual interest payment and calculating the return to maturity.

*Industrial Revenue Bond Financing:* the means by which a municipality or development corporation issues and sells its revenue bonds to build an industrial plant to be leased to a private corporation.

*Interest:* compensation paid or to be paid for the use of money.

*Interest Rate:* the interest payable each year, expressed as a percentage of the principal.

*Inverted Scale:* when the yield is higher on the shorter maturities than on the longer ones.

*Issuer:* a municipal unit that borrows money through the sale of bonds.

*Legal Opinion:* an opinion concerning the legality of a bond issue usually written by a recognized law firm specializing in the approval of public borrowings.

*Limited Tax Bond:* a bond secured by the pledge of a special tax, a group of taxes, or specified portion of the real estate tax that is limited as to rate or amount.

*Liquidity:* the ability to convert a security into cash promptly with minimum risk of principal.

*Marketability:* a measure of the ease with which a security can be sold in the secondary market.

*Maturities Level:* a bond issue in which the same amount of principal becomes due each year during the life of the bonds. This means declining debt service as the bonds are paid off and interest is reduced.

*Maturity:* the date upon which the principal or stated value of a bond becomes due and payable.

*Municipals:* a term used to apply to the bonds issued by a whole range of domestic public agencies and authorities below the level of the United States government (states, counties, cities, town, schools and various special purpose districts or agencies).

*Net Debt:* gross debt less sinking fund accumulations and all self-supporting debt.

*New Housing Authority Bonds:* bonds issued by a local public housing authority to finance public housing and backed by federal funds and the solemn pledge of the United States government to see that this payment is made in full.

*New Issue Market:* market for new issues of municipal bonds.

*Noncash Credit:* an amount representing a payment by a local government or school district for a public improvement contributing to the rebuilding of an urban renewal area. For this the local government may take credit, as part of the "net project cost," in its application for a federal capital grant in an urban renewal program.

*Operating Budget:* the annual budget adopted by a municipality or school district each year, showing an itemized list of proposed operating expenditures, revenues, or other available funds by source.

*Over-the-Counter Market:* a securities market that is conducted by dealers throughout the country through negotiations rather than through the use of an auction system as represented by a stock exchange.

*Overlapping Debt:* that portion of the debt of other governmental units for which residents of a particular municipality are responsible.

*Par Value:* the stated or face value of a bond; the amount of money due at maturity.

*Pay-As-You-Go:* payment on capital improvements from current revenues.

*Premium:* the amount by which price exceeds par amount or maturity value of a bond; also the amount payable to the holder of a callable bond by the issuer, if and when the bond is called.

*Prime Rate:* interest rate charged by banks for loans to their prime or most creditworthy customers.

*Principal:* the face or par value of an instrument, exclusive of accrued interest.

*Priorities:* the order of precedence, in time and importance, among a number of different capital improvements.

*Ratings:* designations used by investors' services to give relative indications of quality.

*Redevelopment:* the process of acquiring land, demolishing existing structures, and making the cleared space available for new development. The purpose of this is to eliminate conditions of blight that cannot be controlled or remedied by regulations (housing codes, sanitation regulations, etc.), and that cannot be dealt with effectively by private enterprise. The acquisition of land, relocation of occupants of the site, and the clearing and replanning of the area is carried out by a public agency. The rebuilding of the site may be undertaken by a private developer or a public agency.

*Refunding:* a system by which a bond issue is redeemed by a new bond issue under conditions generally more favorable to the issuer.

*Registered Bond:* a bond whose owner is registered with the issuer or its agents, either as to both principal and interest or as to principal only.

*Revenue Bond:* a bond payable from revenues secured from a project that pays its way by charging rentals to the users, such as toll bridges or toll highways, or from revenues from another source that are used for a public purpose.

*Scale:* reoffering terms to the public of a serial issue showing price or yields offered to each maturity.

*Self-Liquidating Utility:* a municipal public utility (such as a water or sewer system, toll bridge or public parking lot) in which the cash receipts from fees, rents, or other charges, made during the fiscal year are enough to meet debt service and operating and maintenance costs (excluding depreciation and obsolescence).

*Self-Supporting Debt:* debt incurred for a project or enterprise requiring no tax support other than the specific tax or revenue earmarked for that purpose.

*Serial Bond:* a bond of an issue that has maturities over a period of time for retirement of a debt.

*Sinking Fund:* a reserve fund accmulated over time to liquidate or retire a known obligation on the date of its maturity or call date.

*Special Assessment Bonds:* bonds payable from levies on the property presumably benefited by the improvement being financed; the issuing government agrees to make the assessments and earmark the proceeds for debt service on these bonds.

*Special Tax Bond:* a bond secured by a special tax, such as a gasoline tax.

*Spread:* the gross profit in an underwriting, assuming that all bonds are sold at the initial offering price.

*Staging:* the planning or programming of the construction of capital improvements over time when needed and when the community has the ability to pay.

*Syndicate:* a group of investment bankers who buy (underwrite) "wholesale" a new bond issue from the issuing authority and offer it for resale to the general public.

*Take-Down:* the discount from the list price allowed to a member of an underwriting account on any bonds he sells (sometimes referred to as a takedown concession).

*Tax-Exempt Bonds:* a term applied to municipal bonds of state and local governments or agencies; the interest on municipal securities is exempt from federal income taxes.

*Term Bond:* a bond of an issue that has a single maturity.

*Trading Market:* the secondary market for issued bonds.

*True or Market Value:* the value determined by the state as the true value of taxable real property in a community for the purpose of allocating state aid to education; usually taken as the price at which a willing buyer would purchase the property from a willing seller.

*Trustee:* a bank designated as the custodian of funds and official representative of bondholders.

*Underwriter:* a bank, dealer, or other financial institution that purchases new issues of securities for resale.

*Unlimited Tax Bond:* a bond secured by pledge of taxes that may be levied in unlimited rate or amount.

*Urban Renewal:* undertakings by a local government for the elimination of blight in a designated "urban renewal area". This would be a slum area or a blighted, deteriorated or deteriorating area approved by the Department of Housing and Urban Development as appropriate for an urban renewal project. Urban renewal may involve redevelopment, rehabilitation, or conservation.

*Yield:* the rate of annual income return on an investment, expressed as a percentage. (1) Income yield is obtained by dividing the current dollar income by the current market price for the security. (2) Net yield or yield to maturity is the current income yield minus any premium above par or plus any discount from par in purchase price, with the adjustment spread over the period from the date of purchase to the date of maturity of the bond.

# Author Index

Ackoff, Russell, 245, 266
Advisory Commisson on Intergovernmental Relations, 6, 76, 87, 113
Andrews, Richard B., 64-65, 66, 69-71
Aronson, J. Richard, 89
ASPO Planning Advisory Service, 100-101

Bain, Joe S., 216
Barnard, Chester F., 24
Barrett, Dermot, 24
Baumol, William J., 211
Bavelas, Alex, 24
Beckman, Martin, 51
Blumenfield, Hans, 68
Borts, G.H., 47
Boulding, Kenneth, 209
Burkhead, Jesse, 96

Chatters, Carl H., 111
Chintz, Benjamin, 82
Coughlin, Robert E., 11, 13, 14, 15, 26

Depuit, Jules, 209-210
Deran, Elizabeth Y., 104
Drucker, Peter F., 201
Dubey, Vinod, 47, 48
Due, John F., 199, 230, 264

Eckstein, Otto, 201, 211

Friedlaender, Ann, 199, 230, 264

Gras, N.B.S., 65-66

Hage, Jerald, 24-25
Hanson, Alvin H., 46
Harberger, A.C., 77
Harris, C. Lowell, 76
Harrod, Roy, 204
Hatry, Harry P., 272
Haveman, Robert, 255
Heilbrun, James, 86, 87, 88
Hempel, George H., 112, 193, 194
Hicks, J.R., 204
Hillhouse, A.M., 20, 21, 23, 25, 111
Hinrichs, Harley H., 199, 203, 206, 207
Hirschleifer, Jack, 218

Hochwald, Werner, 61
Howard, S. Kenneth, 20, 21, 23, 25, 267, 271, 274
Hoyt, Homer, 67

Isard, Walter, 47, 58

Johnson, Ronald W., 267, 270, 272
Joint Economic Committee, 5-6, 138-139

Kain, John F., 83
Kaldor, Nicholas, 204
Kennedy, James J., 55
Kepner, Charles, 234
Keynes, John Maynard, 209
Killian, Kathryn W., 22
Krueckeburg, Donald A., 241, 245, 246, 255, 263, 266

Lee, Robert D., 267, 270, 272
Lefeber, L., 47
Leontief, Wassily W., 56
Leven, Charles L., 61
Lewis, Verne B., 273
Little, I.M.D., 205

McClain, Jackson M., 20, 22, 23, 24
McKean, Roland N., 201, 229
Marglin, S.A., 212
Margolis, Julius, 256
Maxwell, James A., 96
Merewitz, Leonard, 202, 205, 208, 209, 214, 217, 272, 273
Meyer, John R., 274
Moak, Lennox L., 22
Moore, Vincent J., 274
Mosher, Frederick C., 24
Munger, Frank J., 17
Municipal Finance Administration, 157, 162, 175, 183, 195, 196, 269
Municipal Finance Officers Association, 169
Musgrave, Richard A., 5
Mushkin, Selma J., 261

National Resources Planning Board, 97

Perloff, Harvey S., 46, 47
Pfouts, Ralph W., 61, 68
Pigon, A.C., 211
Prest, A.R., 232, 233

Quade, E.S., 232
Quesmoy, Françoise, 56

Rabinowitz, Alan, 46, 119, 137, 139, 141, 148
Radner, Roy, 228
Ramo, Simon, 208
Rapoport, Anatol, 201
Reilly, William J., 66
Rodgers, William B., 40

Samuelson, Paul A., 200
Schooler, Eugene W., 59
Schrantz, Roger, 269
Schultz, Charles L., 267
Schwartz, Eli, 89

Scitovsky, Tiber, 204
Scott, Claudia DeVita, 89, 91
Silvers, Arthur L., 241, 245, 246, 255, 263, 266
Simon, Herbert A., 24, 206, 207
Smithies, Arthur, 24
Sosnick, Stephen, 202, 205, 208, 209, 214, 217, 272, 273
Steiss, Alan Walter, 2, 24, 232, 235, 246, 261, 262, 264

Teitz, Michael, 50-51
Tiebout, Charles, 61, 67, 82
Thompson, Victor A., 24-25
Thompson, Wilber, 55-56, 59, 63
Tregoe, Benjamin B., 234
Turvey, Ralph, 232, 233

Wildavsky, Aaron, 272
Woodbury, Coleman, 20

## Subject Index

Accrued interest, 132, 147, 287
Across-the-board structuring, 262
Ad valorem taxes, 129, 133, 287
Amortization, 77, 102, 162, 287
Annual contributions contract, 112
Annual costs of capital improvements, 12
Annual net benefits, 224
Assessed valuation, 75, 95-97, 287
Assessment practices, 96-97, 153
Asset depreciation, 269
Associated costs, 262
Auction bidding, 144
Authorities, 156, 287
Average annual proceeds, 221
Average income on book value, 221

Balloon maturities, 116, 164
Basic and nonbasic industries, 63-68; classification of, 64-65; definition, 64; units of measurement, 66-67
Basis price, 297
Benefit-cost ratio, 25, 78, 81, 207, 209, 215-216; versus net benefits criterion, 223-229
Benefit investment analysis, 214-215, 218-223
Benefit principle, 5, 96-97, 109, 112
Bond anticipation borrowing, 184-185, 288
Bond attorney, 127-128, 179
Bond fund, 174
Bond and interest register, 140, 170-173, 175, 186
Bond issuance, 127-132; buyer requirements, 132; legal requirements, 127-128; maturities, 91, 92, 108; notice of sale, 128-131; timing of, 131-132
Bond ordinance, 128, 133
Bond prospectus, 132-134, 153
Bond ratings, 136-140
Bond service account, 166
Bonded debt ledger, 170, 172, 186
Bonds, 101-121; callable term, 108, 116-117, 130, 164, 190-191, 197, 288; defined, 108, 288; general obligation, 101, 111-112, 288; non-guaranteed, 111-112; production of, 124-125; revenue, 12, 75, 112, 127, 132, 155-168, 170, 292; sale and delivery of, 140-141; serial, 113-116, 288; security of, 111-113; special assessment, 112; term, 113, 164, 293; timing of issue, 121; title transfer, 117; types of maturities, 108, 118, 121, 288. *See also* Municipals
Borrowing, 108-110, 125; appropriate duration of, 109-110, 118; emergency, 76-77, 109, 184; government's capacity, 4-6; justification for, 76-79, 109; long and short term, 12, 79, 108; measuring the capacity of, 79-82; versus pay-as-you-go financing, 4-5, 11-12, 77, 78; statutory limits on, 73-76
Broker, 288. *See also* Underwriter
Budget, 10-20, 261-274; capital, 10, 288; comprehensiveness and unity in, 20-21; execution of, 27; operating, 20; program, 6, 16, 199, 229, 232, 261-274

Callable-term bonds, 108, 116-117, 130, 164, 190-191, 197
Capital budgeting, 6-16, 23-30, 266-274; organizational arrangements for, 23-25; as a political process, 17; and program budgeting, 266-274
Capital construction tax, 79
Capital expenditure decisions, 14-16, 288
Capital facility, definition of, 7, 10, 78; inventory of, 28-30; nonrecurrent nature of, 21
Capital facilities planning, 6-9, 22, 97-100; advantages of, 8; conceptual foundations, 1; delegated responsibilities for, 13-16; lack of theory in, 19; procedures for, 41-43; and program budgeting, 266-274; staff functions in, 13-14, 17, 22, 26, 34-35, 40, 100
Capital improvements tax, 107
Capital reserves, 78, 89, 94, 105-107, 125, 163, 174, 270, 288
Cash basis operation, 79, 183-184
Cash flow, 218, 222-223
Cataloging proposed projects, 30-35
Closed end trust indentures, 167-168

297

Consulting engineer, 133, 165, 179
Contingency analysis, 90, 200, 237, 246, 258
Conversion of debt, 191-197
Corporation bonds, 161
Cost-benefit analysis, 199-230; allocation problem in, 201; criteria for, 208-209; defined, 200; elements of, 200-202; forming objective functions in, 201-208; life-cycle costs in, 209-210; limitations of, 229-230
Cost-constraint analysis, 239-240
Cost-effectiveness analysis, 200, 226, 230-259, 264; attributes of, 232-234; effectiveness measures in, 233-234, 265-266; efficiency versus effectiveness, 231; end product orientation of, 232; and externalities, 255-258; and indivisible projects, 242-243; inputs versus outputs in, 230-231, 264; and program analysis, 236-240; and program impacts, 246-249; and project complementarities, 243-246; ratios, 226
Cost-goal analysis, 237-238
Coupon bonds, 117, 289
Covenants, 133, 159, 161, 162, 164-166
Credit reserve, 77
Credit standing, 79, 121
Criterion of preferredness, 201

Daily Bond Buyer, 128, 142, 144, 146, 184, 288
Dealer's concession, 147, 289
Debt, amortization of, 77, 102, 162; choice of, 111-125, refinancing, 193-197; restrictions in, 73-76; self-supporting, 77-78
Debt administration, 169-199; fund accountability in, 174-175; records and reporting, 169-179
Debt burden, 12, 80-82
Debt equalization, 110
Debt limit, 289-290
Debt policy, 73-83
Debt retirement, 185-191
Debt service, 290
Debt service reserve fund, 166-167
Debt service tax, 107, 174
Default, 159, 193-197, 296
Deferred serial bonds, 116
Deficiency financing, 185
Development rights, 105
Discount rate, 122-123, 288, 290
Discounted cash flow, 222-223
Discounting, 210-215

Earmarked funds, 21

Econometric models, 63
Economic analysis in capital facilities planning, 45-72
Economic base studies, 46, 63-71; criticisms of, 68, 82; delineation of base area, 65-66; multipliers in, 64, 67-68; techniques of measurement, 67-68
Economic dominants analysis, 69-71
Economic impact studies, 52, 55-56
Economic linkages, 50-51, 55, 59
Economic structure, 49, 50-52
Economics, 45-71; descriptive approaches to, 48, 50-51; regional, 47-48, 50-63; urban, 47-50, 63-71; and urban human resources, 49
Economies of scale, 1, 29, 48, 59
Effectiveness measures, 233-234, 265-266
Elasticity of local revenues, 86-87; of local spending, 86; of tax base, 87
Equivalent uniform annual net return, 222-223
Essentiality of service, 37
Excess capital expenditure loans, 110
Excess condemnation, 104-105
Exogenous demand, 56, 61, 83, 91
Expenditures, decision-making framework for, 14-16; forecasts versus commitments, 88-89
Export-base theory, 48, 63-68
Export versus local industries, 63-64
Export specialization, 55
Externalities, 202, 255-258

Face amount of bonds, 118, 124, 290
Financial analysis, 94-100
Financial Reporter, 184
Financial reports, 140, 175-179
Fiscal policy, 22, 24, 98, 100-102, 164
Fixed cost versus fixed benefits, 200, 231, 251

General fund, 174
General obligation bonds, 101, 111-112, 142, 170, 174, 290
Goal-oriented decision making, 230-231, 234
Gross bonding plan, 110
Gross lien or gross income bonds, 166
Gross National Product, 60-61, 85-87, 212
Gross receipts tax, 97

Incidence of program impacts, 246-249
Income and product accounts, 60-62
Income and wage taxes, 97, 98
Incremental costing, 238, 252-253
Industrial complex analysis, 59-60

Industrial revenue bonds, 160–161, 290
Inheritable assets, 253–254
Input-output analysis, 56–59, 82
Interest payable ledger, 170, 173, 186
Interest rate curve, 123
Interest or coupon rates, 119–120, 122–125, 129–131, 144–145, 170–173
Internal rate of return, 209, 216–218
Investment Bankers Association, 127, 133, 153
Investment costs, 210
Investment syndicates, 141–148. *See also* Underwriters
Irregular serial bonds, 116

Joint accounts, 143
Joint production programs, 266

Kaldor-Hicks criterion, 203–205

Law of retail gravitation, 66
Lease-back arrangements, 160
Life-cycle costs and benefits, 118, 202, 209–210, 233, 268
Limited tax bonds, 111, 291
Linkages, economic, 50–51, 55, 59
Little efficiency criterion, 205–206
Location theory, 51–52
Location quotients, 67–68
Long-term investment decisions, 218–219

Maintenance covenants, 165
Management information and program evaluation system (MIPES), 233–234, 262, 264
Maturity, 108–110, 118, 121, 163–164, 288; affecting yield basis, 121; balloon maturity, 116, 164; defined, 92; factors in determining, 118; for revenue bonds, 163–164; refunding of, 191–192
Maturity and interest calendar, 170
Means-ends chains, 206–207, 264
Monetary policy, 123
Money market, 120, 122–123
Moody's Investment Service, 137–138
Multipliers, economic base, 67–68; regional, 61–62
Multiyear programs and plans, 262–263, 266–268
Municipals (municipal bonds), 108–153, 288, 291; callable provisions in, 116–117; costs involved in marketing of, 134–136; defined, 108–110; descriptive criteria of, 111–113; face amount, 118, 124; interest on, 118–119, 122–125, 129–131; investment features of, 109; marketing of, 127–141; maturity determination, 118; methods of redemption, 113–116; ratings on, 136–140; recording and cancellation of, 190; tax exemptions, 109, 149–150; underwriting of, 141–149

Negotiable instruments, 127–128
Negotiated sales of bonds, 142, 148–149
Net benefits criterion, 209, 223–224; versus benefit-cost ratios, 223–224, 225–229
Net cash proceeds, 219–220
Net interest cost, 123–125, 145
Net present value, 222–223
New Haven expenditure model, 89–94
New Housing Authority Bonds, 112
Nodal regions, 50–51
Non-discrimination covenant, 165–166
Nonguaranteed bonds, 111–113
Non-property taxes, 87–88, 98–99, 104, 113
Notice of sale, 128–131

Objective function, 201, 203–208
Open end trust indenture, 167–168
Opportunity costs, 202, 212, 214
Optimum envelope, 249–252
Over-the-counter markets, 149

Par value, 120, 124, 130, 150, 189, 291
Pareto optimality, 203, 204, 205
Pay-as-you-go financing, 4–5, 11–12, 77, 78, 103–104, 108, 125, 291
Payback period, 221
Payment calendar, 186
Performance budgeting, 2, 16
Performance effectiveness 16, 233–234, 265–266
Planning, agency's role, 13–14, 17, 22, 26, 34–35, 40, 100; and budget relations, 2–4; integration of processes, 21–23; versus programming, 9–10, 16
PPBS, 2, 199, 261, 267
Population projections, 3, 7, 22, 98, 267–268
Present value, 210–215
Priorities, 7, 9, 13, 17, 25–26, 35–40, 292
Proceeds per dollar of outlay, 221
Production of bonds, 124–125, 146–148
Program analysis, 263–264, 268–271
Program budgeting, 6, 16, 199, 229, 232, 261–274
Program element, 232, 271
Program impacts, 246–249
Program monitoring procedures, 264
Program planning, 9, 22
Programming period, 10–11
Project complimentary, 243–246

Property tax, 75, 95–97

Rate covenant, 165
Ratio-stepdown methods, 62
Readiness-to-serve charges, 158
Redemption accounts, 167
Referendum for bond authorization, 127, 134–136, 159
Refunding, 191–192, 195–197, 292
Regional accounts, 49, 60–62
Regional economics, 47–48, 50–63
Regional multipliers, 61–62
Registered bonds, 177, 292
Relative debt burden, 80–82
Replacement reserve, 167
Reserve funds, 12, 105–107, 114, 166–167
Reserve maintenance fund, 114, 167
Revenue bonds, 12, 75, 112, 127, 132, 155–168, 170, 292; appropriate uses of, 157–158; authorities and special districts, 156–157; covenants on, 164–166; history of, 155–157; laws governing, 158–159; maturity provisions, 163–164; planning sale of, 161–163; and revenue distribution, 166–167; security of, 155; sources of revenue, 159–161
Revenue funds, 166–167, 174
Revenue of local government, 94–100
Risk and uncertainty, 202

Sales tax, 97, 98
San Francisco Bay Area Rapid Transit District (BART), 119, 124–125, 145–146, 148
Scaling of debt, 195–196, 292
Secondary (or trading) market, 122, 148–149, 192
Self-supporting debt, 153, 157, 292
Sensitivity analysis, 90, 200, 237, 246, 258
Serial bonds, 113–116, 163–164, 292
Service industries, 63–68
Short-term borrowing, 12, 79, 108, 179, 183–185; in anticipation of taxes, 179, 183–184
Sinking funds, 12, 113, 153, 157, 164, 169, 174, 187–190, 292. *See also* Reserve funds
Sinking fund tax, 187
Social costs, 202
Social discount rate, 201, 212, 214
Space-economy analysis, 47, 58

Special assessment bonds, 109, 112, 170, 292–293
Special benefit assessments, 104–105
Special districts, 156–157, 158
Special revenue funds, 174
Special taxes, 159–160, 293
Split-rate bids, 129–130
Spread, 123, 125, 141–142, 146
Staging of capital facilities, 7, 293
Standard and Poor's Corporation, 137–138
Standard Industrial Classification (SIC), 68
Standards of service, 2–3, 4, 13, 28, 36
Strategic planning, 3–4, 7, 22, 26, 261–262
Sunk costs, 252–253
Supplemental coupons, 130–131
Surplus fund, 167
Syndicate account, 143, 293

Take down, 146, 293
Tax anticipation borrowing, 179, 183–184
Tax exempt bond funds, 136, 150–151, 273
Term bonds, 113, 164, 293
Tolls, fees, and concessions, 159
Trading market, 122
Trust funds, 175
Trust indentures, 164, 166

Uncertainty, 202
Underwriters, 118, 123–124, 128, 141–149, 293
Underwriters' spread, 123, 125, 141–142, 146
Unit cost data, 98
Urban economy, 47–50, 82–83
Urban growth, stages in, 55–56
Urban ratchet, 56
Urban renewal, 205, 209
User-benefit equity, 5, 106
User charges, 157, 159

Warrants in short-term borrowing, 108, 149, 179, 183
Welfare economics, 203–208
Working capital fund, 167, 175

Yield or return on investment, 120–121, 146–147, 289, 293

Zero-base budgeting, 253, 272–273

## About the Author

**Alan Walter Steiss** is Associate Dean for Research and Graduate Studies of the College of Architecture and Urban Studies, Virginia Polytechnic Institute and State University. A graduate of Bucknell University (A.B. in Psychology and Sociology) and the University of Wisconsin (M.A. and Ph.D. in Urban and Regional Planning), Dr. Steiss has served at Virginia Tech as Director of the Center for Urban and Regional Studies, Chairman of Urban and Regional Planning and Urban Affairs, and Chairman of the Division of Environmental and Urban Systems. He has been a guest lecturer at several universities, including Rider College, New York University, the University of Wisconsin, Georgia Institute of Technology, Virginia Commonwealth University, and the University of British Columbia. Formerly the head of statewide planning for the State of New Jersey, he has served as a consultant to the states of Wisconsin, New Jersey, Maryland, Virginia, South Carolina, New York, and Hawaii, and the Trust Territory of the Pacific. Dr. Steiss is the author of several books, including PLANNING ADMINISTRATION; A FRAMEWORK FOR PLANNING IN STATE GOVERNMENT; SYSTEMIC PLANNING: THEORY AND APPLICATION (with Anthony J. Catanese); A PUBLIC SERVICE OPTION FOR ARCHITECTURAL CURRICULA; PUBLIC BUDGETING AND MANAGEMENT; MODELS FOR THE ANALYSIS AND PLANNING OF URBAN SYSTEMS; URBAN SYSTEMS DYNAMICS; and DYNAMIC CHANGE AND THE URBAN GHETTO. He has contributed to numerous professional journals in the United States and abroad.

# Related Lexington Books

Czamanski, Daniel Z., *The Cost of Preventive Services: The Case of Fire Departments,* 128 pp., 1975

Greene, Kenneth V.; Neenan, William B.; and Scott, Claudia D., *Fiscal Interactions in a Metropolitan Area,* 288 pp., 1974

Gustely, Richard D., *Municipal Public Employment and Public Expenditure,* 128 pp., 1974

Maciariello, Joseph A., *Dynamic Benefit-Cost Analysis: Evaluation of Public Policy in a Dynamic Urban Model,* 208 pp., 1975

Phares, Donald, and Greytak, David, *Municipal Output and Performance in New York City,* 000 pp., In Press

Ray, Marvin E., *The Environmental Crisis and Corporate Debt Policy,* 128 pp., 1974

Ross, John, and Burkhead, Jesse, *Productivity in the Local Government Sector,* 192 pp., 1974

Slavet, Joseph S.; Bradbury, Katharine L.; and Moss, Philip, *Financing State-Local Services: A New Strategy for Greater Equity,* 128 pp., 1975

Steiss, Alan Walter, *Models for the Analysis and Planning of Urban Systems,* 368 pp., 1975

——, *Public Budgeting and Management,* 368 pp., 1972

——, *Urban Systems Dynamics,* 368 pp., 1974